E X P E R T   A D V I S O R

XyWrite™ *III Plus*

EXPERT ADVISOR

XyWrite™ *III Plus*

Arthur R. G. Campbell

Addison-Wesley Publishing Company, Inc.
Reading, Massachusetts Menlo Park, California New York
Don Mills, Ontario Wokingham, England Amsterdam Bonn Sydney
Tokyo Madrid San Juan

Many of the designations used by manufacturers and sellers to distinguish their products are claimed as trademarks. Where those designations appear in this book and Addison-Wesley was aware of a trademark claim, the designations have been printed in initial capital letters.

XyWrite is a trademark of XYQUEST, Inc.
Lotus 1-2-3 is a trademark of Lotus Development Corp.
PostScript is a trademark of Adobe Systems, Inc.
IBM is a trademark of International Business Machine Corp.
For Comment is a trademark of Broderbund Software, Inc.

Library of Congress Cataloging-in-Publication Data
Campbell, Art.
    Expert advisor.

    1. XyWrite (Computer program)   2. Word
processing.   I. Title.
Z52.5X94C35   1989   652'.5   88-34991
ISBN 0-201-51721-3

Series Editor: Carole Alden
Technical Reviewer: Charles Collinson
Cover Design: Corey & Company
Text Design: Joyce Weston
Production Editor: Amorette Pedersen
Set in 10.5 point Palatino by Benchmark Publications

ABCDEFGHIJK-AL-89
First Printing, April, 1989

With love to Bonnie, for her help and encouragement. And to Felicia and Red, for their help on the keyboards.

Acknowledgments

This book wouldn't exist without the help and support of many people: Amy Pedersen and Chris Williams of Benchmark Productions who spurred, prodded, and brought the book to life; Lorraine and Robert Caristi and C. W. Collinson and Bette Jo Smith, who tested and suggested; Alan Southerton; Gail Freeman, John Hild, Judith Mintz, Brian Pottle, Paul Sarrategui, and Barbara Senese of XYQUEST, who provided lots of help, patience, and answers to many questions.

A number of dedicated XyWriters also participated by crafting programs they uploaded into the public domain on CompuServe's IBM Applications Forum. Tim Baehr, Jay Brent, Ted Eyrick, Jim Franklin, Andy Glass, Edward Mendelson, Paul O'Nolan, Tom Robinson, Pete Strisik, Ernie Wallengren, Robert Woods, and a number of programmers who didn't sign their work all helped. A tip of the floppy to y'all— may your unrecoverable disk errors be few and far between.

Contents

Introduction

This book is intended for XyWriters at all levels of experience. Beginning users can learn a particular function quickly and discover what related topics can help solve their problems. Intermediate users will find new ways to use XyWrite functions and improve their customizing skills. Advanced users will find ways to build fast, effective solutions to complex problems.

The book is an alphabetic listing of all XyWrite functions and commands. The examples show how you can customize XyWrite to make it the most efficient tool for your needs. Each listing in this volume includes several parts:

Overview   This section provides a description of what the function or command does, in simple terms. If you have forgotten what a command does, or want to learn how commands unfamiliar to you work, this section will be helpful.

Procedure   In this section you will find step-by-step instructions on how to use the feature or command most effectively. If you remember a command, but have forgotten how to use it, this section will give you a review.

Examples   Here you will find practical examples for the use of a given command or feature. You will also find other potential uses for the command, many of which you may not have thought of.

Warnings   XyWrite is not free of pitfalls or problems. In this section you will find out where you are most likely to encounter problems. If you can foresee these potential problems, you will probably be able to avoid them.

Tips   This section will make the most interesting reading for users who want to rapidly increase their expertise with XyWrite. The tips may also contain additional techniques and shortcuts, as well as cross-references to other entries in the book.

XyWrite is the best word processor for people who hate to write. It's the best because it's the fastest and most powerful word processor available for IBM PCs and compatibles. You can go into the program, write in the most efficient way, and get out.

XyWrite is also the best writing tool for students, secretaries, reporters, writers, attorneys, and anyone who works with words. Wordsmiths like XyWrite for the same reason hate-to-writers do—because it's the fastest and most powerful word processing tool available. XyWrite lets people play with words, rewrite, revise, access dictionaries and thesauri, change type styles, set up columns, create forms, and perform other fun things.

XyWrite is also powerful in a different sense. People shouldn't have to change the way they work in order to suit a computer program. People who use computers should be in control of the tools they use. XyWrite encourages people to change the program to accomplish the work they do, without having to change the way they do that work. This book explains the inner workings of XyWrite III Plus that make it a powerful writing tool.

Alphabetical
Entries

ABORT OR ABANDON (AB)

Overview   AB removes the currently active file from your computer's memory. It takes effect immediately. It does not affect a saved or stored file that has been written to disk. If you have made any changes to the file on screen since it was last saved, those changes will be lost when you use **Abort**.

Procedure   1. Press **F5** (Clear Command Line).
2. Type **AB**.
3. Press **F9** (Execute).
4. The screen clears.

A La Carte
1. Press **F6** (A La Carte menus).
2. Press **F** or select **File**.
3. Press **B** or select **aBort**.

Examples   AB is the quickest way to leave a file you've opened, but not changed. **Store** closes an open file, but it writes the file back to disk, an operation that takes time.

   AB is the only way to salvage a file if you've made massive mistakes and want to start fresh. **Abort** will "undo" everything you've changed by removing the file from XyWrite's memory. If you've never written the file to disk with a **Save** command, the file you use **Abort** on is totally erased; you can't reopen it. If you used **Save** to write the file to disk, the disk copy remains untouched and stays the way it was when it was last saved. If you have a directory of files on screen and wish to clear the screen, use **AB**.

Warnings   AB is an immediate command, be sure you want to abandon your file before you issue the command. Avoid creating a Save/Get key with **AB** on it; it's too easy to make a mistake and abandon a file you meant to save.

3

Tips   **Abort** automatically closes the window your document occupied if your **New Window** (**NW**) default is set to **1** (**NW=1**). Get the details on managing windows in the Windows section. Information on the default window settings is in the Defaults section and the **New Window** section.

See Store and Quit

APPEND

Overview   **Append** adds a defined block of text or an entire file to the end of a file on disk. It's an immediate command.

　　Append is typically used to add a file (or part of a file) you're working on into a secondary file. **Merge** does just the opposite—it copies a secondary file into your active file.

Procedure   To add your active file to a file on disk:

1. Press **F5** (Clear Command Line).
2. Type **APPEND** D:TARGETFILENAME.
3. Press **F9** (Execute).

To **Append** a defined block of text to a file on disk:

1. Define a block of text.
2. Press **F5** (Clear Command Line).
3. Type **APPEND** D:TARGETFILENAME.
4. Press **F9** (Execute).

To **Append** a file to another file on disk:

1. Press **F5** (Clear Command Line).
2. Type **APPEND** D:SOURCEFILENAME,D:TARGETFILENAME.
3. Press **F9** (Execute).

A La Carte
1. Press **F6** (A La Carte menus).
2. Press **F** or select **File**.

3. Press **A** or select **Append**.
4. The Append to End of File screen displays.
5. Type the name of the target file, the file to which you want to append text, in the blank.
6. Press **Return**.

Examples   **Append** lets you keep some text in two places... you might **Append** an address from a letter into an electronic address book or add several items to your "To Do" list.

It's a great tool to move new information into a document that is always being revised. **Append** is the ideal tool to compile a series of daily sales reports, or project status reports, into a monthly report file. Newspaper reporters often use **Append** to update a developing story.

Warnings   The target file must exist for **Append** to work; it is not created automatically.

See Merge

ARITHMETIC

Overview   XyWrite has a built-in, four-function calculator that can perform independent calculations and insert the result in text.

Procedure   XyWrite can perform math functions on the command line or work with numbers and formula in text. In each case, you have five operators and the use of parentheses to group parts of equation:

+ addition
- subtraction
* multiplication
/ division
= equals

You can actually use the command line as a calculator:

1. Press **Alt** and = (**Clear Internal Calculator**) or execute the **Clearsum (CS)** command.
2. Press **F5** (Clear Command Line).
3. Type the formula you want to solve (**2+4+6=**).
4. Press **F9** (Execute).
5. The answer is displayed on the command line, after the equal sign.

If you want to work with numbers that are part of a document, you have several options. If the numbers are scattered around a sentence or an entire document, you can add or subtract any of the digits from any of the others. Multiplication and division can't be used with this method:

1. Press **Alt** and = (**Clear Internal Calculator**) or execute the **Clearsum (CS)** command.
2. Move the cursor to the first number.
3. Press **Alt** and + (or -) to record the number. It displays on the prompt line.
4. Move the cursor to the second number.
5. Press **Alt** and + (or -) to add or subtract the number. The running total displays on the prompt line.
6. Move the cursor to the next number. Continue using **Alt** and + (or -) to add or subtract the numbers from the running total.
7. When you've completed the calculation, move the cursor to the place where the total should appear in the text.
8. Press **Alt** and = to insert the total.

To add or subtract a group of numbers that can be defined as a block:

1. Press **Alt** and = (**Clear Internal Calculator**) or execute the **Clearsum (CS)** command.
2. Define the block of numbers by pressing **F1** to mark the beginning and end of the block. (You must use **F1**—or **Alt** and **F1**—for a column, other methods of defining a block don't

work.) It can be a group of numbers on a line (4 5 6 7) or a column of numbers:

4
5
6
7

3. Press **Alt** and **+** (or **-**) to add or subtract the numbers. The running total displays on the prompt line.
4. Move the cursor to the place the total should appear in the text.
5. Press **Alt** and **=** to insert the total.
6. Remember to release the define by pressing **F3** (**Release Define**).

To solve a linear expression in text:

1. Press **Alt** and **=** (**Clear Internal Calculator**) or execute the **Clearsum** (**CS**) command.
2. Define the expression or equation by pressing **F1** to mark the beginning and end of the block. The expression cannot include any spaces—**2*(3*3)** is okay; **2* (3*3)** is not.
3. Press **Alt** and **+** (or **-**) to add or subtract the numbers from the running total on the internal calculator. The running total displays on the prompt line.
4. Move the cursor to the place where the total should appear in the text.
5. Press **Alt** and **=** to insert the total.
6. Remember to release the define by pressing **F3** (**Release Define**).

A La Carte A La Carte doesn't provide any special or additional arithmetic tools. Use the standard XyWrite procedures.

Examples   XyWrite's math functions aren't heavy duty calculation tools, but they're adequate for preparing an expense report, making a list of deductions for your accountant, or figuring out how many lines are on the page.

Tips   Two things can mix up your calculations—forgetting to release a defined block of numbers after you're done with them, and forgetting to hit the **Alt** and **=** sequence to clear the internal calculator's memory. If you remember to do those two steps consistently, you'll get accurate results.

Warnings   Most computer keyboards have two sets of number symbols, one arrayed along the top line of the QWERTY keycaps, the other on a number pad along the left side of the keyboard. If you have any trouble using XyWrite's math functions with one set, try the other. Different keyboards send different signals to their computers and some of the signals may not be the ones XyWrite expects.

    If neither set of symbols works, the fault may lie in your keyboard file. Some modified keyboard files may not use the appropriate function calls. If you use a modified keyboard file that includes remapped keys for the math symbols, try loading an original XyWrite keyboard and testing the features with that.

See Clearsum

ASCII, TYPING ASCII CHARACTERS

Overview   Occasionally you'll want to insert graphic characters or printer control codes into your text. XyWrite generates these ASCII characters from the keyboard.

Procedure   You can insert most ASCII characters directly from the XyWrite help screens:

1. Position the cursor where the ASCII character should be inserted.
2. Press **Alt** and **F9** (**Help**).
3. Press **A** or select **ASCII**. Five group are displayed. Press:
   - **F** or select **FOREIGN**.

- **G** or select **GREEK/MATH**.
- **L** or select **LINES**.
- **P** or select **PATTERNS**.
- **S** or select **SPECIAL**.

4. A selection of ASCII characters is displayed. Move the cursor to the one you want to insert.
5. Press **F9** (Execute).
6. The character is inserted in text.

An alternate way to insert the ASCII character is to:

1. Find the ASCII character number on an ASCII character chart or the XyWrite ASCII help screens.
2. Hold down the **Alt** and **Shift** keys.
3. Type the character number. You may have to use the numeric keypad.
4. Release the **Alt** and **Shift** keys.
5. The character displays. Depending on your printer's capabilities, it may or may not print.

A La Carte

1. Press **F6** (A La Carte menus).
2. Press **E** or select **Edit**.
3. Press **A** or select **Ascii**.
4. A screen with several groupings of characters displays.
   - Press **F** or select **Foreign**.
   - Press **G** or select **Greek/math**.
   - Press **L** or select **Lines**.
   - Press **P** or select **Patterns**.
   - Press **S** or select **Special**.
5. The characters in that group display across the top of the screen.
6. Move the cursor to the character you want to insert and press **Return**.
7. When you're through inserting characters, press **Esc** four times to leave A La Carte.

Examples   Everyone is familiar with the 52 Latin characters of our alphabet and the 10 Arabic digits. But in the computer world, these symbols are only part of a larger character set, the 256-character expanded ASCII (American Standard Code for Information Interchange) set.

You can use these symbols for a variety of purposes. There are a number of foreign diacritical characters. Several Greek letters and mathematical symbols are included. Some can be used to draw boxes or lines. Others instruct the printer to do something. ASCII number 12, the universal female symbol, is the form feed character. If it's inserted at the end of a text file, the printer advances the document by one page, making it easier to remove from a dot matrix printer.

If your printer provides special operations that are triggered by escape codes, you can use XyWrite's ASCII insertion capability to embed the codes in your text.

Warnings   Although XyWrite can generate the full complement of 256 characters, few printers print the full range.

AUTO CHECK/CORRECT

Overview   You can set XyWrite's spelling checker to monitor your typing. When you type a questionable word, the computer beeps and you can decide if the word needs help.

Procedure   1. Press **Ctrl-A** to turn **Auto Check/Correct** on. A small "c" appears on the prompt line.
2. Press **Ctrl-A** a second time to toggle it off.

Each time you type a separator (a space, tab stop, or carriage return), **Auto Check/Correct** scans the active dictionaries to see if the word you just typed is listed. If it's not, the computer beeps. You can stop and fix the word if it's a true misspelling; keep on typing until you get to a good stopping point, then return and fix it using the regular spell tools; or ignore the beep if the word is correct.

If you want to finish typing your sentence before checking out the questionable word, use a **Ctrl-F** key combination to return to it. In addition to moving the cursor to the proper spot, **Ctrl-F** invokes the same menu-driven tools the **Spell** command does. From the **Spell** menu, you can correct the misspelled word or add the questionable-but-correct word to any of the active dictionaries.

A La Carte
1. Press **F6** (A La Carte menus).
2. Press **O** or select **Option**.
3. Press **S** or select **Spell**.
4. Press **C** or select **auto Check**.
5. Press **Return**.

Examples   This is one of those features you either love or hate. If you're a methodical typist who likes to fix mistakes as they occur, this is for you. If you're a fast but sloppy typist who puts off proofreading until the writing's done, this feature may drive you crazy. Trying it out is the only way to decide.

Tips   If you've edited your dictionary files and set up replacement words, the misspelled word is automatically corrected when the beep goes off. See the **Spell** listing and the **Auto Replace** listing for more information.

Think the **Auto Check/Correct** beep sounds a bit naggish? You can change it. Both the pitch and duration of the correction beep can be changed by setting a new default **Correction Beep** (**CB**) setting. See the Default section or the **CB** section for more information.

See Spell and Auto Replace

AUTO PAUSE (AP)

Overview   There are two **AP** commands. The one you'll use most often is an embedded command inserted into text. The second is a default setting. When you insert an **AP** in a document, XyWrite pauses as each page prints. To switch **AP** off and enable continuous printing, embed a **No Pause** (**NP**) command in your text after the **AP**'s page number.

Procedure   Since this is a command that's embedded in text, you must have a document open. Pick the page where you want the printer to pause and move your cursor to a point on that page. (Remember that this is *not* an immediate command. The printer won't stop in its tracks when it hits your **AP**. It continues to the bottom of the page, then pauses.)

1. Press **F5** (Clear Command Line).
2. Type **AP**.
3. Press **F9** (Execute).
4. The **AP** appears as a bright command triangle in your text.

When you print the document, the printer pauses at the end of the selected page. You can switch paper, change printwheels, or perform whatever operation you need to do. When you type a plus sign (+), the next page prints. The printer will pause at the end of each page in the document until you turn **Auto Pause** off.

To turn off **Auto Pause** and resume normal continuous printing in the same document, insert a **No Pause** (**NP**) command in the text. Since **AP** is a default setting, you can enter the command in your printer file or in your STARTUP.INT file. If you do, your printer stops after each page it prints. For complete information on setting **AP** as a default, look at the Default section.

A La Carte You cannot set the **AP** default setting from the A La Carte menus.

1. Press **F6** (A La Carte menus).
2. Press **T** or select **Type**.
3. Press **P** or select **type to Printer**.
4. The Type To Printer screen appears. "Pause" is one of the options. If you select it, the document will stop after each page.

Examples   **Auto Pause** is handy if you need to manipulate your printout in any way.

If you need to hand-feed sheets of stationery into your printer, **AP** is the perfect tool to let you align the paper.

If you were writing a letter and wanted to print the envelope at the end of the text as the second page, **AP** instructs the printer to pause while you insert the envelope.

On letter-quality daisy wheel or thimble printers, use **AP** to let you change printwheels when you want to change fonts.

See No Pause (NP) and Pause

AUTO REPLACE

Overview   XyWrite's spelling checker can be set up to exchange a word that you often type incorrectly for the proper text. For example, If you often type "teh" instead of "the," **Auto Replace** will automatically change all the "teh" passages to "the" as you type.

Procedure   Just press **Ctrl-R**. **Auto Replace** takes effect immediately. It is a toggle indicated by an "r" on the prompt line. The first time you press **Ctrl-R**, you turn **Auto Replace** "on"; the second time, it switches **Auto Replace** "off."

Auto Replace is independent of XyWrite's regular spelling facility. The spelling program doesn't have to be loaded for **Auto Replace** to operate, but whatever personal or alternate dictionary you normally use must be in memory. They are normally loaded by the STARTUP.INT file when you start XyWrite.

A La Carte
1. Press **F6** (A La Carte menus).
2. Press **O** or select **Option**.
3. Press **S** or select **Spell**.
4. Press **R** or select **autoReplace**.
5. Press **Return**.

Examples   **Auto Replace** is a real convenience for fast, but sloppy typists. The intended use, of course, is to speed up the proofreading process by fixing minor errors as you type a sentence. You have to be fairly familiar with the way you type to use **Auto Replace** effectively, since you must enter your most common typing mistakes in the spelling dictionary.

Even if you don't use the **Auto Replace** option, the spell check program uses the replacement table you've set up, which speeds the proofreading process a bit.

You can use the **Auto Replace** feature to increase your typing speed if you type a lot of the same phrases over and over. Set up a list of abbreviations for repetitive phrases, matched to the entire phrase. See the Tips section.

Tips   **Auto Replace** works by scanning the dictionary file for a list of words that are frequently misspelled. When it finds an exact match in the misspelled word list, it inserts the correct word. Both words (the incorrect and the correct) are typed on the same line in the dictionary file. Entries from the list look like this:

  teh the
  eth the

Auto Replace works just fine with the replacement list supplied in PERS.SPL, the default supplementary dictionary. The list is fairly short, however, and won't include the spelling and typing mistakes you make most often. To get the most out **Auto Replace**, modify the word list to include your list of "problem" words.

1. **Call** an alternate or supplementary spelling dictionary to the screen. PERS.SPL is the system default.
2. Press **Ctrl** and **End** to go to the end of the dictionary file. You'll see a list of misspelled words followed by their correctly spelled counterparts. This is the **Auto Replace** word list.
3. Type in one of your frequent typing or spelling errors, followed by a space and the correct word. Keep on going to include your most common typing mistakes and their correct counterparts. (Remember that you can spell-check a supplementary dictionary to double-check an entry if you need to.)
4. **Store** the file.
5. Load the modified dictionary.
6. Press **F5** (Clear Command Line).
7. Type **LOAD** DICTIONARYNAME.SPL.
8. Press **F9** (Execute).
9. Toggle **Auto Replace** on by pressing **Ctrl** and **R**. Type one of your words incorrectly. It should be fixed lightning quick!

The only drawback to **Auto Replace** is that your replacement word list has to contain the "correct" incorrect word to substitute the proper spelling. If your fingers include an error that's not in the word list, your **Auto Replace** table won't function as you want it to. When you're setting up the table, try to imagine all the unusual spellings and typing transpositions you might come up with and enter them.

There's a way to insert both the misspelling and the correct spelling in your dictionary file while you run the Spell Check program, if you don't mind modifying your keyboard file. Read the listing on the **IR** function call in the Keyboard File section.

Use **Auto Replace** to dazzle your friends and impress strangers with your blazing typing speed! Type three letters and get a sentence! Try this trick: put an entry in your dictionary file that looks like this:

add. Your Name, Address, and Phone Number

Each time you type **add.** with **Auto Replace** on, the larger phrase is inserted in your text.

You can make each element of your address print on a separate line by putting the ASCII code for a carriage return (character number 13) between the entries. (For information on inserting ASCII characters in text, see the ASCII section.)

If you did, your entry would look like this:

add. Your Name ♪ Address ♪ Phone Number

The expanded entry doesn't have to be your address, of course. It can be any boilerplate phrase, sentence, or paragraph that you're tired of typing.

Warnings   **Auto Replace** doesn't replace the spelling checker. If you're interested in producing a document that's as clean and error-free as possible, don't omit the **Spell** command when you finish your writing.

If whatever you type has to include intentional misspellings, like the last page or so of this text, don't use **Auto Replace** or you'll create a Catch 22 situation.

See Spell and Auto Check/Correct

AUTOMATIC LEADING (AL)

Overview   If you use several sizes of type on a page, **AL** inserts white space above and below each line so your large type won't print over the line above or below it. It's a command that would only be used if you're mixing different sizes of type on a page. **AL** overrides whatever **Line Spacing** (**LS**) settings are in effect.

If you use a dot matrix or daisy wheel printer, you'll have little use for **AL**. If you print on a laser printer or output directly to a typesetting device, you'll probably use **Automatic Leading** very often.

Automatic Leading can be turned on by issuing the **AL** command from the command line or you can keep it active all the time by entering **AL** as a default setting. Since **AL** can be used as a default setting, you can enter the command in your printer file or in your STARTUP.INT file. If you do, **AL** is used each time XyWrite starts. For complete instructions, see the Procedure portion of the Default listing.

Procedure To turn **AL** on from the command line, for a single document:

1. Press **F5** (Clear Command Line).
2. Type **AL**.
3. Press **F9** (Execute).
4. A bright command triangle is inserted.

To set automatic leading for a single editing session:

1. Press **F5** (Clear Command Line).
2. Type **DEFAULT** AL=# (0 turns **AL** off, 1 turns **AL** on).
3. Press **F9** (Execute).
4. "Done" displays on the prompt line.

A La Carte You must be in an empty window (have a blank screen) to access the default menus.

1. Press **F6** (A La Carte menus).
2. Press **X** or select **XyWrite**.
3. Press **D** or select **Defaults**.
4. The View and Change Defaults screen displays.
5. Press **A** or **C** or select **defaults A-C**
6. Move the cursor to the **AL** entry and type **0** to turn **AL** off, or **1** to turn it on.
7. Press **Return**.
8. The Update Default File screen displays. You're asked if you want to make the default settings permanent.

9. Press **Y** or **N**. If you select **Y**, the program writes the new default settings to a special file and returns you to the A La Carte Menu Screen. If you select **N**, the settings are used for the current edit session.

Examples Leading is one of the things that makes typeset documents look better than rough-and-ready typed papers.

If you have a high-quality printer, you can take advantage of XyWrite's sophisticated type handling capabilities to produce professional-looking documents. The best computer printers today can produce many different designs of type in many different sizes.

Regular typed papers usually are printed single- or double-spaced. XyWrite's normal setting prints six lines of type to an inch, dividing each vertical inch of paper into six parts. A professionally typeset document divides each vertical inch into 72 or more parts, so much finer adjustment is possible.

XyWrite provides several tools for adjusting leading, but **AL** is the most automatic. If the normal line space setting is used with different sizes of type, the lines that contain larger sizes print on top of the lines before and after them. The only ways to adjust the amount of white space are to hit the **Return** key several times—a rather crude adjustment; to manually insert extra white space with the **Extra Leading** (**EL**) or **Line Leading** (**LL**) commands; or to toggle **AL** on. When **AL** is invoked, XyWrite ignores the normal line spacing commands in a document and vertically adjusts each line of type according to is size so it doesn't bump its neighbors.

How does **AL** know how much white space to insert? Each printer file XyWrite uses contains size information on each font. One of the entries is the amount of leading to use with that size. The setting can be modified to allow more or less white space. See the Printer File section.

See Line Spacing (LS), Extra Leading (EL), Line Leading (LL), and Printer Files

AUTOMATIC UPPERCASE (AU)

Overview   The **Automatic Uppercase** command (**AU**) instructs XyWrite to capitalize the first letter you type after a punctuation mark.

Procedure   **AU** is a toggle. To turn **Automatic Uppercase** on:
1. Press **F5** (Clear Command Line).
2. Type **AU**.
3. Press **F9** (Execute).
4. A capital "A" appears on the right edge of the prompt line at the top of your screen.

When you begin typing, each word typed after a period, exclamation point, or question mark is capitalized.

To move out of **AU** mode and turn **Automatic Uppercase** off, issue the **AU** again:

1. Press **F5** (Clear Command Line).
2. Type **AU**.
3. Press **F9** (Execute).

A La Carte
1. Press **F6** (A La Carte menus).
2. Press **E** or select **Edit**.
3. Press **C** or select **Case**.
4. Press **A** or select **Automatic uppercase**.
5. Press **Return**.

Examples   **Automatic Uppercase** comes in handy if you want to make writing a little more intuitive or if you are typing too fast to actually think about the information that you are typing. Perhaps when taking notes during a phone conversation, for instance, you mind is ahead of your fingers.

At first glance, **AU** seems to be a gadget, but it's actually quite useful.

Warnings   **Automatic Uppercase** can save you keystrokes during a regular writing session, but it gets in the way if you type a lot of material that uses periods for something besides ending a sentence. Words that follow abbreviations and decimal places are capitalized too, since they follow periods.

See Change case (CC), Lower case (LC), and Upper case (UC)

BACKSPACE CONTROL (BS)

Overview   **Backspace Control** is a default setting you probably won't ever change. The **Backspace Control** setting will compensate for printers (older machines, usually) that can't perform a true backspace.

The correct setting is normally established by XyWrite and installed automatically when you load the proper printer file. Normally, **BS** is set to "on" (**BS=1**).

Procedure   If you need to change the **BS** setting, remember that it's already in your printer file. To change the setting:

1. Press **F5** (Clear Command Line).
2. Type **CA** PRINTERFILENAME.
3. Use **Search** to locate **BS** or move the cursor to the **BS** entry.
4. Type BS=0 to turn the setting off or BS=1 to turn it on.
5. **Store** the file.

If **BS** is not listed in your printer file, see the Procedure portion of the Default listing for complete instructions. You can also issue

BS from the command line to set the attribute for special effects in a single file:

1. Press **Ctrl** and **Home** to move the beginning of the file.
2. Press **F5** (Clear Command Line).
3. Type **DEFAULT** BS=0 to turn the setting off or BS=1 to turn it on.
4. Press **F9** (Execute).
5. "Done" displays on the prompt line.

A La Carte The **BS** default setting is not available through A La Carte menus.

Examples   This is a printer control code, pure and simple. It does not have any other use. It may cause one line to print over another on some printers, but whether it does or not is determined by the printer itself.

Tips   Don't play with the setting unless you want to experiment. If you do switch **BS** settings in a file, make a copy of the original before you modify it.

See Defaults

BACKUP FILES (BK)

Overview   **BK** is a system default setting that specifies whether backup versions of a document should be saved automatically. XyWrite's original default setting is **BK=1**, which saves a backup copy of each document you edit. Each time you use **Call** to edit a document, a backup file with a .BAK extension is created.

Procedure   Since **BK** is a default setting, you can enter the command in your printer file or in your STARTUP.INT file, so backups are created during every editing session.

    To stop XyWrite from making an automatic backup copy of your files, just add a line that reads **BK=0** to your printer file or STARTUP.INT. For complete instructions, see the Procedure portion of the Default listing.

    You can also issue **BK** from the command line to create backups only during your current editing session:

1. Press **F5** (Clear Command Line).
2. Type **DEFAULT** BK=1.
3. Press **F9** (Execute).
4. "Done" displays on the prompt line.

A La Carte You must be in an empty window (have a blank screen) to access this menu.

1. Press **F6** (A La Carte menus).
2. Press **X** or select **XyWrite**.
3. Press **D** or select **Defaults**.
4. The View and Change Defaults screen displays.
5. Press **A** or **C** or select **defaults A-C**
6. Move the cursor to the **BK** entry and type **0** to turn automatic backup off, or **1** to turn the function on.
7. Press **Return**.
8. The Update Default File screen displays. You're asked if you want to make the default settings permanent.
9. Press **Y** or **N**. If you select **Y**, the program writes the new default settings to a special file and returns you to the A La Carte Menu Screen. If you select **N**, the settings are used for the current edit session.

Examples   The automatic backup of files is useful is you need to keep track of previous versions of documents. It can also be a lifesaver if you edit a document, save it, and then decide the changes weren't so hot; that you'd like the first version back.

The drawback to automatic backups is that the feature eats up disk space. Each document takes twice as much space to store if a backup is automatically created, so each of your subdirectories is twice as bulky as it need be.

Tips

Many documents aren't important enough to need an automatic backup for each editing session. There are several other options available that will backup only the files you think are valuable.

If you have a hard disk in your computer, one very good strategy is to use your computer's floppy drive for backups. Dedicate a floppy disk to a subdirectory or a project and copy your important files to the floppy *before* you open them to edit. This has the additional benefit of letting you store your important documents on a disk that can be removed from your computer. If your hard disk crashes, you're still protected.

This strategy can be modified if you're using a double floppy disk system. Normally, your text files would be stored on the "B:" drive and your software on the "A:" drive. When you open a file, before you begin to edit it, remove the text file diskette. Insert a backup diskette, and save the document. Then remove the backup floppy and insert the original text floppy.

If you'd rather not swap floppies all the time, another good strategy is maintaining a subdirectory on your disk (either a hard disk or a floppy) just for backups. Either copying a file before editing to the backup directory or a save to it will keep an extra copy of your data intact. The convenience of this approach has to be weighed against a drawback—the backup data is stored on the same media as the original. If anything happens to the disk, both the original and the backup are gone.

Warning

Making a backup copy of a file is entirely different than making a copy of your current working file on another disk (using XyWrite's ability to save a file to multiple drives). Saving to multiple drives keeps the *current* working copy in two places. Enabling the **BK** command keeps the current working copy and the file from the previous editing session on disk, available for use.

BLOCKS

Overview Many word processing operations affect blocks of text. Underlining a phrase, copying a sentence, moving a paragraph, and deleting a page of text are all block operations. Block operations take effect as soon as a command is executed.

There isn't a fixed size for a block of text. A block can be any portion of a document, from a word to the entire file. It can be any size you want it to be. It may be a word or two, a phrase, sentence, paragraph, or pages of prose.

Procedure Modifying a block of text is a two-stage process. First, define the block. Second, modify the block.

After you modify the block (depending on what you do with it), you may need to release the block. Copying, deleting, and moving a block automatically release the block definitions; the others do not. If you format, print, save, or spell-check a block, you'll have to release it after the operation.

To define the block:

1 Move the cursor to either the beginning or end point of the block of text.
2. Press **F1** to begin defining the block.
3. Move the cursor to the other end point. The text you're defining will display as a different color or shade.
4. Press **F1** again to finish defining the text.

To append the block to a file:

1. Press **F5** (Clear Command Line).
2. Type **APPEND** TARGETFILENAME.
3. Press **F9** (Execute).

To copy the block:

1. Move the cursor through your document to the point you want the block copied.

2. Press **F7** (**Copy**).

If you have more than one document open, you can move a defined block of text from one document to another. Use **Alt** and **F10** or **Shift** and **F10** to move between documents before you press the **F7** key. To delete the block:

1. Press **Alt** and **F6** (**Delete Define**).

Delete something by mistake? You can bring it back with **Undelete**:

1. Press **Alt** and **F3** (**Undelete**). The text you removed snaps back into place.

Format a Block (Method 1) This method works with all text attributes—setting the text to all upper case or lower case letters, and all display modes—boldface, underline, reverse, and so on:

1. Press **F5** (Clear Command Line).
2. Type the format command: **UC** to make the block all capital letters, **MD BO** to make the text boldface, or any of the other mode or type style commands.
3. Press **F9** (Execute).
4. The block displays the new attribute.

Format a Block (Method 2) This method only works with display modes—boldface, underline, and so on. It won't set the block text to upper case or to lower case.

1. Press **Ctrl** and a number key (usually 1 through 9 are defined).

The number key must be one from the top of the keyboard; the number pad keys won't work.

These display modes and matching text attributes are plain vanilla attributes that are set by most XyWrite printer files. The exact attributes can be modified and will vary according to how sophisticated a printer you have.

B

BLOCKS

TABLE 1   **Text Attributes**

TEXT TYPE	CTRL-KEY#	COMMAND	NOTES
Normal	Ctrl-1	MD NM	Sets the block to normal text mode. Use it to restore a block of text with another attribute to match the main text.
Boldface	Ctrl-	MD BO	
Underline	Ctrl-3	MD UL	
Reverse	Ctrl-4	MD RV	Usually used to define part of a form.
Bold Underline	Ctrl-5	MD BU	
Bold Reverse	Ctrl-6	MD BR	Italics, if the printer can support it.
Superscript	Ctrl-7	MD SU	Not usually used on a block of text.
Subscript	Ctrl-8	MD SD	Not usually used on a block of text.

To move a Block:

1. Move the cursor to the point you want the block copied.
2. Press **F8** (**Move**).

If you have more than one document open, you can move a defined block of text from one document to another. Use **Alt** and **F10** or **Shift** and **F10** to move between documents before you press the **F8** key.

To save the block as a separate file:

1. Press **F5** (Clear Command Line).
2. Type **SAD** (**Save Define**), a space, and the file name you want to use: **SAD** C:\DIRECTORYNAME\FILENAME. Note that the drive and the path can be specified, if you don't want to use your current location.
3. Press **F9** (Execute).

26

To save the block as a text Save/Get:

1. Press **F2** (**Make Save/Get**).
2. Select the "hot" key to hold the block.

To call the text back into a document:

1. Move the cursor to the point you want to insert the text.
2. Press **Alt** and the "hot" key you chose when you stored the block.

You can also append a defined block to an existing text Save/Get:

1. Press **Ctrl** and **F2** (**Append** to Save/Get).
2. Select the "hot" key that holds existing text.

To spell-check the block:

1. Press **F5** (Clear Command Line).
2. Type **SPELL**.
3. Press **F9** (Execute).

To print the block:

1. Press **F5** (Clear Command Line).
2. Type **TYPE**.
3. Press **F9** (Execute).

To release the defined block:

1. Press **F3** (Release Define).
2. The screen display will return to normal.

Examples   Once part of a document is defined as a block of text, it can be manipulated and modified. You can:

- **Append** the block to an existing file.
- **Copy** the block.
- **Delete** the block.
- **Format** the block in a particular style—all capital letters, or italic or boldface type.

27

- **Move** the block to a different place in the document.
- **Print** the block.
- **Save** the block as an entirely separate file, or as a macro that can be recalled with a single keystroke.
- **Spell-check** the block.

Tips

Get in the habit of pressing **F3** (Release Define) after you finish a block operation. If you don't, the block can stay defined while you move to a different place in the document. If you issue a command then, it affects the defined block, where you can't see it. It's easy to change the format of a block unintentionally if you don't release the define. There are four shortcuts that define a small block of text quickly. All are based on the **F4** key.

- **Define a line** by pressing **F4**.
- **Define a sentence** by pressing **Ctrl** and **F4**.
- **Define a paragraph** by pressing **Shift** and **F4**.
- **Define a word** by pressing **Alt** and **F4**.

Each of these shortcuts can be repeated. Pressing **F4** twice defines two lines; pressing **Ctrl** and **F4** twice defines two sentences.

The shortcuts cannot be chained together very well. Defining a word with **Alt** and **F4** and expanding the block with **Shift** and **F4** won't work. The block operations discussed here don't function if you're working with text in columns. To define a block of text that's in a column, use the special **Alt** and **F1** combination to define the columnar block. See Column Functions.

One talented XyWriter has written a program that allows you to define unrelated blocks of text and tie them together. COLLECT.PGM is listed in the programming chapter. It works by appending each defined block to a single file. That file can be imported with the **Merge** command. You can, of course, perform the same operation manually.

Warning

If your commands suddenly stop working, for instance, if a **UC** command doesn't create an upper case letter, or a **MD BO** doesn't produce a boldface letter, you probably forgot to release a defined block of text. Press **F3** and double check the last block you defined. There may be a paragraph that's become all capital letters, or all bold!

If you're working with a large blocks of text, in a large document, or on a computer that doesn't have a large memory, you might get a disconcerting error message—"Can't Scroll Define or Display."

The message means that there isn't enough RAM in the computer to run XyWrite, hold the main document, remember what the block is, and perform the block operation at the same time. There is a "work around." Instead of performing the block operation in one phase, park the defined block of text on a Save/Get key. Then delete the block if necessary, release the define block, and use the standard Save/Get procedure to copy or move the "parked" text to its new location.

BLOCK BREAK/NON-BREAKABLE BLOCK (BB/NB)

Overview   The **No Break** and **Block Break** commands are pagination tools. They work together to define a block and to prevent that block from being split across two pages. Both commands are embedded in the text of a document.

Procedure   To see where page breaks occur, activate the **Show Page#-Line#** display by pressing **Shift** and **F9**. When you locate a block that should print on a single page instead of breaking across two pages, do as follows:

1. Move the cursor to the beginning of the text block.
2. Press **F5** (Clear Command Line).
3. Type **NB** (**No Break**) to mark the beginning of the unbreakable block.
4. Press **F9** (Execute).
5. Move the cursor to the end of the text block.

6. Press **F5** (Clear Command Line).
7. Type **BB** (**Break Block**) to mark the end of the unbreakable block.
8. Press **F9** (Execute).

Examples   Automatic pagination is a wonderful thing, but a computer can only do so much. Defining an unbreakable block overrules the computer-mediated pagination.

Many types of text look and read better if they are in one piece on one page. Tables, for instance, can be confusing if they print in two places. It's aggravating to have to flip back and forth between two pages to check column headings or to compare data. More important, this type of page break can hinder your reader's comprehension.

To solve the problem, place a **NB** at the beginning of the table and a **BB** at the end. Defining the table as an "unbreakable block," forces the block to fall on one page instead of the two pages the program would use if it were to paginate the document automatically.

Tips   An alternative to using the **No Break** and **Block Break** commands is the **Page Break** (**PG**) command. If you find yourself in a block that you don't want to break across a page, you can move to the beginning of the block and insert a **PG**. See the **Page Break** section for more details.

The **No Break** and **Block Break** commands are two commands that *must* be used together. If you create documents that contain several unbreakable blocks, think about automating the pagination process.

For instance: if you use XyWrite's column facility to set up tables, or regularly import spreadsheet elements from another program, write a macro or Save/Get to insert a generic command that includes the **NB** and **BB** codes.

If your nonbreakable blocks are paragraphs, a simple three-command program can insert the **No Break** command at the beginning of the paragraph, move to the end of it, and insert and **Block Break** command.

You'll want to look at the Programming Section for more details, but the logical steps of the program flow something like this (assuming you're at the end of a paragraph, keeping your eye on the Page/Line register when you decide it should be a nonbreakable block):

1. The first step in the program is the **Previous Paragraph** (**PP**) function call, to move the cursor to the beginning of the paragraph.
2. The second step inserts the **No Break** (**NB**) command.
3. The third step is the **Next Paragraph** (**NP**) function call, to move the cursor to the next paragraph. To keep things tidy, a single **Cursor Left** (**CL**) moves the cursor to the carriage return between the paragraphs.
4. The final step inserts the **Break Block** (**BB**) command.

There are a number of ways to write the program, but you might end up with something that looks like this:

PP BC nb**XC NP CL BC** bb**XC**

Warning   If the **No Break** and **Block Break** commands aren't used as a pair, the pagination of your document might not come out right. Make sure you complete the operation when you decide to impose page breaks on your own.

See Page Break (PG)

BORDER (WINDOW) COLORS (BX)

Overview   **BX** lets you customize your display screen by color-coding the nine document display window borders, the help screen window border, and the help screen prompt line. It's effective on color monitors; less so on monochrome. **BX** can be issued as a command or used as a default setting. The syntax of the command is long, but not complicated:

BX,#,#,#,#,#,#,#,#,#,#,#,#

The first argument sets the border color for the "active" window, the one that holds the document you're editing. The next nine set border colors for the nine windows that can be open at one time. The eleventh argument sets the border color of your help screen windows. The twelfth controls the help screen prompt line.

A plain vanilla **BX** command for a monochrome display might look like this:

BX,112,7,7,7,7,7,7,7,7,7,112,15

A list of the possible colors and their numbers is in the Display section.

Procedure   Since **BX** is a default setting, you can enter the command in your printer file or in your STARTUP.INT file. If you do, the window borders are set to your color choices every time you start XyWrite. For complete instructions, see the Procedure portion of the Default listing.

You can also issue a **BX** from the command line to set border colors for a single editing session:

1. Press **F5** (Clear Command Line).
2. Type **DEFAULT** BX,#,#,#,#,#,#,#,#,#,#,#,# (# stands for the number of the color you want the window border to be).
3. Press **F9** (Execute).
4. "Done" displays on the prompt line.

A La Carte You can set a **BX** default through A La Carte. You must be in an empty window (have a blank screen) to access the menus.

1. Press **F6** (A La Carte menus).
2. Press **X** or select **XyWrite**.
3. Press **D** or select **Defaults**.
4. The View and Change Defaults screen displays.
5. Press **A** or **C** or select **defaults A-C**.
6. Move the cursor to the **BX** entry and type in the color numbers you want to use. A list of the possible colors and their numbers is in the Display section.
7. Press **Return**.
8. The Update Default File screen displays. You're asked if you want to make the default settings permanent.
9. Press **Y** or **N**. If you select **Y**, the program writes the new default settings to a special file and returns you to the A La Carte Menu Screen. If you select **N**, the settings are used for the current edit session.

Tips

You can see most of the colors your monitor is capable of displaying through XyWrite's Help screens.

1. Press **Alt** and **F9** (**Help**).
2. Press **W** or select **Word**.
3. Type **Color Table** in the blank.
4. Press **F9** (Execute) or **Return**.
5. A display showing the colors your computer and monitor are capable of displaying appears. The numbers on the display are the numbers you can enter in the **BX** settings.

Examples

The **BX** command is cosmetic, but it's nice to have total control of your environment. It's especially useful if you use a color monitor.

See Defaults and Windows

BOTTOM FOOTNOTES (BF)

Overview **Bottom Footnotes** can be either a default entry or an embedded command.

The XyWrite default footnote position forces footnotes to grow downward from the text, like stalactites. On a page that isn't filled with text, such as the last page of a chapter, this setting lets the footnotes float several inches above their usual place on the bottom of a page. With **Bottom Footnotes**, you can make them grow up from the bottom of the page like stalagmites.

Procedure To specify **Bottom Footnotes** in a single document:

1. Press **Ctrl** and **Home** to move to the beginning of the document. (This is optional—you can embed the command at any point in the document, but only footnotes *after* the command will be affected.)
2. Press **F5** (Clear Command Line).
3. Type **BF 1**.
4. Press **F9** (Execute).
5. A bright command triangle is inserted.

If you want to return to the default setting:

1. Press **F5** (Clear Command Line).
2. Type **BF 0**.
3. Press **F9** (Execute).
4. A bright command triangle is inserted.

To set **Bottom Footnotes** as your personal default, insert **BF=1** in your STARTUP.INT or printer file. See the Default listing for more information.

A La Carte **BT** can only be set as a default in A La Carte. You must be in an empty window (have a blank screen) to access the menus.

1. Press **F6** (A La Carte menus).
2. Press **X** or select **XyWrite**.
3. Press **D** or select **Defaults**.
4. The View and Change Defaults screen displays.
5. Press **A** or **C** or select **defaults A-C** (alphabetic listing).
6. Move the cursor to the **BF** entry and type **1** to make footnotes hug the bottom of the page or **0** to let them float up.
8. Press **Return**. The Update Default File screen displays. You're asked if you want to make the default settings permanent.
9. Press **Y** or **N**. If you select **Y**, the program writes the new default settings to a special file and returns you to the A La Carte Menu Screen. If you select **N**, the settings are used for the current edit session.

Examples   **Bottom Footnotes** is a style command. If you like your footnotes on the foot of a page, put your system default set to **BF=1**.

See Footnote Format (FM)

BOTTOM MARGIN (BT)

Overview   The **Bottom Margin** command may be misnamed, since it doesn't have any effect at all on the length of a page of text. **BT** does control where a running footer is placed on a page, but the page length itself is determined by the **Page Length** (**PL**) command.

   BT can be issued as a command or used as a default setting.

Procedure   To issue **BT** as a command that affects a single file:

1. Press **Ctrl** and **Home** to go the beginning of the file.
2. Press **F5** (Clear Command Line).
3. Type **BT #** (# stands for the number of lines from the bottom of the page you want the footer to print—the bottom margin).
4. A bright command triangle appears in the text.

Since **BT** can also be a default setting, you can enter the command in your printer file or in your STARTUP.INT file. If you do, any running footers you use in your documents are placed in the same relative position on every page. For complete instructions, see the Procedure portion of the Default listing.

You can also issue **BT** from the command line to print footers in a unique spot during a single editing session:

1. Press **F5** (Clear Command Line).
2. Press **Ctrl** and **Home** to move the beginning of the file.
3. Type **DEFAULT** BT=# (# stands for the number of lines from the bottom of the page you want the footer to print—the bottom margin).
4. Press **F9** (Execute).
5. "Done" displays on the prompt line.

A La Carte   To issue **BT** as a command that affects a single file:

1. Press **F6** (A La Carte menus).
2. Press **R** or select **foRmat**.
3. Press **S** or select **Status**.
4. Move the cursor to the **BT** entry and enter the number of lines from the bottom of the page you want the footer to print.
5. Press **Return**.
6. A bright command triangle is inserted in the text.

You can also set a **BT** default through A La Carte. You must be in an empty window (have a blank screen) to access the menus.

1. Press **F6** (A La Carte menus).
2. Press **X** or select **XyWrite**.
3. Press **D** or select **Defaults**.
4. The View and Change Defaults screen displays.
5. Press **A** or **C** or select **defaults A-C** (alphabetic listing).
6. Move the cursor to the **BT** entry and enter the number of lines from the bottom of the page you want your footer to print.
7. Press **Return**.

8. The Update Default File screen displays. You're asked if you want to make the default settings permanent.

9. Press **Y** or **N**. If you select **Y**, the program writes the new default settings to a special file and returns you to the A La Carte Menu Screen. If you select **N**, the settings are used for the current edit session.

Examples   **BT** determines where a running footer prints in relation to the bottom of the page, which, in effect, sets a bottom margin. The normal position for a footer is on the line specified as the maximum page length in the **PL** setting. That means **BT** is set to zero (**BT=0**) to place the footer zero lines above the bottom. Changing the setting makes a running footer float upwards into the text according to the number of lines you set.

See Page Length (PL) and Running Footer (RF)

CALL (CA)

Overview   CA, **Call**, **ED**,and **Edit** all open an existing file. Each command does the same thing.

Procedure   1. Press **F5** (Clear Command Line).
2. Type **CA** (or **Call**, **ED**, or **Edit**) FILENAME.
3. Press **F9** (Execute).
4. The file you named displays.

There are two variations that you may encounter, both related to the FILENAME entry. You can call a file from a different disk drive other than the one you're logged onto by preceding FILENAME with the diskname: **CALL A:FILENAME**.

If you use extensions with your filenames, you'll have to include that to select the proper file: **CA FILENAME.EXT**.

If you have a directory listing on the screen, you can call a file by "pointing" to it. This is best done by following the steps listed below

1. With the directory listing on the screen, press **F5** (Clear Command Line).
2. Type **CA** (or **Call**, **ED**, or **Edit**).
3. Press **F10** (Text/Command Line Toggle). The cursor drops into the directory listing.
4. Move the cursor to the file you want to open.
5. Press **F9** (Execute).
6. The file you pointed to displays.

A La Carte
1. Press **F6** (A La Carte menus).
2. Press **F** or select **File**.
3. Press **C** or select **Call**.
4. A screen with a line for you to specify a file name displays.
5. Type the file name and press **Return**. Be sure to include the disk drive letter and directory path if they're different from your current disk/directory location.

Examples The **Call** and **Edit** commands are basic commands. You'll use one or the other almost every time you sit down to the keyboard since editing and rewriting are a central part of all writing.

Tips Because the **Call** and **Edit** commands are used so often, they're prime candidates for automating and enhancing.

Here is a possible Save/Get based on **Call**. Press your **Alt** and **D** keys, and several things happen. First, the program alphabetizes the filenames of whatever directory you're in. Then it displays the directory on screen, puts a **CA** command in place on the command line, and moves the cursor into the directory area. You move the cursor to the file you want to edit. When you press **F9** to execute the **CA** command, the file opens in a new window. The directory remains active in another window in case you want to call another file from that area. (Read the section on Programming for more information on how to create these listings.)

Here's the program listing you can use to do all this:

BC dsort e,f**XC BC** dir**XC BC** ca**CC**

If you wish, you can change the listing to sort your files in a different way (see **Dsort**). Also, you could list a specific disk drive, subdirectory, or file name extension, instead of the generic "dir" that calls all files in the active directory.
This listing sorts the files by date:

BC dsort d**XC BC** dir**XC BC** ca**CC**

This listing pulls a directory listing of the B: drive:

BCdsort e,f**XC BC** dir b:**XC BC** ca**CC**

And this listing lists only those files with a .TXT file name extension:

BC dsort e,f**XC BC** dir*.txt**XC BC** ca**CC**

See Edit , Call-Form, and Call Program

CALL FORM (CAF)

Overview   **CAF** calls an existing file that's been set up as a form. The **Edit Form** (**EDF**) command is the same as the **CAF** command.

Procedure   The basic procedure is the same as the **CA** command:
     1. Press **F5** (Clear Command Line).
     2. Type **CAF** FILENAME.
     3. Press **F9** (Execute).
     4. The form you named displays.

     A La Carte   **CAF** is not available from the A La Carte menus. Use the standard XyWrite procedure.

Examples

A XyWrite form usually has protected areas (labels or identifying fields) and blank areas that can be filled in. The **CAF** command preserves these distinct areas by not letting the cursor enter a label area. If a form was opened with **CA**, it could be corrupted if someone modified the protected information. For more information, look at the Forms topic.

Tips

If you work with forms often, you can write a short macro that displays a directory of all available forms and lets you pick the one you need to open, just as the point-and-shoot macro in the **Call** command does.

Also, if you set up a form for other people to fill out, protect your master forms and data by writing a Save\Get that uses **CAF** to open a file. The program operates the same way the programs mentioned in the **Call** topic do. When you press a Save/Get key combination—**Alt** and **F**, for example—several things happen. First, a directory of the forms stored in a special subdirectory is displayed. The **CAF** command is inserted on the command line, and the cursor is moved into the file listing area. You cursor to the proper form, press the **F9** key to execute the command, and the form is opened. (Read the section on Programming for more information on how to create these listings.)

Here's a program listing some XyWriters use:

BC dsort e,f**XC BC** dir \xywrite\forms*.frm**XC BC** caf**CC**

Warnings

If a form is opened with the normal **CA** command instead of **CAF**, the protected areas of the form can be modified. There isn't a straightforward way to protect a form from being called with a **CA** instead of a **CAF**, so the form information always stands a chance of being corrupted.

See Forms

CALL PROGRAM (CAP)

Overview   **CAP** calls an existing program file. It sets up XyWrite in a slightly different way than it normally operates, since writing a program is different and requires slightly different techniques than editing a text file does. The **Edit Program** (**EDP**) command is the same as the **CAP** command.

Procedure   The basic procedure is the same as the **CA** command:

1. Press **F5** (Clear Command Line).
2. Type **CAP** FILENAME.
3. Press **F9** (Execute).
4. The program you named displays.

A La Carte   **CAP** is not available from the A La Carte menus. Use the standard XyWrite procedure.

Examples   When you write a macro or a program in XyWrite, a special tool to record your keystrokes is available. Using the **CAP** command to call a program file automatically enables the keystroke recorder function. Once it's enabled, you toggle it on and off by pressing the **Scroll Lock** key. For more information on writing programs with XyWrite Programming Language, look at the Programs section.

Warnings   There isn't a straightforward way to keep a program from being called with a **CA** instead of a **CAP**, so the program information stands a chance of being corrupted. Protect your programs by keeping them in a special subdirectory under your XyWrite directory. They'll be a little harder to open by accident.

See Save/Gets, Programs, and Call

CENTERING TEXT

See Flush Center

CHANGE (CH)

Overview   The **CH** command changes existing text within a document from one wording to another. The generic word processing term for this function is "search-and-replace." The program searches for all occurrences of one text string ("red," which includes "RED" and "Red") and replaces each passage with a different set of letters ("green").

A **Change** command affects everything from the point where it's executed to the end of a document. **CH** is not case sensitive.

Procedure   1. Press **F5** (Clear Command Line).
2. Type the **CH** command and a space. After the space, type the characters that exist and those that replace them, enclosed by "separator" characters. (For example, if you type: **CH /this/that/** on the command line, you instruct XyWrite to change all occurrences of "this" to "that.")
3. Press **F9** (Execute).
4. You can watch the progress of the change operation as the program whisks through your document. When all the letters have been switched, the word "Done" displays on the prompt line.

A La Carte
1. Press **F6** (A La Carte menus).
2. Press **S** or select **Search**.
3. Press **R** or select **Replace**.

4. A screen displays that lets you enter your "search" and "replace" strings in fill-in blanks. Fill in the existing text you want to search for first. *Do not press Return yet.*

5. Use the down arrow to move to the "replacement" blank. Fill in the text you want to insert. If you press **Return** now, you'll be asked to verify each replacement.

6. (Optional) Use the down arrow to select a **Change** option—**V** for "verify," the default; **H** to change without verifying; or **I** for "invisible."

7. (Optional) Use the down arrow to select **A** to specify an absolute match for the search string.

8. Press **Return** to implement the changes.

If you're using A La Carte, all members of the XyWrite search-and-replace command family are executed from the same fill-in form.

Examples
One of the greatest benefits word processors have given writers is the ability to change text throughout a document with a couple keystrokes. A misspelled name in a document can be corrected in one fell swoop, and an entire book can be searched for "swell foop" and changed to "fell swoop" at lightning speed.

XyWrite performs text changes faster than most other word processing programs. It also provides a powerful addition to your change options since it can search and replace tab stop characters, carriage returns, and even spaces. This facility lets you change the formatting of a document very quickly.

Suppose you separated paragraphs in a letter with a blank line, indicated by a carriage return. You can remove all those extra carriage returns and indent paragraphs with tab stops very easily.

Shift to expanded display (**Ctrl** and **F9**) and execute a **Change** command like this one:

CH /←←/←./

The carriage returns are generated by pressing the **Ctrl** and **Return** keys, the symbol that indicates a tab stop is generated by the tab key.

Another common formatting change is removing extra spaces between sentences. Many people habitually begin a new sentence with two taps of the spacebar. In many publishing environments, however, editors like to pack slightly more information into their pages by using a single space.

A command like the one below searches for two spaces and replaces them with a single space (the spaces are, of course, invisible):

CH / / /

XyWrite also lets you search for and change its internal formatting commands. In normal text display mode, XyWrite's text formatting commands show up as bright triangles. When you change your text display to "expanded" by pressing **Ctrl** and **F9**, the triangles display the embedded commands you've placed in the text.

In expanded mode, the **Change** command will locate and modify any embedded format commands.

In your Master's thesis, suppose you indented long quotations two inches from your normal left and right page margins. The beginning of a quotation passage might look like this:

«LM30»«RM55»Quoted text begins here and goes on and on and on and on...

Those settings, however, set a very narrow line. Should you decide to widen the measure, a single **Change** command can set a wider line:

CH /«LM30»«RM55»/«LM20»«RM65»/

The European quote marks that XyWrite uses to enclose formatting commands are created by pressing **Ctrl** and the < or > keys.

Other ASCII characters can be used in a **Change** command—look in the ASCII section for more information on how they're generated.

If you want to delete a certain passage in your document, **CH** can take care of it. If you don't put any characters in the second pair of separators, nothing will be inserted, but the "search" characters will be matched and deleted. A **Change** command to delete text looks like this:

CH /text//

Finally, what if you need to search for a passage that includes a slash mark? It's easy. XyWrite requires a separator to set off the old characters from the new, but the separator can be any graphic character. You can use a vertical bar |, backslash \, exclamation point !, or anything else that suits your fancy. A command to modify "and/or" looks like this:

CH | and/or | and |

Tips

Become familiar with the related change commands, especially **Change Absolute (CHA)**. **CH** is extremely useful and is the most powerful of the search-and-replace command family, but its power limits its usefulness for some jobs.

CH is not case sensitive. It ignores the difference between capital and lower case letters.

When you type **CH /red/green/**, XyWrite will change all the "red" character strings it finds to "green"... and all the "RED" and "Red" strings too.

CHA, on the other hand, *is* case sensitive. If you use **CHA** instead of **CH**, as in **CHA /red/green/**, *only* the "red" character strings will change to "green." The "RED" and "Red" strings will not be changed.

Also, remember that a **change** command takes effect at the point in the text where the cursor is and goes on to the end of the document. If you want to do a true "global" change to a document,

C

you'll need to move your cursor to the top of the text by pressing **Ctrl** and **Page Up** before executing the **change** command.

The **Change Invisible (CI)** and **Change Invisible Absolute (CIA)** commands work like **CH** and **CHA** do, but make their changes a little faster.

Another variety of the change commands, **Change Verify (CV)** and **Change Verify Absolute (CVA)**, operate like **CH**, but the program will prompt you before each possible change. You have the opportunity to verify each search-and-replace operation as the program proceeds through your document.

Warnings   It's possible to change too much of a document very quickly. If you execute a **Change** command and realize that the command is running amok, stop the change in its tracks by pressing the **Ctrl** and **Break** keys. On many keyboards, the **Scroll Lock** key doubles as the **Break** key.

If you run through a series of **Change** operations and decide you don't like the end effect, there isn't an easy way to reverse the procedure. You can either plunge onward and undo the most recent change with a second **CH**, keeping on until you get the right effect, or use the **Abort (AB)** command to abort your edits. If you abort before you've saved the bad changes, you can call the previous edit session of your text and begin again.

See Change Absolute (CHA), Change Verify (CV), Change Verify Absolute (CVA), Change Invisible (CI), and Change Invisible Absolute (CIA)

CHANGE ABSOLUTE (CHA)

Overview   **Change Absolute** is a case sensitive search-and-replace command, the picky sibling of **CH**. **CHA** searches through a document to find a particular group of letters or symbols. When they are located, **CHA** removes them and inserts a new group.

CHA works exactly like **CH**, except that **CHA** matches a change string exactly, where **CH** will settle for a close match.

A **Change Absolute** command affects all the text from the point where it's executed to the end of a document.

Procedure   The syntax of a **Change Absolute** command is identical to that of a **Change**:

1. Press **F5** (Clear Command Line).
2. Type the **CHA** command and a space. After the space, type the characters that exist and those to replace them, enclosed by "separator" characters. (For example, if you type: **CHA /this/that/** on the command line, you instruct XyWrite to change all occurrences of "this" to "that.")
3. Press **F9** (Execute).
4. You can watch the progress of the change operation as the program whisks through your document. When all the letters have been switched, the word "Done" displays on the prompt line.

Examples   **Change Absolute** performs all the functions mentioned in the **Change** command section.

   Change Absolute is probably the search-and-replace command you should make a habit of using. Because it's case-sensitive, it is more specific than the simple **Change**. You'll find that **CHA** is less likely to run away and make changes you didn't intend than **CH**. **Change Absolute** can be used in almost all situations where several changes in the text are required. The only situation where you might prefer **CH** is one where you'd like to catch all variations of a word or text string, regardless of case ("red," RED," and "Red") in one pass.

A La Carte
1. Press **F6** (A La Carte menus).
2. Press **S** or select **Search**.
3. Press **R** or select **Replace**.

4. A screen displays that prompts you to enter your "search" and "replace" strings in fill-in blanks. Type in the existing text you want to search for first. *Do not press Return yet!*
5. Use the down arrow key to move into the "replacement" blank. Type in the text you want to insert. If you press **Return** at this point, you'll be asked to verify each replacement.
6. (Optional) You can use the down arrow key to select a **Change** option—**V** for "verify," the default; **H** to change without verifying; or **I** for quick "invisible" replacement.
7. Use the down arrow key to move a little further down the form and select the **A** option to order a change with an absolute case match.

See Change (CH), Change Verify (CV) and Change Verify Absolute (CVA), Change Invisible (CI), and Change Invisible Absolute (CIA)

CHANGE CASE (CC)

Overview   The **Change Case** command capitalizes a lower case letter or changes a capital letter to lower case. The command works on a single letter, word, or a block of text.

Procedure   The **Change Case** command can be executed in two ways. If a block of text has not been defined, the letter under the cursor is changed. If a block of text has been defined, the command switches each letter in the block.

To switch the case of a single letter:

1. Press **F5** (Clear Command Line).
2. Type **CC**.
3. Press **F9** (Execute). The letter under the cursor in the text changes case.

To change the case of every letter in a defined block of text, first define the block, then issue the **CC** command.

To define the block:

1. Put the cursor at the beginning of the text you want to change.
2. Press **F1** (Begin Define).
3. Move the cursor to the end of the text passage.
4. Press **F1** (End Define)

To issue the **CC** command:

1. Press **F5** (Clear Command Line).
2. Type **CC**.
3. Press **F9** (Execute). All the characters in the defined block change case.
4. Release the defined block by pressing **F3**.

A La Carte   To switch the case of a single letter:

1. Press **F6** (A La Carte menus).
2. Press **E** or select **Edit**.
3. Press **C** or select **Case**.
4. Press **C** or select **Change Case**.
5. Press **F9** (Execute) or **Return**.

To change the case of every letter in a defined block of text, first define the block, then issue the **CC** command.
To define the block:

1. Put the cursor at the beginning of the text you want to change.
2. Press **F1** (Begin Define).
3. Move the cursor to the end of the text passage.
4. Press **F1** (End Define)

To issue the **Change Case** command:

1. Press **F6** (A La Carte menus).
2. Press **E** or select **Edit**.
3. Press **C** or select **Case**.
4. Press **C** or select **Change Case**.
5. Press **F9** (Execute).
6. Release the defined block by pressing **F3**.

Examples CC is used most often to correct a typing mistake, typically not capitalizing the first letter in a sentence.

Tips If you find yourself using **CC** very often, consider placing the command on a Save/Get key to save time and keystrokes, or try the **Automatic Uppercase (AU)** command.

Creating the **CC** macro is one of the easiest programs you'll ever write—it's the first example in the Programming section.

Warning Although it's a very basic command, **CC** can backfire. If you're trying to capitalize every letter in every word of a sentence, for instance, you may not want to use **CC**. Here, the **Upper Case (UC)** command will work better.

Defining a sentence and issuing a **Change Case** command makes all the lower case letters into capitals, but it also changes the existing capital letters into lower case. The first word and any names in the sentence will begin with a lower case letter, which probably isn't what you intended.

If you define the sentence and issue the **Upper Case** command, all letters in the sentence become capitals.

See Upper Case (UC), Lower Case (LC), Blocks (Modifying Text), and Automatic Uppercase (AU)

CHANGE DIRECTORY (CD)

Overview The **Change Directory** command in XyWrite works exactly like the DOS or OS/2 change directory command. It's used to change the default directory while you're in XyWrite.

Procedure 1. Press **F5** (Clear Command Line).
2. Type **CD** \DIRECTORYNAME.
3. Press **F9** (Execute).
4. "Done" displays on the prompt line.

A La Carte
1. Press **F6** (A La Carte menus).
2. Press **D** or select **Dir**.
3. Press **C** or select **Changedir**.
4. A screen with a space for you to type in the new path name appears.

Examples   Use **CD** to move around your disk drive while you're running XyWrite. The command eliminates the need to type a file's path name to call it to the screen. It also eliminates the need to leave XyWrite and go to the operating system to change directories.

You may want to change directories to access a file or group of files that aren't your usual documents—perhaps electronic mail messages and replies or entries in a database.

Many people organize their electronic documents like a file cabinet to keep text together. For instance, all the chapters of a book that someone is in the process of writing, could be grouped together in a subdirectory.

Tips   If you're not sure what directory you should move to, or aren't sure of the name, use the **Tree** command instead (the **Dir** command can also be helpful to see a graphic display of the file structure).

Organizing XyWrite directories and compartmentalizing text files is discussed in the **Make Directory (MKDIR)** section.

See Directory (DIR), Make Directory (MKDIR), and Tree

CHANGE DIRECTORY (CHDIR)

See Change Directory (CD)

CHANGE INVISIBLE (CI)

Overview   **Change Invisible** is another member of the search-and-replace command family. **CI** operates just as **Change (CH)** does.

When you execute a **CH** command, the display screen updates the document display as each change is executed. **CI** doesn't update the screen display until all the changes in the text have been made. Since it doesn't update the screen, the search-and-replace procedure is completed more quickly.

Procedure   The syntax of **Change Invisible** is identical to that of a **Change**.

1. Press **F5** (Clear Command Line).
2. Type the **CI** command and a space. After the space, type the characters that exist and those that replace them, enclosed by "separator" characters. (For example, if you type: **CI /this/that/** on the command line, you instruct XyWrite to change all occurrences of "this" to "that.")
3. Press **F9** (Execute).
4. When all the letters have been changed, the word "Done" displays on the prompt line.

Examples   **CI** can be used in any situation where you would use a simple **Change** command to search for a pattern of letters or symbols in a file and replace them with different characters.

Warnings   A **Change Invisible** command, can, if you make a mistake in what to search for or replace, mess up your document. With **CH**, the changes are made and displayed so you can abort the change in midstream, if you notice an incorrect procedure.

Remember that you can always use **AB** to abort an editing session and call the last, previously saved version of your text.

See Change Invisible Absolute (CIA), Change (CH), Change Absolute (CHA), Change Verify (CV), and Change Verify Absolute (CVA)

CHANGE INVISIBLE ABSOLUTE (CIA)

Overview   **Change Invisible Absolute** combines the specificity of a **Change Absolute** (**CHA**) command with the speed of a **Change Invisible** (**CI**).

     CIA conducts a case-sensitive search-and-replace operation in your text without constantly refreshing the screen display.

Procedure   The **CIA** command syntax is exactly like the other **Change** commands:

1. Press **F5** (Clear Command Line).
2. Type the **CIA** command on the command line and follow it with a space. After the space, type the characters that exist and those that replace them, enclosed by "separator" characters. (For example, if you type: **CIA /this/that/** on the command line, you instruct XyWrite to change all occurrences of "this" to "that.")
3. Press **F9** (Execute).
4. When all the characters have been changed, the word "Done" displays on the prompt line.

Examples   **CIA** can be used in any situation where you need a very specific change operation, usually when some similar words contain capital letters and some do not. The command works speedily since the screen display is not updated as the operation proceeds.

Warnings   As with the **Change Invisible** command, messing up the document is possible, see the Warnings section of the last entry.

See Change Invisible (CI), Change (CH), Change Absolute (CHA), Change Verify (CV), and Change Verify Absolute (CVA)

CHECK, SPELLING CHECKER (CK)

Overview   The XyWrite spell check option can operate in four different modes. By setting the **CK** default, you can make the program check words that contain numbers and ignore the automatic replacement feature, ignore all words that begin with a number; use the automatic replacement feature, or ignore all words that begin with a number *and* use the automatic replacement feature.

Procedure   Since **CK** is a default setting, you can enter the command in your printer file or in your STARTUP.INT file. If you do, the spell check option functions as you prefer each time XyWrite starts. For complete instructions, see the Procedure portion of the Default listing.

The syntax of the **CK** command is **CK=#**. The number can be:

- 0 to check words that contain numbers and ignore the automatic replacement feature.
- 1 to ignore all words that begin with a number.
- 2 to use the automatic replacement feature.
- 3 to ignore all words that begin with a number *and* use the automatic replacement feature.

You can also issue **CK** from the command line to set a unique spell check mode for a single editing session:

1. Press **F5** (Clear Command Line).
2. Press **Ctrl** and **Home** to move to the beginning of the file.
3. Type **DEFAULT** CK=# (**0**, **1**, **2**, or **3**).
4. Press **F9** (Execute).
5. "Done" displays on the prompt line.

A La Carte You must be in an empty window (have a blank screen) to access the menus:

1. Press **F6** (A La Carte menus).

2. Press **X** or select **XyWrite.**
3. Press **D** or select **Defaults**.
4. The View and Change Defaults screen displays.
5. Press **A** or **C** or select defaults **A-C**.
6. Move the cursor to the **CK** entry and select **1**, **2**, or **3**. Zero is not an option.
7. Press **Return**.
8. The Update Default File screen displays. You're asked if you want to make the default settings permanent.
9. Press **Y** or **N**. If you select **Y**, the program writes the new default settings to a special file and returns you to the A La Carte menu screen. If you select **N**, the settings are used for the current edit session.

Uses **CK** configures XyWrite's spelling checker to your preference. There are two options: whether or not to spell-check words that include numbers, such as 12th, and whether or not to use words on the auto replace list (see **Auto Replace** for details).

The spell-check numbers option seems of minor importance since most people don't use many words that contain numbers.

The auto replace toggle, however, has some usefulness in day-to-day operation. Briefly, the auto replace option reads a list of often mistyped or misspelled words and quickly substitutes the correct version. A basic list comes with the program and you can add your own words.

If the list is enabled, the proofreading process goes a little faster since the program doesn't pause at each error—it knows how to fix some words by itself.

See Defaults

CLEAR ALL SAVE/GETS (CLRASG)

Overview **CLRASG** is one of a subset of commands related to XyWrite's macro facility.

CLRASG flushes all text and program macros, and all temporary storage buffers, from your computer's memory.

Procedure
1. Press **F5** (Clear Command Line).
2. Type **CLRASG** on the command line.
3. Press **F9** (Execute).
4. The word "Done" will display on the prompt line.

A La Carte
1. Press **F6** (A La Carte menus).
2. Press **E** or select **Edit**.
3. Press **G** or select **save/Get**.
4. Press **C** or select **Clear s/g**.
5. A screen prompts you to enter a single Save/Get key or press **Return** to clear all **Save/Gets**.

Examples
CLRASG and the companion command **CLRSGT** are two commands you never really have to issue. **CLRASG** removes all Save/Get keys, XyWrite's term for a macro procedure or buffer, from computer memory. This includes any text saved temporarily on a Save/Get key and any programs.

You may want to do this before loading a different set of macros from a storage file, but it's not necessary. When the second set is loaded, they supersede all current macros assigned to the same keys.

Warnings
If, for any reason, you issue **CLRASG**, make sure to store any text you have stored temporarily to a file on disk. Otherwise, it will be erased forever.

See Clear Save/Gets (CLRSGT) and Save/Gets

56

CLEAR EDITS (CE)

See Clear Edits (Verify)

CLEAR EDITS, VERIFY (CEV)

Overview   After reviewers or editors have inserted comments in a file with the redlining feature, the original author can erase the comments with **CE** or **CEV**.

Procedure   **CE** and **CEV** are usually the last steps in redlining, the process of inserting hidden comments in a document during the review process. After as many comments as necessary have been inserted with the **Put Edits** (**PE**) and **Put Edits Verify** (**PEV**) commands, the unused comments can be removed with **CE** or **CEV**. **Clear Edits** removes all the comments. **Clear Edits Verify** prompts you before removing a comment.

To remove all comments from a redlined document:

1. Move the cursor to the point when you want to begin clearing edits. Usually, this would be the top of the file.
2. Press **F5** (Clear Command Line).
3. Type **CE**.
4. Press **F9** (Execute).
5. "Done" displays on the prompt line.

To selectively remove comments from a redlined document:

1. Move the cursor to the point where you want to begin clearing edits. Usually, this would be the top of the file.
2. Press **F5** (Clear Command Line).
3. Type **CEV**.
4. Press **F9** (Execute).
5. The cursor moves to the first edit and a menu displays. Select:

- **A** To **Abort** the command, leave the edit in place, and return the cursor to the starting point.
- **Q** To **Quit** the command, leave the edit in place, and keep the cursor where it is.
- **S** To **Stop** the command from executing after this edit is removed.
- **N** To keep the edit in place and continue to the next edit.
- **Y** To remove this edit and continue to the next edit.

6. The process is repeated until all the edits have been reviewed.

A La Carte   Redlining functions aren't available through the A La Carte menus. Use the standard XyWrite procedure.

Warnings   Once you clear any of the comments in a document, it's gone. The only way you might be able to recover the suggestion is to use **Abort** to get out of the current editing session and **Call** to open the file again.

See Redlining and Put Edits

COLUMNS, PARALLEL

Overview   XyWrite's parallel column feature lets you set as many as nine separate, unrelated columns on a page. It's especially useful if you need to build a table or set up a newsletter format with unrelated stories on the same page.

Procedure   Set up parallel columns by issuing a **Column Table (CT)** command. When you issue the **CT**, XyWrite embeds column markers to define each column for you.

The **CT** command requires an argument for each column you're establishing. XyWrite supports up to ten columns.

There's also an argument for offset, the amount of space the columnar text is indented from the left margin.

A sample command syntax looks like this:

CT offset, col. 1 width,col. 2 width, col. 3 width

Given that the typical printed page is 80 characters wide, the command to set up three equal columns would be:

CT 0,26,26,26

To establish the columnar layout in a document:

1. Press **F5** (Clear Command Line).
2. Type **CT** 0,26,26,26.
3. Press **F9** (Execute).
4. Four bright marker triangles will appear on your screen.

The first triangle contains the **CT** command, sets the widths for each column, and marks the beginning of the first column. Each subsequent triangle on that line marks the beginning of a column. If you press **Ctrl** and **F9** to view your document in expanded mode, you'll see that each triangle indicates the appropriate column number—«CT0,26,26,26», «CO2», and «CO3».

An «EC» marker will be on the next line under the column markers. It indicates the end of the column layout and the resumption of the standard full-width environment.

«CT,0,26,26,26»«CO2CO3»
«EC»

When text is inserted, it goes between the markers on the first row.

A La Carte Column functions are not available in A La Carte version 1.0. Use the standard XyWrite procedure.

Examples Parallel columns simplify setting up a table or checklist in a document. For a short table of two or three lines, tab stops give you the desired effect. For anything longer, a column table makes life easier.

This column function does not wrap text from the bottom of one column to the top of the next. Newspaper-style "snaking" columns do that. They're discussed in the next topic. The parallel column function keeps text isolated in its own column, separated from its neighbors.

Many people use a columnar layout to produce newsletters. The XyWrite column functions are powerful enough to approximate more expensive desktop publishing programs. Most newsletters use a mix of parallel columns and snaking columns to create a pleasing design.

Tips

Remember that XyWrite has two types of column modes—this one and **Snaking Columns**, a newspaper-style setting.

Once a column table is established, XyWrite treats the table much as a spreadsheet program does. Each entry in each column becomes a cell in the table.

Column editing commands comprise a small subset of special commands that work only within tables. Most XyWrite editing features work inside a table's column. XyWrite treats each column almost as a separate, narrow page.

TABLE 2

Column Editing Commands

FUNCTION	KEY COMBINATION
Define a text block in a column and end the block	Alt and F1 to begin (Any function mentioned in the"Blocks" section works).
Define current cell	Shift and F1
Move to the nextc olumn over	Shift and î or Ä
Move to the top or bottom of the current cell	Shift and Home or End
Add a row of cells	Shift and Ins
Delete a row of cells	Shift and Del

Change the widths of columns once they're in place by editing the widths in the **CT** marker triangle:

1. The widths of the columns will show up in the **CT** marker («CT0,20,30»). Type in the new entries, making sure you don't inadvertently add a column.

Move existing text into columns in one of two ways. Manually insert the column markers at the appropriate places in the text or set up the column format and move the text into the columns. Inserting column markers works better when the existing text is already arranged properly—block two follows block one and block three follows two. Defining blocks of text before moving them into a column layout works better if the text is spread around a document in bits and pieces. No matter which way you decide to accomplish the task, do the work in expanded mode.

To manually insert column markers in existing text:

1. Press **Ctrl** and **F9** to expand the display.
2. Position the cursor where you want the first column to begin.
3. Type **Ctrl**, <, and > to create a set of embedded command fences. Move the cursor between the fences and type the numbers that specify offset and the width of each column (such as **CT0,20,20**, for two columns). The result should look like this: «CT0,20,20»

Notice that when you type the command directly into the text, the space between the **CT** and the offset entry that's required when issuing the command from the command line, is omitted. To start the next column:

1. Position the cursor where you want the second column to begin.
2. Type **Ctrl**, <, **CO2**, and > to mark the beginning of the second column with «CO2».
3. Position the cursor where you want the third column to begin.
4. Type **Ctrl**, <, **CO3**, and > to mark the beginning of the third column with «CO3».

5. Continue inserting **CO** commands until each column you defined has been marked.
6. Position the cursor at the end of the last column.
7. Type **Ctrl**, **<**, **EC**, and **>** to mark the end of the column environment with «EC».

To move existing text into columns, first establish the columns in the document:

1. Press **F5** (Clear Command Line).
2. Type **CT** 0,26,26,26 (for three equal columns. Modify the entry to suit your needs).
3. Press **F9** (Execute). Five format markers (bright triangles) will appear on your screen.
4. Press **Ctrl** and **F9** to expand the display.
5. Define the block of existing text that will go into the first column. (Move the cursor to the beginning of the text, press **F1**, cursor to the end of the text, and press **F1** again.)
6. Move your cursor to the space just after «CT0,26,26,26» and press **F8**. The text moves into position.
7. Define the text that will go into the next column.
8. Move your cursor to the space just after «CO2» and press **F8**. The text moves into position.
9. Repeat the procedure until all the text is in place.

This is a perfect application for using a "flag" in your text. Insert a unique marker character in the empty column—your flag character. Move away to define your text. Then use a **Search** (**SE**) command to snap back to the proper position, marked by the flag, without cursoring all around.

Justify type in columns if you need to use the available space as completely as possible. See the **Justify** section for details. If you do justify type, you'll be able to fit more words on a line. Remember that justified type is slightly harder to read than type set "flush left" (with a straight and even left margin, but with uneven line endings on the right side of the column or page).

Warnings   Don't build a column table wider than your page margins, or the page itself. If you do, the text will wrap around to the left margin or print off the right side of the page.

Set paragraph indents to zero when you create a column layout with several narrow columns. If you set a column width of 15 spaces but your normal paragraph indent is 5 spaces from the edge of the page, the effective column width of the first line will only be 10. A paragraph indent of 5 which looks good in normal text might be too wide for a column. See the **Indent Paragraph** section for details.

Don't ever erase just one or two column markers. If you need to wipe out the columns, make sure you erase the **CT**, **EC**, and all the **CO** markers or you'll get pagination errors. If one or more markers is deleted accidentally, expand the display with **Ctrl** and **F9** so you can see what's missing. Either delete the survivors and start over or insert the missing commands, using the procedure described earlier.

See Columns (Snaking) and Blocks (Text)

COLUMNS, SNAKING

Overview   The newspaper, or snaking, column feature (the **SN** command) sets up several columns on a single page and flows text into each subsequent column. Text fills the first column, jumps to the top of the second column, fills that, and moves on to the third...

The newspaper column feature is very different from XyWrite's **Column Table** feature. That establishes separate, unrelated columns on a page. It's used to build tables or print stories on the same page. Newspaper columns unify a single story or stream of text on one or more pages.

Procedure   Set up a newspaper-style page format with the **SN** command. **SN** requires an argument for the starting position of each column you're establishing. XyWrite supports up to six snaking columns.

The command syntax looks like this:

SN col. 1 start, col./ 2 start, col. 3 start

Note how different this is from the **CT** command, where you specify the width of each column:

1. Press **F5** (Clear Command Line).
2. Type **SN** 0,26,52.
3. Press **F9** (Execute).
4. A single bright marker triangle appears in your text.

Your page display will not change to reflect the snaking columns, but they'll print properly. If you need to preview the effect, use the **Type to Screen (Type)** command.

To end the snaking column section and return to normal, full-page width text, insert another **SN** command with the starting point set to 0:

1. Press **F5** (Clear Command Line).
2. Type **SN** 0.
3. Press **F9** (Execute).
4. A single bright marker triangle appears in your text.

A La Carte Column functions are not available in A La Carte version 1.0. Use the standard XyWrite procedure.

Examples Snaking columns are great for printing any type of material that doesn't require the full width of the page. Try it with a phone list or index.

If you're publishing a newsletter or flyer of some sort, it's a natural to give your document a professional-looking flair.

See Columns (Parallel)

COMMAND LINE (CM)

Overview   XyWrite displays three reverse video identification blocks in the screen header: CM, PRMPT, and NM. The **CM** command lets you change them to display more useful information: the default disk drive, the current directory path, and the active window number.

Procedure   The **CM** command can be executed from the command line to change the header display for a single editing session, but it's usually included in the STARTUP.INT file so that the header displays useful information each time XyWrite is used.

To execute **CM** from the command line:

1. Press **F5** (Clear Command Line).
2. Type **CM d,w,p** (**D** toggles the **CM** indicator to display the default disk drive, **w** changes PRMPT to display the current directory path, and **p** makes the NM area show the active window number).
3. Press **F9** (Execute).
4. "Done" displays on the prompt line and the display in the three header fields changes.

To include **CM** in a STARTUP.INT file:

1. Press **F5** (Clear Command Line).
2. Type **CA** STARTUP.INT.
3. Press **F9** (Execute).
4. The file opens. Move the cursor to a line that begins with a bold **BC**.
   - Press **F4** (Define Line).
   - Press **F7** (Copy Define).
5. In the new line, move the cursor past the **BC** and type **CM d,w,p**.
6. Erase any text from the original line.
7. Press **F5** (Clear Command Line).
8. Type **ST** (**Store**).
9. Press **F9** (Execute).

65

The next time XyWrite starts, the display in the three header fields shows the new information.

A La Carte A La Carte is installed with all three fields displaying information. To turn any of them off, edit the STARTUP.INT file as described above, but delete the line that contains the **CM** entry.

Examples The **CM** command makes the header more useful to most writers, since it keeps them apprised of where they are and what's going on.

Tips As an added bonus, if you use the **p** option to change the NM display, XyWrite shows the status of any defined blocks. If nothing is defined, only the window number shows. The first time you press **F1** to begin defining a block, a hyphen displays to the right of the window number. The second time you press **F1** to complete the block, an equal sign appears. The equal sign also displays if you use any of the block defining shortcut keys to define a word, sentence, or paragraph.

COMPARING TWO FILES

Overview **Compare** lets you review two similar files and locate differences between them. It doesn't make any changes whatsoever; it just moves the cursor through a document from point of change to point of change.

Procedure Although **Compare** works with any two documents in separate windows, reviewing them side-by-side seems to be the most efficient way. Opening two windows on a single screen lets you track the progress of the comparison.To open windows:

1. Press **Ctrl** and **F10** (Window Menu).

2. Select **V** to split the screen vertically or **H** to split it horizontally.
3. **Call** the first document.
4. Switch to the second window with **Shift** and **F10**.
5. **Call** the second document.
6. If you're going to make more changes in one document, that should be the window you work in. Change windows if necessary.

To begin the comparison:

1. Press **Ctrl** and **-** (**Find Difference**).
2. The cursor stops at the point in the document where it begins to differ from the text in the other window. The other document scrolls along, so you can see the two passages side-by-side.
3. Press **Ctrl** and **=** (**Find Match**).
4. The cursor stops at the point in the document where it begins to match the text in the other window—effectively at the point where the differences stopped.
5. Continue using **Ctrl** and **/-** (**Find Difference**) and **Ctrl** and **=** (**Find Match**) to move through the documents.

A La Carte Comparing files in A La Carte is similar to the standard XyWrite procedure. First, open both files to be compared:

1. Press **Ctrl** and **F10** (Window Menu).
2. Select **V** to split the screen vertically or **H** to split it horizontally.
3. Call the first document.
4. Switch to the second window with **Shift** and **F10**.
5. Call the second document. If you're going to make more changes in one document, that should be the window you work in. Change windows if necessary.
6. Press **F6** (A La Carte menus).
7. Press **S** or select **Search**.
8. Press **F** or select **compareFiles**.

9. A screen with two choices displays: **Find Differences** or **Find Match**. Place the cursor on one and press **Return**.

Examples

Compare is very useful when you're reviewing a document for changes or edits. Used with **Redlining**, XyWrite provides a pretty complete set of editing and document production tools.

You may think that the ability to compare documents would be limited to a few situations—an attorney's office where contracts are constantly being revised, or a writing-and-editing situation where a chapter or article is always being updated. Those are the obvious situations.

Anyone who writes business letters, school papers, recipes, or the Great American Novel, could use **Compare** to find the changes between two drafts of the same document. Once those changes have been located, they're easy to analyze so you can determine which version is better.

Tips

If you want to compare formatting commands, put each document in expanded display mode; otherwise, any differences will be noted, but you won't be able to see what they are. Switch from normal display to expanded with **Ctrl** and **F9**.

Warnings

The location of the cursor is critical to the **Compare** function. It must be at the same point in each document when you begin comparing, or the alternate **Find Match** functions won't work.

Depending on the idiosyncrasies of your computer and keyboard, you might be limited to using the - and = keys above your letter keys, rather than the corresponding keys on the number pad.

See Redlining

COPY A FILE (COPY)

Overview   XyWrite's **Copy** command duplicates a file that is stored on one of your computer's disks. It works just as the DOS command does. You can copy files across directories or disks if you wish. The procedure does not support the DOS wildcards, so only one file at a time can be copied, and you must use the complete fil name.

Procedure   Copy a file to the same or a different location and change its name:
1. Press **F5** (Clear Command Line).
2. Type **COPY** SOURCEFILENAME,TARGETFILENAME.
3. Press **F9** (Execute).

You can precede each filename with a drive and path name:
1. Press **F5** (Clear Command Line).
2.Type **COPY** C:\XYWRITE\BOOK\SOURCEFILENAME, A:TARGETFILENAME.
3. Press **F9** (Execute).

Copy a file to a different location (retaining the original name):
1. Press **F5** (Clear Command Line).
2. Type **COPY** FILENAME,DESTINATION.
3. Press **F9** (Execute).

A La Carte   You must be in an empty window to use the A La Carte **Copy** function. Then:

1. Press **F6** (A La Carte menus).
2. Press **F** or select **File**.
3. Press **P** or select **coPy**.
4. A screen with a **From** and a **To** blank appears. Type the current file name in the **From** blank. Type the name of the new file in the **To** blank.
5. Press **Return.**

Examples   There are hundreds of reasons for copying a file. While you're writing, you may want to make a copy of a document before editing. Another very common application is backup storage, so that if anything happens to the original or the computer it's stored on, you'll be protected.

Tips   If you have several files to copy or aren't sure of the filename, use one of the "directory" variations of **Copy**.

1. Press **F5** (Clear Command Line).
2. Type **Dir** (**Directory**) and, optionally, a source disk and/or path. If you don't specify a disk or path, the current location is used.
3. A list of files will appear.
4. Press **F5** (Clear Command Line).
5. Type **COPY** DESTINATION DRIVE OR PATH (COPY A: or COPY \INVENTORY).
6. Press **F10** to move the cursor into the directory listing.
7. Move the cursor to the file you want to copy.
8. Press **F9** (Execute).
9. "Working..." displays while the procedure is running; "Done" when it's finished.

CORRECT

Overview   The **Correct** command is used near the end of the spell-check process to insert a list of correct words in the target file. **Correct** is only used when a closed file that's stored on disk is spell-checked.

   Correct can also append text to a list of words, a feature that can automate index creation.

Procedure   XyWrite's spell-check program can be used on an open file or a closed file that's stored on disk. When a closed file is spell-checked, a list of words that aren't in the program's dictionaries is created.

After that list is edited and any genuine misspellings are corrected, the **Correct** command inserts the corrections into the target file and removes any misspelled words. After the list of possible misspelled words has been edited:

1. Press **F5** (Clear Command Line).
2. Type **CORRECT**.
3. Press **F9** (Execute).
4. When the changes have been inserted, a prompt displays that asks if you want to save the file to disk. Press **Y** or **N**.

A La Carte Correct operates in A La Carte the same way it operates in XyWrite. To use it, you should have edited the word list generated by the spell-check. You must be in an empty window (have a blank screen) to access the **Correct** command:

1. Press **F6** (A La Carte menus).
2. Press **O** or select **Option**.
3. Press **S** or select **Spell**.
4. Press **C** or select **Correct**.
5. The corrected words are inserted in the target file.

Tips

Using **Correct** to insert corrected words in a closed document is a standard part of the spell-check program. There's another facet to the program that makes **Correct** a plus to anyone who needs to compile an extensive index or concordance.

When the spell-check program checks a closed file, a list of words that don't match known dictionary entries is compiled. That list is a regular ASCII file that can be edited with XyWrite. After the list is edited, the words can be reinserted in the file.

The "list" file can also be created from scratch. It must have the name of the file it's linked to on the first line in reverse type (**MD RV**, usually enabled by pressing **Ctrl** and **4**). Each line under that contains a word, in this case a word that is will appear in an index.

A sample file looks like this:

Q.TXT
Quiller
Wright
nope
yup

To index each of those words in the Q.TXT file:

1. Press **F5** (Clear Command Line).
2. Type **CORRECT** FILENAME,x8 (FILENAME is the name of the word list. The index marker is an optional entry that is appended to each word on the word list, automatically marking each word as an index entry.
3. Press **F9** (Execute).
4. When the words have been inserted, a prompt displays that asks if you want to save the file to disk. Press **Y**.

Using this technique, you can include any text string you want after a list of words, using **Correct** to insert them.

See Spell

CORRECTION BEEP (CB)

Overview   When the spell check function encounters a word it doesn't recognize, it beeps. The length and tone of the beep can be adjusted with the **CB** default setting.

Procedure   Since **CB** is a default setting, you can enter the command in your printer file or in your STARTUP.INT file. If you do, the tone and duration of the spell check's warning will be the sound you want to hear for each editing session. For complete instructions, see the Procedure portion of the Default listing.

You can also issue **CB** from the command line to set a unique beep for a single editing session:

1. Press **F5** (Clear Command Line).
2. Type **DEFAULT** CB=#,# (tone, duration).
3. Press **F9** (Execute).
4. "Done" displays on the prompt line.

The initial settings are **512, 4096**. Either number can be set to any value between 0 and 65534. If you want to turn the beep off altogether, enter a **0,0** value.

A La Carte You must be in an empty window (have a blank screen) to access the menus.

1. Press **F6** (A La Carte menus).
2. Press **X** or select **XyWrite**.
3. Press **D** or select **Defaults**.
4. The View and Change Defaults screen displays.
5. Press **A** or **C** or select **defaults A-C**.
6. Move the cursor to the **CB** entry and type values for tone and duration.
7. Press **Return**.
8. The Update Default File screen displays. You're asked if you want to make the default settings permanent.
9. Press **Y** or **N**. If you select **Y**, the program writes the new default settings to a special file and returns you to the A La Carte Menu Screen. If you select **N**, the settings are used for the current edit session.

Examples The **CB** setting is another way to tailor your copy of XyWrite to your liking. There's no practical value in modifying the beep, but there's a certain amount of satisfaction in being able to play with the program settings.

Tips   The numbers you enter for tone and duration have little relationship to the real world. They were keyed to the original IBM PC speaker, but there have been so many changes in computer hardware since then, tone and duration vary from machine to machine.

See Defaults

COUNTERS (C#)

Overview   The **C** command is used in all XyWrite processes that provide automatic numbering—the numbering of chapters, pages, footnotes, outline entries, and paragraphs.

Procedure   All XyWrite counting processes depend on embedded C commands to keep track of text elements. The **C** commands are issued with a number that identifies a set of counters—**C0**, **C3**, and so on, up to **C14**.

Counters are linked to another command that keeps track of them—a **Reference** command that tracks text passages or chapter, or a **Define Counter** (**DC**) command that sets the format for a numbered list. Depending on what the counter is being used for, the controlling command may have some special requirements, so be sure to review that command. The basic procedure for inserting a **C** command is very simple, however:

1. Move the cursor to the place in the document where the counter should be inserted.
2. Press **F5** (Clear Command Line).
3. Type **C#** (# is the counter set, 1-14. **C0** is reserved for tracking chapters).
4. Press **F9** (Execute).
5. A bright command triangle is inserted in the text.

A La Carte

1. Move the cursor to the point in the text where the counter should be inserted.
2. Press **F6** (A La Carte menus).
3. Press **R** or select **foRmat**.
4. Press **C** or select **Counters**.
5. The Counters screen displays.
6. Move the cursor to the number that represents the set of counters you want to insert.
7. Press **Return**.
8. A bright command triangle is inserted in the text.

Examples   Look at the listings under **Reference Chapter (REC)**, **Reference Page (REP)**, and **Numbering** to see how counters are used in particular situations.

Tips   Most XyWrite numbering procedures allow you to use a set of custom symbols instead of numbers to keep track of text elements. To do this, however, you must create a Counter Table in your printer file:

1. Press **F5** (Clear Command Line).
2. Type **CA** PRINTERFILENAME.
3. Move into the file a few lines to a clear area and type **CS:#** (# is the number of items you're including in the table. For three items, you'd type **CS:3**).
4. Type the first symbol or characters and press **Return**.
5. Type the second symbol or characters and press **Return**. Repeat the procedure until the entire sequence has been entered.
6. Set the table off from other parts of the printer file by typing a semi-colon and pressing **Return**.
7. Press **F5** (Clear Command Line).
8 Type **ST** (**Store**) to close the file.
9. Press **F9** (Execute).

To make the Counter Table active, you must reload the file:

1. Press **F5** (Clear Command Line).
2. Type **LOAD** PRINTERFILENAME.
3. Press **F9** (Execute).
4. "Done" displays on the command line.

This customized counter string is identified by an asterisk or a pound sign in the controlling command that keeps track of counters. The **Define Counter** (**DC**) command calls it out like this: **DC#1**.

In some situations, you might want to insert a counter, but not have it generate a number. If you do this, the program keeps track of the counter, and it increments as it chould. It can be referenced elsewhere. When you execute the **C#** command, add a space and a hyphen:

1. Move the cursor to the place in the document where the counter should be inserted.
2. Press **F5** (Clear Command Line).
3. Type **C#** - (# is the counter set, 1-14. **C0** is reserved for tracking chapters).
4. Press **F9** (Execute).
5. A bright command triangle is inserted in the text.

Warnings   XyWrite only supports a single customized counter string. If you use it for numbering footnotes, for instance, you probably don't want to also use it for page numbers!

See Define Counter, Footnotes, Labels, Numbering, Chapter, Page, and Counter References

---

CURSOR TYPE (CR)

Overview   You can specify what type of cursor you prefer to work with by modifying the **CR** setting.

Procedure   Since **CR** is a default setting, you can enter the command in your printer file or in your STARTUP.INT file. If you do, your favorite cursor display mode is invoked each time XyWrite starts. For complete instructions, see the Procedure portion of the Default listing.

The **CR** setting has two arguments: **CR=#,#**. The first entry is the display mode for normal text-editing display. The second number is the display mode used when you access help screens. A complete list of colors and display modes is in the Display section.

You can also issue **CR** from the command line to set a unique display mode for a single editing session:

1. Press **Ctrl** and **Home** to move to the beginning of the file.
2. Press **F5** (Clear Command Line).
3. Type **DEFAULT** CR=#,#.
4. Press **F9** (Execute).
5. "Done" displays on the prompt line.

A La Carte You must be in an empty window (have a blank screen) to access the menus.

1. Press **F6** (A La Carte menus).
2. Press **X** or select **XyWrite**.
3. Press **D** or select **Defaults**.
4. The View and Change Defaults screen displays.
5. Press **A** or **C** or select **defaults A-C**.
6. Move the cursor to the **CR** entry and enter the appropriate display codes.
7. Press **Return**.
8. The Update Default File screen displays. You're asked if you want to make the default settings permanent.
9. Press **Y** or **N**. If you select **Y**, the program writes the new default settings to a special file and returns you to the A La Carte Menu Screen. If you select **N**, the settings are used for the current edit session.

77

Examples   XyWrite's standard cursor is a blinking block that many people find somewhat distracting. **CR** lets you create a nonblinking cursor or change the color of the cursor (provided you have a color monitor).

Tips   You can see the colors your monitor is capable of displaying through XyWrite's Help screens:

1. Press **Alt** and **F9** (**Help**).
2. Press **W** or select **Word**.
3. Type Color Table in the blank.
4. Press **F9** (Execute) or **Return**.
5. A display showing the colors your computer and monitor are capable of displaying appears. The numbers on the display are the numbers you can enter in the **CR** settings.

See Defaults

DATE (DA)

Overview   The **Date** command creates a "soft" calendar date in text. When you execute **DA**, an embedded command triangle that causes the current date to appear, is inserted into your file. The date is constantly updated so when the file is open, the displayed date will be current. **DA** is not a time stamp that inserts "hard, editable" characters—**Today** does that.

Procedure   Any type of date format can be set with **DA**, but the general command is the same:

1. Press **F5** (Clear Command Line).
2. Type **DA** format (see the possible entries below).
3. Press **F9** (Execute).
4. A command triangle and the current day's date display.

For the format entry, you can mix and match several types of day, month, and year displays.

For Months:

- **M**—Displays the single or double digit number of the current month.
- **MM**—Displays the double digit number of the current month.
- **MMM**—Displays the three letter abbreviation of the current month in capital letters.
- **Mmm**—Displays the three letter abbreviation of the current month with an initial capital letter.
- **MMMM**—Displays the full name of the current month in capital letters.
- **Mmmm**—Displays the full name of the current month with an initial capital letter.

For Days:

- **D**—Displays the single or double digit number of the current day.
- **DD**—Displays the double digit number of the current day.
- **DDD**—Displays the single or double digit number of the current day. If the date is a single digit, this entry also generates a space for the leading digit.

For Years:

- **YY**—Displays the last two digits of the current year.
- **YYYY**—Displays all four digits of the current year.

The date, month, and year can appear in any order. Any type of punctuation can be mixed into the date format information.Here are some of the possibilities generated for a date of November 15, 1990:

- **da Mmm. ddd, yy**, yields - Nov. 15, 90
- **DA MMMM dd, yyyy**, yields - NOVEMBER 15, 1990
- **da dd/mm/yy**, yields - 5/11/90
- **DA yyyy—MM dd**, yields - 1990—11 15

A La Carte
1. Press **F6** (A La Carte menus).
2. Press **E** or select **Edit**.
3. Press **D** or select **time/Date**.
4. The Time/Date screen displays.
5. Press **D** or select **soft Date** to insert the **DA** command.
6. A La Carte inserts a **DA** that produces a standard date format

Examples   **DA** is handy for any type of dating that doesn't require an accurate record on disk. Since the date is constantly refreshed, a memo that you wrote on June 1 and dated with **DA** is going to have a new date when you reopen the file in July.

Templates, master forms and memos, checks, invoices, and all kinds of rotating documents are ideal places for **DA**.

Tips   Where does **DA** get its information? From your computer's operating system. If your computer doesn't have a built-in clock and you have to set the time manually, make sure you do. Don't skip past the time and date prompts or **DA** won't generate the right date.

Compare the **Today** command, which inserts today's date as hard characters that never change. It's better suited than **DA** for a document that must have an accurate place in time for your records.

Although the **DA** command generates a listing that includes days, a month, and a year, you don't have to use all three components. Any can be left out, to generate a date that only includes a month and day, or just a month and year.

See Today, Now, and Time

DECIMAL POINT (DP)

Overview   **DP** is a default setting that specifies what particular character represents a decimal point.

Procedure   Since **DP** is a default setting, you can enter the command in your printer file or in your STARTUP.INT file. If you do, the decimal is used in all math operations whenever XyWrite starts. For complete instructions, see the Procedure portion of the Default listing.

     You can also issue **DP** from the command line to set a unique character for a single editing session:

1. Press **F5** (Clear Command Line).
2. Press **Ctrl** and **Home** to move the beginning of the file.
3. Type **DEFAULT** DP=character.
4. Press **F9** (Execute).
5. "Done" displays on the prompt line.

A La Carte You must be in an empty window (have a blank screen) to access the menus.

1. Press **F6** (A La Carte menus).
2. Press **X** or select **XyWrite**.
3. Press **D** or select **Defaults**.
4. The View and Change Defaults screen displays.
5. Press **D** or **G** or select **defaults D-G** (alphabetic listing).
6. Move the cursor to the **DP** entry and type the character you want to use.
7. Press **Return**.
8. The Update Default File screen displays. You're asked if you want to make the default settings permanent.
9. Press **Y** or **N**. If you select **Y**, the program writes the new default settings to a special file and returns you to the A La Carte Menu Screen. If you select **N**, the settings are used for the current edit session.

Examples   The American and English counting systems use a period as their decimal point, but some currencies and languages use other characters—a comma, for instance. If you need to change the standard period, the **DP** command is your tool.

See Defaults

DECIMAL TAB

See Tab Stops

DEFAULT

Overview   Default settings customize XyWrite to your particular style and needs. You can set standard margins, display parameters, the way windows are opened and shut, what disk drive to use, and in which other parameters of the program. How many settings are controlled by **default**? Seventy-six.

Procedure   Default settings are usually stored in a file. That way, preferred formats are set to your liking every time you use the program.

Defaults can also be set from the command line. If they are, they stay in effect only for the current editing session. When the computer is turned off or you quit XyWrite, "command line" defaults are lost. No markers are inserted in text since you're setting a system default.

As a general rule, set printer and monitor display defaults in your printer file. Format or system settings should go in STARTUP.INT or in a special default settings file (a .DFL file). A file-based entry is typed into the appropriate file just as text is entered into any other file.STARTUP.INT executes a number of commands for you when XyWrite starts. It executes the commands as you do when you issue a command from the command line. Therefore, the command syntax to set a default is the same for both. The syntax is:

DEFAULT COMMAND SETTING (taken from the lists below)

Default entries in STARTUP.INT look like this:

BC DEFAULT BK=0
BC DEFAULT PL=54,60,50
BC DEFAULT TP=6,LM=10,RM=75

Notice that several settings can be strung together on the same line. Just separate them with commas.

If you don't want to take the time to learn XyWrite programming procedures, use the regular text editing tools to modify STARTUP.INT. Open STARTUP.INT with a **Call** or **Edit** command. Define one or two existing lines (with **F4**) that contain "DEFAULT" settings and copy them (with **F7**). Then change the existing settings to your standards.

The syntax of printer file entries is slightly different. The word "DEFAULT" abbreviates to "DF." Otherwise, the syntax is the same:

DF COMMAND SETTING (taken from the lists below)

Default entries in a printer file look like this:

DF EJ=1
DF NW=1
DF LF=1
DF CK=3
DF DT=2
DF ST=1
DF PT=99

To insert commands in a printer file, open the file with **Call** or **Edit**. Then look for the factory default settings listed near the top of a printer file. A number of default settings commonly stored there don't *require* the "DF" prefix, so if you open a file and can't find any, don't be confused. Look for lines that begin with the command entries listed below, when you find them, you'll be in the right neighborhood.

Once you've located the right part of the file, type in your new settings, one to a line, and store the file. To set a default from the command line for a single editing session:

1. Press **F5** (Clear Command Line).
2. Type **DEFAULT** COMMAND ENTRY.
3. Press **F9** (Execute).
4. "Done" displays on the prompt line.

Depending on the setting, the new default may take effect immediately or the next time a file is opened. Setting a default can be confusing simply because there are so many possibilities.

TABLE 3 **Format Settings**

NAME OR COMMAND	ENTRY	ORIGINAL SETTING
Automatic leading	al=1 or 0	0 (off)
Auto Pause	ap	NP (No Pause)
Bottom Footnote	bf=1 or 0	0 (off)
Bottom Margin	bt=# (lines)	0 lines from bottom
Flush Center	fc	(flush left)
Form Depth	fd=## (lines)	66
Flush Left	fl	fl
Flush Right	fr	fr
Footnote Transition	ft=#, (lines)	0
Hyphenation	hy=1 or 0	(1 on)
Indent Paragraph	ip=#,# (spaces)	0,0
Justification	ju	nj (no just.)
Left Margin	lm=# (spaces)	0
Line Spacing	ls=# (lines)	1
Character Mode	md=(setting)	nm (normal)

(Continued)

NAME OR COMMAND	ENTRY	ORIGINAL SETTING
No Justification	nj	nj
No Pause	np	np
Offset	of=#,# (spaces)	0,0
Page Length	pl=#,#,# (lines)	54,60,50
Print Type	pt=(type)	#1
Right Margin	rm=# (spaces)	78
Relative Tabs	rt=1 or 0	0 (right)
Superscript Number	ssc=1 or 0	0 (SS/text)
Top Margin	tp=# (lines)	6
Tab Set	ts=(positions)	8,16,24,...

TABLE 4 Printer and Display Settings

NAME OR COMMAND	ENTRY	ORIGINAL SETTING
Backspace	bs=1 or 0	1 (on)
Window Brd. Colors	bx=(color) #	112,7,7...
Cursor Type	cr=#,#	0,0
Display Blocks	dd=(color)	#8
Discretionary Hyphen	dh=(character)	~
Decimal Point	dp=(character)	. (period)
Display Type	dt=	0,1,2 or 31
Display Units	du=#	10
EGA Control	eg=	0,1 or 20
Eject Last Page	ej=1 or 0	0 (off)
Form Feed	ff=1 or 0	0 (off)
Normal Header Mode	hn=(color)	#7
Reverse Header Mode	hr=(color)	#7
Hyphenation Values	hv=#,#,#	5,2,2
Justify Underline Chs	jl=0 or 1	0 (off)
Justification Type	jt=1 or 0	0 (off)
Margin Unit	mu=#	72
Microspace Factor	ms=#	72
Report Print Errors	ne=1 or 0	0 (off)

(Continued)

D **DEFAULT**

NAME OR COMMAND	ENTRY	ORIGINAL SETTING
Pad Spaces	pd=1 or 0	0 (off)
Screen Length	sl=# (lines)	25
Sequential Page Numbers	sq=1 or 0	0 (off)
Show Tabs	st=1 or 0	0 (off)
Tab Character Prints	tb=1 or 0	0 (off)
Underline Setting	ul=0,1,2 or 3	1
Vertical Unit	vu=#,#,#	0
Word Overstrike	wo=1 or 0	0 (off)
Whole Space Justify	ws=1 or 0	0 (off)
Space Constant	xc=#	4
Space Factor	xf=#	1

TABLE 5   **System Settings**

NAME OR COMMAND	ENTRY	ORIGINAL SETTING
Backup Files	bk=1 or 0	1 (on)
Correction Beep	cb=#,#	513,4096
Spelling Checker	ck=0,1,2 or 3	1
Directory Settings	di=#,#,#	0,6,0
TMP Drive Default	dr=(drive)	varies
Error Beep	eb=#,#	1536,12288
Error Help	eh=1 or 0	0 (off)
Erase Prompt	ep=1 or 0	0 (off)
Footnote Unit	fu=#,#	3,5
Header Size	hs=#	79
Key Click	kc=#,#	0,0 (off)
Display Line Spacing	lf=0 or 1	0 (off)
Normal Carriage Return	nc=0 or 1	1 (on)
New Window	nw=0 or 1	0 (off)
Overstrike Beep	ob=#,#	0,0
Sort Key	sk=#,#	1,80
Ignore Top Margin	tf=0 or 1	0 (off)

A La Carte A La Carte's default setting mechanism is very sophisticated, allowing access to most settings through its menus. It's also radically different from the procedure used in the unadorned XyWrite program. A La Carte stores its defaults in a unique .DFL file instead of writing them to a regular printer file or to STARTUP.INT.

You must be in an empty window (have a blank screen) to access the menus:

1. Press **F6** (A La Carte menus).
2. Press **X** or select **XyWrite**.
3. Press **D** or select **Defaults**.
4. The View and Change Defaults screen displays.
   - Press **M** or select **screen Modes** (monitor display).
   - Press **S** or select **Sort options** .
   - Press **A** or **C** or select **defaults A-C** (alphabetic listing of the settings listed above).
   - Press **D** or **G** or select **defaults D-G** (alphabetic listing).
   - Press **H** or **M** or select **defaults H-M** (alphabetic listing).
   - Press **N** or **S** or select **defaults N-S** (alphabetic listing).
   - Press **T** or **Z** or select **defaults T-Z** (alphabetic listing).
5. Modify the default setting and press **Return**.
6. The Update Default File screen displays. You're asked if you want to make the default settings permanent.
7. Press **Y** or **N**. If you select **Y**, the program writes the new default settings to a special file and returns you to the A La Carte Menu Screen. If you select **N**, the settings are used for the current edit session.

Examples The default settings are your tool for customization. By manipulating XyWrite's default settings, you can create a highly personalized word processor that complements the way you work. Here are more possible default settings. For your STARTUP.INT file:

- **BC** DEFAULT BK=0—Turns off automatic backup of files.

- **BC** DEFAULT PL=54,60,50—Sets the page length to a nominal 54 lines, between a minimum of 50 and a maximum of 60.
- **BC** DEFAULT TP=6,LM=10,RM=75—Sets the top margin to 6 lines (an inch) and left and right side margins to one inch.

For your printer file:

- DF EJ=1—Automatically ejects the last page of a document.
- DF NW=—Automatically opens and closes windows as needed.
- DF LF=1—Screen display mimics the actual line spacing.
- DF CK=3—Spell Check is fully enabled.
- DF DT=2—Page and line numbers are always displayed.
- DF ST=1—Makes tab stops a visible character.
- DF PT=99—Sets Print Type 99 as my default text type.

Tips

Embedded commands in a document take priority over any system defaults. A left margin set to 12 with a **LM 12** command from the command line will override any left margin default settings from any file.

Create several sets of default settings for different situations, store each set in a file, and load whichever one matches the document you're working on.

You may want to do this if you write several radically different types of documents on a regular basis. A legal office may use one set of defaults for letters and memos, a second for briefs (which usually go on legal size paper), and a third for filling out invoices and other forms. A script writer is likely to use a special set of defaults for the highly-specialized script format, but prefer something else for correspondence or outlines.

One way to do this is to make copies of your printer file. Store them under different names to match their different settings. XyWrite's 3EPSONFX.PRN functions just fine as LEGAL.PRN or SCRIPT.PRN. You can do the same thing by copying and renaming STARTUP.INT. Put the second set of defaults in place with the **Load** command for the modified printer file and **Run** for the modified .INT file.

A second, slick strategy is to create files that contain nothing but default settings. XyWrite is not shipped with any of these .DFL files, but A La Carte, the menu-driven add-on product, is. Building your own .DFL file from scratch is pretty easy:

1. Create a new file with a .DFL extension, such as your ARTS.DFL.
2. The first four characters in the file must be **;PR;**. These label the file as a printer file. Press **Return**.
3. Next, type in your default settings, one to a line. Don't use indents, tabs, or spaces.

For the greatest flexibility, type in all the default listings. You won't use all of them, of course, so enter the factory setting on the ones you don't use.

You can add comment lines to each setting which will remind you what each setting does. Begin each comment line with a semi-colon and end each one with a carriage return. Don't use XyWrite's automatic line wrapping feature.

Here's a sample .DFL file listing, with most entries in alphabetic order. (Notice that this file includes some screen display settings too. Everything you need to customize XyWrite to your needs, wrapped up in one file!) Normally, the .DFL listing will be a one column entry. You can then:

1. Store the file.
2. Use the **Load** command with the plus sign option to load the file into memory, *appending it to whatever printer file is already there*. The correct syntax is: **LOAD +YOURARTS.DFL**

If you're satisfied with your .DFL file, add the **Load** command line to the bottom of your STARTUP.INT file, or tack the **+ FILE.DFL** part to the line that loads your regular printer file.

```
;PR;
;This file is generated by A La
Carte.
;
df hl=7
df AL=0
df BF=0
df BK=0
df BT=0
df BX= 112, 7 ,7 ,7 ,7 ,7 ,7 ,7 ,7, 7,
112, 15
df CB=512,4096
df CK=3
df CR=0,0
;
df DD=8
df DH=
df DP=.
df DR=
df DT=2
df EB=1536,12288
df EG=0
df EH=1
df EJ=0
df EP=1
df FD=66
df FF=0
df FT=0
df FU=3,5
;
df HS=79
df HV=5,2,2
df HY=1
df IP=0,0
df JL=0
df NJ
df KC=0,0
df LF=1
```

```
df LL=0,0
df LM=10
df LS=1
;
df NC=1
df NE=0
df NW=1
df OB=0,0
df OF=0,0
df OP=0
df PD=0
df PL=54,60,50
df PT=1
df RM=75
df RT=0
df SC=0
df SL=25
df SQ=0
df ST=1
;
df TB=0
df TF=0
df TB=0
df TF=0
df TP=6
df UL=1
df WD=0
df WO=0
df TS=8, 16, 24, 32, 40, 48, 56, 64,
72, 80, 88
;
;
md nm=7
md bo=15
md ul=1
md rv=112
md bu=9
md br=120
```

```
md su=122            md rv=112
md sd=121            md bu=9
md fn=250            md br=120
df hn=7              md su=122
df hr=112            md sd=121
df WD=0              md fn=250
df WO=0              df hn=7
df TS=8, 16, 24, 32, 40, 48, 56, 64,   df hr=112
72, 80, 88           df dd=8
;                    ;
;                    df sk=1,80,0
md nm=7              ;
md bo=15             ;
md ul=1              ;
```

Warnings   Although there are many default settings that can be modified, the real danger comes in extensively modifying a file without testing the effect as you go. Unless you're sure what the result of a command is, test your new default by issuing it from the command line and observing the effect. When you've got the command figured out, enter it into the file.

Another good idea is to keep a backup copy of whatever file you modify. Before you change one of your files, create an unmodified copy with the **Copy** command. You can return to that file if your modifications don't work out. When you begin to modify your files, add or change one default at a time to gauge the effect. Don't try to make a hundred changes at once—it's easy to end up with a muddle. Even worse, a muddle that's impossible to untangle because you've changed so many things you don't know which one is causing the problem.

Remember that after a printer file or STARTUP.INT has been modified, it has to be reloaded for the changes to take effect. On the command line, issue a **LOAD PRINTERFILE.PRN** command to load the modified printer file. **RUN STARTUP.INT** loads the new startup defaults.

See Restore Defaults, Printer files, STARTUP.INT, and Value of a Variable

---

DEFAULTS, RESTORE XYWRITE DEFAULTS (DM)

Overview   **DM** (Restore XyWrite Defaults) changes any modified default settings to the original "factory settings" established by XYQUEST. The command is usually issued from the command line, so the XyWrite settings stay in effect for a single editing session.

Procedure   1. Press **F5** (Clear Command Line).
2. Type **DM**.
3. Press **F9** (Execute).
4. "Done" displays on the prompt line.

A La Carte   The **DM** command can't be accessed through A La Carte's menus. Use the procedure above.

Examples   If your personal default settings aren't appropriate for a particular writing job, **DM** is a handy command. Instead of having to modify a number of defaults, **DM** implements a set of plain vanilla settings for you.

Although **DM** can be inserted in a printer or in a STARTUP.INT file, most people don't use it that way since those files are the most convenient way to set personal defaults different than the **DM** settings. The original XyWrite settings are:

- Automatic leading   0 (off)
- Bottom Footnote   0 (off)
- Hyphenation   1 (on)
- Indent Paragraph   0, 0
- Justification   NJ (No Justification)
- Left Margin   0
- Line Spacing   1 (single spacing)
- Offset   0

- Page Length   0
- Right Margin   78
- Eject Last Page   0(off)
- Form Feed   0 (off)
- Show Tab Characters 0 (off)
- Make Backup Files   1 (on)

Tips   If you invoke **DM** settings for particular documents, put a note to yourself in those files to ensure you treat them with consistency.

See Defaults

DEFINE COUNTER (DC)

Overview   XyWrite can use up to six different numbering schemes in its automatic numbering feature (see Numbering). **DC** is the command that specifies which set of characters is used. It's also the command that restarts the numbering sequence when you have more than one list in your document or are using sublists.

Procedure   The syntax of the **DC** command depends on how sophisticated your needs are. If you only need a simple numbered list at a single level, the most basic command works well—**DC 1=1**:

1. Press **F5** (Clear Command Line).
2. Type **DC** 1=1 (to set the first level of numbers to Arabic numerals).
3. Press **F9** (Execute).
4. A bright command triangle is inserted in the text.
5. To number items, insert **C1** commands.

This setting automatically sets all subsequent numbers to Arabic numbers too. To restart the numbering sequence when another list begins, enter another **DC 1=1** where the next list begins.

For nested numbering setups you need to determine three parameters. First, decide which of the five supplied numbering schemes you wish to use (or an optional, user-defined scheme). You can use:

- Arabic numerals (1, 2, 3....)
- Upper case Roman Numerals (I, II, III....)
- Lower case Roman numerals (i, i, iii....)
- Upper case letters (A, B, C....)
- Lower case letters (a, b, c....)

Second, decide how many levels you'll nest. XyWrite supports up to 15 levels of nesting:

First level	1
Second level	1-1
Third level	1-1-1
Fourth level	1-1-1-1
Fifth level	1-1-1-1-1

Third, decide if you need punctuation or separators between the numbers. In the preceding example, hyphens are used as separators. Finally, construct the command. The full syntax is:

DC level=style/firstnumber separator style/secondnumber separator style/thirdnumber...

1. Press **F5** (Clear Command Line).
2. Type **DC 1=1-1.1** to set the first level of numbers to Arabic numerals, followed by a hyphen, a second Arabic number, a period, and a third Arabic number. (**DC 1=I.** sets the first level to upper case Roman numerals followed by a period and a space. **DC 2=A.** sets the second level to upper case capital letters followed by a period and a space.)
3. Press **F9** (Execute).

4. A bright command triangle is inserted in the text.

5. To number items, insert **C#** commands.

A La Carte

1. Press **F6** (A La Carte menus).

2. Press **R** or select **foRmat**.

3. Press **C** or select **Counters**.

4. A screen with several numbering options displays.

5. Press **D** or select **Define Counters**. A screen with a blank for you to structure the numbering scheme appears. Fill in the blank and press **Return**. A single **DC** defining one level of the numbering scheme is inserted in text.

6. Press **O** or select **Select Outline Style**. A set of **DC** commands to structure the traditional outline numbering sequence are inserted in text.

7. Press **L** or select **Select Legal Style**. A set of **DC** commands to structure the traditional paragraph numbering scheme used in legal and technical documents is inserted.

Examples   The **DC** command is an integral part of XyWrite's numbering facility. It sets the format for each numbered list, outline, or paragraph numbering scheme. It's also used to automatically number chapters.

See Counters, Numbering, and References

DELETE FILE (DEL)

Overview   XyWrite's **DEL** command erases a file on disk. It functions like the DOS DEL or ERASE command, except it can only be used on one file at a time. The **DEL** and **Erase** commands are used in exactly the same way. All the procedures detailed in the **Erase a File** section are used with **DEL**.

See Erase a File

DELETING TEXT

Overview   XyWrite offers several quick ways to delete varying amounts of text. You can cut a character, word, part of a line, or a whole line by pressing a key or two.

    These shortcuts supplement the two-step "define-and-delete" block operations.

Procedure   Use the following key combination shortcuts:

TABLE 6   **Deleting**

TO DELETE	PRESS
The character under the cursor	Del
The character to the left of the cursor	Back Space
The word under the cursor	Alt and Del
The word to the left of the cursor	Alt and Back Space
The line the cursor is on	F5
The part of the line right of the cursor	Ctrl Del

A La Carte   All these key combinations work in A La Carte.

Tips   When you erase something you shouldn't, remember the "undelete" function— **Alt** and **F3**. Undelete puts whatever was last deleted back into the text wherever the cursor happens to be. If you delete a line, move the cursor up several lines, and then decide to undelete, the missing line is inserted where the cursor is now, not where it was originally.

    Delete other text elements automatically by writing a short macro or modifying your keyboard file.

    Most writers think in sentences, paragraphs, and pages, but XyWrite's writers don't seem to. In the out-of-the-box program, none of those functions can be accomplished with a keystroke or two-key combination.

If you want to delete a sentence, paragraph, screen, or page quickly, you'll have to customize your program a wee bit. The good news is that it's easy!

Write a macro to define and delete a sentence with a two-key combination. To write a macro that defines and deletes a paragraph (more details in the Programming section):

1. Press **F5** (Clear Command Line).
2. Type **NEP** FILENAME.PM.
3. Turn the keystroke recorder on by pressing **Scroll Lock**.
4. Press **Shift** and **F4** (the Define Paragraph combination).
5. Press **Alt** and **F6** (the Delete Define combination).
6. Your screen displays these characters: **DP RD.**
7. Store the file.

To load the macro onto a key:

1. Press **F5** (Clear Command Line).
2. Type **LDPM** FILENAME.PM,# (the # stands for any single letter or number key) to load the program onto a Save/Get key.
3. Press **F9** (Execute).

To delete a paragraph:

1. In a text file, position the cursor in the paragraph.
2. Press **Alt** and **#** (the key you loaded the program) on in Step 2.
3. The paragraph is deleted.

If you want to keep the macro available, store the Save/Get. (See the Save/Get section.)

Modify your keyboard file for the ultimate in convenience. Read the Keyboard File section for more details.

The procedure is fairly basic. Pick a key or key combination you don't use very often. Locate that entry in the keyboard file. Erase the current entry and type in **RP** (the function call for **Delete**

D

Paragraph). Store the file. As soon as the file is loaded, that keystroke combination lets you delete paragraphs.

See Blocks (Modifying Text)

DIRECTORY (DIR)

Overview   The **DIR** command displays a listing of files in the current directory or subdirectory. If you specify a path name or a file qualifier, only those files are listed. The DOS * and ? wildcards are supported.

Procedure   1. Press **F5** (Clear Command Line).
2. Type **DIR**.
3. Press **F9** (Execute).
4. A list of files in the current directory displays.

To list files in a different directory:

1. Press **F5** (Clear Command Line).
2. Type **DIR** Drive:\Path (**DIR** C:\XYWRITE\LETTERS, for example).
3. Press **F9** (Execute).
4. A list of files in the specified directory displays.

To list only those files that end with .TXT:

1. Press **F5** (Clear Command Line).
2. Type **DIR** *.TXT.
3. Press **F9** (Execute).
4. A list of files in the current directory that end with .TXT displays.

A La Carte   You must be in an open window (have a blank screen) to get a directory listing.

1. Press **F6** (A La Carte menus).
2. Press **D** or select **Dir**.
3. Press **D** or select **Dir**.
4. The Display File Directory Screen displays.
5. To list the files in your current directory, press **Return**.
6. To list files in a different directory, type the path, and press **Return**.
7. To view the first view lines of each file, move the cursor to the blank that asks how many lines of each file to view and type a number. Press **Return**.

Examples   **DIR** is a basic command you'll use almost every editing session since it lets you know what files you have available. The directory listing also displays the size of the file, in bytes, and the date and time it was last saved:

.			9-29-88	8:41p
..			9-29-88	8:41p
BOOK			9-29-88	8:42p
PMS			10-01-88	2:34p
XYDOC			9-29-88	8:42p
DICTION		15093	2-22-88	9:21a
GETS		1084	11-14-88	5:55p
READ	ME	8823	2-19-88	1:47p
AUTOEXEC	BAT	19	5-29-87	2:03a
CHSTACK	COM	1753	10-02-87	2:57p
EJECT	COM	128	10-00-80	12:00a
SP20	COM	2176	10-23-85	7:03p
XYKBD	COM	1688	8-19-87	2:24p
EDITOR	EXE	178754	10-18-88	12:04a
GRID	FRM	4768	1-01-80	12:07a
LONG	HLP	200265	1-19-88	8:57a
NEW	HLP	202194	8-24-88	10:33a
CONFIG	INT	14759	2-18-88	11:19a
KAY	INT	96	8-05-87	11:44a
SINGLE	INT	60	8-05-87	11:43a
STARTUP	INT	197	10-01-88	2:42p

DVORAK	KBD	14403	6-15-87	8:55a
IBM	KBD	9530	11-20-87	11:16a
SUPER	KBD	7426	8-24-88	9:25a
TANDY	KBD	5513	6-15-87	8:54a
Z181	KBD	8821	11-10-87	2:02a
LETTER	MAS	217	3-07-88	2:40p
MEMO	MAS	214	3-03-88	9:19a
OUTLINE	MAS	144	5-27-87	3:02p
SPELL	OVR	22432	4-01-87	12:20a
WORD	OVR	22784	5-20-87	1:13a
KBD	PGM	5922	1-04-88	11:35a
3EPSONFX	PRN	8507	10-02-88	1:05a
3IBMPRO	PRN	5251	10-02-88	11:25a
ART	SPL	4278	11-14-88	9:33a
BUSINESS	SPL	6106	6-08-87	12:44a
DICT	SPL	110464	2-04-87	8:55a
LEGAL	SPL	6686	6-08-87	12:08a
PERS	SPL	3885	6-08-87	2:47a
WFBG	SYN	325952	3-04-87	5:22p
PRINT	TMP	145	11-07-88	8:22a
CONFIG	TXT	6695	2-18-88	12:07a

43 Files   1207382 Char.   15949824 Free

The number of files in the directory, the total space they take up, and the amount of free space on the disk display at the bottom of the list.

Tips

DIR is usually the command that's issued just before you open a file for editing. It's a good candidate for automating and enhancing by loading it onto a Save/Get key. Look at the macros listed under the **Call** command for ideas.

Keep a record of a directory listing on disk by issuing a **Store** command once the directory displays. Everything in the listing is written to a file that can be opened later and edited. If you want to create a file that lists other file names for chain printing, this is an easy way to do it.

DIRECTORY, LONG (DIRL)

Overview   **DIRL** functions like **DIR** does, but it gives you more information by displaying the first five or six lines in each file. Path and filename qualifiers can be used with **DIRL** just as they are with **DIR**.

Procedure   1. Press **F5** (Clear Command Line).
2. Type **DIRL**.
3. Press **F9** (Execute).
4. A list of files in the current directory and the first few lines of each file displays.

A La Carte   You must be in an open window (have a blank screen) to get a directory listing.

1. Press **F6** (A La Carte menus).
2. Press **D** or select **Dir**.
3. The Display File Directory Screen displays.
   • To list the files in your current directory, press **Return**.
   • To list files in a different directory, type in the path and press **Return**.
4. Move the cursor to the blank that asks how many lines of each file to view and fill in a number.
5. Press **Return**.

Examples   **DIRL** is more useful than **DIR** when you're prowling through an unfamiliar directory since it provides a peek into each file. And it's worlds better than trying to decipher a cryptic DOS file name. It's great for investigating those old files you wrote months ago and forgot, but suddenly need again.

Tips   Any programs that use **DIR** as a function can also use **DIRL**, although the listing for a large directory can fill several screens.

See Change Directory, Directory, and Find

DIRECTORY SETTINGS (DI)

Overview   **DI** is a default setting that regulates how the **DIRL** command displays a directory listing. **DIRL** displays standard directory information—filename, size, date and time of last save—and the first few lines of the file. (**DI** also has a slight effect on the **DIR** command.)

Procedure   There are three display parameters controlled by **DI**. First, how the file size displays, in bytes or kilobytes; second, the approximate number of text lines to display; and third, whether carriage returns are displayed or removed so more words show.
The syntax of the command looks like this:

DI=k,l,p

Each argument is a number. The default setting for the size display is **1**, to show file size in bytes. If you'd prefer kilobytes, use **1024** as an entry.
The default setting for the number of lines to display is **6**. The third setting, to keep or strip carriage returns, is an on/off setting. Enter **1** to strip carriage returns and **0** to keep them. The XyWrite default is **0**.
DI is a default setting, so you can enter the command in your printer file or in your STARTUP.INT file. If you do, the **DIRL** settings are used. For complete instructions, see the Procedure portion of the Default listing.
You can also issue **DI** from the command line. The settings stay in effect for the current editing session:

1. Press **F5** (Clear Command Line).
2. Press **Ctrl** and **Home** to move to the beginning of the file.
3. Type **DEFAULT** DI=k,l,p.
4. Press **F9** (Execute).
5. "Done" displays on the prompt line.
6. Issue a **DIRL** command to see the effect.

A La Carte DI cannot be set through A La Carte's La Carte Default menus.

Examples   **DI** extends the utility of the **DIRL** command by allowing you to pack more—or less—information into the display. To get the most information from **DIRL**, set **DI** to strip carriage returns. This forces paragraphs to flow together, but gives you more information when you're browsing through a file.

Tips   **DI** also modifies the display of XyWrite's normal **DIR** command, but the only effect is in the file size column. If you set **DI** to display in kilobytes instead of bytes, the setting is read by the **DIR** command as well as **DIRL**.

See Defaults and Directory (Long)

DIRECTORY, SORT DIRECTORY (DSORT)

Overview   The **DSORT** command organizes directory listings alphabetically by file names or extensions, by file sizes, or by date and time the file was last written to disk.

The directory can be sorted in reverse order. You can include a directory identification header in the listing.

The regular DOS listing, organized in the order files that are recorded on disk sectors, is also available.

Procedure The syntax for **DSORT** is **DSORT order,order,modifier,modifier**. Any combination of options and modifiers listed here can be used at the same time. The first one listed takes highest priority. The sorting order possibilities are:

- **f**—Alphabetically by filename
- **e**—Alphabetically by file extension
- **s**—By file size
- **d**—By date and time last written to disk

There are two modifiers:

- **r**—Display the listing in reverse order
- **h**—Add a header to the directory listing

To issue the command:

1. Press **F5** (Clear Command Line).
2. Type **DSORT** e,f,h (for example).
3. Press **F9** (Execute).
4. "Done" displays on the prompt line.
5. When **DIR** or **DIRL** is issued, the directory displays as you specified in **DSORT**.

The sort order stays the same for the editing session or until you issue a new **DSORT** order. The sort order stays the same if you move to a different directory.

A La Carte
1. Press **F6** (A La Carte menus).
2. Press **D** or select **Dir**.
3. Press **S** or select **dirSort**.
4. A screen with several sort options displays. Move the cursor to your choice.
5. Press **Return**.

Examples Large directories make finding a certain file difficult, but **DSORT** helps.

You'll develop a file-naming system eventually, perhaps unconsciously. When you do, **DSORT** lets you modify your directory listing so the files are organized effectively.

To give an example, suppose you have a directory that contains memos (.MEM) files, letters (.LTR), proposals (.PRP), and some odds and ends (no extensions). If you wanted these documents grouped by type and alphabetically by name, specify a **DSORT e,f** to sort the files by extension first, then by filename.

In another scenario, you might want to keep the related documents together by giving them the same name and specifying a different extension. A number of your projects include a memo, letter, and a proposal, so you might want to organize them by project—specifying a **DSORT f,e** order.

If you wanted to keep the most recently edited documents at the beginning of the directory listing, you could specify a **DSORT d,r** order to sort them by dates and display them in reverse order.

If you specify the **h** option for a header, you'll get something like this at the top of your directory listing:

Default drive/directory C:\XYWRITE\LETTERS
Directory of Files C:\XYWRITE\LETTERS*.*

Tips

Once you decide on your favorite sorting order, you can make it permanent by adding the command to your STARTUP.INT file. See the STARTUP.INT section for directions on making the entry.

To clear the sort order and specify a DOS-like listing, simply issue **DSORT** without any options or modifiers. Run a communications program to send or receive electronic mail.

See Directory and Directory (Long)

DISCRETIONARY HYPHEN (DH)

Overview

DH is a default setting that specifies what character indicates a discretionary hyphen.

Procedure   Since **DH** is a default setting, you can enter the command in your printer file or in your STARTUP.INT file. If you do, that character is used whenever you want to indicate a discretionary hyphenation point in a word. For complete instructions, see the Procedure portion of the Default listing.

You can also issue **DH** from the command line to set a unique character for the current editing session:

1. Press **F5** (Clear Command Line).
2. Press **Ctrl** and **Home** to move to the beginning of the file.
3. Type **DEFAULT** DH=character.
4. Press **F9** (Execute).
5. "Done" displays on the prompt line.

A La Carte You must be in an empty window (have a blank screen) to access the menus.

1. Press **F6** (A La Carte menus).
2. Press **X** or select **XyWrite**.
3. Press **D** or select **Defaults**.
4. The View and Change Defaults screen displays.
5. Press **D** or **G** or select **defaults D-G** (alphabetic listing).
6. Move the cursor to the **DH** entry and type the character you want to use as a discretionary hyphen.
7. Press **Return**.
8. The Update Default File screen displays. You're asked if you want to make the default settings permanent.
9. Press **Y** or **N**. If you select **Y**, the program writes the new default settings to a special file and returns you to the A La Carte Menu Screen. If you select **N**, the settings are used for the current edit session.

Examples   Many words are included in the XyWrite hyphenation dictionary, but many are not. When one of the words that isn't included, falls at the end of a line where it might need to be broken, you can mark the best places to hyphenate it. You do that by tapping the discretionary hyphen key. If the word does need to break across two lines, a hyphen is inserted at the break point.

XyWrite's standard discretionary hyphen character is the tilde (~).If you're not fond of tildes or you need to use them regularly in your word processing, you can change the discretionary hyphen character to whatever suits your fancy.

See Defaults

DISK DRIVES

Overview   When XyWrite starts, it uses whatever disk drive the program is on as the default disk drive. Any files you create use that drive as their "home." If you wish, you can specify a different default drive for text files.

XyWrite also allows you to specify a second (even a third or fourth) drive as a "save" drive. When a file is saved or stored on the default drive, a second copy is written to the "save" drive.

Procedure   To change the default disk drive for a single editing session:

1. Press **F5** (Clear Command Line).
2. Type the default disk drive identifier (usually **B:** or **C:**).
3. Press **F9** (Execute).
4. "Done" displays on the prompt line.

To change the default disk drive and name a save drive for a single editing session:

1. Press **F5** (Clear Command Line).
2. Type the default disk drive identifier, a comma, and the save drive identifier. **(C:,B:,** for example).
3. Press **F9** (Execute).
4. "Done" displays on the prompt line.

To set a permanent default drive for every editing session, read the Tips section below.

A La Carte
1. Press **F6** (A La Carte menus).
2. Press **D** or select **Dir**.
3. Press **V** or select **driVe**.
4. A screen with a blank for the new drive entry displays.
5. Type the new drive letter.
6. Press **Return**.

You cannot specify a save drive with the A La Carte menus.

Examples   Specifying a new default drive is especially useful if you're using a computer that has two floppy disk drives but no hard disk. It's standard procedure to keep XyWrite programs on the A: drive and text files on B: because XyWrite can fill (even over-fill) the floppy you keep in A:. Keeping text on the B: drive gives you more room for storage.

The save drive option comes in handy for most writers since it automatically creates a backup copy of your work on a second disk. If you use a save drive when you run XyWrite, you can avoid most of the boring backup procedures people go through to safeguard their text.

Tips   Add a line to your STARTUP.INT file so your disk drive preferences are set each time you start XyWrite.

Open STARTUP.INT with a **Call** or **Edit** command. You'll see something that looks like this:

```
BC LDDICT DICTION
BC LDHELP NEW.HLP
BC DEFAULT BK=0
BC DEFAULT PL=54,60,50
BC DEFAULT TP=6,LM=10,RM=75
BC LP 3IBMPRO.PRN
```

BC LDSGT GETS
BC LOAD ART.SPL
BC LOAD SUPER.KBD
BC CM W
BC

Define the last, empty line by moving your cursor to the line and pressing **F4**. Press **F7** to copy the last line. Move your cursor to the end of the now second-to-last line. Type in your default and save selection as you'd type them on the command line. Store the file. The next time you run XyWrite, your default drives are set automatically.

DISPLAY COLORS

Examples XyWrite provides a broad pallet of display colors and a variety of settings so you can paint a number of screen areas to suit your personal taste.

Each color has a number. The number is used in most display-related settings. For instance, to specify the color of your defined text blocks, you use the **DD** command. The syntax of the command is **DD=COLORNUMBER**, used like this: **DD=240**.

Be aware that not every monitor and computer display colors the same way. These are XyWrite's settings and they work on many IBM PC compatibles, but you may have to experiment to get the best display for your particular setup. In the same vein, although the chart may show different numbers giving the same display results, on your monitor they may not. Treat each combination as a possibility.

Also, notice that some combinations are going to be invisible. Black characters on a black background are obviously difficult to see.

TABLE 7   **Monochrome Monitor Table**

COLOR	NUMBER
Black on Black	0
White Underlined on Black	
White on Black	2-7
Black on Black	8
Bright White Underlined on Black	9
Bright White on Black	10-15
Black on White	112
Black on White	120
(flashing) Black on Black	128
(flashing) White Underlined on Black	129
(flashing) White on Black	131-135
(flashing) Black on Black	136
(flashing) Bright White Underlined on Black	137
(flashing) Bright White on Black	138-143
(flashing) Black on White	140
(flashing) Black on White	248

Color Monitor Table Color selection for a color monitor is different than monochrome selection. You need to pick the color of the text (the foreground) and the color it displays on (the background). Add the two numbers to get your display setting.

Compared to the color choice example given earlier, you could issue commands like **DD=245** (magenta text is 5+white background and with blinking text is 240=245) to make your defined text blocks display as blinking magenta text on a white background. To make each text window display in a different color, you might issue a command like **BX=240,241,242**.

Tips   You can see the colors that your monitor is capable of displaying through XyWrite's Help screens:

1. Press **Alt** and **F9** (**Help**).
2. Press **W** or select **Word**.
3. Type **Color Table** in the blank.
4. Press **F9** (Execute) or **Return**.
5. A display showing the colors your computer and monitor can display appears. The numbers on the display are the numbers you can enter in any of the color-related settings.

TABLE 8 **Foreground Display Settings**

TEXT (FOREGROUND) COLOR	NUMBER
Black	0
Blue	1
Green	2
Cyan	3
Red	4
Magenta	5
Brown	6
Dim White	7
Gray	8
Light Blue	9
Light Green	10
Light Cyan	11
Light Red	12
Light Magenta	13
Yellow	14
Bright White	15

TABLE 9 **Background Display Settings**

DISPLAY (BACKGROUND) COLOR	NUMBER
Black	0
Blue	16
Green	32
Cyan	48
Red	64
Magenta	80
Brown	96
Dim White	112
Black with blinking text	128
Blue with blinking text	144
Green with blinking text	160
Cyan with blinking text	176
Red with blinking text	192
Magenta with blinking text	208
Brown with blinking text	224
Dim White with blinking text	240

See Box Colors, Display Defined Blocks, EGA Support, Header, and Header Reverse

DISPLAY DEFINED BLOCKS (DD)

Overview   DD is the default setting that specifies what color is used to display a defined block.

Procedure   Since **DD** is a default setting, you can enter the command in your printer file or in your STARTUP.INT file. If you do, your personal block display mode is invoked each time XyWrite starts. For complete instructions, see the Procedure portion of the Default listing.

You can also issue **DD** from the command line to set a unique display mode for a single editing session:

1. Press **F5** (Clear Command Line).
2. Press **Ctrl** and **Home** to move to the beginning of the file.
3. Type **DEFAULT** DD=# (the number of the color you want to use). A list of the possible colors and their numbers is in the Display section.
4. Press **F9** (Execute).
5. "Done" displays on the prompt line.

A La Carte You must be in an empty window (have a blank screen) to access the default menus.

1. Press **F6** (A La Carte menus).
2. Press **X** or select **XyWrite**.
3. Press **D** or select **Defaults**.
4. The View and Change Defaults screen displays.
5. Press **D** or **G** or select **defaults D-G** (alphabetic listing).
6. Move the cursor to the **DD** entry and type the color number you want. A list of the possible colors and their numbers is in the Display section.
7. Press **Return**.
8. The Update Default File screen displays. You're asked if you want to make the default settings permanent.
9. Press **Y** or **N**. If you select **Y**, the program writes the new default settings to a special file and returns you to the A La Carte Menu Screen. If you select **N**, the settings are used for the current edit session.

Examples   **DD** provides a way to unmistakably identify a defined block. If you're not satisfied with the bright display on your monochrome monitor or the specific color used on your color screen, this is the best way to change it.

Tips   If you're always forgetting you have a block of text defined somewhere, set your **DD** default to flash, rather than just sit there. You can see the colors your monitor is capable of displaying through XyWrite's Help screens:

1. Press **Alt** and **F9** (**Help**).
2. Press **W** or select **Word**.
3. Type **Color Table** in the blank.
4. Press **F9** (Execute) or **Return**.
5. A display showing the colors your computer and monitor can display appears. The numbers on the display are the numbers you can enter in the **DD** settings.

See Defaults

DISPLAY TYPE (DT)

Overview   **Display Type** is a default setting that determines what type of screen display XyWrite uses when the program starts.

Procedure There are four possible display options:

- **DT=0** sets XyWrite to display text with formatting codes visible and inactive (Expanded Display).
- **DT=1** displays text with codes hidden (Normal Display), with the page and line number display in the upper right hand part of the screen off, and with line-end symbols and embedded command triangles visible.
- **DT=2** is the same as **DT=1**, except the page and line number display is on.
- **DT=3** displays in Normal Display, page and line number display on, and with line-end symbols and embedded command triangles hidden.

Since **DT** is a default setting, you can enter the command in your printer file or in your STARTUP.INT file. If you do, your favorite display mode is invoked each time XyWrite starts. For complete instructions, see the Procedure portion of the Default listing.

You can also issue **DT** from the command line to set a unique display mode for a single editing session:

1. Press **F5** (Clear Command Line).
2. Press **Ctrl** and **Home** to move to the beginning of the file.
3. Type **DEFAULT** DT=# (**0,1,2,**or **3**).
4. Press **F9** (Execute).
5. "Done" displays on the prompt line.
6. The new display setting takes effect the next time the file is opened.

A La Carte You must be in an empty window (have a blank screen) to access the menus.

1. Press **F6** (A La Carte menus).
2. Press **X** or select **XyWrite**.
3. Press **D** or select **Defaults**.
4. The View and Change Defaults screen displays.
5. Press **D** or **G** or select **defaults D-G** (alphabetic listing).
6. Move the cursor to the **DT** entry and type **0**, **1**, **2**, or **3**.
7. Press **Return**.
8. The Update Default File screen displays. You're asked if you want to make the default settings permanent.
9. Press **Y** or **N**. If you select **Y**, the program writes the new default settings to a special file and returns you to the A La Carte Menu Screen. If you select **N**, the settings are used for the current edit session.

Examples   Being able to set the display type of your choice is a handy option. If you're curious about the length of your document and your location in it, keep the page and line number display turned on. Other writers find it distracting and opt for a simpler screen without that display or XyWrite's embedded command triangle. The choice is up to you.

Tips The factory setting for **DT** is **DT=1**—normal display, with page and line numbers turned off, and markers showing.

See Page and Line Numbers

DISPLAY UNITS (DU)

Overview **DU** is a default setting that determines how many points are displayed in the ruler line at the top of the screen. The normal setting is 10 per inch, to match most printers.

Procedure Since **DU** is a default setting, you can enter the command in your printer file or in your STARTUP.INT file. If you do, your standard display mode is invoked each time XyWrite starts. For complete instructions, see the Procedure portion of the Default listing.

You can also issue **DU** from the command line to set a unique display mode for a single editing session:

1. Press **F5** (Clear Command Line).
2. Type **DEFAULT** DU=# (Number of characters per inch to display).
3. Press **F9** (Execute).
4. "Done" displays on the prompt line.

A La Carte The **DU** default setting is not available through A La Carte menus.

Examples The only reason you might want to modify the default setting of **DU=10** is if you *always* use a printer that prints in elite type, rather than pica. Pica width type is set on a 10 character per inch measure, the system default. Elite is set 12 characters per inch. If you want a truer representation when printing with tiny type, you can set **DU=12**.

DO, RUN A PROGRAM

Overview   **DO** allows you to temporarily leave XyWrite, run another program or a **DOS** command under XyWrite, and return to the XyWrite program.

Procedure   To run another program with **DO**; the syntax of **DO** is straightforward, similar to the command you'd use to run a program from **DOS**:

DO PROGRAMNAME FILENAME (optional—if the program requires it).

If the program requires path or drive information you need to supply it just as you would at a DOS prompt:

1. Press **F5** (Clear Command Line).
2. Type **DO** DRIVE:PATH\PROGRAMNAME FILENAME (DO B:\TOOLS\FOGFIND TEXT for example, or **DO** C:\123\HAL).
3. Press **F9** (Execute).
4. After the program is finished, you will be returned to XyWrite.

When running a **DOS** command with **DO**, keep in mind that the syntax required by a DOS command is a little more involved because you must access the DOS COMMAND.COM file and a program:

DO DRIVE:PATH\COMMAND /C DOSCOMMAND OPTION

Again, if path or drive information is required, you must provide it on the command line:

1. Press **F5** (Clear Command Line).
2. Type **DO** DRIVE:PATH\COMMAND /C DOSCOMMAND
   OPTION. (**DO** C:\COMMAND /C FORMAT A: for example).
3. Press **F9** (Execute).
4. After the program finishes, you're returned to XyWrite.

A La Carte You can't execute **DO** commands using A La Carte
menus. Use the standard procedure.

Examples You'll have as many reasons to use **DO** as you have programs on
your computer. Provided you have enough memory to load the
second program, you can temporarily suspend XyWrite and run
another task on your machine. A few examples:

- Format a floppy disk to which you can copy XyWrite text
  files.
- Run a spreadsheet program to generate numbers to include
  in a letter.
- Run a communications program to send or receive
  electronic mail.
- Access a remote database for information to include in
  your document.

Tips It's easy to make typing mistakes and if you make one while
switching between programs with **DO**, it's possible to leave
XyWrite, hang the program at some point, or scramble **DOS**. Also,
some ill-mannered program may usurp memory being used by
XyWrite. Protect yourself! If you're editing a document when you
want to run a program outside XyWrite, write your file to disk
with **Save** first.

Depending on what operation you want to **DO**, you might leave
XyWrite, access DOS, and bomb out of your target program. If that
happens, you're likely to end up staring at a DOS prompt. You can
either go ahead and run your program, or try typing **Exit** at a DOS
prompt and pressing **Return**. Unless DOS completely scrambled
XyWrite, you'll reenter the word processor. If **Exit** doesn't work at
first, check your directory location. Did you land in a different

directory than the one from which XyWrite normally runs? If so, change directories and try **Exit** again.

If you leave XyWrite to run one particular program fairly often, load the **DO** command onto a Save/Get key. You'll be able to run the command with a single key combination and eliminate typing errors. Be extra slick and include a **Save** command in your macro to protect whatever document you're editing. For more information on writing macros and creating Save/Get keys, see the programming section.

Warnings   There are three prerequisites to using **DO**:

- You must have enough memory in your computer to run the second program or command while XyWrite is resident.
- You must be using a version of DOS numbered 2.0 or higher.
- The program you specify must be a .COM, .EXE. or .BAT file; the program must have one of those three extensions.

See DOS

DOS, TEMPORARILY ESCAPE TO DOS

Overview   The **DOS** command lets you suspend XyWrite's operation and exit to DOS to run another program or execute a DOS command. It's similar to **DO**, but limited slightly by it's inability to handle a path command.

Procedure   1. Press **F5** (Clear Command Line).
2. Type **DOS**.
3. Press **F9** (Execute).
4. The XyWrite screen disappears and a DOS prompt displays.
5. Run your second procedure.
6. When you're finished in DOS, return to XyWrite by typing **Exit** and pressing **Return**.

To save a few keystrokes, append the name of your DOS command or batch file to the XyWrite command. The command is executed automatically:

1. Press **F5** (Clear Command Line).
2. Type **DOS** /C DOSCOMMAND (**DOS** /C FORMAT A: for example).
3. Press **F9** (Execute).
4. The XyWrite screen disappears and the DOS command is executed.
5. When the procedure finishes, a DOS prompt displays.
6. At the DOS prompt, return to XyWrite by typing **Exit** and pressing **Return**.

A La Carte You can't exit to DOS using A La Carte menus. Use the procedure above.

Examples   You can use **DOS** for many of the same applications you'd use **DO** for, but **DOS** allows a bit more flexibility. **DO** allows you to perform a single operation; **DOS** drops you into the operating system, so you can accomplish several operations before returning to XyWrite.

Tips   If you're juggling two programs at the same time, you might stumble on one that steals computer memory used by XyWrite. That may cause you to lose part of a file, if you are writing when you exit to DOS. Protect yourself! If you're editing a document when you want to run DOS, write your file to disk with **Save** first.

Warnings   The DOS program COMMAND.COM must be present in the directory you're operating in when you execute the **DOS** command. If it's not, you'll get an error message. Use **Change Directory** (**CD**) to move to a good directory, or make a second copy of COMMAND.COM with XyWrite's **Copy** command.

See Append, Change Directory, Copy, Do, Disk Drives, DEL, Erase, Make Directory, Rename, and Remove Directory

DUMP FOOTNOTES (DF)

Overview   Use **Dump Footnotes** to generate endnotes rather than footnotes in a document. **DF** must be used with the **No Footnotes (NF)** command. If you stop the normal output of footnotes with **No Footnotes,** they'll be saved and printed at whatever point you embed a **Dump Footnotes** bright command triangle, normally on the last page of a chapter or document.

Procedure   To generate endnotes rather than footnotes:

1. Press **Ctrl** and **Home** to go to the beginning of the document.
2. Press **F5** (Clear Command Line).
3. Type **NF** (If you are using more than one set of footnotes, type NF#. The # is the number of the footnote set—1, 2, or 3—you want to use as endnotes.) and press **F9** (Execute).
4. A bright command triangle is inserted in the text.
5. Press **Ctrl** and **End** to go to the end of the document.
6. Press **F5** (Clear Command Line).
7. Type **DF**. (If you are using more than one set of footnotes, type **DF#**. The # is the number of the footnote set—1, 2, or 3—you want to use as endnotes.)
8. Press **F9** (Execute) and a bright command triangle is inserted in the text.
9. Any footnotes in the set begin printing at this point.

A La Carte   To generate endnotes rather than footnotes:

1. Press **Ctrl** and **Home** to go to the beginning of the document.
2. Press **F6** (A La Carte menus).
3. Press **P** or select **Page**.
4. Press **F** or select **Footnotes**.
5. Press **N** or select **No footnotes**.

6. A bright command triangle is inserted in the text.
7. Press **Ctrl** and **End** to go to the end of the document.
8. Press **F6** (A La Carte menus).
   - Press **P** or select **Page**.
   - Press **F** or select **Footnotes**.
   - Press **D** or select **Dump footnotes**.
9. A bright command triangle is inserted in the text.

Note that this procedure is set up to work with footnote set number one, the default set. If you're working with more than one set of footnotes, it may be easier to use the standard procedure.

Examples

Endnotes are a standard arrangement for printing citations or notes in documents, although the old reasoning for the location, that they were easier to type separately, isn't entirely valid any more. Endnotes are still used for a good reason, however—to avoid cluttering the text page with many different references. Also, many types of documents make use of several sets of footnotes, printing one set as endnotes. Separating citations and author's notes is a common application.

XyWrite provides three footnotes "tracks" or sets, so you can use one or two sets for bottom-of-the-page footnotes and the third set for endnotes.

Tips

The **DF** command assumes that you want to place your suppressed footnotes on the final page of your document. You can force output at any other point, simply by inserting the **DF** there.

If you organized a document into several chapters, one chapter to a file, you can use **DF** to print either chapter notes or endnotes. If **Dump Footnotes** is inserted at the end of each chapter, that file's footnotes print before the next chapter begins. If you chain the files together so the entire book prints as a single document, a single **DF** on the final page should print all the notes from all the chapters on that page.

EDIT (ED)

See Call

EDIT FORM (EDF)

See Call Form

EDIT PROGRAM (EDP)

See Call Program (CAP)

EGA SUPPORT (EG)

Overview   **EG** is a default setting that optimizes XyWrite to computers that use Enhanced Graphics Adaptor displays. **EG** is similar to the **SL** default setting, but is limited to EGA displays.

Procedure   Since **EG** is a default setting, you can enter the command in your printer file or in your STARTUP.INT file. If you do, your standard EGA settings are used each time XyWrite starts. For complete instructions, see the Procedure portion of the Default listing.

Use the **EG** default to set up one of three displays:

- **EG=0** establishes a 25-line (normal) screen display on either a color or monochrome monitor.
- **EG=1** sets a 43-line display on a monochrome monitor.
- **EG=2** sets a 43-line display on a color monitor.

You can also issue **EG** from the command line to set the display for the current editing session:

1. Press **F5** (Clear Command Line).
2. Type **DEFAULT** EG=# (**1**, **2**, or **3**).
3. Press **F9** (Execute).
4. "Done" displays on the prompt line.

A La Carte You must be in an empty window (have a blank screen) to access the default settings menus.

1. Press **F6** (A La Carte menus).
2. Press **X** or select **XyWrite**.
3. Press **D** or select **Defaults**.
4. The View and Change Defaults screen displays.
5. Press **D** or **G** or select **defaults D-G**.
6. Move the cursor to the **EG** entry and type **0**, **1**, or **2** (defined above).
7. Press **Return**.
8. The Update Default File screen displays. You're asked if you want to make the default settings permanent.
9. Press **Y** or **N**. If you select **Y**, the program writes the new default settings to a special file and returns you to the A La Carte Menu Screen. If you select **N**, the settings are used for the current edit session.

Examples   If you've spent the extra money for an EGA display, this is the setting that gives you the results you want. The three settings allow you to set a normal 25-line display or pack more text on screen with a 43-line display.

For long hours of writing, most people prefer the larger, easier-to-read characters of the 25-line display. If you have a large screen monitor or need to see more of the document you're editing, the 43-line display will serve you well.

See Defaults

EJECT LAST PAGE (EJ)

Overview Depending on the type of printer you have, the final page of a document may not eject itself from the printer—when the printing stops halfway down the page, the paper movement stops too.

    EJ fixes the situation. If you turn **EJ** on, XyWrite sends a code to the printer that forces the last sheet all the way out.

Procedure **EJ** is a default setting so you can enter the command in your printer file or in your STARTUP.INT file. If you do, the final page of all your documents will roll out of the printer. For complete instructions, see the Procedure portion of the Default listing.

    You can also issue **EJ** from the command line to set the help message display for the current editing session:

1. Press **F5** (Clear Command Line).
2. Type **DEFAULT** EJ=1.
3. Press **F9** (Execute).
4. "Done" displays on the prompt line.

A La Carte You must be in an empty window (have a blank screen) to access the menus.

1. Press **F6** (A La Carte menus).
2. Press **X** or select **XyWrite**.
3. Press **D** or select **Defaults**.
4. The View and Change Defaults screen displays.
5. Press **D** or **G** or select **defaults D-G** (alphabetic listing).
6. Move the cursor to the **EJ** entry and type **0** or **1**.
7. Press **Return**.
8. The Update Default File screen displays. You're asked if you want to make the default settings permanent.
9. Press **Y** or **N**. If you select **Y**, the program writes the new default settings to a special file and returns you to the A La

Carte Menu Screen. If you select **N**, the settings are used for the current edit session.

Examples   Setting **EJ=1** is useful on most printers except page and laser printers. Setting **EJ=1** means you don't have to manually take the printer off line and push the form feed button to get the final page of your document out of the printer.

Tips   The **Eject Last Page** default helps your paper movement, but on some printers, it only rolls the page up to the next perforation. That means you have to rip across a page perforation you can't see or steady with your hand. And that means you could pull the tractor feed paper loose.

To eject another complete sheet of paper, you could end your documents with the ASCII form feed character, character number 12. When the non-printing form feed character hits the printer, your document rolls up a page so you can rip it out of the printer neat and clean. To insert ASCII number 12:

1. Press **Ctrl** and **End** to move to the end of the document.
2. Hold down **Ctrl** and **Alt** while you type **12**.
3. The universal symbol for "female" is inserted.

Type your document the normal way and watch the paper roll.

See Defaults

END COLUMN (EC)

Overview   This command is inserted automatically when a **Column Table (CT)** command is executed.

See Columns

END X-MARKER

See Index Label

ERASE A FILE (ERASE)

Overview   **Erase** deletes a file from a disk, just as the DOS ERASE or DEL command does. It doesn't have an effect on any file that's displayed, even if the display file and the deleted file are the same.

Procedure   1. Press **F5** (Clear Command Line).
2. Type **ERASE** FILENAME. Include a drive designator and extension, if necessary: **ERASE** A:FILENAME.EXT.
3. Press **F9** (Execute).
4. "Done" displays on the prompt line.

   If you have a directory listing on the screen, you can erase a file by "pointing" to it:
1. With the directory listing on the screen, press **F5** (Clear Command Line).
2. Type **ERASE**.
3. Press **F10** (Text/Command Line Toggle). The cursor drops into the directory listing.
4. Move the cursor to the file.
5. Press **F9** (Execute).
6. "Done" displays on the prompt line and the file listing you pointed to disappears.

   A La Carte You must be in an empty window (have a blank screen) to access the Erase menu.

1. Press **F6** (A La Carte menus).
2. Press **F** or select **File**.

3. Press **E** or select **Erase**. The Erase File screen, which has a blank where you enter a filename, displays.
4. Fill in the blank with the filename.
5. Press **Return**.
6. A **Do you want to erase? (Y/N)** prompt displays.
7. Press **Y**.
8. "Done" displays on the prompt line.

If you have a directory displayed on screen, you can point-and-shoot at the file:

1. With the directory listing on the screen, press **F6** (A La Carte menus).
2. Press **F** or select **File**.
3. Move the cursor to the file you want to erase.
4. Press **E** or select **Erase**.
5. Press **Return**.
6. The Erase File screen displays, with the filename you pointed to filled in its filename blank.
7. Press **Return**.
8. A **Do you want to erase? (Y/N)** prompt displays. Press **Y**.
9. "Done" displays on the prompt line.

Examples   Part of basic housekeeping on a computer is removing old, unneeded files. Depending on your inclination, you can always do the job in DOS, but quite often it's easier to manage your directories from XyWrite. The "point-and-shoot" erase method described above provides a quick and easy way to see what you're doing.

Tips   If you have a hard disk drive, you can use the "point-and-shoot" method of displaying a directory and selectively deleting files in non-XyWrite directories. It's a good disk maintenance tool.

While you're cleaning directories with it, remember that you also have **Copy**, and several directory management commands such as **CD**, **MKDIR**, and **RMDIR** available.

Warnings   The **Erase Prompt** (EP) setting provides a smidgen of protection from erasing something valuable, but if you go ahead and zap a file, then discover you shouldn't have... you're still missing a file.

You've got two ways to decrease the likelihood of deleting a valuable file. The best, most secure way is to start a backup program, if not of everything on your disk, of your text files. The second is to purchase a "rescue" program that can recover an erased file.

See Erase and Erase (No Verify)

ERASE PROMPT (EP)

Overview   **EP** generates a "protection" prompt every time you issue an **Erase** command to reduce the chance of erasing a file by accident.

Procedure   Since **EP** is a default setting, you can enter the command in your printer file or in your STARTUP.INT file. If you do, the erase prompt is used each time XyWrite starts. For complete instructions, see the Procedure portion of the Default listing.

You can also issue **EP** from the command line to set a prompt for a single editing session:

1. Press **F5** (Clear Command Line).
2. Type **DEFAULT** EP=# (**0** off or **1** on).
3. Press **F9** (Execute).
4. "Done" displays on the prompt line.

A La Carte   The "**Do you wish to erase?**" prompt is toggled on in A La Carte. To toggle it off, first move to an empty window (have a blank screen) to access the default menus.

1. Press **F6** (A La Carte menus).
2. Press **X** or select **XyWrite**.

3. Press **D** or select **Defaults**.
4. The View and Change Defaults screen displays.
5. Press **D** or **G** or select **defaults D-G** (alphabetic listing).
6. Move the cursor to the **EP** entry and type **0** (**1** turns it on).
7. Press **Return**.
8. The Update Default File screen displays. You're asked if you want to make the default settings permanent.
9. Press **Y** or **N**. If you select **Y**, the program writes the new default settings to a special file and returns you to the A La Carte Menu Screen. If you select **N**, the settings are used for the current edit session.

Examples   If **EP** is "on," a **Do you wish to erase ? (Y/N)** prompt flashes every time you issue the **Erase** command. You must press the **Y** key to actually delete the file.

EP provides a little self-protection for people who go wild with their directory housecleaning chores, deleting too many files. With the prompt toggled on, you have to think an extra time and take an extra second to erase a file.

It's a good idea to enable this setting if people other than yourself, perhaps with less computer experience, use your system. If you don't want to be bothered with answering the prompt question yourself, use the **ERNV** (**Erase, No Verify**) command rather than **Erase** to remove a file.

See Defaults, Erase, and Erase (No Verify)

ERASE, NO VERIFY (ERNV)

Overview   ERNV deletes a file from a disk, just as **Erase** does, but it bypasses the **Do you wish to erase ? (Y/N)** prompt set by the **EP** default setting. Like **Erase**, it doesn't have an effect on any file that's displayed, even if the display file and the deleted file are the same.

Procedure
1. Press **F5** (Clear Command Line).
2. Type **ERNV** FILENAME. Include a drive designator and extension, if necessary: **ERNV** A:FILENAME.EXT.
3. Press **F9** (Execute).
4. "Done" displays on the prompt line.

If you have a directory listing on the screen, you can erase a file by "pointing" to it:

1. With the directory listing on the screen, press **F5** (Clear Command Line).
2. Type **ERNV**.
3. Press **F10** (Text/Command Line Toggle). The cursor drops into the directory listing.
4. Move the cursor to the file.
5. Press **F9** (Execute).
6. "Done" displays on the prompt line and the file listing you pointed to disappears.

A La Carte   A La Carte is installed with the "insurance" prompt active. Unless you want to toggle it off, use **ERNV** to expedite your disk cleanups. **ERNV** is not accessible from the A La Carte menus.

Examples
If you have a number of files to erase and have the **Do you wish to erase ? (Y/N)** prompt toggled on by the **EP** default setting, **ERNV** speeds up your deletions.

Warnings
If you've toggled the **EP** setting "on" to guard against other people accidentally erasing files, you might not want to tell other people about **ERNV**.

See Erase Prompt and Erase

ERROR BEEP (EB)

Overview   EB is a default setting that controls the length and tone of the "beep" that sounds when a program error occurs.

Procedure   Since **EB** is a default setting, you can enter the command in your printer file or in your STARTUP.INT file. If you do, your favorite tone is used each time XyWrite starts. For complete instructions, see the Procedure portion of the Default listing.

You can issue **EB** from the command line to set a unique beep for a single editing session:

1. Press **F5** (Clear Command Line).
2. Type **DEFAULT** EB=#,# (tone, duration).
3. Press **F9** (Execute).
4. "Done" displays on the prompt line.

The initial settings are **1536,12288**. Either number can be set to any value between 0 and 65534. If you want to turn the beep off altogether, enter a **0,0** value.

A La Carte You must be in an empty window (have a blank screen) to access the default menus.

1. Press **F6** (A La Carte menus).
2. Press **X** or select **XyWrite**.
3. Press **D** or select **Defaults**.
4. The View and Change Defaults screen displays.
5. Press **D** or **G** or select **defaults D-G**.
6. Move the cursor to the **EB** entry and type the numbers that specify tone and duration.
7. Press **Return**.
8. The Update Default File screen displays. You're asked if you want to make the default settings permanent.

9. Press **Y** or **N**. If you select **Y**, the program writes the new default settings to a special file and returns you to the A La Carte Menu Screen. If you select **N**, the settings are used for the current edit session.

Tips The numbers you enter for tone and duration have little relationship to the real world. They were keyed to the original IBM PC speaker, but there have been so many changes in computer hardware since then, tone and duration vary from machine to machine.

   If you have a good speaker in a high-speed PC, you might be able to set the tone high enough that your dog barks every time XyWrite hits a system error.

See Default

ERROR HELPS (EH)

Overview When an operator or the computer makes an error, XyWrite usually beeps and flashes a short error message. If you'd like more information, you can make a "help" message appear whenever an error occurs with **EH**.

Procedure EH is a default setting so you can enter the command in your printer file or in your STARTUP.INT file. If you do, help files associated with particular error messages display when an error occurs. For complete instructions, see the Procedure portion of the Default listing.

   You can also issue **EH** from the command line to set the help message display for the current editing session to test the feature:

1. Press **F5** (Clear Command Line).
2. Type **DEFAULT** EH=1.
3. Press **F9** (Execute).
4. "Done" displays on the prompt line.

If you want to turn the help screens off, repeat the procedure and set **EH=0**.

A La Carte   **EH** is turned on as a system default in A La Carte installations. To toggle it off, set **EH=0**. You must be in an empty window (have a blank screen) to access the menus.

1. Press **F6** (A La Carte menus).
2. Press **X** or select **XyWrite**.
3. Press **D** or select **Defaults**.
4. The View and Change Defaults screen displays.
5. Press **D** or **G** or select **defaults D-G** (alphabetic listing).
6. Move the cursor to the **EH** entry and type **0** or **1**.
7. Press **Return**.
8. The Update Default File screen displays. You're asked if you want to make the default settings permanent.
9. Press **Y** or **N**. If you select **Y**, the program writes the new default settings to a special file and returns you to the A La Carte Menu Screen. If you select **N**, the settings are used for the current edit session.

Examples   **EH** provides some useful information, but it tends to slow the system down somewhat because the program has to fetch each help screen from the disk.

     The setting is most useful when you're learning XyWrite or are training someone. After you become proficient, think about toggling **EH** off.

See Default

EXTRA LEADING (EL)

Overview   **Extra Leading** is the manual counterpart of **Automatic Leading** (**AL**). **EL** inserts extra white space after a single line of type to set off the line or make room for larger-than-normal headline type.

Procedure   1. Move the cursor to the line *after* the one that needs extra leading.
2. Press **F5** (Clear Command Line).
3. Type **EL #** (# is the number of lines to add; partial lines use decimal).
4. Press **F9** (Execute).
5. A bright command triangle is inserted on the line. The display won't change to reflect the increase in white space, but the line will print as you specified.

A La Carte
1. Press **F6** (A La Carte menus).
2. Press **R** or select **foRmat**.
3. Press **L** or select **Linespace**. A screen with several options displays.
4. Move the cursor to the **Extra Space** (**EL**) entry and fill in the blank with the number of lines to insert after the current line.
5. Press **Return**.
6. A bright command triangle is inserted in the text.

Examples   **EL** is a very precise command to add white space after a single line of text. You might want to use **Extra Leading** if you've used a line of expanded type as a headline, used a larger font on one line, or if you simply want to separate two unrelated lines of text.

The amount of vertical space you insert is measured in lines. XyWrite assumes that each line is a sixth of an inch. You can split that sixth into any proportion, using decimal values as small as hundredths. If your printer can provide vertical movements that small, XyWrite can make it happen.

As an example, adding a line of white space would be set by issuing a **EL 1** command. A line and a quarter would be **EL 1.25**. A line and a third, **EL 1.33**.

It's especially useful if you have a laser printer that generates a wide variety of fonts and sizes. **EL** gives you a professional typographic tool to make sure everything prints just right.

See Leading and Automatic Leading

135

FIELD IDENTIFICATION (FI)

Overview   FI is used in mail merge operations. **Field Identification** identifies, by name, the fields that contain data which is merged into a main file (for example, names and addresses in a data file into a form letter in a main file). **FI** is entered in the data file.

FI and **PF** are complementary commands. The **Put Field** (**PF**) command identifies the fields in the main file.

Procedure   1. Move to the beginning of the file by pressing **Ctrl** and **Home**.
2. Press **F5** (Clear Command Line).
3. Type **FI** fieldname1,fieldname2,fieldname3.... The field names are listed in the order they appear in the data file, and not in the main file.
4. Press **F9** (Execute).
5. A bright command triangle displays.

A La Carte   FI is not available through A La Carte Menus. Use the standard XyWrite procedure.

Examples   FI is an optional command. Use it only if you want to name the fields in your data file. If you refer to them by number, you wouldn't use **FI**; the fields read out automatically.

If anyone besides yourself is going to use the mail merge files you set up, **FI** becomes very useful since the field names you specify can describe the type of data each contains.

If an entry in your data file reads—

P.G.E. Smith
Alan Allen
Red's Cat Food
71 High St.
Columbus
Ohio
38321

—the entry would work fine in a mail merge operation, and you would know what each line means, but no one else would.

If you labeled each field with **FI** instead of using the number of their position in the file, anyone else could read your **FI** statement:

FI salesman, soldto, itembought, shipadd, shiptown, shipst, shipzip

They would know what each entry meant.

Tips　　　　If you're working with a data file generated by another program, or used for another purpose before you got the file, you might have data entries you don't want to use. For instance, in the example above, you might want to print an address label and omit "salesman" and "itembought." Just leave the position blank:

FI ,,soldto,,shipadd,shiptown,shipst,shipzip

See Mail Merge and Put Field

FIELD SEPARATOR (FS)

Overview　　　XyWrite uses a carriage return to mark the end of each field in each record of a mail merge data file. You can change this default with the **FS** command.

Procedure　　The **Field Separator** (**FS**), must be entered in a printer file. When the file is loaded into memory, the command take effect.

NOTE: By changing the **FS** setting, you change the parameters of any existing data files that use the default. If you don't want to change your data files to match the new setting, consider building a printer file with nothing in it but your maverick separator settings (see the Tips section for details):

1. Open the printer file just as you would a text file, with the **Call** command.
2. Your printer file may already have a **FS** entry. Check by issuing a **Search** command:
   - Press **F5** (Clear Command Line).
   - Type **SE** /FS/.
   - Press **F9** (Execute).
   - The search will probably fail and return a "Not Found" message. If an entry exists, your cursor moves to it (if you have entry, skip the next few "creation" steps and modify your existing settings).
3. Move your cursor to a clear area near the top of the printer file.
4. Type a semi-colon and a brief note describing the new separator setting. If your note is longer than one line, end each line with a carriage return and begin each one with a semi-colon.
5. Type **FSARATOR** (separator is whatever character you want to insert between data, for example, to separate names from addresses from city, state, and zip codes).
6. Use the **Store (ST)** command to close the file.
7. Load the file with the **Load** command.

A La Carte   There aren't any special A La Carte menu commands for the **FS** command. Use the standard XyWrite procedure.

Examples   Unless you import a data file from a very unusual program, you'll probably never have to change this setting, since most database programs use the same default field separator as XyWrite.

    If you do import a file that uses an unusual separator that's not a carriage return, it may be more practical to execute a **Change (CH)** command in the data file, to replace the native character with XyWrite's carriage return.

Tips   If, for whatever reason, you need to change the defaults with **FS**, think about putting the setting in a separate printer file from the one you normally use. That way the XyWrite default is preserved for use with mail merge files that don't require the unusual default. And you can load the small special file in an instant when you need to.

Creating the file is simple. Just create a file as you normally do. Convention dictates that the file have a .PRN extension for identification, but even that's not required.

The first line of the file must have an identifying code of a semi-colon, a PR, and another semi-colon, like this:

;PR;

After that unique first line, follow the procedure outlined in the first part of this section for inserting the **FS** command and the new separator character. Remember that any comment lines must fit on one line, begin with a semi-colon, and end with a carriage return; word wrap is not allowed.

See Defaults, Mail Merge, and Record Separator

FINAL PAGE (FP)

Overview   **FP** is an embedded command, usually used in running footers or headers. If you ever have to generate a line that reads something like:

Page 2 of 10

FP is the command that generates the number "10."

Procedure   Pick the point in your text where you want the total number of pages to print. If you like, type in any lead-in words (Page X of...). Then:

1. Press **F5** (Clear Command Line).
2. Type **FP**.
3. Press **F9** (Execute).
4. A bright command triangle is inserted.

The total number of pages does *not* display. When you print the file or preview it with **Types**, the correct number is inserted.

While **FP** can be used in the actual text of a document, most people insert it in a header or footer that prints at the top or bottom of each page. (Creating a running header or footer is covered in the Headers/Footers section.) To generate the line—

Page 2 of 10,

—combine **FP** with a **Page Number** (PN) command:

1. Type **Page** .
2. Press **F5** (Clear Command Line).
3. Type **PN** (**Page Number**).
4. Press **F9** (Execute).
5. A bright command triangle displays.
6. Type **of** .
7. Press **F5** (Clear Command Line).
8. Type **FP** (**Final Page**).
9. Press **F9** (Execute) and a bright command triangle displays.

A La Carte
1. Press **F6** (A La Carte menus).
2. Press **P** or select **Page**
3. Press **C** or select **Page#**.
4. The Insert Page Number screen appears. Move the cursor to the Insert Final Page Number Automatically entry.
5. Press **Return**.
6. A bright command triangle is inserted in the text.

Instead of executing Step 4, A La Carte offers another option, to insert the codes that automatically generate the line: **Page # of #**. Just move the cursor to that entry and press **Return**.

Examples   Many types of documents require the total number of pages to be printed on each page, to insure that no pages are overlooked or lost. **FP** does away with the drudgery of counting the pages and inserting the number after everything is typed.

Warnings   The **FP** command doesn't work if you're printing a series of linked files with the **Type @** command. XyWrite doesn't have a way of finding out how many pages are in the bundle of files, so it can't fill in the number **FP** requires.

See Running Footer (RF) and Running Header (RH)

FIND FILE (FIND)

Overview   **Find** searches an entire disk for a filename. If it finds any files with names similar to those you specified, it displays a directory list of them and prompts you to call one.

Procedure   1. Press **F5** (Clear Command Line).
2. Type **FIND** FILENAME.
3. Press **F9** (Execute).
4. A directory listing of files that meet your specification displays, **Call** displays on the command line, and "Done" displays on the prompt line.
5. Move the cursor to the file you want to open.
6. Press **F9** (Execute).
7. The file displays.

The **Find** command supports both standard wildcard characters—the **?** that stands for any single character and the ***** that represents a multiple-character string. Since the usual reason for using **Find** is that you've forgotten a file name, using wildcards is standard procedure.

Assume you're looking for a file that begins with the letter "C." You'd probably type **FIND c*.*** to pull all files that begin with "C." If it ends with a "C," type **FIND *c.***. If the letter "C" was in the middle of the name, you could type **FIND *c*.***. If the file has a .TXT extension, type **FIND *.TXT**.

A La Carte You must be in an empty window (have a blank screen) to access the **Find** command.

1. Press **F6** (A La Carte menus).
2. Press **S** or select **Search**.
3. Press **F** or select **findFile**.
4. The Search Disk for Files screen displays.
5. If you know any part of the filename, type it in the blank.
6. Press **Return**.
7. A directory listing of files that meet your specification displays, **Call** displays on the command line, and "Done" displays on the prompt line.
8. Move the cursor to the file you want to open.
9. Press **F9** (Execute) and the file displays.

Examples   If you've got a hard disk drive full of files, or lots of small files stored on floppy disk, **Find** makes life much simpler. Everyone misplaces files... and the longer a file remains unneeded, the harder it is to recall just which subdirectory holds it. **Find** prowls the entire disk for you, not just the XyWrite directories.

Tips   If you have a bad case of brain fade and can't recall enough of the name for **Find** to score a hit, use the multi-file **Search**. Although **Search** won't prowl through all subdirectories like **Find** does, it will open each file in a particular directory and look for a unique text string, such as a person's name.

See Directory, Directory (Long), and Search

142

FLUSH CENTER (FC)

Overview   **FC** is an embedded command that centers text.

Procedure   1. Move the cursor to the line where centering should begin.
2. Press **F5** (Clear Command Line).
3. Type **FC**.
4. A bright command triangle is inserted in the text. The line with the **FC**, and all lines after it, automatically center themselves between the left and the right margins.

To turn off centering, issue a **Flush Left** (**FL**) command to return to the program's normal text-positioning mode or a **Flush Right** (**FR**) command to make the text hug the right margin.

A La Carte
1. Press **F6** (A La Carte menus).
2. Press **R** or select **foRmat**.
3. Press **A** or select **Alignment**.
4. A screen with several options displays. Move the cursor to the **Center** entry and press **Return**.
5. A bright command triangle is inserted in the text. The line with the **FC**, and all lines after it, automatically center themselves between the left and the right margins.

Examples   Centered text is useful for headings and special effects; it is in most writer's repertoire of standard word-processing tools.

Tips   There's a little-used default command (also called **FC**) that starts XyWrite in "centering" mode. See the Defaults section.

See Flush Left (FL) and Flush Right (FR)

FLUSH LEFT (FL)

Overview   **FL** makes lines of text begin flush with the left margin of a page. It's the default text position for XyWrite.

Procedure   1. Move the cursor to the line where flush left text should begin.
2. Press **F5** (Clear Command Line).
3. Type **FL**.
4. A bright command triangle is inserted in the text. The line with the **FL** and all lines after it begin at the left margin.

A La Carte
1. Press **F6** (A La Carte menus).
2. Press **R** or select **foRmat**.
3. Press **A** or select **Alignment**.
4. A screen with several options displays. Move the cursor to the **Left** entry and press **Return**.
5. A bright command triangle is inserted in the text. The line with the **FL** and all lines after it align with the left margin.

Examples   Embed the **FL** command to return text positioning to the default position after you've centered text with **FC** or made it align on the right margin with **FR**.

See Flush Center (FC) and Flush Right (FR)

FONTS

Overview   XyWrite does not have a command called "fonts." Instead, the **Print Type** (**PT**) command selects different sizes or styles of type.
        Your printer ultimately determines what styles and sizes of type you can use. XyWrite can control and manipulate whatever your

printer can supply. You can customize this ability to meet your requirements by editing your printer file.

See Printer Files and Print Table (PT)

FOOTER

See Running Footer

FOOTNOTE (FN)

Overview   **FN** is an embedded command that creates a footnote.

Procedure   Put the cursor at the place in the text where you want to generate the footnote:

1. Press **F5** (Clear Command Line).
2. Type **FN** (if you're using several sets of footnotes, type **FN1**, **FN2**, or **FN3**—**FN** without a number identifies footnote set number one.)
3. A horizontal window opens in the text. Type in the text of your footnote.
4. Press **F3**.
5. The footnote window closes and a bright number, the number of the footnote, is inserted in the text.

The text of the footnote itself is not visible. You can view it by putting your cursor on the bright number and pressing **Ctrl** and **F3** (Open Footnote) or by shifting to expanded display with **Ctrl** and **F9**.

A La Carte

1. Press **F6** (A La Carte menus).
2. Press **P** or select **Page**.
3. Press **F** or select **Footnotes**.
4. Press **E** or select **Enter Footnote**.
5. A horizontal window opens in the text. Type in the text of your footnote.
6. Press **F3**.
7. The footnote window closes and a bright number, the number of the footnote, is inserted in the text.

Examples

FN creates footnotes. XyWrite automatically tracks footnotes, numbering them in the proper order. If you move a block of text that contains a footnote, the numbering adjusts itself automatically.

XyWrite provides three sets of footnotes, so you have all the tools you need to create references, citations, author's notes, or any other notation device you're likely to use. It's easy to make one set of footnotes different by altering the format of the set. See the **Format Footnotes** listing.

Footnote placement is controlled by the **Bottom Footnote (BF)** command. XyWrite normally places footnotes up against the body text, rather than down against the bottom of the page.

Placement of chapter notes or endnotes is controlled by the **Dump Footnotes (DF)** and **No Footnotes (NF)** commands. XyWrite's default places footnotes on the page that contains the reference.

The numbering format of footnotes calls for small superscript digits in text and normal text-size corresponding numbers with the footnote. You can make both sets of digits print in superscript by changing the **SC** setting.

The footnote separator, a (usually) short line of hyphens that separates the body text from the footnotes, is set by the **FS** command. If you don't specify a footnote separator, none will be used.

Tips Most style guides call for the number that identifies a footnote at the bottom of the page to be set off with a period and a space. XyWrite only supplies the number, so you'll have to remember to insert the period and space. The time to do it is when you first create the footnote, in the open window. If you forget to insert the period and space, your footnote number merges into the first word of your footnote.

It's easy to move a footnote—just define the number as a block of text, and move it wherever you like.

The easiest way to create *ib*, *ibid*, and *op. cit.* listings is by loading them onto Save/Get keys. That way, the entire footnote and its contents are inserted with a single keystroke combination. Just create one listing, define it as a block of text, and load it to a key. See Save/Gets for more information.

You can create footnotes that are not numbered, but are identified by a symbol—say a dagger, for author's notes. Set up a counter string specifying which symbols to use. See the Counter section for details.

Once you've created the counter string, you'll need to enter a **Set Footnote (SF)** command. The syntax for the command is **SF** **#* (the # stands for the footnote set number —**1**, **2**, or **3**). Insert it at the front of the file if you want the symbols in your counter string to keep incrementing. That would generate one dagger for the first footnote, two daggers for the second, and so on.

To repeat the symbol string on each page without incrementing, insert the **SF** on each page that contains that type of footnote.

Warnings XyWrite only supports a single customized counter string. If you use it for identifying footnotes, you probably don't want to also use it for page numbers!

See Footnote Format (FM) and Footnote Separator (FS)

FOOTNOTE FORMAT (FM)

Overview   The **Footnote Format** establishes printing and display parameters for footnotes. You would embed **FM** in text to make footnotes look different than the rest of the text on a page.

Procedure   **FM** can handle, but does not require, up to ten arguments. Specify:

- Left and right margins (**LM** and **RM**)
- Tab stop locations (**TS**)
- Paragraph indent (**IP**)
- Line spacing (**LS**)
- Offset (**OF**)
- Align text flush left, centered, or flush right (**FL**) (**FC**) (**FR**)
- Turn text justification on or off (**JU**) (**NJ**)
- Specify footnote placement on the page (**BF**)
- Set the amount of space between footnotes (**FT**)
- Set the style of the footnote's numbers (**SC**)

XyWrite supports three sets of footnotes so you can use a different style for each one. The general syntax of the command is:

FMset# command,command,command...

The commands don't have to be in any particular order. **FM** affects footnotes that appear after it. You'll usually issue the command at the beginning of the file:

1. Move to the beginning of the file by pressing **Ctrl** and **Home**.
2. Press **F5** (Clear Command Line).
3. Type **FM2 LM=10,RM=70,JU,FT=.5** (footnotes in set two have a left margin of 10 spaces, a right margin of 70, justified text, and have an additional half a line of white space between stacked footnotes).
4. Press **F9** (Execute).
5. A bright command triangle is inserted.

A La Carte

1. Move to the beginning of the file by pressing **Ctrl** and **Home.**
2. Press **F6** (A La Carte menus).
3. Press **P** or select **Page.**
4. Press **F** or select **Footnotes.**
5. Select **Formats.**
6. A screen with possible options for footnote formats displays.
7. Move the cursor to the entry you want to modify and make your changes.
8. Press **Return.**
9. A bright command triangle is inserted in the text.

Examples   Making your footnotes stand out from the main text in some way makes good graphic sense; it separates them visually to reinforce their distance from the text. This can be especially important if you have several sets of footnotes that apply to different things—author's notes, citations, or other references.

With **FM**, you can set a distinctive style for a herd of footnotes, instead of embedding the same commands in each one.

Tips   You don't have to specify a different footnote format if you don't want to. Whatever type of text settings you have in effect are used for footnotes if a **FM** isn't used. **FM** doesn't have any effect on the footnote separator.

See Footnotes

FOOTNOTE SEPARATOR (FS)

Overview   The footnote separator is the small graphic device at the bottom of a page that shows where the text stops and the footnote begins. You can create whatever device you want with **FS**.

Procedure

1. Move to the beginning of the file by pressing **Ctrl** and **Home**.
2. Press **F5** (Clear Command Line).
3. Type **FS** (if you're using several sets of footnotes, type **FS1**, **FS2**, or **FS3**—**FS** without a number identifies footnote set number one.)
4. A horizontal window opens in the text. Type in the text of your footnote separator. A common separator is one or two blank lines, 10 hyphens (to make a line an inch long), and one or two more blank lines.
5. Press **F3**.
6. The window closes and a bright command triangle is inserted.

The separator itself is not visible. You can view it by putting your cursor on the bright triangle and pressing **Ctrl** and **F3** (Open Footnote) or by shifting to expanded display with **Ctrl** and **F9**.

A La Carte
1. Move to the beginning of the file by pressing **Ctrl** and **Home**.
2. Press **F6** (A La Carte menus).
3. Press **P** or select **Page**.
4. Press **F** or select **Footnotes**.
5. Press **S** or select **Separator**.
6. A horizontal window opens in the text. Type in the text of your footnote separator. A common separator is one or two blank lines, 10 hyphens (to make a line an inch long), and one or two more blank lines.
7. Press **F3**.
8. The window closes and a bright command triangle is inserted in the text.

The separator itself is not visible. View it by putting your cursor on the bright triangle and pressing **Ctrl** and **F3** (Open Footnote) or by shifting to expanded display with **Ctrl** and **F9**.

Examples

Footnote separators are used in most documents to isolate the footnotes from the main text. They're a standard device in many papers, and the **FS** command makes using them easy.

FOOTNOTE TRANSITION (FT)

Overview   The **FT** setting controls how much white space is left between footnotes.

Procedure   **FT** can be entered as a default setting in your printer file or in your STARTUP.INT file. If you do, the setting is invoked each time XyWrite starts. For complete instructions, see the Procedure portion of the Default listing. To set a **Footnote Transition** that applies to a single document, make an **FT** entry in the **Footnote Format (FM)** command.

You can also issue **FT** from the command line to set a unique display mode for a single editing session:

1. Press **F5** (Clear Command Line).
2. Type **DEFAULT** FT=# (number of lines to put between footnotes).
3. Press **F9** (Execute).
4. "Done" displays on the prompt line.

A La Carte   You must be in an empty window (have a blank screen) to access the default menus.

1. Press **F6** (A La Carte menus).
2. Press **X** or select **XyWrite**.
3. Press **D** or select **Defaults**.
4. The View and Change Defaults screen displays.
5. Press **D** or **G** or select **defaults D-G**.
6. Move the cursor to the **FT** entry and type the number of lines to use between footnotes.
7. Press **Return**.

8. The Update Default File screen displays. You're asked if you want to make the default settings permanent.

9. Press **Y** or **N**. If you select **Y**, the program writes the new default settings to a special file and returns you to the A La Carte Menu Screen. If you select **N**, the settings are used for the current edit session.

To modify the **FT** setting for a file, access the **FT** setting that's embedded in the **FM** command.

Examples   **FT** is useful in documents that have several footnotes on a page. A little bit of white space, even just half a line, separates them nicely and makes them easier to read.

See Footnote (FN) and Footnote Format (FM)

FOOTNOTE UNIT (FU)

Overview   **FU** is a default setting that instructs the program to reserve space for a footnote or a reference number.

Procedure   Since **FU** is a default setting, you can enter the command in your printer file or in your STARTUP.INT file. If you do, that footnote unit setting is established each time XyWrite starts. For complete instructions, see the Procedure portion of the Default listing.
　　You can also issue **FU** from the command line to set a unique display mode for a single editing session:

1. Press **F5** (Clear Command Line).
2. Type **DEFAULT** FU=#,# (the number of spaces to allow for footnote and reference numbers).
3. Press **F9** (Execute).
4. "Done" displays on the prompt line.

A La Carte You must be in an empty window (have a blank screen) to access the default menus.

1. Press **F6** (A La Carte menus).
2. Press **X** or select **XyWrite**.
3. Press **D** or select **Defaults**.
4. The View and Change Defaults screen displays.
5. Press **D** or **G** or select **defaults D-G**.
6. Move the cursor to the **FU** entry and type the number of character spaces you want to reserve for footnote numbering.
7. Press **Return**.
8. The Update Default File screen displays. You're asked if you want to make the default settings permanent.
9. Press **Y** or **N**. If you select **Y**, the program writes the new default settings to a special file and returns you to the A La Carte Menu Screen. If you select **N**, the settings are used for the current edit session.

Examples   **FU** is (usually) only used with a printer that supports micro-spaced justification. The command inserts enough space to package the footnote or reference in a tidy block without letting the number hang into the margin area.

See Footnote (FN) and Defaults

FOOTNOTE WRAP SEPARATOR (FW)

Overview   Footnotes that are too long to fit at the bottom of a page are continued to a second. The **Footnote Wrap Separator** generates a unique separator that fits between the text and the continued footnotes, just as the regular footnote separator does.

Procedure   1. Move to the beginning of the file by pressing **Ctrl** and **Home**.
2. Press **F5** (Clear Command Line).

3. Type **FW** (if you're using several sets of footnotes, type **FW1**, **FW2**, or **FW3**—**FW** without a number identifies footnote set number one.)

4. A horizontal window opens in the text. Type in the text of your footnote wrap separator. A common separator is one or two blank lines, 10 hyphens (to make a line an inch long), the word "continued," and one or two more blank lines. Make sure that the footnote wrap separator uses the same number of lines that the regular footnote separator does.

5. Press **F3**.

6. The window closes and a bright command triangle is inserted.

The separator itself is not visible. You can view it by putting your cursor on the bright triangle and pressing **Ctrl** and **F3** (Open Footnote) or by shifting to expanded display with **Ctrl** and **F9**.

A La Carte

1. Move to the beginning of the file by pressing **Ctrl** and **Home**.

2. Press **F6** (A La Carte menus).

3. Press **P** or select **Page**.

4. Press **F** or select **Footnotes**.

5. Press **W** or select **Wrap Separator**.

6. A horizontal window opens in the text. Type in the text of your wrap separator. A common separator is one or two blank lines, 10 hyphens (to make a line an inch long) the word "continued", and one or two more blank lines. Make sure that the footnote wrap separator uses the same number of lines that the regular footnote separator does.

7. Press **F3**.

8. The window closes and a bright command triangle is inserted in the text.

See Footnote (FN) and Footnote Separator (FS)

FOREIGN CHARACTERS

Overview   A number of Latin letters with diacritical marks are included in the ASCII character set. These can all be used in XyWrite documents. Not all printers can print all the special characters.

Procedure   There are two ways to insert foreign characters in text files: from the help screens, or by typing the number of the ASCII character. To insert characters from the help screen:

1. Position the cursor where the foreign character should be inserted.
2. Press **Alt** and **F9** (**Help**).
3. Press **A** or select **ASCII**.
4. Press **F** or select **FOREIGN**. (Or press **G** or select **GREEK/MATH**.)
5. A selection of characters is displayed. Move the cursor to the one you want to insert.
6. Press **F9** (Execute).
7. The character is inserted in text.

To insert characters by typing their ASCII number:

1. Find the foreign character number on an ASCII character chart or the XyWrite ASCII help screen (Call the help screen with **Alt** and **F9**).
2. Hold down the **Alt** and **Shift** keys.
3. Type the character number. You may have to use the numeric keypad.
4. Release the **Alt** and **Shift** keys.
5. The character displays. Depending on your printer's capabilities, it may or may not print.

A La Carte
1. Press **F6** (A La Carte menus).
2. Press **E** or select **Edit**.

3. Press **A** or select **Ascii**.
4. A screen with several categories of characters display.
   - Press **F** or select **Foreign**.
   - Press **G** or select **Greek/math**.
5. The characters in that group display across the top of the screen.
6. Move the cursor to the character you want to insert and press **Return**.
7. When you're through inserting characters, press **Esc** four times to leave A La Carte.

Examples   Many words used in English-speaking countries are borrowed from European languages—résumé, for instance. It's easy to add the proper diacritical marks to these words in XyWrite. If your printer can print the character, there's no reason not to spell the word correctly.

Tips   If you type a fair number of foreign characters, modify your keyboard file to insert the characters with one keystroke. See the sections on Function Calls and Keyboard Files.

See ASCII and Printer Files

FORMAT (FO)

Overview   **FO** is the same command as **Typef**, used to preview a document or create a print file by writing a formatted file to disk.

The **Format** command was changed to **Typef** in an early version of XyWrite, but **FO** and **Format** still work. Some people find the older commands less cryptic and easier to remember.

See Typef.

FORMS

Overview   XyWrite can be used to fill in pre-printed forms. It can also generate original electronic forms to be filled in on the computer.

Procedure   XyWrite provides tools to work with two broad categories of "forms"—pre-printed for you to fill out, and those you create for others to fill out, either on-screen or on paper. XyWrite provides several powerful tools.

Edit prepared forms with a **NEF**, **Callf**, **CAF**, **EDITF**, or **EDF** commands. When you do, XyWrite treats the file differently than it does a normal text file. A form file can contain two types of text, "fixed" and "fill-in." Fixed text is usually material that identifies a blank in the form to the typist. Fill-in text is the information that goes into a blank.

When a form file is opened with a forms command, special display modes are used to enter fixed text. You can make the fixed text print or not print when the form is typed.

Printing Fixed Text   Text that's entered as bold or underlined is fixed text that can't be typed over, erased, or moved, but can be printed. Use it to identify form fields when you want the labels to print. Before you type the label, press **Ctrl** and **2** (for bold) or **Ctrl** and **3** (for underlined). Text created in bold mode prints bold; text created in underline mode prints as underlined.

Non-printing Fixed Text   Text that's typed in reverse video mode is also fixed text. It does not print. Use reverse video text to identify form fields for a typist or to provide non-printing instructions. To enter reverse video mode while typing, press **Ctrl** and **4**.

Technique #1   To create an original form (blanks can be filled out in XyWrite):

157

1. Press **F5** (Clear Command Line).
2. Type **NEF** (**New Form**) FILENAME.
3. Press **F9** (Execute).
4. The FILENAME displays on the prompt line. The screen is empty.
5. Use the print modes described above to create fixed text field labels.
6. Create blank space where data can be entered:
   - Shift to normal display mode (press **Ctrl** and **0** or **Ctrl** and **1**).
   - Press the spacebar until enough space exists. Do not use the **Tab** key.
   - To limit the blank to just the defined space, shift back to the display mode you used to enter the blank's label. Press **Return**.
   - To allow the blank to grow as information is typed in, stay in normal display mode and press **Return** to insert a carriage return character.
7. Repeat the procedure until the form is complete.
8. Store the file.

Technique #2 Most pre-printed forms are designed to be filled out by hand. They use weird line spacing, unusual line breaks, and multiple columns. XyWrite can handle all these things, but it takes some time to set up the format the first time through.

It is only worth doing if you're going to fill out a number of forms or if it's critical that the few forms you run off look professional. It's perfect for filling out repetitive insurance, legal, billing, or other bureaucratic paperwork. The time you spend setting the form up is paid back in time savings later.

You'll need several "original" forms to experiment with. Copies are fine. You also need a line and column grid file called GRID.FRM that's supplied by XYQUEST. You may have copied it to your XyWrite directory when you installed the program or it may still be on your master floppy disk. If it's not in your master directory, copy it from the floppy disk.

1. Call GRID.FRM to the screen (**CA GRID.FRM**). A screen of numbers displays. Each line and column of the page is numbered.
2. If you have standard default margins set, you may need to change them to get GRID.FRM to display without its full-page width lines wrapping over to a second line. Set your left margin to 0 and your right margin to 80 (**LM 0** and **RM 80**).
3. Print GRID.FRM (**Type**).
4. Compare the typed grid with the form you want to fill in. Check the top and bottom margins. Does the grid start high enough on the page and end low enough so that all the fill-in blanks are covered? If not, go back to GRID.FRM and adjust the top margin (**TP**) and page length (**PL**).
5. Print GRID.FRM again and compare it to the form. If all blanks on the form are covered by a grid coordinate, go ahead to the next step. Otherwise, go back and adjust the GRID.FRM file.
6. Load one of your original forms or a copy into your printer. Pay careful attention to where the top of the page lies in relation to the printhead. Most printers have a reference line somewhere in the mechanism to align the page... use it.
7. Print GRID.FRM again, this time on top of the form. Quite a few line and column coordinates should print right where there are blanks on the form.

Now you have to make some formatting decisions. If the form has columns, do the lines in each column line up evenly? If they do, you can use spaces or tab stops to put the information in the right spots. If the lines don't line up, a XyWrite column table may be necessary, since the line spacing in each column can be set independently. See the **Column Table** command.

Many forms are designed to be filled out by hand, and their lines are placed unevenly on the vertical axis. If you have occasional XyWrite grid lines that don't align exactly, adjust them with the **Extra Leading** (**EL**) command. If you have masses of narrowly-separated lines, try the **Line Spacing** (**LS**) command. Remember that you aren't tied to single or double spacing—you can use fractions of a line in your **LS** command, or even *less* than single spacing.

1. If necessary, adjust the lines on GRID.FRM and type the grid on top of your fill-in form. Keep adjusting until you have a very close match. It's much easier to work with GRID.FRM than real text.
2. When you're happy with the result, store GRID.FRM under a different name so you don't have to recreate the grid again. That also leaves the original, unaltered GRID.FRM file ready for the next form you set up.
3. Press **F5** (Clear Command Line).
4. Type **NEW** FILENAME,NEWGRIDNAME. (This opens a new file and copies your new working grid into it.)
5. Press **F9** (Execute).
6. Toggle your display so "Overwrite Text" is on.
7. Shift to the non-printing field mode (**Ctrl** and **4**). Keeping the final version of your form-with-grid printout as a guide, use the spacebar and text keys to overwrite the line and column identifiers with blank space or non-printing labels that identify the fields. Take care not to overwrite or erase any of the bright command triangles that control line or column positions.
8. When you reach a place that should contain text, shift to normal mode (**Ctrl** and **0** or **Ctrl** and **1**). Either type in the text, or create room for the text with the spacebar so it can be entered later.
9. Store the blank master form.

A La Carte XyWrite's Forms facility is not available through A La Carte menus. Use the standard XyWrite procedure.

Examples   If you generate forms of any type—invoices, time sheets, bills—anything at all, XyWrite's ability to build an easy-to-generate electronic form can save you hours of time. By repeatedly filling in a master electronic form and saving the working copies on disk, you create a compact and precise record of your transactions.

In a separate vein, XyWrite's precise text-positioning capabilities can make life easier for anyone who must fill out pre-printed forms. Insurance, medical, legal forms, even tax papers can be handled efficiently using the program's form-handling capability.

The instructions and field labels on XyWrite's electronic forms can be set so a typist can't modify the form when it's filled out. The instruction and identification areas can be set to print or not to print.

Tips

If you need to make changes in your master forms, be sure you open the form with the standard **Call** command, not **Callf**. Several editing tools are disabled in forms mode.

If you need to fit more information onto a form, remember that most XyWrite printer files contain an entry for elite type. Elite packs 12 characters into an inch; standard pica type only fits 10.

Many people massage the information they gather in forms with a database program. Moving the data from XyWrite to a database program is usually very easy. XyWrite creates pure ASCII files that can be edited and delimited with the word processor to build an easy-to-import "comma-delimited" data file.

Warnings

The procedures outlined here are just the front half of XyWrite's form capability. After master files are created, working files that use the masters as templates are a snap to create. Using the master files created here is discussed in the **NEF** section.

See Call Form(CAF)

FORM DEPTH (FD)

Overview **Form Depth** is the absolute length of the page of paper you're working with, measured in lines.

Procedure **FD** can be a default setting, but you can insert it as an embedded command to control the depth of a single file, such as an envelope. To insert **FD** in a document:

1. Press **F5** (Clear Command Line).
2. Type **FD** # (# is the number of six-per-inch lines that fit on a page). Sixty-six is the normal entry for 11-inch paper.
3. Press **F9** (Execute).
4. A bright command triangle is inserted in the text.

A La Carte You must be in an empty window (have a blank screen) to access the default menus.

1. Press **F6** (A La Carte menus).
2. Press **X** or select **XyWrite**.
3. Press **D** or select **Defaults**.
4. The View and Change Defaults screen displays.
5. Press **D** or **G** or select **defaults D-G**.
6. Move the cursor to the **FD** entry and type the number of lines on the paper size you're using.
7. Press **Return**.
8. The Update Default File screen displays. You're asked if you want to make the default settings permanent.
9. Press **Y** or **N**. If you select **Y**, the program writes the new default settings to a special file and returns you to the A La Carte Menu Screen. If you select **N**, the settings are used for the current edit session.

Examples If all you ever type are standard document pages, you'll probably never touch **FD**. If you print envelopes, legal documents, tractor-feed checks, or other forms, you'll probably need to adjust the form depth for each.

XyWrite allows six lines per inch to set the form depth. To get an accurate setting, simply multiply the length of the form by six.

The **FD** settings for some common paper lengths:

- Standard 11-inch paper—66
- Legal size 14-inch paper—84
- Business envelopes (4 1/8 inch)—25

Tips   When you enter the page length, don't add a line here or there to create more white space... that's handled by the **Page Length** (PL) command. All you'll do is throw off all your page measurements.

See Page Length (PL)

FORM FEED (FF)

Overview   The **FF** default setting compensates for different printers' hardware-controlled form feed settings. If your printer begins printing text at lower and lower positions from page to page, you may need to change this setting.

Procedure   This particular default setting should be entered in your printer file. For complete instructions, see the Procedure portion of the Default listing.

If you're not sure whether you need to change your setting, issue **FF=1** from the command line to try the setting during a single editing session. If that stops the printer creep, enter the **FF** setting in your printer file:

1. Press **F5** (Clear Command Line).
2. Type **DEFAULT** FF=1 (**0** is the factory default setting form most printers.).

3. Press **F9** (Execute).
4. "Done" displays on the prompt line.

A La Carte You must be in an empty window (have a blank screen) to access the default menus.

1. Press **F6** (A La Carte menus).
2. Press **X** or select **XyWrite**.
3. Press **D** or select **Defaults**.
4. The View and Change Defaults screen displays.
5. Press **D** or **G** or select **defaults D-G**.
6. Move the cursor to the **FF** entry and type **1**.
7. Press **Return**.
8. The Update Default File screen displays. You're asked if you want to make the default settings permanent.
9. Press **Y** or **N**. If you select **Y**, the program writes the new default settings to a special file and returns you to the A La Carte Menu Screen. If you select **N**, the settings are used for the current edit session.

Examples   The **FF** default setting fine-tunes your printer to match XyWrite's settings. XyWrite normally sends carriage returns to advance paper to the next sheet. Some dot matrix and laser printers require an ASCII form feed character (ASCII 12) to end pages.

If your printer seems to position text progressively lower on the page, perhaps just half a line or so, you should change the default **FF** setting from **0** to **1**.

Tips   Some Hewlett-Packard Laserjet printers and some recent Epson dot matrix printers need this setting.

XYQUEST has incorporated this setting in many of the printer files that require it. If you find the text creeping down the page, you might have an out-of-date printer file. Contact XyWrite's technical support people to see if a newer one has been written for your printer.

See Default and Eject Last Page (EJ)

FUNCTION CALLS

Overview   Function calls are the link between the keyboard and what happens in the program. When you press a command key, a specific two-letter command is executed.

    If you really want to learn how XyWrite works, or you want to craft the word processor of your dreams, studying the function calls can take you a giant step in that direction.

    A number of these two-letter commands are not mapped to keys as XyWrite is supplied. They're all available to you for customizing, however. In fact, many of the best ones aren't implemented! Read the Keyboard File section for some ideas.

Procedure   Function calls can either be inserted in a keyboard file, to be executed when a key is pressed, or used with the **Func** command from the command line. They're also key elements of many programs or macros you'll write.

Examples   This is a listing of all function calls, current through version 3.54 or XyWrite III+. A **NA** entry means the function is available but is not assigned to a key.

    Unassigned function calls are explained in a separate table.

TABLE 10   **Assigned Function Calls**

FUNCTION NAME	FUNCTION CALL	ASSIGNED KEY(S)
Auto Check/Correct	AC	Alt A
Append Define to Save/Get	AD	Shift F2
Auto Replacement	AR	Ctrl R
Alternate Screen	AS	Alt F10
Blank Command Line	BC	F5
Backspace Delete	BD	Backspace
Bottom of File	BF	Ctrl End
Break	BK	Ctrl Break
Bottom of Screen	BS	End
Toggle Between Header/Text	CC	F10
Cursor Down	CD	Down Arrow
Cursor Left	CL	Left Arrow
Toggle Expanded/Normal Display	CM	Ctrl F9
Copy Defined Block	CP	F7
Cursor Right	CR	Right Arrow
Cursor Up	CU	Up Arrow
Define Column	DC	Alt F1
Define Block	DF	F1
Define Line	DL	F4
Define Paragraph	DP	Shift F4
Display Ruler	DR	Alt Tab
Define Sentence	DS	Ctrl F4
Display Total	DT	Alt =
Define Word	DW	Alt F4
End Column	EC	Shift End
Erase Entry	EE	Shift Del
Edit Footer, Header, Footnote	EF	Ctrl F3
Express Left Cursor	EL	Crtl Left Arrow
Edit Next File	EN	Ctrl N
Express Right Cursor	ER	Crtl Right Arrow
Exit	EX	Ctrl Alt Del
Find Difference	FD	Ctrl -
Find Match	FM	Ctrl =
Fix Spelling	FS	Ctrl F
Home Column	HC	Shift Home
Cursor to Home Position	HM	Home
Display Mode 0 (reset)	M0	Ctrl 0

(Continued)

FUNCTION NAME	FUNCTION CALL	ASSIGNED KEYS
Display Mode 1 (normal)	M1	Ctrl 1
Display Mode 2 (bold)	M2	Ctrl 2
Display Mode 3 (underline)	M3	Ctrl 3
Display Mode 4 (reverse)	M4	Ctrl 4
Display Mode 5 (bld underline)	M5	Ctrl 5
Display Mode 6 (bld reverse)	M6	Ctrl 6
Display Mode 7 (superscript)	M7	Ctrl 7
Display Mode 8 (subscript)	M8	Ctrl 8
Mark Cell	MC	Shift F1
Move Down	MD	Ctrl Down Arrow
Memory Usage Menu	ME	Ctrl M
Momentary Insert	MI	Ctrl Ins
Move Up	MU	Ctrl Up Arrow
Move Defined Block	MV	F8
Next Formatted Page	NF	Alt Pg Dn
Num Lock Toggle	NK	Num Lock
Next Tab	NT	Ctrl Tab
Next Window	NX	Shift F10
Old Prompt	OP	Alt Shift F9
Page Down	PD	Pg Dn
Previous Formatted Page	PF	Alt Pg Up
Print Screen	PR	Shift PrtSc
Previous Tab	PT	Shift Tab
Page Up	PU	Pg Up
Previous Word	PW	Alt Left Arrow
Spelling Menu Functions	Q1-Q8	F1-F6, Esc, Return
ASCII 0	R0	Alt Shift 0
ASCII 1	R1	Alt Shift 1
ASCII 2	R2	Alt Shift 2
ASCII 3	R3	Alt Shift 3
ASCII 4	R4	Alt Shift 4
ASCII 5	R5	Alt Shift 5
ASCII 6	R6	Alt Shift 6
ASCII 7	R7	Alt Shift 7
ASCII 8	R8	Alt Shift 8
ASCII 9	R9	Alt Shift 9
Rubout Character	RC	Del
Rubout Defined Block	RD	Alt F6
Rubout to End of Line	RL	Ctrl Del
	(Continued)	

FUNCTION NAME	FUNCTION CALL	ASSIGNED KEYS
Rubout Word	RW	Alt Del
Save/Get Directory	SD	Alt F2
Show Help	SH	Alt F9
Show Save/Get Key	SK	Ctrl F2 (key)
Sum	SM	Alt +
Spell One Word	SO	Ctrl S
Show Page/Line Number	SP	Shift F9
Subtract Value	SU	Alt -
Save Define	SV	F2 (key)
Show Window Menu	SW	Ctrl F10
Thesaurus	SY	Ctrl T
Table Entry	TE	Shift Ins
Top of File	TF	Ctrl Home
Toggle Insert	TI	Ins
Table Column Left	TL	Shift Left Arrow
Toggle Num Lock	TN	Num Lock
Toggle Overstrike	TO	TO
Table Column Right	TR	Shift Right Arrow
Toggle Scroll Lock	TS	Scroll Lock
Toggle Word	TW	TW
Undelete	UD	Alt F3
Wild Alpha-Numeric	WA	Alt Shift A
Wild Letter	WL	Alt Shift L
Wild Number	WN	Alt Shift N
Wild Separator	WS	Alt Shift S
Wild String	WW	Alt Shift W
Wild Any Character	WX	Alt Shift X
Execute	XC	F9
Cancel Define	XD	F3
Cancel Define	XD	F3
Save/Get Key	@A-@Z	Alt A Z
Save/Get Key	@0-@9	Alt 0-9

TABLE 11   Unassigned Function Calls

FUNCTION NAME	FUNCTION CALL	EXPLANATION
Counter Commands	C0-C9	Inserts a counter command in text, just as the **C#** command does. See the DC and Numbering sections.
Clear Num Lock	CN	Turns off Num Lock. Used in programming to get the effect of pressing **Num Lock** when **Num Lock** is active.
Comma	CO	Inserts a comma in text, or as part of a keystroke. Commas are used as separators when several characters are mapped to a key so they can't be inserted directly.
Clear Scroll Lock	CS	Turns off Scroll Lock. Used in programming to get the effect of pressing **Scroll Lock** when it is active.
Display On	DO	"Thaws," or frees the screen display after freezing it with the DX function call.
Display Off	DX	Freezes the screen display.
Define Row	ED	Defines a row in a Column Table.
Force Fill	FF	Forces the screen display to refresh.
Go To Header	GH	Moves the cursor from the text to the cursor's last position on the command line.
Go To Text	GT	Moves the cursor from the command line to the cursor's last position in the text.
Help	HL	Displays the help screen related to the first word that's on the command line.
Insert Replacement	IR	Calls the spell check menu, but doesn't check for errors. Lets you access the spell check menu functions to enter corrections into a dictionary file.
Line Begin	LB	Moves cursor to the left margin of the current line. Won't move the cursor up a line with the word wrap.
Linear Down Cursor	LD	Moves cursor straight down one line, whether text is present or not. Usually used if a mouse or similar pointing device is used.

(Continued)

FUNCTION NAME	FUNCTION CALL	EXPLANATION
Line End	LE	Moves cursor to the end of the current line on the right side of the screen. Won't move the cursor down with the word wrap.
Linear Left Cursor	LL	Moves cursor one column to the left, whether text is present or not. Usually used if a mouse or similar pointing device is used.
Linear Right Cursor	LR	Moves cursor one column to the right, whether text is present or not. Usually used if a mouse or similar pointing device is used.
Line Spacing	LS	Toggles screen display between single line spacing (to show as much text as possible) and true line spacing (that more closely reflects how text prints). See the **LF** default setting.
Linear Up Cursor	LU	Moves cursor straight up one line, whether text is present or not. Usually used if a mouse or similar pointing device is used.
Not IBM-Sensitive	NI	Isolates a keystroke sequence from DOS, so keys usually protected keys can be used in XyWrite.
Next Line	NL	Moves the cursor to the start of the next line.
No Markers	NM	Hides bright command triangles, carriage return indicators and the page/line number display. See the **DT** default listing..
No Operation	NO	Used to map several alpha-numeric characters to a single key. Precedes the characters.
Next Paragraph	NP	Moves the cursor to the first character of the next paragraph.
Next Ruler	NR	Toggles between the normal "ruler" line in the header and a straight line.
Next Word	NW	Moves the cursor to the first character of the next word.
Previous Line	PL	Moves the cursor to the start of the preceding line.
Previous Sentence	PS	Moves the cursor to the first character of the previous sentence. (Continued)

FUNCTION NAME	FUNCTION CALL	EXPLANATION
Toggle Redlining On/Off	RO	Works just like the **RED ON** and **RED OFF** commands. See Redlining.
Rubout Paragraph	RP	Erases the paragraph the cursor is in.
Rubout Sentence	RS	Erases the sentence the cursor is in.
Review	RV	Types the current file to the screen. See TYPES.
Acute Accent	S1	These six entries all generate their corresponding character.
Grave Accent	S2	
Umlaut	S3	
Circumflex	S4	
O Accent	S5	
Tilde	S6	
Underline	S7	All the S function calls generate diacritical marks over certain letters. When an S call is issued, the next alpha key generates that letter with the chosen accent. This works with all vowels, the y, and upper and lower case n's.
Set Insert	SI	Turns on Insert mode. Used in programming to get the effect of pressing **Ins** when Overstrike mode is active.
Set Num Lock	SN	Turns on Num Lock. Used in programming to get the effect of pressing **Num Lock.**
Set Scroll Lock	SS	Turns on Scroll Lock. Used in programming to get the effect of pressing **Scroll Lock.**
Toggle Page Normal/Expanded	TP	Toggles between normal and expanded text display, but keeps the Page/Line number displayed when you return to normal display.
Unpad Spaces	UP	Deletes spaces between the cursor and the first character to its left.
Normal Mode	WG	Turns on normal display without the Page/Line number display.
Expanded Mode	XP	Turns on expanded display.
Cancel Define; leave notes open	YD	Releases a defined block of text, but leaves headers, footers, and footnotes open. Usually it's only used in programming.
Save/Get Key	&A-&Z	

(Continued)

171

FUNCTION NAME	FUNCTION CALL	EXPLANATION
Save/Get Key	&0-&9	All the Save/Get entries are used specifically when a program is loaded to a Save/Get key. If they're executed, the program that's assigned to the key is run.
Window Number	#1-#9	Moves directly to the window number of the command, bypassing the window menu.
Call Help	$A-$Z	All the Call Help calls display the help screen that's linked to the particular command..
Call Help	$0-$9	

Tips   Having access to all XyWrite's function calls lets you customize your keyboard. If you're not happy with a particular function... say that **Alt-F5** doesn't automatically release a defined block before it deletes a line, you can fix it! Just add the Release Define function to the Alt Keyboard Table's **F5** key.

If you're not positive what a function does, try it out using the **FUNC** command.

See Function Calls, Command and Keyboard Files

FUNCTION CALL COMMAND (FUNC)

Overview   Func executes any XyWrite function call as a one-shot command.

Procedure
1. Press **F5** (Clear Command Line).
2. Type **FUNC COMMAND**.
3. (Optional) If the function call inserts a character, press **F10** to move the cursor into the text and move the cursor to the proper location.
4. Press **F9** (Execute).
5. The command is executed, but depending on its nature, you may not get any visual feedback.

A La Carte The **Func** command is not available through A La Carte menus. Use the standard XyWrite procedure.

Examples Function calls are explained in detail in the Function Calls section, but briefly, they're two-letter commands that represent specific keyboard actions.

When you're writing and you press the (Up Arrow) key, function call **Cursor Up** (**CU**) is executed by XyWrite; the cursor moves up one line. Press **F7** and function call **Copy Defined Text** (**CP**) is executed.

Func is ideal for trying out a particular function call before you bother entering it in a keyboard file. It's a quick and easy way to see if a function call does what you want it to.

The command's also handy for executing a function call that's not assigned to a particular key.

See Function calls, Keyboard Files, and Programming

FUNCTION KEYS

Overview IBM and compatible computers usually have 10 or 12 dedicated function keys on their keyboards. A number of important XyWrite functions are controlled by them.

A La Carte The only difference between A La Carte's function key assignments and the straight XyWrite program's is the **F6** key. In A La Carte, pressing **F6** brings up the special A La Carte menus. In XyWrite, **F6** clears the command line just as **F5** does.

Examples If a key combination doesn't have a listing, it usually repeats the function key's primary definition. For example, **Shift F1** is not assigned a unique function. **Shift F1** can begin or end a defined text block, just as **F1** by itself does.

TABLE 12   **Function Key Assignments**

KEY (S)	FUNCTION
F1	Begin/End Text Define
Alt F1	Begin/End Column Define
Shift F1	(primary definition)
Ctrl F1	(primary definition)
F2	Make (load) a Save/Gets
Alt F2	Display All Current Save/Gets
Shift F2	Append to a Save/Get
Ctrl F2 (key)	Displays Save/Get on one key
F3	Release Define
Alt F3	Undelete
Shift F3	(primary definition)
Ctrl F3	Open a footnote or header
F4	Define Line
Alt F4	Define Word
Shift F4	Define Paragraph
Ctrl F4	Define Sentence
F5	Clear Command Line
Alt F5	Delete Line
Shift F5	(primary definition)
Ctrl F5	(primary definition)
F6	Clear Command Line
Alt F6	Delete Define
Shift F6	(primary definition)
Ctrl F6	(primary definition)
F7	Copy Defined Block
Alt F7	(primary definition)
Shift F7	(primary definition)

KEY (S)	FUNCTION
Ctrl F7	(primary definition)
F8	Move Defined Block
Alt F8	(primary definition)
Shift F8	(primary definition)
Ctrl F8	(primary definition)
F9	Execute Command
Alt F9	Help Screens
Shift F9	Show Page/Line Numbers
Ctrl F9	Toggle Normal/Expanded Display
F10	Toggle Command Line/Text
Alt F10	Go To Previous Window
Shift F10	Go To Next Window
Ctrl F10	Window Menu

Tips   If you're not fond of XYQUEST's function key assignments, change them! Some keyboards have **F11** and **F12** keys. These aren't assigned a particular function by XYQUEST. You can, however, map any function you want to these keys. See the Keyboard File section.

See Text Blocks

175

GO

Overview　　Go is an immediate command that moves the cursor to whatever page and line position you specify.

Procedure　　The **Go** command works with both page and line numbers, but if you're not sure of the line number, it can be omitted. If you only specify a page number, the cursor jumps to the first line on that page:

1. Press **F5** (Clear Command Line).
2. Type **GO** P#-L# (**P#** is page number; **L#** is line number).
3. Press **F9** (Execute).
4. The cursor moves to the specified page and line number.
5. The Page/Line display is toggled on.

A La Carte
1. Press **F6** (A La Carte menus).
2. Press **S** or select **Search**.
3. Press **P** or select **gotoPage**.
4. The Go To Page screen displays. Type in the page number, and optionally, the line number you want to move to.
5. Press **Return**.
6. The cursor moves to the specified page and line.

Examples　　Go is normally used when editing existing text, particularly if you're keying in corrections marked on hard copy. It eliminates a lot of all around a document.

See Mark, Page/Line Numbers, and Search (SE)

HEADERS

See Running Header (RH)

HEADER NORMAL (HN)

Overview The **HN** default setting determines how the "active" areas of the two header lines and the ruler line display. The default setting is normal text mode.

Procedure **HN** is a default setting you can enter in your printer file or in your STARTUP.INT file. If you do, your favorite display mode is invoked each time XyWrite starts. For complete instructions, see the Procedure portion of the Default listing.

You can also issue **HN** from the command line to set a unique display mode for a single editing session or to test out different settings:

1. Press **F5** (Clear Command Line).
2. Type **DEFAULT** HN=# (the color number of your choice, from the listing in the Display section).
3. Press **F9** (Execute).
4. "Done" displays on the prompt line in the new color.

A La Carte The **HN** setting isn't available through A La Carte's menus. Use the standard XyWrite procedure.

Examples Changing the header display can be helpful, especially on laptop computers that don't have a great contrast range. Change the display to a brighter mode that stands out from the screen.

Tips　　　You can see the colors your monitor is capable of displaying through XyWrite's Help screens:

1. Press **Alt** and **F9** (**Help**).
2. Press **W** or select **Word**.
3. Type **Color Table** in the blank.
4. Press **F9** (Execute) or **Return**.
5. A display showing the colors your computer and monitor are capable of displaying appears. The numbers on the display are the valid entries for the **HN** setting.

See Header Reverse (HR) and Display

HEADER REVERSE (HR)

Overview　　The **HR** default setting determines how the "inactive" areas of the two header lines display. This includes the "CM," "PRMPT," "P-L," and the various indicator letters. The default setting is reverse mode, black on white.

Procedure　　**HR** is a default setting you can enter in your printer file or in your STARTUP.INT file. If you do, your favorite display mode is invoked each time XyWrite starts. For complete instructions, see the Procedure portion of the Default listing.

　　You can also issue **HR** from the command line to set a unique display mode for a single editing session:

1. Press **F5** (Clear Command Line).
2. Type **DEFAULT** HR=# (the color number of your choice, from the listing in the Display section).
3. Press **F9** (Execute).
4. "Done" displays on the prompt line in the new color.

A La Carte　The **HR** setting isn't available through A La Carte's menus. Use the standard XyWrite procedure.

178

Examples   Changing the header display can be helpful, especially on laptop computers that don't have a great contrast range. Change the display to a brighter mode that stands out from the screen.

Tips   You can see the colors your monitor is capable of displaying through XyWrite's Help screens:

1. Press **Alt** and **F9** (**Help**).
2. Press **W** or select **Word**.
3. Type **Color Table** in the blank.
4. Press **F9** (Execute) or **Return**.
5. A display showing the colors your computer and monitor are capable of displaying appears. The numbers on the display are the valid entries for the **HR** setting.

See Header Normal (HN) and Display

HEADER SIZE (HS)

Overview   **Header Size** lets you narrow the full-width header field to display information from another program.

Procedure   Since **HS** is a default setting, you can enter the command in your printer file or in your STARTUP.INT file. If you do, the header display is set short each time XyWrite starts. For complete instructions, see the Procedure portion of the Default listing.

You can also issue **HS** from the command line to set a unique display mode for a single file:

1. Press **F5** (Clear Command Line).
2. Type **DEFAULT** HS=# (the default is **79** spaces wide).
3. Press **F9** (Execute).
4. "Done" displays on the prompt line.

A La Carte You must be in an empty window (have a blank screen) to access the default menus.

1. Press **F6** (A La Carte menus).
2. Press **X** or select **XyWrite**.
3. Press **D** or select **Defaults**.
4. The View and Change Defaults screen displays.
5. Press **H** or select **defaults H-M**.
6. Move the cursor to the **HS** entry and enter the width of the header in spaces.
7. Press **Return**.
8. The Update Default File screen displays. You're asked if you want to make the default settings permanent.
9. Press **Y** or **N**. If you select **Y**, the program writes the new default settings to a special file and returns you to the A La Carte Menu Screen. If you select **N**, the settings are used for the current edit session.

Examples If you use memory resident programs or "background" programs that display information in the upper right-hand corner of the monitor screen, you can clear the XyWrite header so they have a clean display. **HS** has no effect on header placement, which is always flush left.

Warnings If you use programs that put information anywhere on the command line without shortening the header, that information actually becomes part of your commands.

See Defaults

HELP, ACCESSING

Overview Quick on-line directions and advice are available by pressing the **Alt** and **F9** keys.

Procedure
1. Press **Alt** and **F9** (Access Help).
2. The ruler line is replaced by several keywords that identify different categories of assistance.
3. Press the key that is the first letter of the keyword or move the cursor to the keyword and press **F9** (Execute) or **Return**.
4. Depending on the help file that's loaded and on the topic, you'll see another screen offering more detailed selections.
5. Move the cursor to the correct keyword and press **F9** (Execute) or **Return**.

When you've found the answer to your question, you have two choices:

• Step back up the menu tree by pressing **Esc**.
• Return directly to the text by pressing **Alt** and **F9**.

If you go the **Alt** and **F9** route back to your text, you can return directly to the last help screen by pressing **Alt**, **Shift**, and **F9**.

A La Carte   Access Help screens in A La Carte the same way, by pressing **Alt** and **F9**.

Examples
At the basic level, XyWrite's help function provides quick answers to questions that pop up when you're writing. Two versions are available, LONG.HLP and SHORT.HLP. LONG.HLP is a physically larger file that's more comprehensive. The XyWrite manual implies that it's intended for novice users, but there's no reason for a knowledgeable user not to have it available, provided disk storage and computer memory aren't issues.

Tips
At a more sophisticated level, XyWrite's help feature can be customized to guide other users through almost any operation. You can modify the original screens or create your own help screens from scratch. XYQUEST has used the help screen facility to great advantage in its A La Carte menu interface. Point-and-shoot command execution, fill-in-the-blank text

insertion, and chained help screens are all used to good advantage. And they're all things you can adapt to your own applications.

For example, suppose you're setting up XyWrite in a medical office to fill out insurance forms. You've created the necessary electronic forms. You can also create help screens that guide a typist through the filling out procedure from beginning to end. Details on customizing help screens are in the next section.

See Help Files

HELP FILES

Overview   Help Files are not commands. They are the menus, messages, and information that pop up when you press **Alt** and **F9** to call **Help**. Change the factory-supplied files or write your own, tailored to your particular needs.

Procedure   In this section, you'll learn how to modify XyWrite's help messages. Your modifications can be used in an existing XyWrite help file or installed in a built-from-scratch help file.

Like XyWrite's other customizable features, help files are quite extensive, though not really complicated. If you have any programming experience, the logic used to create a chain of help files will feel very natural. If you've never done any programming, don't be intimidated. If you take a few minutes to become familiar with the existing help screens and can visualize your information up there on the screen, you'll do fine.

There are several types of help screens, roughly divided into two categories. When you call **Help,** the first thing you see are **menu screens** that list topics to look at or commands to execute. These lead to **information screens** that hold information or instructions, or perform an operation on your document.

In operation, help screens are arranged like a disk directory. Think of the first menu screen as your root directory, the second layer of menus as your primary directories, and the lower layers of screens as subdirectories. Keep this image in mind when you begin writing your own help sequences. To make the process as easy as possible, plan what screen leads to what other screens, and what you need to type or select to get there.

A complete set of help screens is contained in a single ASCII file. They don't have to be in any particular order within the file. If they're written correctly, the program cross-indexes them and brings the right screen up at the right time.

XyWrite allows up to 14 levels of screens (in XyWrite terminology, help screens are "frames"). As they're invoked, they stack on top of each other in windows, so you can page up and down the particular "tree." See Help for movement instructions.

Become familiar with XyWrite's LONG.HLP file that uses most of these screen types. If you're not using it, load the file so you can get the feel of it. It's helpful to print the file, but it's huge—more than 200 kilobytes. If you don't want to print it, call the file to the screen (as you'd call any other text file) so you can see the hidden codes. To load LONG.HLP:

1. Press **F5** (Clear Command Line).
2. Type **LOAD** LONG.HLP. (If the file isn't in your XyWrite directory, specify the disk or directory where it's stored: **LOAD** A:LONG.HLP).
3. Press **F9** (Execute).
4. "Done" displays on the prompt line.

To print LONG.HLP (Remember— it's a big file):

1. Press **F5** (Clear Command Line).
2. Type **TYPE** LONG.HLP. (If the file isn't in your XyWrite directory, specify the disk or directory where it's stored: **TYPE** A:LONG.HLP.)
3. Press **F9** (Execute).

Here's a list of the 12 types of help screens, or frames. Pay particular attention to Type 0, the screen you'll use for most menus at the top of your structure, and Type 6, the screen that carries instructions or information.

In the example below the listing, note the identifying code— the first characters of the screen. Comment lines begin with semicolons. The syntax of the identification code is critical; the program uses the code to tie the screens together. Each frame begins with {{**TYPE,KEYWORDS**}}. The keyword is the name of the screen and the link between menus. Some screens have optional arguments entered after the KEYWORD. These begin with a dollar sign; they control what conditions must exist for the frame to be used (when no file is open, when a file is open, when a directory listing is displayed, etc.). The arguments are explained at the end of this listing.

Type 0 When you press **Alt** and **F9**, a Type 0 screen displays. It's a single line of topics, called **keywords**, that replaces the ruler line. You can cursor to each word to see a brief description of the topic. When you press **Return**, you call another screen that's further down the hierarchy. Here is the first menu from LONG.HLP:

```
;
{{0$D,$F,$N,$B}}
INDEX, Alphabetical listing of the topics covered by help
WORD, Help information by key words or phrases
KEY, Help information for a particular key
ASCII, Complete set of ASCII characters
ERROR, Gives you a fuller description of the most recent error message
HELP, Information on how to use HELP
COMMANDS, Complete listing of all the XyWrite commands
FUNCTIONS, Complete listing of all two-letter function calls
TEMPLATE, Description of the function keys
DOS, Menu of important DOS functions
```

The first, capitalized, words are the topics that display on the ruler line. The description of the topic is separated from its keyword by a comma. When you call help, move the cursor to **INDEX,** and press **Return**, the Type 6 Index screen appears.

Type 1 Type 1 frames are multi-purpose, fill-in-the-blank frames. A brief message displays, along with a blank for the user to fill in. When they enter information, it's inserted as text in an open file, used to execute a XyWrite program from the cursor location, or to put a command on the command line.

Type 1 in LONG.HLP—Execute DOS Commands These three short sample screens issue commands from the command line. They allow an operator to specify how or where the command should be executed. Notice that the syntax of the command is the same as if you manually typed the command on the command line.

The second line is the only line that appears on the screen. When the operator fills in the blank, that character is passed to the third line, which contains the command. The character is passed with a variable that's identified by a percent sign. Percent One (%1) is the contents of the first fill-in blank; %2 the contents of the second, and so on.

```
{{1CHKDSK}}
Which drive do you want to check: _
do chkdsk %1:

{{1DOS}}

dos

{{1DISKCOPY}}
copying from drive _ to drive _
do diskcopy %1: %2:
```

In each case, the fill-in blank is created by shifting to underline display mode by pressing **Ctrl** and **3**. Press the spacebar until a large enough blank has been created. Then shift back to normal display by pressing **Ctrl** and **1** or **Ctrl** and **0**. End the line the blank is on by pressing **Return**.

Type 1 To Insert Text in a File The syntax of this variant is the same. The first line is the standard header. The second line contains a fill-in blank that's displayed on screen. The third line takes the contents of the blank and inserts it in text at the cursor location.

There's one specific difference in the third (executable) line—the first character must be the ASCII 1 character, the smiley face. It's created by holding down **Ctrl** and **Alt** and typing **1**. Follow it with whatever text you want to insert. Remember that it can only be one line long. The contents of the fill-in blanks are passed with the same variables—%1, %2, and so on.

```
;This line inserts editing information in a file.
{{1EDITED}}
Enter your name and today's date, please_____,_____
☺ This story was edited by %1 on %2.
```

Type 1—Execute a Program from the Cursor Location Again, the syntax of this screen is the same as the other Type 1 variations. The first line is the standard header; the second line contains a fill-in blank that's displayed on screen, and the third line takes the contents of the blank and inserts it in a XyWrite program.

If the listing ends with the execute function call and if the program affects text, the program works on the text at the cursor location.

In a program listing, the third executable line must begin with the ASCII 2 character, the reverse video smiley face. After that comes the program listing. Rather than editing the entire help file in program mode, create your program in a file by itself, then use **Merge** (**ME**) to bring it into the file.

Type 2 A Type 2 frame inserts special (or foreign) ASCII characters in text. This screen is limited to two lines, but that allows access to 80 different characters.

Type 2 screens are used in the help file's ASCII area. When you step down the help screen tree, you end at a screen that asks what category of character you want to look up or insert. When you specify, "foreign" characters, a line of accented letters displays. Move the cursor to one, press **F9** and it's inserted in the text at the cursor.

The two line format is simple. The first line is the standard header. The second is the list of characters that display and can be inserted.

Type 2 screen in LONG.HLP:

;
{{2foreign}}
ÄäâàáÅåªæÇçëéêèÉéïîìíñÑôÖöòóºûùúÜüÿ£Æ¥

Type 3 A Type 3 frame lets a user search for keywords in the help file. It usually summons a Type 7 screen. Type 3 displays a single line of text on the ruler line. A fill-in blank is part of the line, so a user can type in a keyword that links to other screens.

You see it in the second set of menus, after you choose **Word** from the initial help screen. When you type in a word and press **Return**, the program searches all keyword fields for a match and displays that help screen.

The Type 3 screen in LONG.HLP:

{{3word}}
Enter phrase _____(for example—PRINT for info on printers)

Create the blank in underline mode, just as the blank in a Type 1 screen is created.

Type 4 Type 4 screens show what function or character is mapped to a key. When a user selects a Type 4 screen, they're usually prompted to press a key. When they do, the key's character or function is displayed. If that function also has a Type 8 information screen linked to it, to interpret the function, that screen displays next.

The Type 4 screen in LONG.HLP:

{{4key}}
Strike a key for Help frame of that key. Strike **ESC** to Exit.

Type 5 A Type 5 screen is similar to a Type 1, in that it inserts text into a file or executes a program, but you're not limited to a single line. You can set up a Type 5 so a user can enter text in several blanks.

When you create the screen, you'll see the syntax is similar to the Type 1. The first line contains the usual header information: double curly brackets enclosing the number 5 and any keywords. The next lines are the text passage that displays on screen, with blanks to be filled in. After the message text, on a line by itself, should be an ASCII 1 or ASCII 2 character. An ASCII 1 indicates the next lines are text to be inserted. An ASCII 2 indicates a XyWrite program or programs to execute.

Immediately after that comes the actual text to be inserted. The contents of the blanks are carried down into the insertion with percent sign variables (%1, %2, %3). No Type 5 screens are used in XyWrite's supplied help files, but this one is representative:

```
{{5SHIP}}
This form generates a shipping label.

What's the customer's company name? _____
To whose attention should this go? _____
Street address?_____
City?_____ State__ Zip_____-____
[·]
%1
Att. %2
%3
%4, %5   %6-%7
```

To insert XyWrite programs, separate the help screen display lines from the program listing with an ASCII 2 character. The easiest way to bring a program into the help file is to write it in a file by itself, then use **Merge** (**ME**) to import it.

Type 6 A Type 6 screen is the type of screen you're likely to use most often. It's usually called from a Type 0 screen.

A Type 6 provides a full screen to work in. You can either type in information and instructions, or list keywords that take a user to the next screen in the sequence. Consider this index frame, taken from LONG.HLP:

```
{{6index}}
INDEX TO XYWRITE
```

This help file provides you with an alphabetical index of all of the topics covered by Help. Type the first letter of the topic in which you are interested. With each topic there is a phrase in bold. The bold represents one of four things:

A descriptive phrase or keyword

The command name

The key combination that activates that function

The two-character function call for keyboard commands

Put your cursor on the topic that you want and hit return.

A B C D E F G H I J K L M
N O P Q R S T U V W X Y Z

The keywords are the bold-face letters at the bottom of the screen. When you cursor to one and press **Return**, another Type 6 screen displays. That screen uses a single letter as its keyword.

Here's the "one" screen. Notice how it also has keywords that lead a user farther down the hierarchy of help files.

{{6l}}

laser printers	**laser**
leadering	**ld**
line spacing	**ls**
linear cursor movement	**lr**
load command	**load**

When you write a Type 6 screen, indicate which choices are keywords by typing them in bold mode. Shift to bold mode by pressing **Ctrl** and **2**. Return to normal mode by pressing **Ctrl** and **1** or **Ctrl** and **0**.

Type 7 The Type 7 help screen executes file management commands while a directory listing is displayed. Any file-related command that can be issued from the command line could be an entry: **Call, Erase, Load.**

The screen displays the keywords instead of the ruler line. Comment lines for each keyword are displayed above the list.

A Type 7 is created much as the Type 0 screen. The first line is the standard header information: {{7KEYWORD}}. Subsequent lines begin with the keyword that displays on the ruler line. After the keyword, type a comma and the comment line you want displayed. This frame is from the ALACARTE.MNU file. It's used to guide users through the different spell-check options executed from a set of lower level screens.

```
{{7,option}}
Spell,-spell Spellfile Correct Loaddict
soRt,-Sort sort and order list
mailMerge,-mm Mainfile Datafile mergetoPrinter mergetoFile mergetoScreen
```

When the screen is called up, the command that's chosen is executed on the file in the directory that the cursor was on.

Type 8 Type 8 screens display information about function calls. They're usually accessed from a Type 6 or Type 4 screen. This screen interprets the **AR** function call. It's from LONG.HLP. Note the boldfaced keywords at the bottom of the screen. They're links to other frames.

```
{{8ar,auto-replace,auto-expand,shorthand}}
    AUTO REPLACE


Auto-Replace is similar to Auto Check, but it does not check for spelling errors.
CTRL-R turns Auto-Replace (AR) ON and OFF. "R" appears when Replace is ON.
```

Type 9 A Type 9 is a help screen that's actually more of a command. In most cases, you wouldn't need to modify the existing Type 9 frames because they're usually program-specific; they don't lend themselves to customizing. It's a simple one-line entry in the help file that causes XyWrite to display a message (in a Type 6 frame) that explains a program error. Each XyWrite program error is numbered, and the resulting Type 6 frame usually is identified by the associated error code number. Naturally, there must be a linked Type 6 frame keyed to that error number in order for something to be displayed.

This Type 9 frame and two related Type 6 frames are taken from the ALACART.MNU file. In the second Type 6 frame, notice how the same frame is used to explain several program errors.

```
{{9,error,$e}}

{{6022}}
Too many mode entries

You have defined too many printing modes. Reduce the number of MODE
 definitions in the PT Tables in the Printer File.

The maximum number of mode entries is 300

{{6079,183,232,233,245,292}}
No memory . . .

You need to take some text out of memory by storing or aborting.

Either STore this file or other files that you have open for editing.

Go to the beginning of the file with CTRL-HOME. Return to where
you are and continue.
```

Although it's not strictly part of the Help frame, remember that XyWrite has a built-in feature controlled by the **EH** default setting that automatically calls up an explanation of whatever program error occurs. See the **EH** listing for more information.

Type A A Type A screen is a cousin to a Type 4, which lets you know what happens when you push a particular key. When a Type A is called up, you would usually have a message display to tell the user to press the key they want interpreted. The Type 4 screen is limited to the key's function call. The Type A screen reads the key's number, its physical location. When they press the key, the help screen for that key displays.

A Type A is a two-line screen. The first line is the standard header. The second is the message that displays on the ruler line.

Type B Type B screens are used to execute XyWrite programs or insert text in files. They provide more choices than Type 1 screens do. Type B screens can provide several choices of commands, each numbered from 1 through 9. When the user types the number of a command it is executed or its text is inserted.

Type B screens are full-screens. Begin with the standard header. Enter the numbered lines that display on screen next. Follow those with the actual commands, one for each numbered entry. Program lines must begin with an ASCII 2 character, then the program string. Each line that inserts text must begin with an ASCII 1 character, followed by the text.

Keywords These are usually single words, although they can be any length. You can include single spaces between them. There are several "special" keywords that control when a help frame can be accessed. These arguments can be put into the header line of any frame type that provides access to the help file:

$B   Available only when a block of text is defined.
$D   Available only when a directory is displayed.
$F   Available only when a file is open on screen.
$N   Available only when no file is open on screen.
$*   Available anytime.

The asterisk is a wildcard that can be included in a keyword field to broaden the range of words that call it. The asterisk stands for any number of characters.

You might use one in a Type 3 frame where people enter a topic on which they want more information. Different people enter different words to describe the same thing. If a person wanted information on "disk drives," think of all the possibilities: disk, diskette, hard disk, soft disk, floppy, floppy disk, and so on. If you use a keyword like **dis*** in your disk drive help frame header, many of the different words connect with the proper frame.

Type C Type C frames are the same as Type 1 frames, except they're not loaded into memory; they remain stored on disk until called. Like the Type 1 frame, a Type C can execute a program or insert text into a file.

192

A Type C can include an underlined blank where text can be entered or placed automatically by a XyWrite variable. Just as in the Type 1 frame, a line that inserts text needs to begin with an ASCII 1 symbol; a line that executes a program must begin with an ASCII 2.

This Type C frame is taken from XYQUEST's SAMPLE.HLP file. It's intended to open a new document file in a specific window. The lines are shown in expanded mode, so the codes are visible. Just as in the Type 1 frame, text that's entered is identified as %1 or %2 when it's reused in the program line.

```
{{CC}}
⊡ New file: «MDUL»     «MDNM» In window «MDUL»$wn «MDNM»
«HF2»BC window % 2XC «EI»«HF1»BC ne %1XC «EI»[CR]
```

Type D Type D frames help identify and explain function calls, in a fashion similar to Type 8 frames. A Type D can be linked only to a Type 8, however; a Type 8 can call a Type 6 frame to provide a full screen of information. This example is from a XYQUEST help file called SAMPLE.HLP. The keywords in the frame are the three bold function calls at the bottom of the frame. They link to the Type 8 screens that follow.

```
{{DD}}
TYPE D FRAMES

What Function Calls Mean
Select the function call you want to know more about: XP  XM  LB

{{8XP}}
FUNCTION CALL XP
The function call XP (Expanded Mode) forces text into expanded mode.

Press Esc. to return to the Type D Help Screen.
Press F6 to clear the screen.

{{8XM}}
FUNCTION CALL XM
The function call XM moves the cursor to the midpoint of the current line, based
on number of characters on that particular line. XyWrite counts the number of
```

characters and moves to the midpoint of that number, regardless of proportional widths.

Press Esc to return to the Type D Help Screen.
Press F6 to clear the screen.

Type F A Type F frame contains a list of keywords. When a user selects one, a XyWrite command is executed. In the example below, also from SAMPLE.HLP, when you move your cursor to one of the boldfaced keywords, the corresponding command in the lower part of the frame is executed. Note that the command strings must begin with the ASCII 2 character to set them off from text.

```
{{FF}}
TYPE F FRAME
```

Executing commands from a list of keywords.

TMP   Delete all files on this drive with .TMP extension
BAK   Delete all files on this drive with .BAK extension
BOTH   Delete all files on this drive with either .TMP or .BAK extension.

 ⬚ **BC** find *.tmp**XC** iferexei**BC** del**CC** lbloop**XC** ifer**BC** ab**XCBC**exeiglloop
 ⬚ **BC** find *.bak**XC** iferexei**BC** del**CC** lbbloop**XC** ifer**BC** ab**XCBC**exeiglbloop
 ⬚ **BC** find *.tmp**XC** iferglbakei**BC** del**CC** lbcloop**XC** ifer**BC** glbakeiglclooplbbak
 BC find *.bak**XC** iferexei**BC** del**CC** lbdloop**XC** ifer**BC** ab**XC BC** exeigldloop

Type G Type G frames are two-line frames that call a specific file from disk storage. This could be a large text file that provides detailed information on the "help" subject.

The first line of the G frame is the normal identification code, "G" followed by a keyword, both enclosed in double curly brackets. The second line is the name of the file that's called. The first character of the file that's called must be the number or letter that identifies the type of help frame the file is. In this case, the "5" that's several lines under the "G" represents the first line of the file named MORE.HLP. In this example, MORE.HLP is a Type 5 frame.

```
{{GMORE}}
c:\xy\more.hlp
```

```
5
The text for MORE.HLP goes here...
```

A La Carte There's no special facility in A La Carte for editing help files. Follow the procedures outlined here.

Examples Altering help screens is a powerful tool for customizing XyWrite to your particular application. The regular help screens are sufficient for most purposes, but if you plan on doing extensive programming, keyboard modifications, or using XyWrite for special applications (having untrained typists fill in forms), the help files should be fine-tuned.

If you make modifications, finish the job by updating the help files to support other people. If you don't, you're either going to spend a lot of time answering the same questions or you're going to handicap the other users because they won't be able to use the full power of the program.

Tips You can tie a help frame directly to a key, so that when the key is pressed, a specific help screen displays. In the screen's keyword field, enter a dollar sign followed by a single number or capital letter (**$1**, **$K**). Then, modify a keyboard file by entering the same combination as a function call. See the Keyboard File section for more information.

This example shows how you might modify a XyWrite-supplied help screen to reflect changes you make in a keyboard file:

1. Press **F5** (Clear Command Line).
2. Type **CA** LONG.HLP (or SHORT.HLP if you prefer).
3. Near the top of the file, find the key Type 0 frame that appears when you call for help. It looks like this:

```
{{0$D,$F,$N,$B}}
INDEX, Alphabetical listing of the topics covered by help
WORD, Help information by key words or phrases
KEY, Help information for a particular key
ASCII, Complete set of ASCII characters
ERROR, Gives you a fuller description of the most recent error message
```

HELP, Information on how to use HELP
COMMANDS, Complete listing of all the XyWrite commands
FUNCTIONS, Complete listing of all two-letter function calls
TEMPLATE, Description of the function keys
DOS, Menu of important DOS functions

4. At the bottom of the frame, under the DOS line, enter your keyword and a description:

KEYBD, Changes to the SUPER keyboard by John Doe.

5. Next, create a help screen that appears when **KEYBD** is selected:

{{6KEYBD}}

CONTROL KEYS	**CONTROL KEYS**
OUTLINE	**OUTLINE**
WINDOWS	**WINDOWS**
OTHER KEYS	**OTHER KEYS**

6. You've defined four categories, so you need to create four help screens, one for each:

{{6CONTROL KEYS}}

Ctrl-Shift-A	Auto/Check On/Off
Ctrl-C	CALL file from directory
Ctrl-D	Call DIRECTORY of default drive
Ctrl-Shift-F	Spell check last incorrect word (Auto Check)
Ctrl-F	Start Footnote Entry
Ctrl-H	Flush Left
Ctrl-J	Flush Center
Ctrl-K	Flush Right
Ctrl-L	Start numbered list - 1.1.1.1.1.1.1.1
Ctrl-Shift-M	Memory Usage Menu
Ctrl-M	Memory Usage Menu
Ctrl-N	Edit Next file in multi-file call (as in CMca *.prn)
Ctrl-O	Start Outline list format - I A 1 a (1) (a)
Ctrl-P	Page Eject
Ctrl-Shift-R	Auto Replace

Ctrl-Shift-A	Auto/Check On/Off
Ctrl-R	Reset Screen to NOT IN USE
Ctrl-Shift-S	Spell check 1 word
Ctrl-S	SAVE current file, don't store
Ctrl-T	Thesaurus
Ctrl-X	Start Index Entry

{{6OUTLINE}}

CAP-1	Outlining (numbered list) Level 1
CAP-2	Outlining (numbered list) Level 2
CAP-3	Outlining (numbered list) Level 3
CAP-4	Outlining (numbered list) Level 4
CAP-5	Outlining (numbered list) Level 5
CAP-6	Outlining (numbered list) Level 6
CAP-7	Outlining (numbered list) Level 7
CAP-8	Outlining (numbered list) Level 8
CAP-9	Outlining (numbered list) Level 9

The Cap Lock is a Shifting Key, not a Toggle. Use it to insert outline or numbered list counters. In this table use the Cap Lock and a Number Pad to move to a window number:

{{6WINDOWS}}

CAP-1	Go to Window 1
CAP-2	Go to Window 2
CAP-3	Go to Window 3
CAP-4	Go to Window 4
CAP-5	Go to Window 5
CAP-6	Go to Window 6
CAP-7	Go to Window 7
CAP-8	Go to Window 8
CAP-9	Go to Window 9

{{6OTHER KEYS}}

NORMAL (Number Pad) -	moves to next sentence
NORMAL (Number pad) +	moves to next paragraph
SHIFT (Number Pad) -	moves to previous sentence
SHIFT (Number Pad) +	moves to previous paragraph
CAPS LOCK (Number Pad) -	deletes current sentence
CAPSLOCK (Number Pad) +	deletes current paragraph
SHIFT PgUp	moves you 2 pages up
SHIFT PgDn	moves you 2 pages down

7. Store the file under a different name, to avoid corrupting your original help file (**STORE** JOHN.HLP).
8. Load the new file: **LOAD** JOHN.HLP.
9. Push **Alt** and **F9** to call help and test your new screens.

Building a new help file from scratch takes more planning than modifying an existing screen does. If you're planning a large project, take the time to outline the project on small pieces of paper, one screen to a sheet. Move them around on a wall until you're satisfied with what screen pulls up what information. Then begin typing.

Folk singer Pete Seeger maintains "Plagiarism is essential to all culture." That's especially true when you're writing a new help file, and doubly true if you're doing it for the first time.

The previous example demonstrated how an existing file can be modified. The best strategy for creating a brand new file is to modify an existing file—extensively. Instead of simply adding screens, of course, you'll want to delete a number of existing screens.

Replace existing screens with your own a few at a time. Your first step might be to change a keyword on the Type 0 screen. Pick a keyword that emulates the actions you want to copy—filling in blanks, or providing information. Remove the existing keyword and insert your own. Then use **SE** to find the old keyword in other screen's headers. Insert your own keywords in their place, and rewrite the screens to suit your new application.

Warnings   Always name your new help file something unique so you don't corrupt a XyWrite file you may need in six months. Always test as you go—don't get so caught up in your project that you make too many changes at once. Save, load, and test the new file periodically, so you can fix problems as you go.

See Help (Accessing), Auto Check, and Loading Personal Dictionary

---

HYPHENATION (HY)

Overview   XyWrite automatically hyphenates words if a hyphenation dictionary is loaded, unless you turn the feature off with **HY**. Once automatic hyphenation is off, it can also be turned back on with **HY**.

Procedure   Turn off hyphenation in a single file:

1. Move the cursor to the place where you want to turn hyphenation off.
2. Press **F5** (Clear Command Line).
3. Type **HY** OFF (or **ON**, if you're restarting the feature).
4. Press **F9** (Execute).
5. A bright command triangle is inserted in the text.

If you decide that you never want hyphenation to be invoked automatically, you can enter a default setting to keep it turned off. See the default section for details on entering the command in your printer file or in STARTUP.INT. To turn off hyphenation for a single editing session, enter **DEFAULT HY=OFF** at the command line. NOTE: If you permanently disable automatic hyphenation, you can do without the hyphenation dictionary the feature requires. **DICTION** is the default hyphenation dictionary name; it's usually loaded by the STARTUP.INT file when XyWrite starts.

To stop it from loading, open STARTUP.INT as you would any text file. Look for a line like this:

BC LDDICT DICTION

Then delete it. Then use **Store** to save the modified STARTUP.INT. The next time you load XyWrite, the hyphenation dictionary won't be loaded. To turn off hyphenation for a single editing session:

1. Press **F5** (Clear Command Line).
2. Type **DEFAULT** HY=OFF.
3. Press **F9** (Execute).
4. "Done" displays on the prompt line.

A La Carte Hyphenation can be controlled in a single file through the A La Carte menus:

1. Press **F6** (A La Carte menus).
2. Press **R** or select **foRmat**.
3. Press **A** or select **Alignment**.
4. Move the cursor the Hyphenation line and select **On** or **Off**.
5. A bright command triangle is inserted in text.

You can also modify the default setting to turn hyphenation off or on for either a single editing session or all editing sessions. You must be in an empty window (have a blank screen) to access the default menus.

1. Press **F6** (A La Carte menus).
2. Press **X** or select **XyWrite**.
3. Press **D** or select **Defaults**.
4. The View and Change Defaults screen displays.
5. Press **H** or select **defaults H-M**.
6. Move the cursor to the **HY** entry and type **0** to turn hyphenation off, or **1** to turn it back on.
7. Press **Return**.

8. The Update Default File screen displays. You're asked if you want to make the default settings permanent.
9. Press **Y** or **N**. If you select **Y**, the program writes the new default settings to a special file and returns you to the A La Carte Menu Screen. If you select **N**, the settings are used for the current edit session.

Examples

You might want to turn hyphenation off in several situations:

- If you were writing headlines that you didn't want to break in the middle of a word.
- To maximize the effect of a flush left or flush right setting.
- To manually hyphenate words.

Tips

XyWrite hyphenates words with an algorithm and an exception dictionary. If a word is listed in the exception dictionary, those break points are used. If the word isn't listed, the algorithm is used.

If you're unhappy with a word's breaking point, you can insert a hyphen manually that overrides the default hyphenation points supplied in the hyphenation dictionary. XyWrite provides three types of manual hyphens: non-breaking hard hyphens, breaking hard hyphens, and soft hyphens.

A *non-breaking hard hyphen* stays firmly attached to whatever word or character "owns" it. It won't become separated if the word falls on the end of a line. Use it to indicate a negative number, or in a hyphenated word that you won't allow to break, such as a company name or a person's compound last name. Create a non-breaking hard hyphen by holding down the **Alt** and **Shift** keys and typing **45**. When you release the keys, the hyphen appears.

A *breaking hard hyphen* is the character produced by the hyphen key or the minus sign on the numeric keypad. It's the character most people automatically type to indicate a hyphen. If you have a word that's the last word on a line and you want to force a hyphenation at a particular point, insert the breaking hard hyphen.

A *soft hyphen* indicates a conditional hyphenation point. If you're typing a word that you want to hyphenate in a particular spot, but you're not sure it will fall at the end of a line, type a tilde at the hyphenation point. (The tilde is inserted at the left edge of the cursor, so put the cursor on the letter *after* the break point.) The tilde won't display, but it'll be in place. If your word falls at the end of a line, the word breaks at the spot you marked. If you need to delete a soft hyphen because you changed your mind, shift to expanded mode by pressing **Ctrl** and **F9**. The tilde appears as a regular character.

(If you need to type a real tilde, you must use the ASCII character insert procedure. Hold **Alt** and **Shift** down and type **126**. When you release the keys, a visible tilde displays.)

If you like the convenience of automatic hyphenation but dislike some words' breakpoints, you can modify just those words in the hyphenation dictionary. Also, if some words you use aren't in the hyphenation dictionary, you can add them and select their breakpoints as you do.

The standard hyphenation dictionary is named DICTION. It's usually loaded at the beginning of a session by the STARTUP.INT file. DICTION is a regular ASCII file, so you can call it to the screen for editing as you would any other text file.

The dictionary format is very straightforward—just one word to a line. When you open the file, you'll see something similar to this:

```
aban-do*n-ment
abrup*t-ly
aca-dem-ic
acad-emy
ac-cept-a*bil-ity
ac-com-plish-
ac-coun-tant
ac-cord-ing-ly
ac-knowl-edge*
adap*t-abil-ity
```

The hyphens are the preselected breakpoints. To change a word's hyphenation points, type hyphens where you want the word to break. To remove a breakpoint in an existing word, delete the hyphen. To prevent hyphenation in a word, remove the hyphens.

To keep XyWrite fast, the hyphenation dictionary doesn't load the entire word into memory—just the first seven characters. Asterisks in or after a word override that rule. If you have a long word, you might want the entire word to be considered for hyphenation points, rather than just the first seven characters. Enter an asterisk after the word or segment you want considered.

After the dictionary is modified, it must be stored and reloaded for the changes to take effect. Execute the **LOAD DICTION** command from the command line.

See Hyphenation Value and Non-Breaking Space

HYPHENATION VALUE (HV)

Overview   XyWrite uses the **HV** command to provide high-level control over how words are hyphenated at the end of a line. XyWrite uses **HV** to set the size of words that can be hyphenated and how many characters can appear on a line before a hyphen or after a hyphen.

Procedure   Since **HV** is a default setting, you can enter the command in your printer file or in your STARTUP.INT file. If you do, the program follows your rules for word hyphenation each time XyWrite starts. For complete instructions, see the Procedure portion of the Default listing.

You can also issue **HV** from the command line to set a unique display mode for a single edit session:

1. Press **F5** (Clear Command Line).

2. Type **DEFAULT** HV=#,#,# (the initial settings specify five letter words as the minimum length to hyphenate, and two characters before and after a hyphen—**HV=5,2,2**).
3. Press **F9** (Execute).
4. "Done" displays on the prompt line.

A La Carte You must be in an empty window (have a blank screen) to access the default menus.

1. Press **F6** (A La Carte menus).
2. Press **X** or select **XyWrite**.
3. Press **D** or select **Defaults**.
4. The View and Change Defaults screen displays.
5. Press **H** or select **defaults H-M**.
6. Move the cursor to the **HV** entry. Type the three numbers that represent the shortest word length to hyphenate and the minimum number of characters to leave before and after the hyphen.
7. Press **Return**.
8. The Update Default File screen displays. You're asked if you want to make the default settings permanent.
9. Press **Y** or **N**. If you select **Y**, the program writes the new default settings to a special file and returns you to the A La Carte Menu Screen. If you select **N**, the settings are used for the current edit session.

Examples   XyWrite has enough built-in flexibility to generate as high a quality typography as you want. If you're using microjustification to fine-tune the space between letters, you may have strong feelings about where a word is hyphenated when it ends a line. Generally, the fewer the breaks in a word, the better.

XyWrite's original settings allow hyphenation of a five-letter word. That can leave three letters on one line and two on the next. You may want to increase XyWrite's minimum settings by a letter or two to create a stricter hyphenation table.

Tips   If you're quite serious about your hyphenation and don't like the way XyWrite does things, modify the program to suit your fancy:

- Use **HV** to increase the minimum word length.
- Review the **Hyphenation (HY)** section.
- Modify the hyphenation dictionary.

See Hyphenation and Show Hyphenation

INCLUDE (IN)

Overview   IN imports files from other software packages into a XyWrite document. Use it to include a spreadsheet, database report, or graphic.

Procedure   Don't use **Include** to bring a raw data file from a foreign software package into XyWrite. The command only works with files that have been printed to disk (like those created with **Typefs** in XyWrite). Most software packages can print a file to disk; if you use one that can't, you may be out of luck.

The first step is to prepare the file in the foreign software package. In Lotus 1-2-3, you'd select PRINT, then FILE. Lotus creates a file with a .PRN extension. Other software packages use different extensions. Remember the file name.

Second, send the .PRN file to your printer. Align your printer paper. At a DOS prompt, type **COPY FILENAME.PRN LPT1** (if your printer is wired to parallel port number one). When you press **RETURN** to execute the command, the file is copied to your printer. Measure the depth of the insert, the amount of vertical space it takes on a page (a graphic may be three inches deep, a spreadsheet printed sideways may be 6.5 or 14 inches).

Third, convert the insert's depth to lines-per-inch. XyWrite usually measures its page depth in lines, six lines to an inch. Multiply your depth measurement by six. Your three-inch graphic would be 18 lines deep; the spreadsheet 39 lines or 84. Fourth, open your main document in XyWrite:

1. Move the cursor to the point where the insert should go.
2. Press **Return** once to give yourself a clean line.
3. Press **F5** (Clear Command Line).
4. Type **IN** FILENAME.PRN,DEPTH (such as **IN** COSTS.PRN,39).
5. Press **F9** (Execute).
6. A bright command triangle is inserted, but the foreign file won't display. When you use **Type** to send the file to the printer, the insert prints properly. Unfortunately, **Typef** and **Types** don't display the insert, although they leave blank lines to indicate where the insert goes.

A La Carte The A La Carte menus don't differentiate between the **IN** command and the **Merge** command. If you've prepared the foreign file as a printer file, try the built-in **Merge** facility. If it doesn't work, use the regular XyWrite procedure given here:

1. Press **F6** (A La Carte menus).
2. Press **F** or select **File**.
3. Press **M** or select **Merge**.
4. A screen displays that prompts you to enter the name of the file you want to import. Type in the filename.
5. Press **F9** (Execute).
6. The foreign file is inserted in the open file.

Examples **Include** is one of the tools that makes XyWrite a major-league word processor. It allows you to integrate information from several software applications into a single document without a lot of hassle or messy manual cut-and-paste procedures.

When you get really proficient with **Include**, you can produce pages that look as if they came from an expensive desktop publishing package.

Tips
If you generate a lot of letters, think about having the sender's signature scanned as a graphic. If you have a good printer, the signature can be inserted as the letter rolls off the printer.

Non-graphic files that are printed to disk usually contain generic ASCII characters. The first time you import a file from a new piece of software, take the time to experiment a bit. If the file is made up of true ASCII characters, you'll have more flexibility if you use **Merge** to import the data. With **Merge**, the foreign file is copied into, and becomes a part of, the XyWrite file. It can be manipulated with XyWrite. If you use **IN**, the foreign file remains semi-independent. Any changes you make must be made in the foreign file.

Most inserted files print on the left margin of your XyWrite document. There are several tools you can use to move the insert further towards the center or right side of the page. The file format of the insert is going to vary from one software package to the next, so you may need to try several of these commands before you achieve the right effect.

If you want to center the insert, try XyWrite's **Flush Center** command. If that distorts the insert, the incoming file format's line lengths probably vary. The other way to move the insert over is to change your left margin to a wider setting.

To move the insert all the way over to the right edge of the page, try XyWrite's **Flush Right** command.

Warnings
Every software package treats files differently. Some embed printer control codes, even in a file that's printed to disk. If your printer begins acting more independent than it should when it hits an insert, suspect the imported file.

Hidden printer control codes could let the insert print, but print XyWrite text on top of it. Get around the problem by inserting an **Extra Leading** (**EL**) command and changing the depth setting in the **IN** to **0**.

If the insert uses an alternate type style (bold, italic, expanded...) and doesn't return control to XyWrite after the insert prints, embed the appropriate XyWrite mode command on the line after the insert.

When you create the printed-to-disk file, make sure the file is formatted for the same printer your XyWrite document is going to print on. A graph created for a Postscript printer isn't going to work on your Epson.

See Merge and Extra Leading

INDENT PARAGRAPH (IP)

Overview   The **Indent Paragraph** command automatically indents (or outdents) the first line of a paragraph.

Procedure   The **IP** setting can either be inserted in a file or used as a default setting to control hyphenation in all documents. If you write the same style of text all the time, you might want to use **IP** as a default. If you're constantly changing styles of text, **IP** would probably be used more often as an embedded command. You can also use both—set a default **IP** value to take care of most situations and override it with an embedded **IP** in special documents. Either style of **IP** takes two values.

The syntax of the command is: **IP #,#**. The first number sets the number of spaces to indent the first line of the paragraph. The second controls the amount of indent of all succeeding lines. If you omit the second number, XyWrite uses **0** and sets all following lines at the left margin. To issue **IP** as a default value, you can enter the **IP** command in your printer file or in your STARTUP.INT file. If you do, your standard paragraph indent is used for all documents each time you use XyWrite. For complete instructions on modifying either of these files, see the Procedure portion of the Default.

You can also issue **IP** from the command line to set a unique display mode for a single editing session:

1. Press **F5** (Clear Command Line).
2. Type **DEFAULT** IP=#,#.

3. Press **F9** (Execute).
4. "Done" displays on the prompt line.

   To embed **IP** in a document:

1. Move the cursor to the point where you want to begin the new indent.
2. Press **F5** (Clear Command Line).
3. Type **IP #,#** (for example, **IP 5,0** indents the first line five spaces and sets the following lines flush with the left margin. An **IP 0, 10** creates a hanging first line at the left margin and insets all following text ten spaces.)
4. Press **F9** (Execute).
5. A bright command triangle is inserted. Existing paragraphs following the triangle change their format to reflect the new setting.

A La Carte   To issue **IP** as a default value, you must be in an empty window (have a blank screen) to access the default menus.

1. Press **F6** (A La Carte menus).
2. Press **X** or select **XyWrite**.
3. Press **D** or select **Defaults**.
4. The View and Change Defaults screen displays.
5. Press **H** or **M** or select **defaults H-M**.
6. Move the cursor to the **IP** entry and type in the two line values for your indent.
7. Press **Return**.
8. The Update Default File screen displays. You're asked if you want to make the default settings permanent.
9. Press **Y** or **N**. If you select **Y**, the program writes the new default settings to a special file and returns you to the A La Carte Menu Screen. If you select **N**, the settings are used for the current edit session.

   To embed **IP** in a document:

1. Move the cursor to the point where you want to begin the new indent.

2. Press **F6** (A La Carte menus).

3. Press **R** or select **foRmats**.

4. Press **I** or select **Indents**.

5. A screen displays with a blank for you to enter the number of characters you want to indent the first and the subsequent lines. Type in the number of characters, separated by a comma.

7. Press **Return**.

8. A bright command triangle is inserted in the text.

Examples   **IP** is a basic formatting command. Many people like to indent the first line of paragraphs, and **IP** eliminates using the tab key to set the line manually. Using the **IP** command instead of the tab key allows you to change the formatting of all paragraphs in the document at once, instead of going through all the paragraphs with a **CH** command.

Any text after a carriage return is viewed as a paragraph by XyWrite. If you type a line and end it with a carriage return, the next thing you type is viewed as a separate paragraph.

Tips   If there's already an **IP** command in place in a document and you want to change the setting, shift to expanded display by pressing **Ctrl** and **F9**. Move the cursor to the **IP** entry and type in your new numeric setting directly.

See Style Sheets

INDEXING

Overview   Generating an index in XyWrite is easy. It's a three-step procedure that involves marking text with the **X#** command, setting the index format with the **I#** command, and building the index itself with the **Index Extraction** (**IX**). The process is very similar to building a table of contents.

I

XyWrite uses the term "index" to mean an alphabetically sorted list of words or phrases. A XyWrite "table of contents" is a list that's sorted by page numbers. You can generate up to nine indexes and tables per document.

Procedure   Remember that creating an index involves three steps: marking text, setting the index format, and extracting the index. There are three ways to create index entries. You can index a word or phrase in the text, or build a paraphrased entry that doesn't appear in the text. To list a single word in the text:

1. Move the cursor to the space just *after* the target word. There can be no spaces or hidden mode commands between the cursor and the word.
2. Press **F5** (Clear Command Line).
3. Type **X#** (**#** is the number of the index set, **1** through **9**).
4. Press **F9** (Execute). A window opens, but don't type anything into it.
5. Press **F3**.
6. A bright command triangle is inserted in the text.

To list a phrase in the text, the phrase you want to list must end with a carriage return. This is how a title, headline, or subtitle is often written—on a line by itself:

1. Move the cursor to the space just *before* the target phrase. The cursor must have a space, a tab stop, or a carriage return in front of it. The phrase must end with a carriage return.
2. Press **F5** (Clear Command Line).
3. Type **X#** (**#** is the number of the index set, **1** through **9**).
4. Press **F9** (Execute). A window opens, but don't type anything into it.
5. Press **F3**.
6. A bright command triangle is inserted in the text.

To build a paraphrased entry (Option 1):

1. Move the cursor to the spot that the entry should reference.

2. Press **F5** (Clear Command Line).
3. Type **X#** (**#** is the number of the index set, **1** through **9**).
4. Press **F9** (Execute). A window opens.
5. Type the phrase or word you want to use as the entry.
6. Press **F3**.
7. A bright command triangle is inserted in the text.

To build a paraphrased entry (Option 2):

1. Move the cursor to the spot that the entry should reference.
2. Press **F5** (Clear Command Line).
3. Type **X#** (**#** is the number of the index set, **1** through **9**) and the phrase or word you want to use as the entry (for example—**X1 Rubble, Barney**).
4. Press **F9** (Execute).
5. A bright command triangle is inserted in the text.

When an index is generated, all marked text that appears before the embedded command is included. To index an entire document, move the cursor to the end of the main document by pressing **Ctrl** and **End**:

1. Move the cursor to the place in the document where the indexing should end. (Press **Ctrl** and **End** to move the cursor to the end of the main document).
2. Press **F5** (Clear Command Line).
3. Type **X#** (**#** is the number of the index set, **1** through **9**).
4. Press **F9** (Execute). A window opens.
5. Enter the page format of the index. You can use any formatting commands, such as **Left Margin (LM)**, **Right Margin (RM)**, or **Line Spacing (LS)**.
6. Enter the line format of the index with the **Set Record (SR)** command. A typical entry might be:
   - Press **F5** (Clear Command Line).
   - Type **SR** IX (Place Marked Text).
   - Press **F9** (Execute).
   - Press **F5** (Clear Command Line).
   - Type **LD.** (Use Periods As Leadering)
   - Press **F9** (Execute).

- Press **F5** (Clear Command Line).
- Type **SR** CH- (Place Marked Text's Chapter and Page Number).
- Press **F9** (Execute).

7. Instead of generating a chapter number, you might want just the page number:
   - Press **F5** (Clear Command Line).
   - Type **SR** PN (Place Marked Text's Page Number).
   - Press **F9** (Execute).

8. When the format looks good, press **F3**. The window closes.

9. Store the document.

You can build the index as part of the main document or as a separate file. To build the index in a separate file you need to include a **No Index** (**NI**) command in the main document. To extract the index, see the **IX** command.

To build the index as part of the document:

1. Press **F5** (Clear Command Line).
2. Type **TY** MAINFILENAME.
3. Press **F9** (Execute). As the file prints, the index is generated and printed as part of the document.

A La Carte   Indexing is not supported in the A La Carte menus. Use the procedures outline here.

Examples   Many types of documents, especially academic papers and books, require indexes. XyWrite's ability to generate nine separate sorted lists lets you create a subject index, an author index, a reference index, an index to special features or passages of text—almost anything that's in a document can be referenced.

As XyWrite builds the index, it automatically removes duplicate entries and combines multiple page numbers on one line.

Tips   Marking text is usually the most time-consuming part of building an index. If you plan ahead and embed markers as you go, it makes the process go faster. In the SUPER.KBD file, XyWrite provides dedicated keys for beginning index and table of contents entries. You can pirate these entries to your own keyboard, or adopt the SUPER. See the Keyboard section for more information.

At the very least, consider writing a short macro so your index entries can be accomplished with a single keystroke. Read the Save/Get section for instructions.

To generate a multi-level index that groups items under a general heading, see the **Index Label** (**IL**) command.

To group index entries by the letters of the alphabet or any other grouping, see the **Index Break** (**IB**) command.

If you want to cross-reference index entries, or refer to another index entry, read the listing on the **End X-Marker** (**EX**) command.

See Index Break, Indexing (Cross Referencing), Index Label, Index Extraction, No Index, Table of Contents, Set Record, and Text Marker

---

INDEXING, CROSS REFERENCING (EX)

Overview The **EX** command suppresses the page number that usually prints with an index entry. It's used to cross reference to other index entries or to insert headings.

Procedure **EX** is inserted in text after a regular index entry that contains the cross reference information. **EX** can be embedded in any of the three types of index entries: for a word, a text passage, or a descriptive phrase. Compare this procedure to the "Build a paraphrased entry (Option 1)" in the Indexing section:

1. Move the cursor to the spot that the entry should reference.
2. Press **F5** (Clear Command Line).
3. Type **X#** (**#** is the number of the index set, **1** through **9**).
4. Press **F9** (Execute). A window opens.
5. Type the phrase or word you want to cross reference to (for example—**See Rubble, Barney**).
6. Press **F5** (Clear Command Line).

7. Type **EX**.
8. Press **F9** (Execute) and press **F3**.
9. The **EX** command is inside the regular index entry, the bright command triangle that's inserted in the text.

Follow the same procedure to suppress the page number of a word or phrase that actually appears in text. In those cases, the **EX** command would be the only entry in the window.

A La Carte Indexing is not supported in the A La Carte menus. Use the procedures outlined here.

Examples   Extensive indexes, especially if several are used to list many types of items, routinely use cross referencing to make sure no information escapes a reader. **EX** entries can also generate group titles for the index entries, to display a message or provide parenthetical information.

Tips   To generate two separate cross references for the same entry, simply repeat the procedure outlined above.

See Indexing

INDEX BREAK (IB)

Overview   The **IB** command separates an index into alphabetized sections. It inserts a separator (including the key capital letter of the group) between each group of index entries.

Procedure   1. Go to the first line of the text file by pressing **Ctrl** and **Home**.
2. Press **F5** (Clear Command Line).
3. Type **IB**.
4. Press **F9** (Execute).

5. A formatting window opens. Type the separator you want to use between groups of entries (a carriage return, a **Flush Center** command, a pound sign) to activate the **IB's** lettering sequence, and another carriage return.
6. Press **F3** to close the window.
7. A bright command triangle is inserted in text.

A La Carte Indexing is not supported in the A La Carte menus. Use the procedures outlined here.

Examples Breaking each set of alphabetized index entries gives your document a professional touch. **IB** goes a step further by inserting capital letters to identify each group of entries for you.

Tips The **IB** command provides a useful tool by inserting a capital letter at the beginning of each group of indexed entries. But what if you don't want that?

With XyWrite's ability to give you control over all parts of a document, you don't have to use capital letters as separators. In the **IB** procedure, don't insert the pound sign that toggles the letters on. A carriage return or two provide a nice separator on their own.

Another nice separator starts with the normal capital letter on the left margin, but includes an underline all the way across, set with the **Leadering** command.

See Indexing, Index Label, and Index Extraction

INDEX EXTRACTION (IX)

Overview The **IX** command generates a document index as a separate file.

Procedure In order to generate an index in a separate document, you have to include a **No Index** (**NI**) command in each of the text files that contains the index entries. Once that's done, you can extract the index:

1. Press **F5** (Clear Command Line).
2. Type **IX#** MAINFILENAME,INDEXFILENAME (**#** is the number of the index set, **1** through **9**). If you don't supply a name for the source file, XyWrite uses whatever file is displayed in the active window. If you don't supply a name for the index file, XyWrite supplies one.
3. Press **F9** (Execute).
4. After the index has been generated, it can be opened and edited as any other text file can.

The procedure for extracting an index from a series of linked files is the same as it is for a single file, with one difference. Instead of typing a single filename, type the "parent" filename. The parent file is a short text file that lists the names of each linked file, one to a line.

NOTE: A parent file is used to print linked files as a single document, so it may already exist. It's fully discussed in the **Type @** section. The **Type @** command allows one option you may not want to use in your index. In **Type @**, files can be grouped into sets within the larger document. If this option is used when an index is generated, a separate index is generated for each set instead of a single index for the entire document.

To create the parent file:

1. Press **F5** (Clear Command Line).
2. Type **NEW** PARENTFILENAME.
3. Press **F9** (Execute).
4. Type the names of the files you want to link together, in the order they should be printed. Put just one filename on a line. Your file should look something like this:
   FILENAME.1
   FILENAME.2
   FILENAME.3
   FILENAME.4
5. Press **F5** (Clear Command Line).

6. Type **ST** (**Store**).

7. Press **F9** (Execute).

To process the series of files:

1. Press **F5** (Clear Command Line).

2. Type **IX#** @PARENTFILENAME,TARGETFILENAME (**#** is the number of the index set, **1** through **9**).

3. Press **F9** (Execute).

4. The index is extracted and placed in the target file you specified.

5. After the index has been generated, it can be opened and edited as any other text file can.

A La Carte Indexing is not supported in the A La Carte menus. Use the procedures outlined here.

Examples This is the final step in generating an index. XyWrite also allows the generation of an index as part of a document file, but for larger documents, this is usually more convenient.

Tips If you plan to use **IX**, remember to include **No Index** commands in your main document files, so extra indexes won't be generated each time the file is printed.

See Indexing

INDEX LABEL (IL)

Overview Use the **IL** to build a multi-layered index, with sub-entries stacked under a general descriptor, in outline fashion.

Procedure The **IL** command must be preceded by the index entry that defines the general category of the listing. If you were creating an index

218

that includes a sub-category of town names under one of state or province names, you would want to list these under a primary index entry of a country name. The country name index entry must exist before anything can be put under it.

Once the country entry (USA, in this case) has been created with **X#**, here's the procedure to create the sub-categories with **IL**:

1. Move the cursor to the first sub-entry (for a state) and press **F5** (Clear Command Line).
2. Type **X8** (to create an index entry in index number 8). A format window opens.
3. Press **F5** (Clear Command Line).
4. Type **IL USA** (the primary index entry) and press **Return**.
5. To indent the sub-entry, press **Tab** and type the sub-entry (**New Hampshire**), then press **F3**.
6. Move the cursor to the second sub-entry (for a town) and type **X8** (to create an index entry in index number 8). A format window opens.
7. Press **F5** (Clear Command Line).
8. Type **IL USA**, press **Tab**, and type **New Hampshire** and press **Return**. Then press **Tab**, **Tab**, and type the second sub-entry: **Exeter**.
9. Press **F3**.

When the index is generated, the entry should look something like this:

```
USA
    New Hampshire  32, 56, 66
        Exeter 56
```

A La Carte   Indexing is not supported in the A La Carte menus. Use the procedures outlined here.

Examples   This is one more part of the index procedure. If you've a need for multiple levels, this is the way to do it.

Tips   Building a multi-level index entry can take a lot of keystrokes. It's a prime candidate for automation with a Save/Get sequence.

Warnings   The **IL** entry itself is very straightforward. Just make sure you have the primary index entry in place.

               See Indexing

INSERT SAVE/GET (IS)

Overview   A block of text stored on a Save/Get key can be inserted into a document with the **IS** command.

Procedure   1. Press **F5** (Clear Command Line).
               2. Type **IS** KEY (the alpha or numeric key that controls the Save/Get where the text is stored).
               3. Press **F9** (Execute).
               4. A bright command triangle and **IS KEY** are inserted in the text.

               A La Carte This feature isn't supported through the A La Carte menus. Use the regular XyWrite procedure.

Examples   **IS** can be used to assemble a new document from various pieces of text that are stored on different Save/Get keys. It's generally used in a controlled situation where the same document or a variation is used repeatedly. If you have a template for letters, for instance, you could use **IS** to insert your return address and the salutation.

Tips   If you or your office generates a lot of form letters, **IS** makes your
                  life easier. Build Save/Gets from your master form letter. Then
                  create a new master that uses **IS** commands instead of the actual
                  text. When the letter is printed, the Save/Gets dump their contents
                  in the right places.

                  See Save/Gets

JUMP (JMP)

Overview   **JMP** moves the cursor to a specific spot in a file identified by the
                  number of characters it is from the beginning of the file.

Procedure   1. Press **F5** (Clear Command Line).
                  2. Type **JMP** # (# is the number of characters into the file you
                     want to move. For example—**JMP 11223** would move the
                     cursor to the spot that's 11223 characters from the beginning
                     of the file).
                  3. Press **F9** (Execute).
                  4. The cursor moves to the specified location.

                  A La Carte **JMP** isn't available through the A La Carte menus.
                  But there are built-in "Mark" and "Go To Mark" functions that use
                  Jump. Access them this way:

                  1. Press **F6** (A La Carte menus).
                  2. Press **S** or select **Search**.
                  3. Press **M** or select **Mark** to insert a marker in text.
                  4. Press **G** or select **Gotomark** to jump to the marker from
                     another location.

Examples   Most people use the **Go** command to move around their files since
                  thinking in pages and lines is often easier than thinking in the

hundreds or thousands of characters that the **JMP** command requires.

Tips   **JMP** is useful in programming, however. You can move away from the marker, then use a companion program that contains the **JMP** command to "jump" to the original location. See the section on programming for instructions.

See Go

JUSTIFICATION TYPE (JT)

Overview   This is a mystery command. It exists, but no printer requires it! Yet. It provides a way for XYQUESTS's programmers to use more than one method of implementing microjustification.

See Microjustification

JUSTIFY ON (JU)

Overview   Justification is a typesetting term that means each line of type is printed to the same width, like most magazines and newspaper columns are.

To use this style of printing rather than the normal ragged right text, which lets each line end in a different location, insert the **JU** in text.

Procedure   1. Move the cursor to the point where you want justification to begin.
2. Press **F5** (Clear Command Line).
3. Type **JU**.
4. A bright command triangle is inserted in text.

5. Your screen display won't change, but the justification setting is reflected when you print the document.

A La Carte

1. Move the cursor to the point where you want justification to begin.
2. Press **F6** (A La Carte menus).
3. Press **R** or select **foRmat**.
4. Press **S** or select **Status**.
5. Move the cursor to the "Justify text" entry.
6. Type **JU** to turn justification on.
7. Press **Return**.
8. A bright command triangle is inserted in text.

Examples   Justification gives a document a more formal appearance than regular typed text. It also allows you to pack slightly more text into the available space, since it eliminates unused white space at the end of each line. It's also slightly harder to read.

You might use it occasionally to set off a particular passage of text from the surrounding document. Combined with narrower margins, it's great for setting off a fairly long quotation in an academic paper.

Justification looks best with proportionally-spaced type. If your printer supports a proportionally spaced font or two, your documents can look really dynamite.

XyWrite supports two types of justification, whole-space and microjustification. Whole space justification evens out lines by adjusting the white space between words. Microjustification evens out lines by adjusting the space between each letter and the larger spaces between words.

Microjustification looks better since whole-space justification can leave some unnaturally large gaps between words, but not all printers support it.

Tips   Justification tends to be a personal thing. Some people don't particularly like whole-space justification. Microjustification is useful in certain situations, but unless you have a printer that supports that mode, don't bother experimenting.

See Justify Off (NJ) and Microjustification

JUSTIFY UNDERLINE (JU)

Overview This is an old setting that's been renamed Justify Underlined Text.

See Justify Underline Text (JL)

JUSTIFY UNDERLINED TEXT (JL)

Overview The Justify Underlined Text setting is a default setting that determines whether text that's underlined should be microjustified.

Procedure JL is a default setting that's normally entered in your printer file. For complete instructions, see the Procedure portion of the Default listing.

To see what the mode does with your printer, you can also issue JL from the command line. The setting stays in effect for a single editing session:

1. Press **F5** (Clear Command Line).
2. Type **DEFAULT** JL=# (**0** turns the feature off; **1** turns it on).
3. Press **F9** (Execute).
4. "Done" displays on the prompt line.

A La Carte You must be in an empty window (have a blank screen) to access the default menus.

1. Press **F6** (A La Carte menus).
2. Press **X** or select **XyWrite**.
3. Press **D** or select **Defaults**.
4. The View and Change Defaults screen displays.
5. Press **H** or **M** or select **defaults H-M**.
6. Move the cursor to the **JL** entry and type **0** to turn underline justification off or **1** to turn it on.
7. Press **Return**.
8. The Update Default File screen displays. You're asked if you want to make the default settings permanent.
9. Press **Y** or **N**. If you select **Y**, the program writes the new default settings to a special file and returns you to the A La Carte Menu Screen. If you select **N**, the settings are used for the current edit session.

Examples   This setting is used only if you have a high-quality printer that can adjust the amount of white space between letters in a word.

You'll have to experiment with your printer to determine whether your **JL** setting should be **0** (off), or **1** (on). If you turn the setting on, your printer may not generate the correct width of the underline that goes beneath a narrow or wide character. Look for an underline that has gaps of white space or doesn't fit under the word properly. If that happens, turn the setting off. The characters in the underlined word won't be adjusted as precisely as the normal text, but the underlining will match their width.

Tips   In early versions of XyWrite, this setting was called **JU**. That mnemonic has been changed to indicate whether justification should be on or off.

See Microjustification

KEY CLICK (KC)

Overview   Most computer keyboards don't give you any audible feedback when you press a key. If you'd like to change that and give yours a sound, set up the **KC** default.

Procedure   Since **KC** is a default setting, you can enter the command in your printer file or in your STARTUP.INT file. If you do, your keyboard will click away each time XyWrite starts. For complete instructions, see the Procedure portion of the Default listing.

The **KC** setting, like all beep-related XyWrite settings, takes any setting up to 65534 in either argument. The numbers don't really mean anything, since each personal computer runs at a different speed and has a different speaker. You'll have to experiment to determine what's a pleasing sound on your machine.

You can also issue **KC** from the command line to try out different settings or to set a click for a single editing session:

1. Press **F5** (Clear Command Line).
2. Type **DEFAULT** KC=#,# (the tone and duration of the click).
3. Press **F9** (Execute).
4. "Done" displays on the prompt line.

A La Carte You must be in an empty window (have a blank screen) to access the default menus.

1. Press **F6** (A La Carte menus).
2. Press **X** or select **XyWrite**.
3. Press **D** or select **Defaults**.
4. The View and Change Defaults screen displays.
5. Press **H** or select **defaults H-M**.
6. Move the cursor to the **KC** entry. Type the numbers that represent the tone and duration of the key click you want.
7. Press **Return**.

8. The Update Default File screen displays. You're asked if you want to make the default settings permanent.

9. Press **Y** or **N**. If you select **Y**, the program writes the new default settings to a special file and returns you to the A La Carte Menu Screen. If you select **N**, the settings are used for the current edit session.

Examples   The original XyWrite settings for key click are 0,0—no noise at all. If you want to make your computer sound more like a typewriter, however, you can.

See Defaults

KEYBOARD FILES

Overview   XyWrite uses a device called a keyboard file to turn keystrokes into text or commands. These files are edited and changed to suit a particular application or person's fancy.

Procedure   Any function call or combination of calls can be mapped to any key or key combination, so you can easily create the word processing tools you need, but XYQUEST didn't include. You can map several letters or numbers to a key, so a word or phrase is inserted when it's pressed, rather than a single character.

For example, as it comes from the box, XyWrite doesn't have a feature to delete a sentence or a paragraph. The program does have Function Calls for those two tasks, but they aren't in a keyboard file. In less than five minutes, you can add both functions to your keyboard:

1. You need two pieces of information to enhance a keyboard file: the function call you're going to use and the number of the key you're going to use. Look in the Function Call section to find the listings. They're also in the LONG.HLP file, if you

have it loaded. ("Delete Sentence" is **Rubout Sentence (RS)**, "Delete Paragraph" is **Rubout Paragraph (RP)**.)

2. Decide what key or keystroke combination you're going to use. **Alt** and **F5** is already used to **Delete Line**, so you could map **Delete Sentence** to **Ctrl F5** and **Delete Paragraph** to **Shift F5**.

3. Use **Call** to open your keyboard file (example—**Call** IBM.KBD).

NOTE: If you're not sure what keyboard file you're using, **Call** your STARTUP.INT file. Look for a line in that file that loads a file with a .KBD extension. Abort the STARTUP.INT file, then open whatever .KBD file was listed. If there isn't a .KBD file listed, see the following Warnings section.

The first thing you'll see is either a graphic representation of the keyboard, with each key numbered, or several comment lines explaining what that particular keyboard file does.

The IBM.KBD file begins with two graphics that number each key on both the 83 and the 104 key keyboards. You may have to adjust the margins of the file so it displays properly. A left margin of 0 and a right margin of 80 work well. Be sure that the line you insert the margin settings on begins with a semi-colon. Check the diagram for the key you want to map your function to.

Under the graphic, you'll see several "Definition" lines that may look like this:

```
;    DEFINITIONS
;
KEYS=104
CTRL=29,99
ALT=56,98
SHIFT=42,54
CAPS=58,T:C
;
```

Don't change these settings at this time.

Just under the definitions are a series of tables. Each line begins with a number (a key), followed by an equal sign, and then a character or function call. The first table usually has the regular keys that generate characters without any **Shift**, **Alt**, or **Ctrl** keys held down. The beginning looks like this:

```
;
;
TABLE=
1=
2=1
3=2
4=3
5=4
6=5
7=6
8=7
```

Toward the end of the table, you'll see the F keys and their function calls:

```
58=
59=Q1,DF
60=Q2,SV
61=Q3,XD
62=Q4,DL
63=Q5,BC
64=Q6,BC
65=CP
66=MV
67=XC
```

Under the regular keystroke table are separate tables for **Ctrl**, **Alt**, and several other key combinations.

4. Move the cursor down in the file until you see the TABLE=CTRL heading. Then find the entry for key number 63. Unless your keyboard file is an old one or has been modified, it should read: 63=Q5,BC.

5. Define the "63" line (press **F4**) and copy it (press **F7**). Change the original entry by adding a semi-colon to make it read ;63=Q5,BC (the semi-colon makes it into a comment line). Change your new line to 63=Q5,RS to enable the Rubout Sentence Function Call. (Two functions are mapped to this particular key. The first one, Q5, is used by the spell checker. Keep it in place.)

6. Move the cursor down in the file until you see the TABLE=SHIFT heading. Then find the entry for key number 63. It probably reads 63=Q5,BC just as the CTRL table entry did.

7. Define the "63" line (press **F4**) and copy it (press **F7**). Change the original entry by adding a semi-colon to make it read ;63=Q5,BC. Change your new line to 63=Q5,RP to enable the Rubout Paragraph Function Call.

8. Use **STORE** to close the file.

9. Load the file:
   • Press **F5** (Clear Command Line).
   • Type **LOAD** IBM.KBD.
   • "Done" displays on the command line.

You should then open a document that you're not attached to and test your two new keys.

A La Carte Keyboard re-mapping is not supported through the A La Carte menus. Use the standard XyWrite procedure. A La Carte comes with a standard keyboard file, ALACARTE.KBD.

Examples The name of the keyboard game is modification. XYQUEST provides several keyboards with each XyWrite package. Several are for particular computers—IBM compatibles with old 84 key keyboards or the newer AT-style 104 key keyboards, Zenith, DEC, or Tandy machines. A Dvorak keyboard for people who dislike the standard QWERTY layout is available.

At least one, SUPER.KBD, is a modified keyboard that includes a host of typing shortcuts for serious XyWriting. Before extensively modifying your standard keyboard file, open

SUPER.KBD and read the list of functions it provides. It's filled with good ideas.

Customizing a keyboard is less likely to be dependent on a particular application—legal work, or academic writing—than it is personal typing preferences. Just as a good carpenter always picks the right tool for a job, someone with XyWrite can craft the right tool for their writing tasks. The words and documents you produce day in and day out are easier to create on a custom keyboard.

Tips

Use SUPER.KBD as a base to build a word processor that suits the way you work. The keyboard file is so easy to modify and test, it's constantly evolving.

Some of the changes are detailed in the Procedure area here. Other possibilities include:

- Changing the ,/ (comma/less than) and ./ (period/greater than) keys so commas and periods are generated when you've got the **Shift** key down to type capital letters. (Move the greater than and less than signs, which aren't used very often, to the **Ctrl** table.)
- Changing the automatic outlining feature of the SUPER to insert periods and spaces after its numbers.
- Automatically releasing a define when deleting a line, sentence, or paragraph with an "unmapped" rubout function call.
- Moving through a document by sentence, paragraph, or by double screenfulls.
- Retain the SUPER keyboard's linear up and down cursor movement, but do away with the linear left and right unless you use a mouse.

You can stack several function calls on one key, to execute one after the other. If you wish, you can make your cursor move up six or eight lines at a time by stringing several **Cursor Up (CU)** function calls together. When you map a number of calls to a single key, separate them with commas: 72=CU,CU,CU,CU,CU,CU.

If you'd like to insert regular letters or numbers, you can do that too. A remapped keyboard is ideal for inserting words or phrases with a single key combination. A **Ctrl** table key—"A," for instance—could be mapped to insert your address. Each key must begin with a function call, however. XyWrite has provided the **No Operation** (**NO**) call for those situations when you want to insert text. When you're editing the table, remember to separate the individual characters with commas: 30=NO,2,9, ,J,o,n,e,s, ,B,e,a,c,h, R,o,a,d

Spaces are inserted as any other character is. If you want to break the text into several lines, insert ASCII character 13 as a carriage return between two commas. (To generate ASCII 13, hold **Ctrl** and **Alt** down, type **13**, and release **Ctrl** and **Alt**.)

Finally, you can combine function calls and letters or numbers to execute commands. These lines from SUPER.KBD accomplish a number of tasks:

```
30=BC,A,:,XC,CC
31=BC,S,A,XC
32=BC,D,I,R,XC
33=BC,F,N,XC
```

Key number 30 switches the default disk drive to drive A: by clearing the command line (**BC**), inserting the characters "A" and ":" and executing the command (**XC**). Thirty-one saves a file, 32 calls a directory, and 33 begins a footnote.

At the top of the keyboard file is a short list of the keys that file defines as "shifting." In the definition section from the IBM.KBD file, **Ctrl**, **Alt**, **Shift**, and **Caps** are defined:

```
; DEFINITIONS
;
KEYS=104
CTRL=29,99
ALT=56,98
SHIFT=42,54
CAPS=58,T:C
```

(The "KEYS=104" line refers to the highest numbered key that can be defined in the keyboard file.)

The keyboard files' tables are linked to different combinations of shifting keys. The priority of the key combination is set by the order they appear in the definition section of the file.

Most keyboards have at least four shifting keys that, when pressed, generate different characters. The **Shift** key is the most obvious—when it's held down, capital letters are generated. The other three are **Ctrl**, **Alt**, and **Caps Lock**.

If you like, you can also add other "shifting" keys to the standard set of **Shift**, **Ctrl**, and **Alt**. The **Caps Lock** key is originally a "toggle" key, but it can be changed to an unlocked key that functions only when held down. If that change is made, the key's perpetual capitalization function is disabled. You get an additional keyboard table of specialized function calls by making the change, a keyboard that can be used for specialized functions.

You can pick one or two other keys from your keyboard, keys that you don't use very often, and make them shifting keys too. XyWrite supports up to six shifting keys and up to 20 tables. To add a totally new shift key, make up a short one-word title for the key and its table. Follow the format of the Definition section and add it, followed by an equal sign and the key's number.

If you didn't use the number pad's five for anything, you could make it a shifting key by adding **FIVE=76** in the definition section. Go through all the tables, searching for key number 76, and replace the "5" character with a space. Then copy an existing table, rename it to "**FIVE**" and change the entries.

Each shifting key can be modified by specifying one of three options:

- Adding a **,N** to a shift key definition lets another key toggle the Num Lock setting on or off.
- Adding a **,T** makes a shifting key into a toggle key, as the **Caps Lock** key usually is. One push turns it on; a second turns it off.
- Adding a **,S** changes one of the shift keys into a "single-shot" shift key that doesn't have to be held down to operate. If a shifting key is changed to single-shot,

whatever key is struck after the shifting key is processed as if the shifting key had been held down. If the **Shift** was turned into a single-shot, you could press **Shift**, let go, press the **k** key, and have a capital **K** generated. The single-shot mode is good for people who have difficulty typing, particularly people with physical handicaps.

- The **,T** and **,S** options have an optional argument that displays a reminder letter on the prompt line whenever that particular key is active. It's the same thing that generates the capital I or O to reflect whether the program is in **Insert** or **Overtype** operation, or the Num Lock or Scroll Lock function is on. To generate the reminder letter, follow the **,T** or **,S** with a colon and the letter you want to use. The Caps Lock key from the standard IBM file is set up to display a C whenever the key is "on"—**CAPS=58,T:C**.

Foreign Character Keyboards If you use many math, Greek, or foreign characters, why not create a special keyboard for them? Pick or create a table and insert the appropriate ASCII characters as you would in a document. Look at the discussion on creating new shifting keys and tables in this section.

Comment Lines In the procedure above, the original keys are saved as comment lines and not erased. If something doesn't turn out as you expected, the comments are invaluable for restoring a file. In the same vein, if you plan to do extensive modifications to a file, copy and rename it so the original isn't corrupted. You can convert any existing line to a comment line by preceding it with a semi-colon. You can also insert a written comment by beginning a text line with a semi-colon. NOTE: XYQUEST doesn't recommend inserting comment lines in the middle of tables.

Unusual Computers XYQUEST constantly updates their keyboard file library as new computers are introduced. If you have a slightly unusual keyboard layout, like those on some Toshiba portables, it's worth a call to the technical support department to see if they've created something special for your machine.

If you have a keyboard with an unusual number of keys, you can match your keyboard to a file by modifying the KEYS line that's in the definition section of each keyboard file. Then add the required number of keys to whatever tables you want to enhance.

XYQUEST has a prepared treat called TEST.KBD, which identifies each key you press by its number. It's a temporary file that's not intended for writing. You can make your own copy easily—here's a listing from the CTRL table that does the mapping. Just copy the format into a renamed keyboard file of your own:

```
TABLE=CTRL
1=ni,bc,k,e,y, ,1
2=ni,bc,k,e,y, ,2
3=ni,bc,k,e,y, ,3
4=ni,bc,k,e,y, ,4
5=ni,bc,k,e,y, ,5
6=ni,bc,k,e,y, ,6
7=ni,bc,k,e,y, ,7
8=ni,bc,k,e,y, ,8
9=ni,bc,k,e,y, ,9
10=ni,bc,k,e,y, ,1,0
```

After you load TEST.KBD, press **CTRL** and a key. The key's number displays on the command line.

Warnings   XyWrite works without a keyboard file being loaded; there's a transparent plain-vanilla one built into the program. If you want to customize a keyboard, however, you must load a keyboard file.

If your installation doesn't include a keyboard file in its STARTUP.INT file, get out the XyWrite master floppy disks. Several keyboard files are usually on the main program disk. Copy one or more of those (IBM.KBD and SUPER.KBD, for instance) into your main XyWrite directory. Open your STARTUP.INT file, define a line that begins with a bold **BC** (press **F4**), and copy it (press **F7**). Release the defined line by pressing **F3**. Cursor past the bright **BC** to the text. Change the line to read **BC LOAD FILENAME.KBD**. Store the file. Whatever file you named will load as part of the XyWrite start up procedure. In some older versions of XyWrite, the keyboard is not loaded with **Load**; it's loaded with **LDKBD**. You can remap the **Alt** key table if you wish, but that set of keys is used by the program to implement Save/Get keys. You may be limiting your options if you remove these keys from the Save/Get repertoire.

See Function Calls

KILL TYPING (KT)

Overview   The **KT** command stops a printing operation that's in progress.

Procedure   1. Press **F5** (Clear Command Line).
2. Type **KT**.
3. Press **F9** (Execute).
4. Printing may not stop immediately if you have a printer that holds data in its own memory. No more data is sent after the command is executed.

A La Carte
1. Press **F6** (A La Carte menus).
2. Press **T** or select **Type**.
3. Press **K** or select **Killtype**.
4. A screen displays to verify that you want to stop printing.
5. Press **Return**.

Examples   Printing sometimes needs to be stopped in mid-document if you see an error, queue the wrong document to the device, or simply change your mind.

Tips   If you want to stop printing dead in its tracks, you need to clear whatever text is in your printer's buffered memory. On most machines, the only way to do that is to cut the power.

See Type

LABEL (LB)

Overview   The **Label** command identifies part of a document so it can be referenced in another part of the same document.

Procedure   Label a text passage:

1. Move the cursor to the beginning of the text you want to keep track of, the text that is referred to in another part of the document.
2. Press **F5** (Clear Command Line).
3. Type **LB** NAME (the **NAME** must be unique).
4. Press **F9** (Execute).
5. The label is inserted in the text. It does not print.

When a reference command refers to the label, the position of the text in the document is reported back.

To reference a footnote from another part of a document, the label must be the very first thing in the footnote, before the actual text. If you're writing the footnote:

1. Press **F5** (Clear Command Line).
2. Type **FN** (Create Footnote).
3. A window opens so the text can be inserted.
4. Press **F5** (Clear Command Line).
5. Type **LB** NAME (the **NAME** must be unique).
6. Press **F9** (Execute).
7. The label is inserted. Go ahead and type the text of the footnote.
8. Press **F3** to close the footnote window.

If the footnote is already in place:

1. Put the cursor on the footnote reference number.
2. Press **Ctrl** and **F3** (Open Window) or shift to expanded mode by pressing **Ctrl** and **F9**.

3. Position the cursor so it's on the very first space in the footnote.
4. Press **F5** (Clear Command Line).
5. Type **LB** NAME (the **NAME** must be unique).
6. Press **F9** (Execute).
7. The label is inserted.
8. Press **F3** (Close Window) or return to normal display mode by pressing **Ctrl** and **F9**.

When a reference command refers to the label, the position of the footnote is reported back. To label a counter:

1. Move to the counter position.
2. If a plain unlabeled counter is in place put the cursor on the counter's bright command triangle.
3. Press **Ctrl** and **F3** (Open Window) or shift to expanded mode by pressing **Ctrl** and **F9**.
4. You'll see something that looks like this: «**C2**». Put the cursor on the closing quote mark.
5. Type in the label. The modified command should look like this: «**C2NAME**».
6. Press **F3** (Close Window) or shift back to normal mode by pressing **Ctrl** and **F9**.

If a counter isn't in place:

1. Press **F5** (Clear Command Line).
2. Type **C#** NAME (# is the number of the counter).
3. Press **F9** (Execute).
4. A bright command triangle is inserted in text.

A La Carte
1. Press **F6** (A La Carte menus).
2. Press **E** or select **Edit**.
3. Press **R** or select **Reference**.
4. The Reference Labels screen displays.
   - Press **T** or select **insert label in Text**, or
   - Press **C** or select **label tied to Counter**.

5. A screen with a blank for you to enter the label appears. Type in the label and press **Return**.
6. A bright command triangle is inserted in text.

Examples   Putting a unique label on text, a footnote, or a counter is the first step in building a reference to it. Once a label is attached to an element of a document, that element can change pages, chapters, or even files, and its position will still be tracked and reported properly.

The **LB** command is used with a reference command to build statements like these:

- **See Chapter 5, Page 88**
- (Table 5-6)
- Refer to Footnote 34, Page 189

No matter how the document changes, the proper chapter numbers, page numbers, or table numbers are always referenced—thanks to the labels.

Tips   Be sure each labeled element has a unique name. The reference command won't search for duplicate names—it simply picks the first one it comes to.

See Footnotes, References, Reference to Page Number, Reference to Chapter Number, and Reference to Counter Number

LEADERING (LD)

Overview   The Leadering command separates text items into two columns set against the left and right margins, like this:

See note #7   Page 111

Procedure   You can specify a particular character to be used as the leading character. If none is specified, XyWrite uses spaces.

1. Type the text that should be set against the left hand side of the page.
2. Press **F5** (Clear Command Line).
3. Type **LD**. To specify a leading character, type **LD**, a space, and the character (for example—to generate a dotted line of periods across the page, type **LD**) .
4. Press **F9** (Execute).
5. A bright command triangle is inserted in the text and the cursor moves to the right margin. If a leading character was specified, they display.
6. Type the right side text.

A La Carte
1. Press **F6** (A La Carte menus).
2. Press **E** or select **Edit**.
3. Press **L** or select **Leadering**.
4. The Select Leadering screen displays. Type the character you want to use in the blank.
5. Press **Return**.
6. A bright command triangle is inserted in the text.

Examples   Leadering is often used to create indexes, tables of contents, phone lists, and the like:

Savings   p. 67
Software   p. 594

If you design forms, **LD** generates a set of even "fill-in" lines for you. Use the underbar character as your leading character:

NAME_____

ADDRESS_____

Tips If you're in a hurry to build a document with a few columns or several fill-in blanks, you can use several **LD** commands on the same line. The width of the columns varies depending on how much text separates the **LD** commands, but it's quite acceptable in many situations.

See Indexing and Table of Contents

LEADING

See Automatic Leading, Extra Leading, and Line Leading

LEADING, LINE (LL)

Overview The **Line Leading** command sets the amount of white space XyWrite inserts between lines, paragraphs, or both. This provides a finer degree of control than the **Line Spacing** command.

Procedure 1. Move the cursor to the point in the document where the new line leading setting should take effect.
2. Press **F5** (Clear Command Line).
3. Type **LL #,#** (the first # controls the amount of white space between paragraphs; the second between lines—either can be omitted).
4. Press **F9** (Execute).
5. A bright command triangle is inserted. If your **LF** default setting is set to reflect the real line spacing on screen, your display shifts to reflect the change.

A La Carte
1. Press **F6** (A La Carte menus).
2. Press **R** or select **foRmat**.

3. Press **L** or select **Linespace**.
4. The Line Spacing screen displays.
5. Move the cursor to the **LL** entry. Type in values for paragraph and line leading. Press **Return**.

Examples

XyWrite supplies a very high degree of control over how your words appear on paper, a higher level of control than many people are used to. Most people are familiar with "single-spaced" or "double-spaced" documents. It's common in business correspondence, for instance, to single space a document but separate paragraphs with a line of blank space created with two taps of the carriage return.

"Leading" (pronounced "leding") is a typographic term that means the amount of white space inserted between lines. Using the **Line Leading** command, you can achieve a finer setting that looks better than you can with regular line spaces.

For instance, you can improve on the single-space or double-space business letter format with a **LL 2.5,1.25** setting. That makes your typing easier to read by inserting a line-and-a-half of white space between lines while still separating your paragraphs with twice as much white space. The other difference is that you don't have to tap the **Return** key twice between paragraphs—once does the trick.

Tips

When you're using the **LL**, remember that XyWrite usually splits a vertical inch of paper into six lines. The numbers you enter are parts of that sixth-of-an-inch. A **LL 1.25** inserts a line and a quarter between paragraphs; that translates into .209 of an inch. XyWrite supports a line leading setting up to hundredths of a line, provided your printer can.

If you have a laser printer or similar high-quality output device, the **LL** command can really make your documents shine. Used judiciously, you can set type almost as accurately as a typesetter. The resolution differs greatly, of course, but the amount of control you have over your type is the same.

See Automatic Leading, Extra Leading, and Line Spacing

LEFT MARGIN (LM)

Overview   The **Left Margin** command determines where the left edge of type falls relative to the left edge of the page of paper or monitor screen.

Procedure   XyWrite provides a default left margin setting of 0 (and a right margin of 78). Many people replace that with a standard left and right margin using a default command in their printer file or in the STARTUP.INT file. That way, their margins are set the amount they prefer each time XyWrite is used. See the Default section for instructions. You can also change margins through the Tab and Margin Selection menu. It provides a good visual tool to show you just where the margins fall relative to the ruler line and any tab stops on the page.

   If you're going to modify your default settings, begin the numbered steps from an empty window. If you want to modify the tab settings in a specific document, move your cursor to the point you want to set new tab stops before you perform the numbered steps:

1. Press **Alt** and **Tab**.
2. The Tab and Margin Selection Menu displays. The cursor displays on the ruler line across the top of the screen.
3. Set either margin moving the cursor to the correct position and pressing **L** (for the left margin) or **R** (for the right margin).
4. When you've set the margins, press **F9** (Execute) or **Return**.
5. If you accessed the menu from an open document, a bright command triangle is inserted in text. If you accessed the menu from an open window to change default settings, they're written to memory and used for that editing session. They're not permanently stored in a file.

   Margins can easily be adjusted to modify a particular document or different parts of a document.
   To change the left margin for a particular document:

1. Move the cursor to the beginning of the line where the margin should take effect.
2. Press **F5** (Clear Command Line).
3. Type **LM** # (# is the number of spaces or margin units to indent the type from the edge of the page. Most printers generate pica type which is 10 characters per inch. To set an inch-wide left margin, type **LM 10**).
4. Press **F9** (Execute).
5. A bright command triangle is inserted and the line moves to reflect the margin change.

A La Carte
1. Press **F6** (A La Carte menus).
2. Press **R** or select **foRmat**.
3. Press **M** or select **Margins**.
4. The Set Margins Screen displays.
5. Type in a number for the new Left Margin. You must also enter a number for the Right Margin.
6. Press **Return**.
7. Two bright command triangles are inserted in the text.

Examples   There's no limit to how many margin changes you can make in a XyWrite document. A common reason to shift margins mid-document is to set off a long quotation or excerpt from the main text. If your normal margins are **LM=10** and **RM=75** (to give an inch margin on each side), you might want to set off a long quotation with **LM=15** and **RM=70**. Remember to reset your normal margins after the quotation ends.

Tips   Normally, tab stops are in fixed places that are independent of the left margin setting. For instance, a **LM=10** setting is two characters farther in than one of XyWrite's original tab settings, at 8 spaces. You can use the **Relative Tab** (**RT**) command to make the tab stops fall into position at a constant distance from the left margins, if you prefer.

See Right Margin and Defaults

LINE SPACING (COMMAND)

Overview　　　The **LS** command sets the line spacing of the document—single-spaced or double-spaced, for instance.

Procedure　　　1. Move the cursor to the point in the document where you want the line spacing to change.
2. Press **F5** (Clear Command Line).
3. Type **LS #** (# is the number of lines. Fractions of lines are acceptable—**LS 1.5** gives line-and-a-half spacing.)
4. Press **F9** (Execute).
5. A bright command triangle is inserted. If the **LF** default setting is turned "on," the text on-screen shifts to reflect the new setting.

A La Carte
1. Press **F6** (A La Carte menus).
2. Press **R** or select **foRmat**.
3. Press **L** or select **Linespace**.
4. The Line Spacing screen displays.
5. Move the cursor to the **LS** entry. Type in a value for line spacing.
6. Press **Return**.

Examples　　　For simple typing, **LS** is all you need to determine how your text will print. It's the same as the line space switch on a typewriter.

See Line Leading

LINE SPACING, ON-SCREEN (LF)

Overview   The **LF** default setting makes your screen display show an accurate image of whatever line spacing is in effect.

Procedure   **LF** is a default setting that's usually entered in your printer file or in your STARTUP.INT file. If you put it there, your favorite display mode is invoked each time XyWrite starts. For complete instructions, see the Procedure portion of the Default listing.

You can also issue **LF** from the command line to see the effect or to set a unique display mode for a single file:

1. Press **F5** (Clear Command Line).
2. Type **DEFAULT** LF=1 (**0** is the "off" setting).
3. Press **F9** (Execute).
4. "Done" displays on the prompt line and any text that's not single-spaced moves to reflect its true position.

A La Carte   A La Carte's original default is with **LF** "on," so a 0 turns it off. You must be in an empty window (have a blank screen) to access the default menus.

1. Press **F6** (A La Carte menus).
2. Press **X** or select **XyWrite**.
3. Press **D** or select **Defaults**.
4. The View and Change Defaults screen displays.
5. Press **H** or select **defaults H-M**.
6. Move the cursor to the **LF** entry and type **0** to turn **LF** "off."
7. Press **Return**.
8. The Update Default File screen displays. You're asked if you want to make the default settings permanent.
9. Press **Y** or **N**. If you select **Y**, the program writes the new default settings to a special file and returns you to the A La Carte Menu Screen. If you select **N**, the settings are used for the current edit session.

Examples   XyWrite, as it's usually installed, packs as many words as possible on to the screen. Double-spaced text is displayed exactly the same as single-spaced is, to make editing somewhat easier.

     Many people prefer a more WYSIWYG (What You See Is What You Get) display. XyWrite won't give you 100 percent accuracy, but it will faithfully mimic the text as your printer prints it. If you want to see double-spaced text display on your screen as double-spaced, toggle **LF** "on."

See Defaults

LOAD

Overview   **Load** makes XyWrite support files available to the program by placing them in the computer's memory. Help, keyboard, printer, sort table, spelling dictionary, hyphenation dictionary, and character substitution files can be installed with **Load**.

Procedure   Load can either load a file into memory or append a file to a similar file type that's already resident. More than one file can be loaded with the same command. Whether the file is loaded or appended, the basic procedure is the same.

     Files are usually loaded by the STARTUP.INT file when XyWrite begins, but there are a number of occasions when they need to be loaded manually. A **Load** line in STARTUP.INT might look like this:

       LOAD ARTS.SPL,ARTS.KBD,ARTS.PRN

     To load files into memory manually:

1. Press **F5** (Clear Command Line).
2. Type **LOAD** FILENAME,FILENAME,FILENAME. Note that the filenames are separated by commas.
3. Press **F9** (Execute).
4. "Done" displays on the prompt line.

To append files to those already in memory:

1. Press **F5** (Clear Command Line).
2. Type **LOAD** +FILENAME+FILENAME+FILENAME. Note that the filenames begin with plus signs (including the first file).
3. Press **F9** (Execute).
4. "Done" displays on the prompt line.

You can load files and append to files with the same load command. You'd use a command line like this:

Type **LOAD FILENAME,FILENAME+FILENAME**

The first two files are loaded; the third is appended.

A La Carte There's no provision for loading any file but a new printer file through the A La Carte menus. Use the standard XyWrite procedures, or see the **LDPRN** section for instruction on manually loading a printer file.

Examples   Depending on how you like XyWrite configured, you might load one or more of each support file type. XyWrite will run without help, keyboard, printer, sort table, spelling dictionary, hyphenation dictionary, and character substitution files, but it will serve you better if you use the available tools.

Beginning with XyWrite III, **Load** replaced a host of "dedicated" **load** commands mentioned in the See section of this listing. It also is used to load any supplementary spelling dictionary files, a feature that didn't exist before version III Plus.

You can streamline your loading operation somewhat by using **Load**, but if you're familiar with the older commands, there's no compelling reason to change.

Tips   The one feature that's extremely handy is **Load**'s append feature. It allows you to place two printer files into memory and have both of them active. It isn't used to place to printer files that both drive

L

printers. It's used to load one printer driver and a second printer-type file, such as a file that lists a number of default settings—a .DFL file.

XyWrite uses this feature in their A La Carte interface, and in their implementation of the Hercules Graphics Card +, both of which use a number of unique calls not normally listed in a regular printer driver file.

See Load Help, Load Keyboard, Load Printer, Load Sort Table, Load Dictionary, and Load Character Substitution File

LOAD CHARACTER SUBSTITUTION FILE (LDSUB)

Overview
A character substitution file changes characters in a text file to different characters when the file is printed. A typical change might be English characters to French accented characters. **LDSUB** loads the table into memory so the change can take place.

Procedure
1. Press **F5** (Clear Command Line).
2. Type **LDSUB** FILENAME. A directory or path name can precede the FILENAME, if necessary.
3. Press **F9** (Execute).
4. "Done" displays on the prompt line.

A La Carte There's no provision in the A La Carte menus to load a character substitution table. Use the standard XyWrite procedure.

Examples
Character substitution tables are usually a part of a printer file, so **LDSUB** isn't used very often. See the Printer File and the Substitution File sections for more information.

Tips In versions of XyWrite beginning with the XyWrite III revision, you can use **Load** to load all support files with a single command. See the **Load** section for information.

Warnings A substitution table that's part of a printer file takes priority over a separate substitution table. If the **LDSUB** command doesn't seem to have an effect on the typed copy, that may be the reason.

See Load

LOAD DICTIONARY (LDDICT)

Overview **LDDICT** loads the hyphenation dictionary into memory so XyWrite's automatic hyphenation feature can work. It can also unload the dictionary.

Procedure The hyphenation dictionary is usually loaded automatically by STARTUP.INT when XyWrite is first started.

To load the hyphenation dictionary manually:

1. Press **F5** (Clear Command Line).
2. Type **LDDICT** DICTIONARYNAME (DICTION is the default dictionary name). A directory or path name can precede DICTIONARYNAME, if necessary.
3. Press **F9** (Execute).
4. "Done" displays on the prompt line.

To unload the hyphenation dictionary:

1. Press **F5** (Clear Command Line).
2. Type **LD**DICT.
3. Press **F9** (Execute).
4. "Done" displays on the prompt line.

A La Carte The hyphenation dictionary is loaded automatically by A La Carte's STARTUP.INT file. There's no provision in the menus to load another dictionary manually. Use the standard XyWrite procedure.

Examples XyWrite's automatic hyphenation feature requires a hyphenation dictionary. When XyWrite is first installed, a line is created in the STARTUP.INT file, which configures the program, to load the default dictionary: LDDICT DICTION. If the line is missing from your STARTUP.INT file, and you want the convenience of automatic hyphenation, insert it.

1. Press **F5** (Clear Command Line).
2. Type **CA** STARTUP.INT.
3. Move the cursor to a line that begins with a bold **BC**.
4. Press **F4** (Define Line).
5. Press **F7** (Copy Define).
6. Move the cursor past the **BC**, delete the command that's there, and type **LDDICT** DICTION.
7. Store the file.

The next time XyWrite is loaded, the hyphenation dictionary is loaded automatically.

Tips In versions of XyWrite beginning with XyWrite III revision, you can use **Load** to load all support files with a single command. See the **Load** section for information.

See Hyphenation On and Load

LOAD HELP (LDHELP)

Overview **LDHELP** loads a help file into memory so instructions and online help are available when you press **Alt** and **F9**.

Procedure   A help file is usually loaded automatically by STARTUP.INT when XyWrite is first started.

To load the help file manually:

1. Press **F5** (Clear Command Line).
2. Type **LD**HELP FILENAME (SHORT.HLP and LONG.HLP are the default filenames).
3. Press **F9** (Execute).
4. "Done" displays on the prompt line.

A La Carte A La Carte has a special help file that's loaded automatically by STARTUP.INT. There's no provision in the menus to load other help files manually. Use the standard XyWrite procedure, if necessary, but be careful, since a modified file could disable some A La Carte features.

Examples   XyWrite's built-in online help facility must access a help file to work.

When XyWrite is first installed, a line is created in the STARTUP.INT file, which configures the program, to load a help file: LDHELP LONG.HLP. If the line is missing from your STARTUP.INT file, it's easy to insert it:

1. Press **F5** (Clear Command Line).
2. Type **CA** STARTUP.INT.
3. Move the cursor to a line that begins with a bold **BC**.
4. Press **F4** (Define Line).
5. Press **F7** (Copy Define).
6. Move the cursor past the **BC**, delete the command that's there, and type **LD**HELP FILENAME.
7. Store the file.

The next time XyWrite is loaded, the help feature will be available.

Tips   In versions of XyWrite beginning with the XyWrite III revision, you can use **Load** to load all support files with a single command. See the **Load** section for information.

See Help and Load

LOAD KEYBOARD (LDKBD)

Overview   **LDKBD** loads a keyboard file. These are optional files, usually containing customized instructions that interpret keystrokes and perform a variety of operations.

Procedure   Keyboard files are often loaded by STARTUP.INT when XyWrite is started. To load a keyboard file manually:

1. Press **F5** (Clear Command Line).
2. Type **LDKBD** FILENAME.
3. Press **F9** (Execute).
4. "Done" displays on the prompt line.

A La Carte   A La Carte's special keyboard file is loaded automatically by its STARTUP.INT file. There's no provision in the menus to load another file manually. Use the standard XyWrite procedure.

Examples   Keyboard files can be extensively modified to reflect a particular application. A person who often works with tabular material might have a customized keyboard just for tables. They may prefer a second table for writing, the XyWrite-supplied SUPER.KBD. To switch from one keyboard to the other, they could load the new keyboard manually.

   XyWrite usually loads a keyboard file when the STARTUP.INT file configures the program at start up. A typical line might read:

LDHELP LONG.HLP. If the line is missing from your STARTUP.INT file, it's easy to insert it:

1. Press **F5** (Clear Command Line).
2. Type **CA** STARTUP.INT.
3. Move the cursor to a line that begins with a bold **BC**.
4. Press **F4** (Define Line).
5. Press **F7** (Copy Define).
6. Move the cursor past the **BC**, delete the command that's there, and type **LDKBD** FILENAME.
7. Store the file.

Tips   In versions of XyWrite beginning with XyWrite III, you can use **Load** to load all support files with a single command. See the **Load** section for information.

See Keyboard Files and Load

LOAD PRINTER FILE (LDPRN)

Overview   **LDPRN** loads a printer file, something that must be done in order to print a document. This command can also be used to load the special default file discussed in the Default section.

Procedure   Printer files are often loaded by STARTUP.INT when XyWrite is started. If your computer drives more than one type of printer, you'll probably need to load the second printer file manually. To load a printer file manually:

1. Press **F5** (Clear Command Line).
2. Type **LDPRN** FILENAME.
3. Press **F9** (Execute).
4. "Done" displays on the prompt line.

A La Carte You must be in an empty window (have a blank screen) to load a new printer file.

1. Press **F6** (A La Carte menus).
2. Press **T** or select **Type**.
3. Press **L** or select **Load**.
4. The Load Printer Driver screen displays.
5. Press **Return**.
6. A list of the printer files in the main A La Carte directory displays.
7. Move the cursor to the printer file you want to load.
8. Press **Return**.
9. "Done" displays on the prompt line.

Examples   XyWrite uses printer files to carry special default settings. These can either be attached to real printer files that actually drive printers, or to dummy printer files that only contain lists of defaults (these are discussed in the Defaults section). This means that several printer files might be used in during a single editing session, if the writing jobs are highly specialized.

Tips   In versions of XyWrite beginning with XyWrite III, you can use **Load** to load all support files with a single command. See the **Load** section for information.

If you use several printers or sets of defaults and switch between them frequently, create Save/Get keys that hold the **LDKBD** command you use. You'll save typing time and speed up the change-over process.

See Load and Defaults

LOAD PROGRAM (LDPM)

Overview   **Load program** can either attach a XyWrite Program Language (XPL) program to a Save/Get key so it can be executed with a single keystroke combination or load a XPL program into memory for faster execution.

Procedure   To attach a program to a Save/Get key:

1. Press **F5** (Clear Command Line).
2. Type **LDPM** PROGRAMNAME,# (# stands for the single alpha-numeric key the program is attached to, or the function call the program is attached to, such as &A-&Z or &0-&9). A drive or path can precede the PROGRAMNAME, if necessary (for example—**LDPM** C:\PGM\PROGRAMNAME,A).
3. Press **F9** (Execute).
4. "Done" displays on the prompt line.

Attaching a program to a key this way creates a temporary Save/Get that stays in effect for your current editing session. To make the Save/Get permanent, you must store the current set of Save/Gets and reload them for each editing session. See Save/Gets for information. To load a program into memory:

1. Press **F5** (Clear Command Line).
2. Type **LDPM** PROGRAMNAME. A drive or path can precede the PROGRAMNAME, if necessary (for example—**LDPM** C:\GM\PROGRAMNAME).
3. Press **F9** (Execute).
4. "Done" displays on the prompt line.

Loading a program into memory speeds program execution incrementally because the program doesn't have to be read from a disk.

A La Carte There's no provision in A La Carte's menus for **LDPM**. Use the standard XyWrite procedures.

Examples   The **LDPM** is normally used to create Save/Get keys that run XyWrite programs. Any program written in XPL can be executed by pressing **Alt** and whatever letter or number key the program is attached to. This is a standard way to customize XyWrite for a particular application or personal style, since the single keystroke combination is quick and easy.

See Programs and Save/Get

LOAD SAVE/GETS (LDSGT)

Overview   **Load Save/Get** makes a set of Save/Gets keys stored on disk the active set.

Procedure   An initial set of Save/Get keys is usually loaded by STARTUP.INT when XyWrite is started. Many people use more than one set of Save/Gets, however. If you want to switch between sets, you'll use the manual loading method:

1. Press **F5** (Clear Command Line).
2. Type **LDSGT** FILENAME. A directory or path name can precede the FILENAME, if necessary.
3. Press **F9** (Execute).
4. "Done" displays on the prompt line.

A La Carte
1. Press **F6** (A La Carte menus).
2. Press **E** or select **Edit**.
3. Press **G** or select **save/Gets**.
4. Press **L** or select **Load s/g**.

5. A screen displays with a blank for the name of the Save/Get file. Type the file name.
6. Press **Return**.
7. "Done" displays on the prompt line.

Examples   When XyWrite is first installed, a bare bones set of Save/Get keys named Gets is included. Gets is loaded automatically by the STARTUP.INT file each time XyWrite starts.

Tips   If you load more than one set of Save/Get keys, the sets do not replace each other, they supplement each other. Only those keys in the last set to be loaded (that are were used by the earlier set) are changed. Any keys that were active in the first set and are not used in the second stay in effect. For example, if the first set contained a Save/Gets assigned to keys number 1 and 2 and the second set contained assignments to keys number 2 and 3, key number 1 from the first set remains active after the second set is loaded because nothing in set number two overwrites it. Key number 2 in the first set is superseded by key number 2 from the first set.

To completely replace a set of Save/Gets with another set, use the **Clear Save/Get** (**CLRSGT**) command before loading the second set.

If you use several sets of Save/Gets for different applications, attach the **CLRSGT** and **LDSGT** commands to a unique Save/Get key in each of your sets. Switching between the sets will be quicker.

See Save/Gets and Clear Save/Gets (CLRSGT)

LOAD SORT TABLE (LDSORT)

Overview   **LDSORT** loads an alternate sort table so that XyWrite can arrange indexes and tables of contents in an order different from the program's alphabetic default.

Procedure   1. Press **F5** (Clear Command Line).
2. Type **LDSORT** FILENAME. A directory or path name can precede the FILENAME, if necessary.
3. Press **F9** (Execute).
4. "Done" displays on the prompt line.

A La Carte There's no provision in the A La Carte menus to load a sort table manually. Use the standard XyWrite procedure.

Examples   XyWrite supplies a standard sort table as part of the program. It doesn't have to be loaded. **LDSORT** is used to override the program's default with a different table. Directions on creating an alternate table are in the Sort Table section.

Once the table has been created, **LDSORT** is used to activate it. If the alternate table is the one that's always going to be used, the command can be added to the STARTUP.INT file so it's installed each time XyWrite is started.

1. Press **F5** (Clear Command Line).
2. Type **CA** STARTUP.INT.
3. Move the cursor to a line that begins with a bold **BC**.
4. Press **F4** (Define Line).
5. Press **F7** (Copy Define).
6. Move the cursor past the **BC**, delete the command that's there, and type **LDSORT** FILENAME.
7. Store the file.

Tips   In versions of XyWrite beginning with XyWrite III, you can use **Load** to load all support files with a single command. See the **Load** section for information.

See Load and Sorting

LOWER CASE (LC)

Overview   The **LC** command makes a capital letter, or all the capital letters in a defined block of text, lower case.

Procedure   To change a single letter:

1. Put the cursor on the capital letter you want to make lower case.
2. Press **F5** (Clear Command Line).
3. Type **LC**.
4. Press **F9** (Execute).
5. The letter changes to lower case.

To make a defined block of text lower case:

1. Define the block.
2. Press **F5** (Clear Command Line).
3. Type **LC**.
4. Press **F9** (Execute).
5. All letters in the block change to lower case.
6. Release the defined block by pressing **F3.**

A La Carte
1. Press **F6** (A La Carte menus).
2. Press **E** or select **Edit**.
3. Press **C** or select **Case**.
4. Press **L** or select **Lower case**.
5. The cursor returns to the text. Move it to the character you want to change. Press **F9**.

Examples   LC is a quick fix for many typing errors. If you hold the **Shift** key down a second to long or don't notice the Caps Lock key is "on," you'll generate more capitals than necessary. Go over them with **LC** instead of retyping them.

If you receive electronic mail, download stock or business information from videotex services, or access private bulletin boards, you've probably noticed that many systems use only capital letters. All upper case passages stand out too much in most regular printed documents, so **LC** can be used to quickly reformat electronic documents.

Tips   In single-character correction situations, **LC** does the same thing as **Change Case** (**CC**). It's just a question of which command is easier to remember.

Warnings   Be careful if you're using the **LC** on a large block of text. There always seem to be proper nouns hiding where you least expect them, so proofread your material thoroughly.

See Change Case and Upper Case

LV#

Overview   The **LV#** command works just as **C#** when you're numbering sections or chapters for a table of contents. The only difference is that **LV** does not output a number when the document is printed. The number only appears in the table of contents.

Procedure   Follow the same procedure used with the **C#** when you identify a chapter or section number. **C0** is reserved for numbering chapters, so the corresponding non-printing counter is **LV0**. When the table of contents is extracted, the **LV#** is read by XyWrite as a **C#**. Follow the procedure described in **C#**, but substitute **LV0** for **C0**.

A La Carte   There isn't a procedure in the A La Carte menus for the **LV** command. Use the standard XyWrite procedure.

See Counters and Numbering

MAIL MERGE

Overview A "Mail Merge" is the process of creating many unique, customized copies of the same document. A typical example is merging a list of names and addresses with a form letter. XyWrite's Mail Merge facility can be used to insert any type of information, not just names and addresses, into a standard letter or document.

Procedure Generating a form letter mailing takes three steps:

1. Create the Main File (the letter).
2. Create the Data File (the addresses, or other information).
3. Merge the two files to create the final documents.

When create the main file, the **Put Field** (**PF**) command is the XyWrite tool you'll use in this step. It identifies each place in the main file where a name, address, or other personalized information goes. The actual name, address, or bit of information is stored in the Data File.

1. Create a regular text file using the **New** command.
2. At each place in the main file where you want an entry from the data file inserted, place a **PF** embedded command:
   - Press **F5** (Clear Command Line).
   - Type **PF** FIELDNAME or NUMBER.
   - Press **F9** (Execute).
   - A bright command triangle is inserted.
3. Continue until each field has been identified with a **PF** command. If you used field names, you must execute a **Field Identification** command. If you used field numbers, skip steps 4-8.
4. Press **Ctrl** and **Home** to move the cursor to the beginning of the file.
5. Press **F5** (Clear Command Line).

6. Type **FI** fieldname1,fieldname2,fieldname3. NOTE: It is important to list field names in the order they appear, or will appear, in the data file, not the main file.
7. Press **F9** (Execute).
8. A bright command triangle is inserted in the text.
9. Store the file.

When creating the data file, the data file may be a file you've imported from a database, a list that was originally created for another purpose, or a XyWrite file. The only real requirement is that the file be made up of ASCII characters. XyWrite can convert any ASCII file into the propcr format.

The data file format is simple. Just follow these three rules:

- Each field entry is on a line by itself.
- Each group of fields, or record, is separated from the next record by two carriage returns.
- The data file must end with a single carriage return.

Here's an example of two records from a data file:

«FIsalesman,soldto,company,shipadd,shiptown,shipst,shipzip»
P.G.E. Smith
Alan Allen
Red's Cat Food
71 High St.
Columbus
Ohio
38321

Nancy Dennis
Glendale Pets
Leather Collars, Inc.
1408 Dayton St.
Portland
Maine
01022

Here's a sample main file that can pull the data file information and use it to generate a mailing label or an envelope address.

ΔPF:company
Att. **ΔPF:soldto**
ΔPF:shipadd
ΔPF:shiptown, **ΔPF:shipst**
ΔPF:shipzip

Merging the files to create the final documents is the easiest part of the operation. The files are merged automatically when you execute any flavor of **Type** command (**Type, Typef**, or **Types**).

The syntax of the **Type** command is slightly different from the command used to print a single file. Link the data file to the main file with a plus sign. The command to merge the files and print the documents looks like this:

TYPE DATAFILENAME+MAINFILENAME.

To preview the merge operation and bring electronic documents to the screen, use **Types:**

TYPES DATAFILENAME+MAINFILENAME.

To generate a third file of documents with all the blanks filled in, use the **Typef** command:

TYPEFDATAFILENAME+MAINFILENAME,TARGETFILENAME.

If you have the data file on the screen, you can omit its name and just specify the main file:

TYPE +MAINFILENAME.

And if the main file is open, you can omit its name:

TYPE DATAFILENAME+.

A La Carte
1. Press **F6** (A La Carte menus).
2. Press **O** or select **Option**.
3. Press **M** or select **mailMerge**.
4. The Mail Merge screen displays. You can either edit files or merge them.
5. Create a data file by pressing **D** or selecting **Datafile.**
6. Create a main file by pressing **M** or selecting **Mainfile**.
7. Press **P** or select **merge to Printer** to print the documents.
8. Press **F** or select **merge to File** to merge the documents into a third file.
9. Press **S** or select **merge to Screen** to preview the documents.

If you select an output option, you'll be prompted for the names of the data and main files.

Examples   Mail Merge is used most often in a business situation when a mailing is sent to a prepared list of clients. XyWrite's tools are designed to generate customized letters or forms, but you can also use the program to address envelopes, fill in forms, or type labels.

Tips   Remember that **FI** is an optional command. It's needed only if you name the fields in your data file. If you refer to them by number, don't use **FI**; the fields read out automatically. **FI** is a great help if the file is going to be used by anyone else since the field names annotate the fields.

If you do a fair amount of mail merge operations, you may want to explore different ways of sorting your data files—by zip code, for instance, or by state or town.

You can reorder your files in XyWrite. XYQUEST has produced an Application Note (number 159) with detailed instructions. XYQUEST recommends modifying the original data file with several **Change** operations to remove extra carriage returns, then sorting it by resetting the **Sort Key** default setting to pick up the new data.

Depending on the structure of your data files, you might also be able to do the job by constructing a "main file" that calls out the fields in the data file in a different order. If that output file is printed to screen with **Types** or to a third file with **Typef**, another file that you can edit is created. You may be able to run the sort that way and use the revised data file instead of the original.

Warnings   The most common mistake made during a Mail Merge operation is miscounting or misnaming the fields, which can cause the program to put the wrong information in the wrong place, or skip blanks. The XyWrite procedure can be a trifle clumsy, since one of the first things you need to do in identifying blanks, is refer to a data file that might not exist. Write down each field so you don't have to do lots of debugging.

See Field Identification, Field Separator, Put Field, Type, and Record Separator

MAKE DIRECTORY (MKDIR)

Overview   XyWrite's **MKDIR** operates exactly as the DOS **Make Directory** command does. It allows you to modify your disk's directory structure without leaving the program.

Procedure   1. Press **F5** (Clear Command Line).
2. Type **MKDIR \DIRNAME** (include the entire new path, or XyWrite creates the new directory under your root directory).
3. Press **F9** (Execute).
4. "Done" displays on the prompt line.

A La Carte
1. Press **F6** (A La Carte menus).
2. Press **D** or select **Directory**.
3. Press **M** or select **Makedir**.

4. A screen appears so you can enter the name of your new directory.

5. Press **Return**.

Examples   **MKDIR** is a great organizational tool. Since you can create directories on the fly, you can store documents in the best places.

Everyone has their own scheme for organizing documents on a disk, just as everyone has a unique paper document filing system. **MKDIR** lets you compartmentalize your documents as new organizational solutions occur to you.

Tips   To really manage your hard disk effectively, combine the **MKDIR** command with **Tree** to work with a graphic representation of your electronic filing cabinet. **Tree** lets you check the effect of **MKDIR** instantly and change to a new directory immediately.

Warnings   The end effect of XyWrite's **MKDIR** is the same as the DOS command, but there's an important difference. DOS makes a directory under whatever directory you happen to be in when the command is issued. XyWrite always creates the directory under the root directory. Remember to specify the full path when creating a new directory in XyWrite.

See Change Directory and Tree

MARGINS

See Bottom Margin, Left Margin, Right Margin, and Top Margin

MARGIN UNITS (MU)

Overview   The **Margin Unit** setting is a default setting that provides a base for other printer movement calculations. XYQUEST sets **MU** at 10 to match other 10-character per inch system settings and discourages users from modifying it.

Procedure   Since **MU** is a default setting, you can enter the command in your printer file or in your STARTUP.INT file, so the proper margin unit is invoked each time XyWrite starts. For complete instructions, see the Procedure portion of the Default listing.

You can also issue **MU** from the command line to set a unique display mode for a single editing session:

1. Press **F5** (Clear Command Line).
2. Type **DEFAULT** MU=# (**12** is the usual elite type alternate to the standard entry of **10** pica type).
3. Press **F9** (Execute).
4. "Done" displays on the prompt line.

A La Carte   The **Margin Unit** default isn't available through the A La Carte menus. Use the standard XyWrite procedure.

Examples   Margin units might be more accurately described as printer units. They are the unit of measure XyWrite uses to figure out its justification movements. A single margin unit is the widest letter a printer can print, according to the Proportional Space Width Table in the XyWrite printer file. The number entered with the **MU** setting is the number of these letters that fit into an inch.

The standard setting is 10, to correspond to most pica-based fonts. If you use elite type that sets characters 12 to the inch, you might want to change the setting, but XYQUEST discourages it since it can throw off other system settings.

See Defaults, Display Units, and Microjustification

MATH

See Arithmetic

MEMORY USAGE MENU (CTRL M)

Overview   The Memory Usage Menu shows how much of your computer's memory is in use and how much is available for writing or running other programs. Within that overall information, it also shows how much memory XyWrite components and supporting data files are using on an individual basis. Finally, The Memory Usage Menu allows you to load or unload those XyWrite components and supporting data files—printer files, keyboard files, and so on.

Procedure   To access the menu, press **Ctrl** and **M**. A screen like this one displays:

```
MEMORY USAGE
or selects a functionUNLOAD PROGRAM
0-7,- performs that function on the designated feature UNLOAD FILE
 if LOAD function is selectedLOAD FILE
Esc  key will remove menu
```

#	Feature	ProgramFile	Expanded
-	Standard dictionary		
0	All features		
1	Load (keyboard, help, etc.)	4	
2	Math and Programming	5	
3	Spelling and Use dictionary	12	7
4	Help	6	12
5	Hyphenation	3	11
6	Sorting	1	
7	Printing	17	15

Available Memory **319**

The sample menu above shows a situation just after XyWrite loaded in a computer with 640K of memory. To free computer memory, you might want to unload a program or file. Generally, supporting data files are larger and free more memory when removed. To unload a file:

1. Move the cursor to the "**UNLOAD FILE**" entry.
2. Type the number of the feature you want to unload, or a hyphen to unload the standard spelling dictionary.
3. The Memory Usage Menu display changes when the file is removed.

To unload a program:

1. Move the cursor to the "**UNLOAD PROGRAM**" entry.
2. Type the number of the feature you want to unload, or a hyphen to unload the XyWrite code that runs the spell-check feature.
3. The Memory Usage Menu display changes when the program is removed.

The procedure to load a file isn't really accomplished from the menu because the supporting data files can carry any name you give them; XyWrite can't know which file you intend to load:

1. Move the cursor to the "**LOAD FILE**" entry.
2. Press **Return**.
3. The Memory Usage Menu disappears and the **Load** command is entered on the command line. You're prompted to enter the name of the file to load into memory. (Each file carries a unique identification code, so it's not necessary to specify the type of file with a number or hyphen from the menu.)
4. Type the name of the file to load.
5. Press **F9** (Execute).
6. "Done" displays on the prompt line.

Examples   The sample menu above shows a situation just after XyWrite is loaded in a computer with 640K of memory. As soon as the **Spell** command was issued the large spelling dictionary file was loaded, eating up almost 110K of memory. Once the dictionary file is loaded, it stays loaded—unless you use the Memory Usage Menu to remove it.

Working with small files, or in a computer that has a lot of RAM, this might not be necessary. If you were working with large files, printing (which generates additional files), or working on a computer with limited memory, unloading inactive files can make XyWrite operate faster since it has more room to move.

You might also want to remove programs or remove files if you were loading additional files to perform a different variation of a procedure. For example, XyWrite can only use one sort file at a time. Loading a customized sort table that arranges a file of mailing list data can interfere with the indexing process. To generate an index, you'd have to unload the customized sort table.

The same principle applies to printer files, keyboard files, Save/Get files, or any other supporting data file. Loading a new version of the file doesn't remove the first version that was used. Only those parts of the old file that are used by the new file are overwritten; unduplicated features or keys from the first file can remain active if they're not removed or overwritten.

Tips

In day-to-day operation, the first real warning you may have that the program needs more memory is a "Can't Scroll, Define, or Display" message appearing on your prompt line. Nothing is destroyed when XyWrite displays that message, but the operation you're attempting may not be completed. Check the Memory Usage Menu to see if there are a few things you can live without.

Warnings

If you load several versions of a single file type, juggling several printer or keyboard files, or several sets of Save/Gets, remember how XyWrite works (outlined in the Examples section above). If you load some of your files over another version, and they don't behave as you expect them too, try removing the first version before loading the second.

See Load and Save Code

MERGE (ME)

Overview   The **Merge** command copies a file from disk into whatever file you have open on screen. It's inserted at the point where the cursor is.

Procedure   1. Move the cursor to the point where the second file should be inserted.
2. Press **F5** (Clear Command Line).
3. Type **ME** FILENAME. Include a disk or directory designator, if necessary (for example, **ME** A:\WILLS\STOCK.SEC).
4. Press **F9** (Execute).
5. The file is inserted at the cursor location.

A La Carte
1. Move the cursor to the place in the file the second file should be inserted.
2. Press **F6** (A La Carte menus).
3. Press **F** or select **File**.
4. Press **M** or select **Merge**.
5. The Merge File screen displays. Enter the name of the file you want to insert.
6. Press **Return**.

Examples   **Merge** is especially useful in a business or legal environment where identical boilerplate paragraphs or document sections are used in contracts or standard documents. For example, many leases contain a small amount of unique language, such as names, addresses and rates, and a large amount of standard contract language. The standard contract is written up once and stored in a file. When a new lease is drawn up, the unique part of the document is typed in and the boilerplate is inserted with a **ME**.

Tips   If you'd like someone who doesn't know much about XyWrite to be able to pick from several documents and merge them into a working document, think about modifying a help file to let them point-and-shoot at the boilerplate. Also remember that it's easy to store short pieces of text on Save/Get keys for instant insertion with a single keystroke combination. See the section on Save/Gets.

MODE, DISPLAY AND PRINT (MD)

Overview   XyWrite controls your monitor display and, indirectly, your printer, with the **MD** command. Each type of printing that your printer is capable of displaying—normal, underlined, bold, and so on—is turned on with a different **MD** command that is reflected on the monitor.

Procedure   XyWrite sets up nine display modes and maps these to different printer attributes. The link between a display mode and a printer mode is in the printer file. Each mode can be entered from the command line or by a special **Ctrl**-key combination.

   The printer attributes linked to the display modes vary from printer to printer, since not all printers are capable of producing the same types of letters. The attributes listed in the following table are the ones that are usually supplied.

TABLE 13   **Printer Attributes**

MODE	MD COMMAND	CTRL-KEY	PRINT ATTRIBUTE
Normal	**MD NM**	**Ctrl** and **1**	Normal
Bold	**MD BO**	**Ctrl** and **2**	Bold
Underline	**MD UL**	**Ctrl** and **3**	Underline
Reverse	**MD RV**	**Ctrl** and **4**	Hidden (Not Printed)
Bold Underline	**MD BU**	**Ctrl** and **5**	Bold Underline
Bold Reverse	**MD RV**	**Ctrl** and **6**	Italic
Superscript	**MD SU**	**Ctrl** and **7**	Superscript (small)
Subscript	**MD SB**	**Ctrl** and **8**	Subscript (small)
Reset to normal	**None**	**Ctrl** and **0**	Normal

273

There are also several display modes that are not assigned to **Ctrl**-key combinations by XYQUEST. These modes are only reflected in the monitor display; they're not linked to a printer mode until you modify your printer file and assign them. If you use one without modifying the printer file, the text that's displayed in that mode will print as "normal" text. These additional modes are explained in the Examples section below.

To set a new display mode for text as you're typing it in either press **Ctrl** and the number key that's linked to the mode (for example—**Ctrl** and **2** to make the new text bold) or execute a **MD** command from the command line:

1. Press **F5** (Clear Command Line).
2. Type **MD** BO (or the two-letter code for the mode).
3. Press **F9** (Execute).
4. The text you type to the right of that point takes on the new mode attribute.

To turn off that mode and switch to another mode, such as the previous mode, repeat the process. Press **Ctrl** and **0** to reset to the previous mode, or **Ctrl** and the number of the next mode you want to use.

There are two ways to set a mode for existing text: by defining a block and changing it, or by inserting **MD** commands at the points you want the text to switch modes.

Block Method:

1. Define the block of text
2. Press **Ctrl** and # (the number of mode you want to set).
3. Press **F9** (Execute).
4. The block of text takes on the attributes of the new mode.

Command Method:

1. Move the cursor to the point the new mode should begin.
2. Press **F5** (Clear Command Line).
3. Type **MD** BO (or the two-letter code for the mode).
4. Press **F9** (Execute).

5. All the text to the right of the cursor changes modes.

6. Move the cursor to the point the mode should stop.

7. Press **F5** (Clear Command Line).

8. Type **MD** NM (to return to normal text, however, you can use any two-letter mode command).

9. Press **F9** (Execute).

A. The text to the right of the cursor takes on the new mode.

A La Carte Switching type modes is not supported in A La Carte Menus. Use the standard XyWrite procedures.

Examples Making text change modes and attributes is a straightforward process, but there are several other things you can do with display modes.

Not all display modes control a printer mode. The two activities are not related until they're linked in a printer file. Modifying a printer file is discussed in a separate section, but become familiar with the other display modes before you modify them in a printer file.

XyWrite provides several additional display modes that are not installed on **Ctrl**-keys. If you customize the program, you can substitute any of these monitor display modes for those assigned by XYQUEST, or if your printer supports additional print modes, you can link them to those print modes in your printer file.

TABLE 14   **Additional Print Modes**

MODE	MD	COMMAND
Footnote	MD	FN
Flashing	MD	FL
Flashing Underline	MD	FU
Flashing Reverse	MD	FR
Flashing Bold (Called "Standout" by XyWrite)	MD	SO

In addition to these, you can make your own modes with any of the 255 colors the program can display. Any color in the color table can be used as a mode by typing **MD #** (# is the number of the color), for example—**MD 254**.

If you have a monochrome monitor but need to define additional modes, you can use the color settings. Check the Color table display through the Help feature, or look at the Color table in the Display section. Either pick one color number from the program's color table display, or pick one foreground and one background color from the monochrome color table and add the numbers together. Use that number to define the mode.

Even beyond these modes, XyWrite uses an entirely different set of modes to indicate edit changes when you use its redlining feature. These are explained in the **Redlining** section.

Tips

MD commands are embedded in the text, but aren't marked by the bright command triangles. If you need to delete or change one, shift to expanded mode by pressing **Ctrl** and **F9.**

If you choose to modify the mode displays in your printer file, keep in mind that each computer display/printer combination can give you different results, so you may have to do a fair amount of experimentation.

One change that's easy is generating an on-screen representation of italics for italic text. The modification simply involves a certain amount of testing. Calling the Color Table display available through the help file's keyword option, shows you what's available. Confirm the modes by issuing **MD** commands using the unassigned modes listed in Examples until you find one that generates slanted letters on your monitor. Then open the printer file and changed all occurrences of the **BR** mode to the newly found mode.

You might notice that hyphens in words which break at the end of a line don't usually print in the same mode as the word's letters. If you'd like them to, open your printer file and go to the Font Table section. Change the **FO** entry to read **FO=4**. Store and reload the file, and the hyphens should match their words. See the Printer File section for more information.

Warnings   It's possible to get carried away defining modes. XyWrite has a limit of 255 regular display modes. This is based in part on the requirements of the redlining feature, because for each mode you define, the program builds two more modes to define redlining's insert and delete modes for your new mode. The 255 limit allows room for the "hidden" redlining modes.

See Display and Printer Files

NEW FORM (NEF)

Overview   The **NEF** opens a new file and establishes XyWrite in forms mode.

Procedure   Although **NEF** can simply open a file in forms mode, it is normally used to copy a blank form that's filled in and saved as a unique file. To call a form to fill in:

1. Press **F5** (Clear Command Line).
2. Type **NEF** NEWFILENAME,MASTERFORMNAME.
3. Press **F9** (Execute).

Of course, this only works when you've already created the master form, as described in the Forms section. To create a blank file and enter forms mode:

1. Press **F5** (Clear Command Line).
2. Type **NEF** NEWFILENAME.
3. Press **F9** (Execute).

A La Carte The A La Carte menus don't have a provision for forms handling. Use the standard XyWrite procedure.

See Forms

NEW PROGRAM (NEP)

Overview   The **NEP** opens a new file and establishes XyWrite in program mode.

Procedure   1. Press **F5** (Clear Command Line).
2. Type **NEP** NEWFILENAME.
3. Press **F9** (Execute).

A La Carte The A La Carte menus don't have a provision for programming. Use the standard XyWrite procedure.

See Programs

NEW WINDOW (NW)

Overview   The **NW** setting determines whether document windows are automatically opened and closed as required or are manually controlled.

Procedure   Since **NW** is a default setting, you can enter the command in your printer file or in your STARTUP.INT file. If you enter it in one of these places, XyWrite will handle windows as you wish each time you start the program. For complete instructions, see the Procedure portion of the Default listing.
    You can also issue **NW** from the command line to try different settings during a single editing session:

1. Press **F5** (Clear Command Line).
2. Type **DEFAULT** NW=# (**0**, **1**, or **2**). The **0** is the original XyWrite setting, which disables automatic window functions.

A **1** enables automatic window opening and automatic closing. A **2** enables automatic opening, but not closing.
3. Press **F9** (Execute).
4. "Done" displays on the prompt line.

A La Carte You must be in an empty window (have a blank screen) to access the default menus.

1. Press **F6** (A La Carte menus).
2. Press **X** or select **XyWrite**.
3. Press **D** or select **Defaults**.
4. The View and Change Defaults screen displays.
5. Press **N** or select **defaults N-S**.
6. Move the cursor to the **NW** entry and type **0**, **1**, or **2**. The A La Carte default is **1**, which enables automatic opening and closing.
7. Press **Return**.
8. The Update Default File screen displays. You're asked if you want to make the default settings permanent.
9. Press **Y** or **N**. If you select **Y**, the program writes the new default settings to a special file and returns you to the A La Carte Menu Screen. If you select **N**, the settings are used for the current edit session.

Examples   Turning automatic window handling on can make your life a little easier if you shift between several documents and directory listings while you're using XyWrite.

With a **NW=1** entry in place, a new window is opened whenever you need one—when you issue a **Call** or **New** command while a document is open on screen, when you issue a **DIR** command to look at a directory; or when you execute a **Typef** or **Types** command to preview a document.

The window is closed when you issue an **Abort** (**AB**) or **Restore Screen** (**RS**) command.

Tips   To keep track of what document window you're in when several are open, issue a **Command** (**CM**) to display the current window number on the command line. You always have the window menu available too—just hit **Ctrl** and **F10**.

See Defaults and Windows

NEXT STYLE (NS)

Overview   The **NS** command switches from whatever style sheet is in use in a document to the next predetermined style sheet.

Procedure   To use **NS**, you must have:

- Set up more than one style sheet with the **Save Style (SS)** command.
- Invoked one of the style sheets in your current document with the **Use Style (US) command.**

1. Press **F5** (Clear Command Line).
2. Type **NS**.
3. Press **F9** (Execute).
4. A special **NS** marker is inserted in the text and the style sheet you defined after the one that was in use is invoked.

A La Carte Style commands are not available through the A La Carte menus. Use the standard XyWrite procedure.

Examples   XyWrite allows you to group a number of formatting commands together so they can be put into a document with one command. You might create a style sheet for letters, a second for expense accounts, and a third for journal articles... and combine them all in one document, using the **NS** and **Previous Style** (**PS**) commands. (Creating a style is discussed in the Save Style section.) XyWrite keeps track of the order in which the sheets are created.

When the **NS** command is issued, the program checks to see what style is the current one and invokes the one that was created after that one.

Tips   It's easy to forget in what order the style sheets come. When you're naming them, it helps to include a number in the name.

Since it is easy to forget the order, most people find it's easier to use the **Use Style (US)** command rather than **NS** or **PS**. If you can keep your styles straight or always create a document in one set format, **NS** and **PS** will serve you well.

If you use several style sheets, think about setting up a menu-driven point-and-shoot custom help file to make inserting the proper style file easier. You can write a new help screen using Type 1 and 5 screens that insert the appropriate style command.

See Previous Style, Style Sheets, and Use Style

NO FOOTNOTES

Overview   The **No Footnotes** command stops footnotes from printing. It's usually used with the **Dump Footnotes** (**DF**) command to produce chapter notes or endnotes.

Procedure   To stop footnotes from printing:

1. Move the cursor to the top of the document by pressing **Ctrl** and **Home**.
2. Press **F5** (Clear Command Line).
3. Type **NF**. (If you are using more than one set of footnotes, type **NF#**. The **#** is the number of the footnote set you want to use as endnotes, either 1, 2, or 3.)
4. A bright command triangle is inserted in text.

To generate chapter notes or endnotes, follow the procedure for inserting the **NF** command. If you're working in a document made up of chained-together files, the **NF** must be inserted in each file.

Then, generate the chapter notes or endnotes with the **DF** command:

1. Move the cursor to the point the where footnotes should print. If you want them on the last page of the file, press **Ctrl** and **End** to go to the end of the document.
2. Press **F5** (Clear Command Line).
3. Type **DF**. (If you are using more than one set of footnotes, type **DF#**. The **#** is the number of the footnote set, either 1, 2, or 3, that you want to use as endnotes.)
4. Press **F9** (Execute).
5. A bright command triangle is inserted in the text.
6. Any footnotes in the set begin printing at this point. If you're working on a document made up of chained-together files and you want chapter notes, repeat the **DF** command sequence at the end of each chapter file.

A La Carte To stop footnotes from printing:

1. Press **Ctrl** and **Home** to go to the beginning of the document.
2. Press **F6** (A La Carte menus).
3. Press **P** or select **Page**.
4. Press **F** or select **Footnotes**.
5. Press **N** or select **No footnotes**.
6. A bright command triangle is inserted in the text.

To generate chapter notes or endnotes follow the procedure for inserting the **NF** command. If you're working in a document made up of chained-together files, the **NF** must be inserted in each file. Then, generate the chapter notes or end notes with the **DF** command:

1. Move the cursor to the point where the footnotes should print. If you want them on the last page of the file, press **Ctrl** and **End** to go to the end of the document.

2. Press **F6** (A La Carte menus).

3. Press **P** or select **Page**.

4. Press **F** or select **Footnotes**.

5. Press **D** or select **Dump footnotes**.

6. A bright command triangle is inserted in the text.

Note that this procedure is set up to work with footnote set number one, the default set. If you're working with more than one set of footnotes, it may be easier to use the standard procedure.

Examples   Endnotes are a standard arrangement for printing citations or notes in documents, although the old reasoning for the location, that they were easier to type separately, isn't entirely valid any more. Endnotes are still used to avoid cluttering the text page with many different references. Also, many types of documents make use of several sets of footnotes, printing one set as endnotes. Separating citations and author's notes is a common application.

XyWrite provides three footnotes "tracks" or sets, so you can use one or two sets for bottom-of-the-page footnotes and the third set for endnotes.

Tips   The description of the **DF** command assumes that you want to place your suppressed footnotes on the final page of your document. You can force output at any other point, simply by inserting the **DF** there.

See Dump Footnotes and Footnotes

NO INDEX (NI)

Overview   The **NI** command is inserted in a document to prevent an index from being generated when that document is printed. It's required if you want an index or table of contents generated as a separate document.

Procedure
1. Move the cursor to the beginning of the document by pressing **Ctrl** and **Home**.
2. Press **F5** (Clear Command Line).
3. Type **NI**.
4. A bright command triangle is inserted.

A La Carte   Index tools are not available through the A La Carte menus. Use the regular XyWrite procedure.

Examples
There are two reasons to use the **NI** command. First, to prevent an index from being generated before you're ready for it, and second, to force the index into a separate document with the **Index Extract (IX)** command.

If you're creating an index as part of a document, an index is generated every time you use **Type** to print the paper. This can be a nuisance while you're writing—the index isn't needed until the document is complete.

To prevent an index from being generated until you're ready for it, insert an **NI** command while you're writing. When you're finished, remove it to generate the index.

XyWrite lets you include the index as part of the main document or as a separate file. If you want the index in a separate file, you need to insert the **NI** to prevent an index from being built in your main document. The separate file is generated when you issue the **IX** command to extract the index. The **NI** has no effect on the extraction; it can stay in place.

If you're generating a common index from a number of chained-together files, you must have the **NI** command at the beginning of each document file in the set.

Warnings
At the end of writing, it's easy to forget that you've inserted a **NI** command at the front of the document. Attach a non-printing reminder to the command so you won't wonder why the index doesn't extract properly.

See Index and Index Extraction

NO JUSTIFICATION (NJ)

Overview   **No Justification** is the companion command to **Justify On** (JU). NJ turns justification "off" and returns the document format to standard ragged right text.

Procedure   1. Move the cursor to the end of the text element you want set in justified type.
2. Press **F5** (Clear Command Line).
3. Type **NJ**.
4. A bright command triangle is inserted in the text.

A La Carte
1. Move the cursor to the end of the text element you want set in justified type.
2. Press **F6** (A La Carte menus).
3. Press **R** or select **foRmat**.
4. Press **A** or select **Alignment**.
5. The Alignment screen displays.
6. Move the cursor to the **No Justification** entry and press **Return**. A bright command triangle is inserted in the text.

Examples   If you want to print just part of a document with justified type to create a graphic effect, **JU** is essential for returning to your normal text mode. You might want to use justification to set off a long quotation or other excerpt from the main body of a paper. Narrowing your margins and justifying the excerpt make it stand out.

See Justify On

NON-BREAKABLE BLOCK (NB)

Overview   The **NB** command is used only in conjunction with the **BB** command, to protect a paragraph or other text element from breaking across pages.

See Block Break

NORMAL CARRIAGE RETURN (NC)

Overview   The **Normal Carriage Return** (**NC**) default is used only if you're outputting directly to a typesetter rather than a printer. Some typesetters require that a carriage return be sent in the same print mode as the line of type it ends. The **NC** default lets XyWrite meet that requirement.

Procedure   Since **NC** is a default setting, you can enter the command in your printer file or in your STARTUP.INT file so the carriage return setting is established each time XyWrite is started. For complete instructions, see the Procedure portion of the Default listing.

You can also issue **NC** from the command line to set the carriage return for a single editing session:

1. Press **F5** (Clear Command Line).
2. Type **DEFAULT** NC=0. (**0** generates a carriage return in whatever mode is in effect. A **1** is XyWrite's default entry, which generates a carriage return in normal model.)
3. Press **F9** (Execute).
4. "Done" displays on the prompt line.

A La Carte You must be in an empty window (have a blank screen) to access the default menus.

1. Press **F6** (A La Carte menus).
2. Press **X** or select **XyWrite**.
3. Press **D** or select **Defaults**.
4. The View and Change Defaults screen displays.
5. Press **N** or **S** or select **defaults N-S**.
6. Move the cursor to the **NC** entry and type **0** or **1**.
7. Press **Return**.
8. The Update Default File screen displays. You're asked if you want to make the default settings permanent.
9. Press **Y** or **N**. If you select **Y**, the program writes the new default settings to a special file and returns you to the A La Carte Menu Screen. If you select **N**, the settings are used for the current edit session.

Examples The **NC** setting is something 99.9 percent of XyWrite users never use, since they drive printers, not typeset equipment, with their computers. For the few people who send copy directly to typesetters, the **NC** setting lets them fine-tune XyWrite to meet the special needs of their machines.

If you run a typesetter directly from your computer, look for unusual characters at the end of some lines or short lines. If you're getting this symptom, try switching the **NC** setting from it's normal **1** entry to **0**. The **1** setting sends a carriage return in normal print mode; the **0** sends it in whatever mode is in effect in the surrounding text.

Tips XyWrite was originally developed as part of the Atex front-end system for large scale editorial jobs, including type setting. XYQUEST has experimented with writing device drivers for some typesetters. If you're serious about using XyWrite as a front-end system, contact the corporation through the customer support department.

See Defaults

NOW

Overview   The **Now** command inserts the current time when the command is executed.

Procedure   1. Move the cursor to the point where the time should print.
2. Press **F5** (Clear Command Line).
3. Type **Today**.
4. The current time is inserted in text.

A La Carte
1. Press **F6** (A La Carte menus).
2. Press **E** or select **Edit**.
3. Press **D** or select **time/Date**.
4. The Time/Date screen displays.
5. Press **F** or select the **Fixed time** entry.
6. Press **Return**.
7. The current time is inserted in text.

Examples   The **Now** command inserts a "hard" time that doesn't change. It works like a time stamp, showing when the document was processed.

The **Time (TM)** command inserts a "soft" time that changes to reflect the current time whenever the file it's in is opened or printed.

Tips   To work properly, all XyWrite's time-related commands depend on the system clock in the computer. Some computers and versions of DOS let you skip over entering the correct date and time when they start up. If you use **Now** or any of the other time and date commands, don't skip entering the correct date and time.

See Date, Time, and Today

NUMBERING

Overview XyWrite provides a large toolkit of automatic numbering tools. You can set up outlines, number sections, paragraphs, or anything else your application requires.

Procedure XyWrite uses two commands for all numbering schemes, **Define Counter (DC)** and **Counter (C#)**. The **DC** command defines what type of numbering is going to take place. The **C#** generates the number called for by the **DC**.

The syntax of the **DC** command is as involved as the numbering scheme you need to structure. If you're generating a simple numbered list with only one set of Arabic numerals—1,2,3,4, and so on, it can be omitted. If you're structuring an outline, a legal or technical document, or some other type of involved project, **DC** commands are essential.

To insert a **DC** command, first determine how many levels deep your numbering will go, and what type of symbol you'll use for each.

You can set up to 14 numbering levels and you can use regular Arabic numbers, upper or lower case Roman numerals, or upper or lower case letters for numbering. You can also define your own set of symbols, if necessary.

If you want the numbering to be continuous, you'll only need one **DC** command. If you want the numbering to reset itself on different levels, you'll need one **DC** for each level. The first, top level, includes a reference for every level. The second level includes a reference for all levels *except* the top level. The third has all levels except the first and second.

Once a **DC** command has been inserted, the numbering scheme continues until a second **DC** is encountered. If you have two separate, unrelated numbered lists in a document, you'll use two **DC**s at the beginning of each.

The basic syntax of the command runs like this:

DC LEVEL=SYMBOL

The "SYMBOL" entry specifies both what type of numbers to use and what the first digit will be. An "I" means upper case Roman numerals beginning with I; a "2" means Arabic numerals starting with 2.

To build an outline structure of six levels, using a standard numbering scheme, insert a series of **DC** commands with this procedure:

1. Move the cursor to the point where the outline begins, normally the beginning of the document.
2. Press **F5** (Clear Command Line).
3. Type **DC** 1=I A 1 a (1) (a). (This is the first level **DC** command, identified by the 1 in the "LEVEL" position. The command specifies that the first level of the outline will be upper case Roman numerals beginning with "I." The second level will be upper case Latin letters beginning with "A." The third level will be Arabic numerals starting with "1;" the fourth will be lower case Latin letters; the fifth, Arabic numerals in parentheses; the sixth, Latin letters in parentheses.)

4. Press **F9** (Execute) and a bright command triangle is inserted.
5. Press **F5** (Clear Command Line).
6. Type **DC** 2=A 1 a (1) (a).

7. Press **F9** (Execute) and a bright command triangle is inserted.
8. Press **F5** (Clear Command Line).
9. Type **DC** 3–1 a (1) (a).

10. Press **F9** (Execute) and a bright command triangle is inserted.
11. Press **F5** (Clear Command Line).
12. Type **DC** 4=a (1) (a).

13. Press **F9** (Execute) and a bright command triangle is inserted.
14. Press **F5** (Clear Command Line).
15. Type **DC** 5=(1) (a).
16. Press **F9** (Execute) and a bright command triangle is inserted.

17. Press **F5** (Clear Command Line).
18. Type **DC** 6=(a).
19. Press **F9** (Execute) and a bright command triangle is inserted.

The full outline structure is in place, contained in those six bright command triangles. Notice that punctuation seems to be able to be inserted automatically, as the parentheses are. *Only* parentheses (and brackets, braces, or angle brackets) can be typed after a number, although any punctuation symbol can be used *between* numbers. When the outline is typed, the structure looks like this:

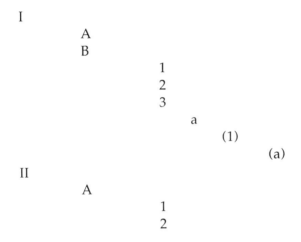

```
I
            A
            B
                        1
                        2
                        3
                    a
                        (1)
                            (a)
II
        A
                        1
                        2
```

Legal (Paragraph) Numbering Compare the outline structure to this procedure, which sets up a standard six-level legal numbering system:

1. Press **F5** (Clear Command Line).
2. Type **DC 1=1.1.1.1.1.1.**
3. Press **F9** (Execute).
4. A bright command triangle is inserted in text.

This command generates a structure that looks like this:

```
1.
          1.1.
          1.2.
                    1.2.1.
                              1.2.1.1.
                              1.2.1.2.
2.
          2.1
```

Notice that in the outline structure, the numbering is reset on each level. In the legal structure, only the first level is reset. The difference is in the first **DC** command. In the outline, the repetitive **DC**s instruct the program to reset lower levels automatically.

Once the **DC** structure is in place, the **Counter (C#)** commands are executed to generate the numbers:

1. Move the cursor to the point where the number should appear.
2. Press **F5** (Clear Command Line).
3. Type **C#** (the # is the numbering level). Type **C1** for the first level, **C2** for the second, **C12** for the twelfth.... The **C0** counter is reserved for chapter numbering—see the Examples section below.
4. Press **F9** (Execute).
5. A bright command triangle is inserted.

A La Carte

1. Move the cursor to the point in the text where the number list should be.
2. Press **F6** (A La Carte menus).
3. Press **R** or select **foRmat**.
4. Press **C** or select **Counters**.
5. The Counters screen displays. You can choose to insert a set of predefined "Outline" format **DC** commands, a set of predefined "Legal" **DC**s, a **DC** of your own design, or a **C#**. Move the cursor to the appropriate entry and press **Return**.
6. The appropriate command is inserted as a bright command triangle.

Examples **Chapter Numbering** XyWrite uses a special counter, number 0, for chapter numbering. Insert a **DC 0=1** (or **DC 0=I**) at the beginning of the very first chapter. Follow that up with a **C0** command before all additional chapter titles.

If you're working on a document that has multiple chapters, each in a separate file, use a special **DC** command at each chapter title—**DC 0=?1**. The question mark tells the program that the current chapter number is unknown. When the chapters are printed as one document with a "chained files" **Type@** command, they will be numbered properly.

Tips **Simple Lists** Remember that for a simple numbered list, all you have to do is issue the appropriate **C#** (usually a **C1**) command. The **DC** setting will default to Arabic numerals.

Using Letters The normal XyWrite numbering scheme using letters runs A through Z, then AA through ZZ, AAA through ZZZ, and so on. If you prefer, you can make the list run A through Z, then AB, AC, AD, and so on. To do this see the Numbering Style section.

There's a special procedure for starting a "lettered" list with a letter that is also a Roman numeral—an I, C, M, or any of the others. Precede the letter with a double quote mark in the **DC** command: **DC="C**.

Custom Numbering Sequences If you want to use symbols other than the numbers and letters XyWrite makes available, you can define your own unique set. Do it by defining a Counter String table in your printer file (you may want to read the Counters and Printer File sections for complete instructions):

1. Open the printer file.
2. Move the cursor to a clear point in the file.
3. Type:
   CS:#
   symbol/string
   symbol/string

symbol/string
symbol/string
symbol/string
symbol/string
4. Store the file and reload it if necessary.

When you enter your **DC** command in your document, use one of these formats:

- **DC 1=*1** causes the counter string to recycle itself by multiplying the number of symbols as they're needed.
- **DC 1=#1** recycles the list without doubling the entries.

XyWrite only supports a single customized counter string. If you use it for numbering footnotes, for instance, you probably don't want to also use it for page numbers!

The XyWrite numbering function is somewhat limited if you want to include automatically-generated punctuation in your lists or outlines.

An easy way to generate periods and spaces after outline letters or numbers is to either map the **C#**, the punctuation, and a trailing space to a Save/Get key or to a modified keyboard file. See the Save/Get or the Keyboard section for more information.

Some lists require entries that don't generate numbers, but still reset counters below them. To do this, substitute an exclamation point for the number of the list level in your **DC** command:

DC =1 ! 1

This makes the second list level an unnumbered level, but still allows a **C2** command to reset any counter levels under it.

See Counters, Define Counter, and References

NUMBERING STYLE (AZ)

Overview   The **AZ** default setting determines how numbered lists that use letters as indicators, increment.

Procedure   Since **AZ** is a default setting, you can enter the command in your printer file or in your STARTUP.INT file. If you do, your numbering scheme is used each time XyWrite starts. For complete instructions, see the Procedure portion of the Default listing.

You can also issue **AZ** from the command line to set a unique display mode for a single editing session, or to test the setting:

1. Press **F5** (Clear Command Line).
2. Type **DEFAULT** AZ=# (**1** to change the incrementing sequence, or **0** to switch back to the default setting). The difference between the two settings is explained in the Examples section below.
3. Press **F9** (Execute).
4. "Done" displays on the prompt line.

A La Carte The **AZ** default isn't available through the A La Carte menus. Use the standard XyWrite procedure.

Examples   Normally, when letters are specified as indicators, the letters increment from A (or a) to Z. The twenty-seventh indicator is AA, then BB, and so on. If you toggle **AZ** to **1** instead of the default entry of **0**, the twenty-seventh indicator is still AA, but it's followed by AB, AC, AD, and so on.

Tips   The **AZ** setting, if altered, also effects numbering systems that use lower case letters as counters.

See Counters, Defaults, Footnotes, and Numbering

OVERSTRIKE BEEP (OB)

Overview The **Overstrike Beep** is a default setting that controls the sound your computer makes when you're typing in "Overstrike Text" mode and you type over a character. XyWrite doesn't make any noise unless you turn on a beep with this setting.

Procedure Since **OB** is a default setting, you can enter the command in your printer file or in your STARTUP.INT file. If you do, your computer will beep each time you start XyWrite and type over any text. For complete instructions, see the Procedure portion of the Default listing.

You can also issue **OB** from the command line to try out the setting during a single editing session:

1. Press **F5** (Clear Command Line).
2. Type **DEFAULT** OB=#,# (tone and duration of the beep). Any number up to 65,534 is acceptable.
3. Press **F9** (Execute).
4. "Done" displays on the prompt line.

A La Carte You must be in an empty window (have a blank screen) to access the default menus.

1. Press **F6** (A La Carte menus).
2. Press **X** or select **XyWrite**.
3. Press **D** or select **Defaults**.
4. The View and Change Defaults screen displays.
5. Press **N** or select **defaults N-S**.
6. Move the cursor to the **OB** entry and type in the setting you want to use for tone and duration.
7. Press **Return**.
8. The Update Default File screen displays. You're asked if you want to make the default settings permanent.

9. Press **Y** or **N**. If you select **Y**, the program writes the new default settings to a special file and returns you to the A La Carte Menu Screen. If you select **N**, the settings are used for the current edit session.

Examples   If you turn the **Overstrike Beep** on, it functions as a warning when you overwrite text. Many people habitually type in Overstrike mode however, so for those people, the setting is less intrusive in the standard setting—off.

Tips   If your copy of XyWrite is being used by a visually-impaired person, or by someone who's not familiar with computer operation, you might want to toggle **OB** on.

The numbers you enter for tone and duration have little meaning in the real world. They were keyed to the original IBM PC speaker, but there have been so many changes in computer hardware since then that tone and duration vary greatly from machine to machine. You'll have to experiment to get the effect you want.

See Defaults

OFFSET (OF)

Overview   The **OF** command shifts all text a specified number of spaces away from either the right or left margins when a document is printed. It's usually used to provide extra room on a page for binding a document.

Procedure   1. Move the cursor to the beginning of the document.
2. Press **F5** (Clear Command Line).
3. Type **OF** #,# (# is the number of spaces you want to shift the type). The first entry controls the right-hand pages; the

second, the left-hand pages. If you only enter one number (for example—**OF 5**), the setting is used for all pages.
4. Press **F9** (Execute).
5. A bright command triangle is inserted.

A La Carte
1. Press **F6** (A La Carte menus).
2. Press **R** or select **foRmat**.
3. Press **S** or select **Status**.
4. The Status screen displays.
5. Move the cursor to the **OF** entry and type in the number of spaces you want to offset right and left hand pages.
6. Press **Return**.
7. The new settings are installed.

Examples　　Although **Offset** seems to duplicate the regular margin commands, it's really quite different. **Offset** isn't reflected on the monitor screen as margins are. It's only used when a document is printed.

　　If anything you write is bound directly as it rolls from the printer, **OF** allows you to position your words for greatest legibility, away from the gutter created by the binding.

Tips　　Unless your printer is capable of double-sided printing, you're going to feed your pages through your printer twice, or the sheets are going to be duplicated in some way, you can ignore the double entry in the **OF** command.

ORPHANS (OP)

Overview　　When a paragraph begins at the bottom of a page and concludes on the next page, the first few lines at the bottom are "orphans." The **OP** sets the minimum number of lines you think are acceptable.

Procedure   Orphan control is dependent on the settings you've entered in the **Page Length** entry. **PL** sets the minimum acceptable page length, the nominal page length and the maximum page length in lines .

XyWrite's preset default values for **PL** are 54, 60, and 50, meaning that XyWrite tries to fit 54 lines on a page, is satisfied if 50 fit, and will not permit more than 60. The preset default **OP** entry is 2, meaning that the first two lines of a paragraph are permitted on the bottom of a page, but that a single line never appears by itself.

You can calculate the greatest number of lines you can enter in your **OP** command by subtracting the minimum entry in your **PL** from the nominal entry and adding a line.

Using the preset values, 50 lines from 54 leaves 4, plus 1, meaning your largest possible orphan entry is 5 lines. If you use that entry, XyWrite would place the first five lines of a paragraph at the bottom of a page, but never print fewer than five there.

Once you've checked your **PL** entry (it's usually found in the STARTUP.INT file, but can be embedded in a single document) and figured the maximum allowable orphan entry, execute the command:

1. Move the cursor to the first line of your document by pressing **Ctrl** and **Home**.
2. Press **F5** (Clear Command Line).
3. Type **OP** # (# is the minimum number of lines).
4. A bright command triangle is inserted in the text.

A La Carte
1. Move the cursor to the beginning of the file by pressing **Ctrl** and **Home**.
2. Press **F6** (A La Carte menus).
3. Press **R** or select **foRmat**.
4. Press **S** or select **Status**.
5. The Status screen displays.

6. Move the cursor to the **OP** entry and type in the number of lines you want to specify for orphan lines.
7. Press **Return**.
8. The new setting is installed.

Examples

"Orphans" and "widows" are typographic terms that describe parts of paragraphs that are split so they print on two pages. The "orphan" controlled by **OP** is the first part of a paragraph that prints at the bottom of a page. The "widow" is the rest of the paragraph that prints at the top of the next page.

In almost all documents, you'll want to make sure that at least the first two lines of a paragraph are printed at the bottom of a page. A single line by itself, with the rest of the paragraph at the top of the next page, makes it hard for your reader to follow the idea expressed in the sentence. Two lines, the XyWrite preset, is the minimum. Three is a better setting for general purpose work.

For complex documents, or those that have been designed to very strict standards, you'll want to increase the **OP** setting to insure that more of a paragraph prints before the page break.

Warnings

The **Orphan Control** setting is linked to the **Page Length** setting. If you modify the **PL** setting or increase the number of lines used in **OP**, check your **PL** settings. For **OP** to work properly, the difference between the **PL** "nominal" and "maximum" numbers must be greater than the **OP** or **WD** setting. For instance, the XyWrite default entry for both **OP** and **WD** is two lines. The difference between the modified **PL** setting's nominal and maximum values should be at least three.

See Page Length and Widow Control

PAD SPACES (PD)

Overview   **Pad Spaces** inserts spaces between the last word you typed and your current cursor location *if* you have your keyboard set for linear cursor movement.

Procedure   Since **PD** is a default setting that's dependent on a keyboard file setting, you should enter the command in your printer file or in your STARTUP.INT file. That way, the pad space setting and the linear cursor setting mesh each time XyWrite starts. For complete instructions, see the Procedure portion of the Default listing.

You can also issue **PD** from the command line to test the setting during a single editing session:

1. Press **F5** (Clear Command Line).
2. Type **DEFAULT** PD=# (**0** or **1**). The effects are explained in the Examples section.
3. Press **F9** (Execute).
4. "Done" displays on the prompt line.

A La Carte   You must be in an empty window (have a blank screen) to access the default menus.

1. Press **F6** (A La Carte menus).
2. Press **X** or select **XyWrite**.
3. Press **D** or select **Defaults**.
4. The View and Change Defaults screen displays.
5. Press **N** or select **defaults N**.
6. Move the cursor to the **PD** entry and type **0** or **1**.
7. Press **Return**.
8. The Update Default File screen displays. You're asked if you want to make the default settings permanent.
9. Press **Y** or **N**. If you select **Y**, the program writes the new default settings to a special file and returns you to the A La

Carte Menu Screen. If you select **N**, the settings are used for the current edit session.

The standard A La Carte keyboard, ALACARTE.KBD, does not use linear cursor movement. You should modify it if you use a mouse or want to use the **Pad Spaces** setting.

Examples

The **Pad Spaces** setting is valid only if you use linear cursor settings in your keyboard file. These special cursor movements are often invoked if your computer has a mouse or if you use XyWrite' SUPER.KBD. To see if your keyboard file uses them, review the Keyboard File section.

When a keyboard file uses linear cursor settings, you can move the cursor around in the area to the right of XyWrite's carriage return arrow, out beyond the "end" of a line. You can also type while the cursor is out there. If the **PD** setting is **0**, any text you type snaps back behind the carriage return, next to the last word you typed. When the **PD** setting is **1**, the space between the last word and your newly typed text is padded with spaces so your words stay put.

Tips

Pad Spaces is useful if you're writing poetry or any other free-form text where aesthetic word placement is important. It's also handy if you work with files that have been imported from other programs. If, for instance, you've imported part of a spreadsheet or a graphic, the linear cursor and **PD** let you annotate the file quickly and easily.

If you do decide to use the **Pad Spaces** setting, map the **Unpad Spaces** function call to a key on your keyboard. (See the Keyboard File section.) **Unpad Spaces** deletes extra spaces between the cursor location and the word to its left. It's not assigned to a key by XyWrite, but is very useful when paired with **PD**.

See Defaults

PAGE BREAK (PG)

Overview   The **PG** command forces a page break. The line after the one where the **PG** is inserted becomes the first line of the next page.

PG can also count the number of lines on a page and end the page only if the page contains the number of lines you have preset.

Procedure   To create an unconditional page break:

1. Put the cursor at the end of the line you want to be the last line of the page.
2. Press **F5** (Clear Command Line).
3. Type **PG**.
4. Press **F9** (Execute) and a bright command triangle is inserted in the text. If the Page-Line Number display is turned on, you can verify the page change by pressing the down arrow key.

To create a conditional page break:

1. Put the cursor at the end of the line you want to be the last line of the page.
2. Press **F5** (Clear Command Line).
3. Type **PG #** (# is the number of lines the page should contain before it breaks). A **PG 25** command forces a page break only if the page contains 25 lines. What would be the 26th line becomes the first line of the next page.
4. Press **F9** (Execute) and a bright command triangle is inserted in the text.

A La Carte
1. Move the cursor to the point where the page break should occur.
2. Press **F6** (A La Carte menus).
3. Press **P** or select **Page**.
4. Press **B** or select **pageBreak**.
5. The Force Page Break Screen displays.
6. A bright command triangle is inserted.

Tips   Both types of **PG** commands are very useful if you're assembling a complex document that involves cut-and-paste work. For instance, if you want to leave half a page blank so a photograph can be inserted later, **PG** saves the place.

Warnings   If you unaccountably get a blank page in the middle of your document, a badly-placed **PG** could be causing it. Look for a **PG** on a line by itself at the bottom of the page, before the blank one.

PAGE LENGTH (PL)

Overview   The **PL** setting controls the number of lines of text on each printed page.

Procedure   The **PL** setting has three parts: the nominal page length, the maximum page length, and the minimum page length. When **PL** is issued as a command, the syntax is:

                  PL NOMINAL,MAXIMUM,MINIMUM.

                  XyWrite is shipped with a default **Page Length** setting of 54,60,50 in the STARTUP.INT file.
                  NOTE: all the numbers in this section are based on a standard 11-inch long sheet of paper that holds 66 lines of text. These settings don't have anything to do with whether you're writing a single, double, or triple-spaced document. The **PL** simply tells the program how many lines fit on a sheet, whether they're blank lines or not.
                  "Nominal" is the number of lines of text you want on a normal page.
                  "Maximum" is the absolute maximum number of lines that can be printed on a page. The program uses this number to place footnotes. It's also used by the **Orphan** (**OP**) setting.

P

"Minimum" is the minimum number of lines that appear on a page which has several footnotes pushing up from the bottom. This number is also used by the **OP** (**Orphan**) setting.

The **PL** setting counts lines of text down from the top of the sheet of paper. It includes the lines taken up by a top margin, a running header, body text, and footnotes. It doesn't include a bottom margin or footnotes.

To determine a **PL** setting, first decide how many lines of text are needed by the bottom margin and the running footer. Many people pick 6 as the entry for the bottom margin, since that translates into an even inch of white space. A single line is usually sufficient for a running footer, although some document designs use two. Subtract those figures (6 and 1) from 66 (the number of lines that can fit on an 11-inch sheet of paper) to yield the "maximum" entry—59.

Nominal is an arbitrary number. Use your "maximum" number less two or three lines if you're planning a single-spaced document, or three or four if you normally write double-spaced. For this example, say the nominal is 56.

Minimum is another arbitrary figure, this one based on the "nominal" number. If you use many footnotes, you'll want to pick a "short" minimum to give them room. If you rarely use footnotes, allow another two or three lines. For this example, the minimum is 52.

To set a **PL** for a single document, with the above planning out of the way, **PL** is entered as any other command is:

1. Move the cursor to the beginning of the document by pressing **Ctrl** and **Home**.
2. Press **F5** (Clear Command Line).
3. Type **PL** 56,59,52 (the numbers from the examples above).
4. Press **F9** (Execute).
5. The setting is inserted in the text.

If you modify the **PL** setting XyWrite installed in the STARTUP.INT file, the same **PL** is used for all documents, unless a unique **PL** is inserted in a particular document.

To reset the "standard" **PL** in the STARTUP.INT file:

1. Press **F5** (Clear Command Line).
2. Type **CA** STARTUP.INT.
3. Press **F9** (Execute).
4. Move the cursor to the line that reads: DEFAULT PL=54,60,50.
5. Change the entry to read: DEFAULT PL=56,59,52 (the numbers from the examples above).
6. Press **F5** (Clear Command Line).
7. Type **STORE**.
8. Press **F9** (Execute).

The next time XyWrite is started, the new settings will be used.

A La Carte
1. Press **F6** (A La Carte menus).
2. Press **P** or select **Page**.
3. Press **L** or select **Layout**.
4. Move the cursor to the **PL** entry and insert the three numbers that represent the nominal, maximum, and minimum number of lines for the page layout.
5. Press **Return**.
6. A bright command triangle is inserted in text.

You can also set a new default **PL** setting through A La Carte's menus. You must be in an empty window (have a blank screen) to access the default menus:

1. Press **F6** (A La Carte menus).
2. Press **X** or select **XyWrite**.
3. Press **D** or select **Defaults**.
4. The View and Change Defaults screen displays.
5. Press **N** or select **defaults N-S**.
6. Move the cursor to the **PL** entry and enter the settings for nominal, maximum, and minimum.
7. Press **Return**.
8. The Update Default File screen displays. You're asked if you want to make the default settings permanent.
9. Press **Y** or **N**. If you select **Y**, the program writes the new default settings to a special file and returns you to the A La

Carte Menu Screen. If you select **N**, the settings are used for the current edit session.

Tips

Many times you'll write what should be a single-page document, a letter, for instance, but several lines loop over on to the next page. You can cram them onto a single sheet by entering a "long" **PL** on the first line of the document—say a **PL 80**. It's usually not necessary to enter a maximum or minimum setting since letters usually don't contain footnotes.

Warnings

If you modify the **PL** setting, particularly if you modify the default setting in the STARTUP.INT, you should review the sections on the **Orphan Control** (**OP**) and **Widow Control** (**WD**) settings. For these two settings to work, the difference between the **PL** "nominal" and "maximum" numbers must be greater than the **OP** or **WD** setting. For instance, the XyWrite default entry for both **OP** and **WD** is 2 lines. The difference between your modified **PL** setting's nominal and maximum values should be at least 3.

See Breakable Blocks, Orphan Control, Running Headers/Footers, and Widow Control

PAGE-LINE NUMBER DISPLAY (CTRL-F9)

Overview

XyWrite displays the page number and line number the cursor is on at the top, right side of the screen.

Procedure

The Page-Line Number display is toggled on and off by pressing **Ctrl** and **F9**.

If you shift into expanded display mode, the Page-Line Number display is toggled off (since an accurate count can't be done in expanded mode).

It's easy to set up XyWrite so the Page-Line Number display is on all the time. The status of the display is controlled by the **DT** default setting.

See Command and Defaults

PAGE NUMBER (PN)

Overview The **PN** is an embedded command that generates the current page number. It's normally used in a header or footer, but can be inserted in regular text.

Procedure 1. Press **F5** (Clear Command Line).
2. Type **PN**.
3. Press **F9** (Execute).
4. A bright command triangle is inserted. The page number won't display, but when the document is printed, it is typed.

A La Carte
1. Move the cursor to the point where you want the page number printed.
2. Press **F6** (A La Carte menus).
3. Press **P** or select **Page**.
4. Press **P** or select **Page#**.
5. The Insert Page Number screen displays.
6. Move the cursor to the Insert Page Number Automatically entry.
7. Press **Return**.
8. A bright command triangle is inserted.

Tips XyWrite assumes that you want to begin page numbering with "1." If you don't, use the **Set Page Number** (**SP**) command to tell the program where to start.

To generate a "Page 23 of 89" line in your document, use the **PN** command combined with the **Final Page** (**FP**) command. Full instructions are in the **FP** section.

You can combine the **PN** with other counters to generate other page number formats. For instance, a 4-123 number that indicates chapter number and page number is generated by using the **C0** counter and the **CH-** command, explained in the Numbering section.

See Final Page, Numbering, Running Headers/Footers, and Set Page Number

---

PAUSE, A PROGRAM DURING EXECUTION (P)

Overview   **P** is used only in a program. It can be used either to simply slow down program execution or to display a message.

Procedure   In a program file:

1. Move the cursor to the point in the program where you want the pause inserted or the message displayed.
2. Turn the keystroke recorder on by pressing **Scroll Lock**.
3. Press **F5** (Clear Command Line).
4. Type **P** MESSAGE. The MESSAGE is optional.
5. Press **F9** (Execute).
6. Turn the keystroke recorder off by pressing **Scroll Lock**.
7. **Store** the file.

A La Carte   Programming functions aren't available through the A La Carte menus. Use the standard XyWrite functions.

Examples   **P** is normally used to display messages that let a user know what's happening while a long program runs. There are few things more unsettling than staring at a blank or inactive screen while a program plays in your computer.

Good programmers keep their audience at ease by displaying progress reports as the program does its work.

Tips   On the original IBM PC, **P** caused a pause that lasted about one second. As computers got faster, the pause got shorter. If you're operating with a speedy machine, a single **P** will flash by before your message can be read. The first time you use **P**, plan on testing the display time.

Lengthen the pause by pressing **F9** several times when you enter the command, instead of the single press used in the procedure here.

See Programming

PAUSE PRINTER (PA)

Overview   You can make your printer pause while it's printing a document by embedding a **PA** command at the point where the printer should stop.

Procedure   1. Move the cursor to the point where the printer should pause.
2. Press **F5** (Clear Command Line).
3. Type **PA**.
4. Press **F9** (Execute).
5. A window opens so you can type in the message you want displayed when the pause occurs. Enter your message.
6. Press **F3** (Close Window).
7. A bright command triangle is inserted in the text. When you use a **Type** command to print the document, the printer pauses when it hits the embedded **PA**. Press the + key to restart the printer.

You can also use the **PA** command to display a message on the prompt line when the printer hits the **PA**—"Change the Printwheel" or "Insert the Envelope":

1. Move the cursor to the point where the printer should pause.
2. Press **F5** (Clear Command Line).
3. Type **PA** MESSAGE GOES HERE.
4. Press **F9** (Execute).
5. A bright command triangle is inserted in the text. When you print the document, the printer pauses at the embedded **PA** and the message displays on the prompt line. You still press the + key to restart the printer.

A La Carte There isn't a menu function in A La Carte to insert a **PA** command. Use the standard XyWrite procedure.

Examples   The **PA** is intended for printing documents that require a printer adjustment part of the way through the document. It could be something like inserting an envelope after a letter is typed, changing a printwheel to a different font, or switching a laser cartridge to print in a second color.

Tips   If you're hand-feeding stationery or performing a very extensive printer operation between every page of a document, read the section on **Automatic Pause** (**AP**). It's intended for situations where you need a pause after every page.

See Automatic Pause and Type (with the p option)

PREVIOUS STYLE (PS)

Overview   The **PS** command switches from whatever style is in use in a document to the one that precedes it in the document's series of styles.

311

Procedure To use **PS**, you must have:

- Set up more than one style with the **Save Style** (**SS**) command.
- Invoked one of the style sheets in the set in your current document with the **Use Style** (**US**) command.

1. Press **F5** (Clear Command Line).
2. Type **PS**.
3. Press **F9** (Execute).
4. A special **PS** marker is inserted in text and the style sheet you defined before the one that was in use is invoked.

A La Carte Style commands are not available through the A La Carte menus. Use the standard XyWrite procedure.

Examples XyWrite allows you to group a number of formatting commands together so they can be put into a document with one command. You might create a style sheet for letters, a second for expense accounts, and a third for journal articles... and combine them all in one document, using the **PS** and **Next Style** (**NS**) commands. (Creating a style is discussed in the Save Style section.) XyWrite keeps track of the order in which the sheets are created.

When the **PS** command is issued, the program checks to see what style is the current one and invokes the one that was created before that one.

Tips It's easy to forget what order style sheets come in. When you're naming them, it helps to include a number in the name.

Since it is easy to forget the order, most people find it's easier to use the **Use Style** (**US**) command rather than **NS** or **PS**. If you can keep your styles straight or always create a document in one set format with a regular progression of styles, **NS** and **PS** will serve you well.

If you use several style sheets, think about setting up a menu-driven, point-and-shoot custom help file to make inserting the proper style file easier. You can write a new help screen using

Type 1 and 5 screens that should insert the appropriate style command.

See Next Style, Style Sheets, and Use Style

PRINTER CONTROL (PC)

Overview   If you have a heavy-duty printer that does tricks such as selecting paper from several different bins, the **PC** command lets you orchestrate everything from XyWrite.

Procedure   To use the **PC** command, you must create a table of special Printer Control strings in your printer file.

Every printer file can be edited since it's a standard ASCII text file. The strings you'll insert in the PC Table are groups of commands the printer requires in order to perform a function. They vary greatly from machine to machine, but are almost always documented in the printer manual:

1. Press **F5** (Clear Command Line).
2. Type **CA** PRINTERFILENAME.
3. Press **F9** (Execute).
4. The printer file opens on the screen. The PC table can be inserted almost anywhere in the file, but the end of the file is good, since it won't disrupt anything else there. Move the cursor to the end of the file by pressing **Ctrl** and **End**.
5. You'll probably see a few lines that looks like these:

    ;
    ; **END OF PRINTER FILE**
    ;

1. Move the cursor to the semi-colon above the end of printer file message.
2. Type **PC:** and press **Return**.

3. After locating the printer control strings you need in your printer manual, type a single control code string into the file.
4. Press **Return**.
5. Continue typing in control code strings, one to a line, until you've inserted all the commands you need.
6. Count the number of lines you've created.
7. Move the cursor to the carriage return arrow after the **PC:** that begins the table, and type in the number of lines (for example, **PC:5** or **PC:18**).
8. (Optional) It's a good idea to add a note below the PC Table explaining what the strings are and what they do. Begin each line with a semi-colon and end each line with a carriage return. Don't allow the lines to word wrap. When you're through, the table might look like this:

```
;
PC:4
string 1
string 2
string 3
string 4
;This is a memo line, explaining the four printer control lines.
;Memo lines must begin with semi-colons and end with carriage
;returns. Word wrap is not allowed.
;
; END OF PRINTER FILE
;
```

1. Before you close the file, make a note to yourself identifying what each line does.
2. Press **F5** (Clear Command Line).
3. Type **ST** (**Store**).
4. Press **F9** (Execute).

The printer file needs to be reloaded to activate the PC Table. See the **Load** command section for instructions.

After the printer file has been reloaded, you're ready to embed **PC** commands in your text files. Each Printer Control string is on a line by itself. The number of the line in the Printer Control Table is used by the **PC** command:

1. Move the cursor to the point in the file where the printer action is needed.
2. Press **F5** (Clear Command Line).
3. Type **PC** # (# is the line number of the command from the Printer Control Table).
4. Press **F9** (Execute).
5. A bright command triangle is inserted.

When you issue a **Type** command to print the file, the printer control string from the PC Table is sent to the printer.

A La Carte   There isn't a menu function in A La Carte to generate a **PC** command. Use the standard XyWrite procedure.

Examples   If your printer is capable of emulating several types of devices, say a graphics printer or plotter, as well as typing text, you could construct a Printer Control Table containing the commands that switch it between the two modes.

Inserting a **PC 1** in your document could move the printer to graphics mode to print an inserted graphic and **PC 2** could move it back to text.

Another common application for the **PC** command involves printers that draw paper from several sheet feeder bins. If the printer has three bins, you could build a Printer Control table containing the software commands to switch between them. When printing a long letter, you can insert a **PC** command to print the first page on letterhead, a second **PC** command to print the second page on matching stationery, and finally draw the envelope from the third bin.

Tips   The **PC** command is useful for printer commands that are used over and over. If you're in a situation where you need to specify a printer trick, such as drawing a rule, that's only going to be used occasionally, use the **Printer Insert (PI)** command instead. The **PI** sends the printer code directly to the printer—you don't have to set up a Printer Control Table.

If you'd like to check to make sure the control codes are being inserted in the document in the right place and include the proper characters, remember the **Typef** command. **Typef** prints a copy of a text file to disk and includes all printer control and formatting codes, just as they're sent to the printer.

See Printer File and Printer Insert

PRINTER FILE

Overview XyWrite's printer files contain unique information the printer requires to properly format and type a document. XYQUEST supplies more than 100 printer files with the XyWrite software. More than 150 additional drivers are available through the customer support department.

A printer file can also set default values, manage the monitor display, and implement several other program functions.

Perhaps because they do so many things, questions about printer files generate about half the calls XYQUEST's Technical Support Department receives.

Printer files and all the functions they control can be modified to fine-tune XyWrite or a particular machine to a specific application. Keep in mind that just as each printer differs from other printers, each printer file differs from its cousins. Each of them controls a different printer, so each printer file contains different information. The Epson FX is a popular printer that boasts a typical printer file, so it's used here as an example.

Printer files are edited just as text files are. To make modifications or just browse to see what your printer is capable of, call the file to your screen:

316

1. Press **F5** (Clear Command Line).
2. Type **CA** FILENAME.PRN.
3. Press **F9** (Execute).
4. The file opens.

Printer files usually have nine or ten distinct parts, but they're really not that complicated. XYQUEST usually places a version number and an identifying memo at the very top of the file. The different capabilities of the printer are also listed. When you open a printer file, notice that a number of lines begin with semi-colons. These are comment lines that don't have an impact on printer file operation. This is the header information from the Epson FX file:

```
;PR;;REV 3.2A                            EPSON FX-80, FX-100
;
; AvailableATTRIBUTES:
 UNDERLINE                               DOUBLE EMPHASIZED
;SUBSCRIPT                               SUPERSCRIPTFORMS
;ITALIC
;
; Available FONTS:PICA(10pitch) ELITE(12pitch)PROPORTIONAL
;PICA/EXPANDED                           COMPRESSED
;ELITE/EXPANDED
;COMPRESSED/EXPANDED PROPORTIONAL/ITALIC
;PROPORTIONAL/EXPANDED
;PROPORTIONAL/ITALIC/EXPANDED
;
;
```

A printer attribute is a printer function. On most (but not all) printers, it is a mechanical operation that's not entirely software-controlled. For instance, the Epson FX described above has seven attributes. The machine can:

- Underline text.
- Double strike letters.
- Emphasize type (usually this means each letter is double-struck slightly out of register, so the letters are wider than normal).

- Print small letters in subscript or superscript positions (below and above regular text).
- Operate in forms mode.
- Generate slanted letters.

These are all things the printer does mechanically, by moving the print head in some way.

A font is not the same thing as an attribute. A font is a set of characters that share a similar design. The Epson generates 10 styles of type. Fonts are more likely to be generated by software than hardware. The available fonts are:

- Pica, normal 10 character per inch letters.
- Elite, the slightly smaller 12 character per inch type.
- Proportional, letters of different widths like those used to create the type of this book.
- Pica/Expanded, large letters, used for special applications, like a speaker's reference notes or headlines. These are twice the size of normal Pica type—five characters per inch.
- Compressed, squeezed-into-a-smaller-than-normal space letters.
- Elite/Expanded, large letters similar to the Pica/Expanded, but based on the 12 character per inch standard. Generates six characters per inch.
- Compressed/Expanded, is based on the compressed font, again printed double-size.
- Proportional/Italic, a companion font to the regular proportional font. Note that this is a distinct type design different from the proportional font with the italic attribute.
- Proportional/Expanded, the large "headline" type based on the variable-width Proportional font.
- Proportional/Italic/Expanded, the final member of the font family, a large companion to the Proportional/Italic font.

Each of the 10 fonts can be printed with any of the seven attributes. The combining is done in the Print Tables of the printer file, an area that comes after a few lines that normally list default settings. If you modify your system default settings and insert your preferences in your printer file, this is the best place to put them. You can even label the area as your default area by inserting a note on a line that begins with a semi-colon.

The Epson default section falls just under the printer information. It's not labeled, but looks like this:

```
;
; Substitution Table: FOREIGN
;DF WS=1
MD MM=255
LE¶
PE¶
FE<►2 ¶
;
```

In this case, the Epson supports a foreign character substitution table. The next line (DF WS=1) is a default setting that turns whole-space justification off in favor of the more aesthetic (but slower) micro-spaced justification mode (see the Justification section). If you want to turn whole-space justification on, simply erase the semi-colon.

The MD MM=255 line is a setting that controls how microspacing is performed when microjustifying text. It shouldn't be changed. The next three lines are the characters the printer needs to receive to end a line, paragraph, and file.

Just after this information comes the meat of the file, the Print Type table definitions. As a general rule, XYQUEST supplies three basic Print Type tables, for pica, elite, and proportional fonts. These are enough to give you a good base for modifications or building additional tables. Here are the three standard tables from the Epson file:

```
PT=1
MD NM+PICA
MD BO+PICA+EMPHASIZED+DOUBLE
MD BU+PICA+EMPHASIZED+DOUBLE+UNDERLINE
MD UL+PICA+UNDERLINE
MD RV+PICA+FORMS
MD BR+PICA+ITALIC
```

```
MD SU+PICA+SUPERSCRIPT
MD SD+PICA+SUBSCRIPT
MD MM+MICRO
;
PT=2
MD NM+ELITE
MD BO+ELITE+EMPHASIZED+DOUBLE
MD BU+ELITE+EMPHASIZED+DOUBLE+UNDERLINE
MD UL+ELITE+UNDERLINE
MD RV+ELITE+FORMS
MD BR+ELITE+ITALIC
MD SU+ELITE+SUPERSCRIPT
MD SD+ELITE+SUBSCRIPT
MD MM+MICRO
;
PT=3
MD NM+PROPORTIONAL
MD BO+PROPORTIONAL+EMPHASIZED+DOUBLE
MD
BU+PROPORTIONAL+EMPHASIZED+DOUBLE+UNDERLINE
MD UL+PROPORTIONAL+UNDERLINE
MD RV+ELITE+FORMS
MD BR+PROPORTIONAL+ITALIC
MD SU+PROPORTIONAL+SUPERSCRIPT
MD SD+PROPORTIONAL+SUBSCRIPT
MD MM+MICRO
;
```

As you look at each table, you might recognize another XyWrite command, the mode setting. The MD NM, MD BO, MD UL, and the other lines are linked to the commands that trigger a change in type style. For instance, you'd insert a **MD BO** command while typing to indicate a boldface word or letter (see the Mode section for complete information).

In each table, the **MD NM** (normal type) setting is linked to a particular font's unadorned printing mode. When the **MD NM** command is inserted in a document, it is always going to generate "plain" type, no matter if the font is pica, elite, or proportional.

P

The lines after the normal mode build on the main font by adding attributes. To take the second line of each table as an example, the **MD BO** setting stands for boldfaced type. When you make a word bold in your text by issuing a **MD BO** command, XyWrite instructs the printer to generate bold type by striking each letter twice. If you inserted a **Print Table** (**PT**) **2** command, you'd generate bold elite type; a **PT 3** calls for bold proportional type.

Notice that you can chain several attributes together. That's the way the **Bold Underline** (**BU**) print mode is put on paper.

Below the Print Type Tables is an Attribute Definition section. These lines record the characters that are sent to the printer to order the special operations that generate an attribute. The Epson FX section includes these entries:

```
; ATTRIBUTE DEFINITIONS
;
AT:INSERT
AT<[
AT>]
ET
;
AT:DELETE
AT#♣\
AT<➤ — ▯
ET
;
AT:UNDERLINE
AT< ➤-
AT> ➤-
ET
;
AT:EMPHASIZED
AT<➤E
AT>➤F
ET
;
```

Attribute definitions very rarely, if ever, have to be modified. Following the Attribute Definitions are the Font Definitions, the characters that are sent to the printer when a specific font is called for by a Printer Type Table. From the Epson FX file:

```
; FONT DEFINITIONS
;
FO:PICA
FO< ➤p ➤P
UW:PICA
US:FOREIGN
ET
;
FO:ELITE
FO<➤p ➤M
UW:ELITE
US:FOREIGN
ET
;
FO:COMPRESSED
FO<❀
FO>↕
UW:COMPRESSED
US:FOREIGN
ET
;
```

After the fonts come font width tables. They specify how wide each letter is to be printed:

```
; WIDTH TABLES
;
WD:PICA
SW=12
ET
;
WD:ELITE
SW=10
ET
;
```

```
WD:PICA/EXPANDED
SW=24
ET
;
```

Next come any character substitution tables the printer may use. Remember the "FOREIGN" character substitution table in the first part of the Epson FX file? This is where the table actually lives.

The structure of a substitution table is straightforward. The special character you insert in your text file is listed along with the command string the Epson needs to receive to print the foreign character. When XyWrite formats your text file for printing, it reads the special character (say the yen or pound sign) and embeds the printer control string in the text as it's sent from your computer to the printer.

;SUBSTITUTION TABLE TO ACCESS FOREIGN CHARACTERS

```
;
SU:FOREIGN
¥≠➤R♣\➤R
£=➤R♥#➤R
ì=➤R♠~➤R
°=➤R♠[➤R
¡=➤R♦[➤R
¿=➤R♦]➤R
ñ=➤R♦|➤|
Ñ=➤R♦/➤/
Ρ=➤R♦#➤R
É=➤R✪@➤R
✪=➤R✪$➤R
Å=➤R✪]➤R
å=➤R✪}➤R
Æ=➤R✪[➤R
```

After the substitution tables come Vertical Space Settings, the numbers and characters that move the printer's print head up and down to create lines and place the superscript and subscript characters. Again, these are specific instructions to the printer to accomplish this single function:

```
;VERTICAL SPACING SETTINGS
;
;Movement in 216ths of an inch.
VU=36,36,100
VS:36
```

At the end of the file is one more section, the group of settings that determine how microjustification is implemented. These are system settings, picked because of printer capability.

```
;
; MICROJUSTIFICATION SETTINGS
SC=3
SF=1
JT=0
JU=0
;
MU=12
DU=12
MS=6
```

Procedure   The most common modification to a printer file involves building additional Print Type tables so XyWrite can take advantage of each print mode a printer offers. All you need is an understanding of the Print Table structure and the font and attribute information.

First, make a copy of your printer file. Make your changes in the copy. This keeps your original file intact and uncorrupted in case you make a mistake:

1. Press **F5** (Clear Command Line).
2. Type **COPY** FILENAME.PRN,NEWFILENAME.PRN.
3. Press **F9** (Execute).
4. "Done" displays on the prompt line.

Second, open the new printer file:

1. Press **F5** (Clear Command Line).
2. Type **CA** NEWFILENAME.PRN.
3. Press **F9** (Execute).
4. Make a note of the fonts and attributes your printer supports. (You can define that portion of the printer file as a block and print it, just as you would a text file.) Decide what font you want to add. Using the Epson FX file, you might decide on a pica-based large type font, the PICA/EXPANDED.
5. Move the cursor down to the Print Table area. Define a print table, in this case, PT=1, the print table that defines the Pica font.
6. Press **F7** to copy the table.
7. Change the "PT=1" identifier to "PT=4" and change each occurrence of "PICA" to "PICA/EXPANDED."
8. Add a comment line at the head of the file to remind yourself what you've done. Make sure it begins with a semi-colon.
9. Store the file.

Third, load the file and test the new Print Type table on one of your documents:

1. Press **F5** (Clear Command Line).
2. Type **LOAD** NEWFILENAME.PRN.
3. Press **F9** (Execute).
4. "Done" displays on the prompt line.
5. Open one of your document files,move the cursor into the text and press **F5** (Clear Command Line).
6. Type **PT 4** and press **F9** (Execute).
7. A bright command triangle is inserted in the text and the line lengths will adjust to accommodate the new font.
8. If you wish, move the cursor down a few more lines and switch back to normal type by inserting a **PT 1** command.
9. Print the document, or define a block that contains your commands and print that.

If you like the effect and want to use the new printer file all the time, modify the line in your STARTUP.INT file that loads the printer to load your NEWFILENAME.PRN.

A number of printers, usually the more expensive ones, handle their fonts differently than does the Epson described here. XYQUEST usually provides enhanced files with more Print Type tables to drive these sophisticated machines. When you open your printer file, you're likely to see a Print Type table that looks more like these, taken from a PostScript printer file:

```
PT=4
MD NM+12AVANT-GARDE
MD BO+12AVANT-GARDE-BOLD
MD UL+12AVANT-GARDE+UNDERLINE
MD RV+12AVANT-GARDE+FORMS
MD BU+12AVANT-GARDE-BOLD+UNDERLINE
MD BR+12AVANT-GARDE-OBLIQUE
MD SU+12AVANT-GARDE+SUPERSCRIPT
MD SD+12AVANT-GARDE+SUBSCRIPT
;
PT=5
MD NM+12BOOKMAN
MD BO+12BOOKMAN-BOLD
MD UL+12BOOKMAN+UNDERLINE
MD RV+12BOOKMAN+FORMS
MD BU+12BOOKMAN-BOLD+UNDERLINE
MD BR+12BOOKMAN-ITALIC
MD SU+12BOOKMAN+SUPERSCRIPT
MD SD+12BOOKMAN+SUBSCRIPT
;
```

"AVANT-GARDE" and "BOOKMAN" are fonts, but beyond that, each font is described in points, a typesetting measurement. Each size of type is a different font. (There are 72 points to an inch. These two fonts are 12 point type, so they print six lines to an inch if Automatic Leading is "on.")

XYQUEST provides specific information on modifying these special printer files, but the basic procedure is the same: copy the file, then add Print Tables by copying and modifying the point size or font. An additional step, creating a new Font Definition to match the new Print Table, is usually required.

Here are several Font Definitions from the same PostScript file. Each font is part of the Avant-Garde family, but is a separate entity:

```
;
FO:12AVANT-GARDE
FO) s A 12 f (
VL=14
UW:12*AVANT-GARDE
US:SUB
ET
;
FO:12AVANT-GARDE-BOLD
FO) s AB 12 f (
VL=14
UW:12*AVANT-GARDE-BOLD
US:SUB
ET
;
FO:12AVANT-GARDE-OBLIQUE
FO) s AO 12 f (
VL=14
UW:12*AVANT-GARDE-OBLIQUE
US:SUB
ET
;
FO:12AVANT-GARDE-BOLD-OBLIQUE
FO) s ABO 12 f (
VL=14
UW:12*AVANT-GARDE-BOLD-OBLIQUE
US:SUB
ET
;
```

There are two steps to building a new font for one of these printers. Say you'd like to have a 14 point Avant-Garde, a slightly larger font than the standard 12 point.

First, create a Print Type table following the procedure outlined above. Instead of changing the *name* of the font, you'd simply change the "12" in each line to "14." Don't store the file yet.

Move your cursor down to the font definition section of the file. Define and copy the entire group of Avant-Garde font definitions. In the newly copied definitions, change all the "12" entries to "14" again. They're in the lines that begin FO:, FOL, and UW.

Notice the one line in each font definition that's labeled VL=14. The VL stands for Vertical Leading, the amount of space between lines. In the standard tables, there are 14 points of leading. The type is 12 points high, so there are two points of white space ($2/72$ of an inch) between lines. For relatively small type like this, two points of leading is adequate. Change the setting of the VL line from "14" to "16" points. For large type, such as 24 point, 36 point, or larger, increase the amount of leading proportionally.

After you've entered the new font definition, store the file, then load and test the new font.

The printer file is an ideal place to insert your own personal system default settings, since they're invoked each time XyWrite is run. Here's a file, with several system defaults in place. Remember that the lines with semi-colons are comment lines; they're here to explain what the settings are:

```
;DEFAULT SETTINGS - A.C. 9/88
;EJ=1 ejects the last page of the document
;NW=1 enables automatic opening and closing of windows
;LF=1 sets line spacing so document format is reflected on-screen
;CK=3 sets the spell check function to all features on
;DT=2 sets the Page/Line Number display to "always on"
;ST=1 sets the show tabs setting to visible
;DF PT=99 sets Print Type table 99 as the default
DF EJ=1
DF NW=1
DF LF=1
```

DF CK=3
DF DT=2
DF ST=1
DF PT=99

The actual procedure for entering settings is easy, and similar to the one used for adding a Print Type table.

Again, make a copy of your printer file to hold your changes and keep your original file intact. Second, open the new printer file:

1. Press **F5** (Clear Command Line).
2. Type **CA** NEWFILENAME.PRN.
3. Press **F9** (Execute).
4. Move the cursor down to the unnamed "defaults" section, and add comment lines describing what you're going to do.
5. Type in the settings (discussed in detail in the Default section.
6. If you're changing an existing default setting, don't erase it! Just put a semi-colon in front of the old command, to turn it into a comment line.
7. Store the file.

Third, load the file and test the new defaults:

1. Press **F5** (Clear Command Line).
2. Type **LOAD** NEWFILENAME.PRN.
3. Press **F9** (Execute).
4. "Done" displays on the prompt line. If you made any errors while editing the file, error messages will display, but they flash by quickly—stay alert the first few times you load the file, to see if any pop up.

A La Carte A La Carte doesn't have any special menu functions for editing printer files. There is a special command associated with printer file loading, explained in the **Load** section. There is a special set of menus to set default values in the .DFL file, a special printer file for default values. See the Default section.

Examples   Printer files are used for many things in XyWrite. They're one of the main tools used in customizing the program to a specific application, since they're a ready vehicle for carrying default commands.

Tips   If you use several printers, remember that the default settings from the first printer file aren't automatically erased when the second printer file is loaded. They're not overwritten unless the same commands (they can have different settings, of course) are duplicated in each file. If you have unaccountable printer errors, check to make sure the system default commands in each file match.

　　Also, remember that loading different printer files can affect the way files appear on screen, due to differences in the print tables. One printer file may think **PT 5** is 12 point Helvetica; a second may interpret it as huge **72** point poster type.

　　If your printer doesn't work in XyWrite, go to DOS and issue a DIR command. Then press **Shift** and **PrtSc** to send whatever is on your monitor screen to the printer. If the directory listing doesn't print either, the problem is probably in the printer or cable. If you get the print screen function to work, but XyWrite doesn't, the problem may be in the printer file or the installation.

　　Some printers generate minor, non-fatal printer error messages. XyWrite usually interprets any printer error message as fatal and halts printing. If XyWrite interprets minor errors, try entering the line **NE=1** as a default setting in the printer file. **NE** is the **No Errors From Printer** setting. Entering the default value of **1** instructs XyWrite to ignore minor messages from the device.

Warnings   XyWrite takes full control of the printer through the printer file. It's usually a mistake to try to take control by punching the buttons on the front of the printer.

　　In the same vein, always align the perforation of tractor-feed paper with the print head. XyWrite expects to begin its page there. If you move the perforation up and down, you'll throw off all the automatic pagination and automatic line-counting features.

If your printer prints very slowly, or goes crazy when you're printing microjustified text, don't worry. It's normal for some printers to jerk, shudder, and shake. This is caused by the printer trying to adjust to the tiny partial spaces that microjustification requires. Also, microjustification, because it requires a lot of printer adjustments, can dramatically slow down the printing process.

There is a 64K file size limit on printer files. It's easy, especially for laser printer files, to reach that limit. The Hewlett-Packard, for example, has so many fonts available that three or four separate printer files are used to make them all available. If you find that you're running out of room in a file, try renaming the fonts with shorter names. You might change "PICA" to "P," or "HELVETICA" to "H."

See Counters and Printer Control

PRINTER INSERT (PI)

Overview The **PI** command lets you embed special printer commands in a text file. The printer command can be any set of characters up to 80 characters long. It can be used to shift between printer modes, draw lines or graphics, shift between different color ribbons, or draw paper from different paper bins.

Procedure The **PI** command and the **PC** command do the same thing—send special instructions to your printer. The two commands just send the message differently.

PI differs from the **PC** command in that you don't need special Printer Control strings in your printer file. The printer command is inserted with the **PI** and stays with the command:

1. Move the cursor to the point in the file where the printer action is needed.
2. Press **F5** (Clear Command Line).

3. Type **PI** PRINTERCOMMAND. The command can be up to 80 characters, one line, long.

4. Press **F9** (Execute).

5. A bright command triangle is inserted.

A La Carte The **PI** command isn't supported by the A La Carte menus. Use the standard XyWrite procedure.

Examples Every printer has slightly different features and modes of operation. You might find **PI** useful for printing multiple copies of the same document, if your printer has a "copy" function.

Other printer features you can juggle are those listed in the **PC** command section: deciding which type of device the printer should emulate, whether it should operate in text or graphics mode, which paper bin to draw from, and so on. Your printer manual should list them all, along with the printer command character strings.

Tips The **PI** command is useful for sending occasional instructions to your printer. If you need to send very long strings of characters, longer than the 80 character maximum afforded by **PI**, you should use the **PC** command.

If you send short strings, but do it fairly often, you have a choice. You could use the **PC** command, but an equally quick way to insert the commands is be to load the **PI** and its string onto a Save/Get key, so the whole command is inserted with a single key stroke combination.

See Printer Control and Printer File

PRINTING

Overview XyWrite prints a document with a **Type** command.

See Type, Typef, and Types

PRINT TYPE (PT)

Overview   Use the **PT** command to change type styles or fonts.

Procedure   The exact number of print types you have available depends on two things:

- How versatile your printer is.
- Whether your printer file supports all the printer's features and capabilities.

Modifying the standard XyWrite printer files to take advantage of all your printer has to offer is discussed in the Printer File section.

Most of the printer files that XYQUEST supplies with XyWrite support pica, elite, and proportionally spaced type. The only exceptions are those printers that are fully mechanical—daisy wheel printers, thimble printers, converted typewriters, and some laser and high-end printers.

The procedures outlined here are based on the standard XyWrite printer file configuration that's shipped with the program. That configuration calls pica type Print Type (or Print Table) 1, elite type is Print Type 2, and proportionally spaced type is Print Type 3. Pica type has 10 characters per inch and elite type has 12 characters per inch. Proportionally spaced type has letters of varying widths. To change Print Types:

1. Move the cursor to the point in the document where the type style should change.
2. Press **F5** (Clear Command Line).
3. Type **PT** # (# is the number of the Print Type—for this example, **1** [pica], **2** [elite], or **3** [proportional space]).
4. Press **F9** (Execute).
5. A bright command triangle is inserted in the text. Depending on the size of the type, the line lengths of text beyond the embedded command may adjust themselves.

A La Carte There isn't a direct link between the A La Carte menus and the printer file that's in use, so there isn't any way to pick a specific Print Table through the menus.

If you know what Print Type tables exist, you can insert a **PT** command with the menus:

1. Move the cursor to the point in the file where the font should change.
2. Press **F6** (A La Carte menus).
3. Press **R** or select **foRmat**.
4. Press **F** or select **Fonts**.
5. The Switch Font Print Type screen displays. Enter the number of the Print Table you want to use.
6. Press **Return**.
7. A bright command triangle is inserted in text.

If you're not sure what print types are available, try PT1, 2, and 3—or open the printer file following the procedure in the Printer File section.

Examples The more powerful your printer, the more you'll use the **PT** command. Most laser printers, for instance, can produce what seems to be an infinite variety of type fonts and sizes. Even the least expensive printer is usually capable of several modes. Most printer manuals usually provide samples of the full range and XyWrite's printer files usually list all the types the printer is capable of.

The **PT** command switches from one type style to another. This means that one type style can be used for main headlines, a second for sub-heads, a third for main text, a fourth for pull-outs, and so on. The number of print types available and the number of fonts you use in a document is limited only by your printer and your sense of design. Remember that a page with too many styles of type is cluttered and hard to read, not good design.

Tips   If you choose a **PT** that doesn't exist, the file may print using **PT 1** or the **PT** that was in effect just before the erroneous command was inserted.

See Printer File

PROGRAMMING

Overview   XyWrite provides two powerful programming tools. The first and the easier to use, is a keystroke recording function. This is used to automate repetitive tasks. When it's enabled, each keystroke you make is recorded and stored in a special program file. After you've stepped through a procedure, store the file. When you need to repeat the task, the program can be executed so the keystrokes are played back and the task is performed automatically.

In addition to its facility of recording keystrokes, XyWrite provides a richly-featured programming language. This section outlines the programming tools that are available.

A separate chapter of this book provides a catalog of several programs written by talented XyWriters and released into the public domain. They're excellent references and good examples of the XyWrite Program Language (XPL) at work.

These are very useful little programs. They can be executed with the **Run** command, but they're much handier if they're loaded on Save/Get keys so they can be executed with a single keystroke combination. Check the Save/Get section for directions.

The Keystroke Recorder This is an easy-to-use, almost foolproof way to write a program. And *no* programming experience is needed! All you have to know are what keys you press to perform a task.

This example shows how to write a short program that un-transposes letters:

1. Think through the steps you'd take if two letters in a word were transposed and you wanted to reorder them:
   - Put the cursor on the second letter. You'd do this manually.
   - Press **F1** to begin a defined block.
   - Press the right arrow once to move the cursor one character to the right.
   - Press **F1** again to end the defined block.
   - Press the left arrow twice to move the cursor two characters to the left.
   - Press **F8** to move the defined block.
2. Press **F5** (Clear Command Line).
3. Type **NEP** PROGRAMNAME.PGM.
4. Press **F9** (Execute).
5. Turn the keystroke recorder on by pressing **Scroll Lock**.
6. Begin pressing the keys to execute the steps you outlined. (It's safe to assume that your cursor is already on the second letter.) As you press each key, the Function Call assigned to that key is automatically entered in your file.
7. At the end of your procedure, there should be a single line of text on your screen that looks like this: **DF CR DF CL CL MV**.
8. Turn the keystroke recorder off by pressing **Scroll Lock**.
9. Store the file.

If you press the wrong key while you have the keystroke recorder on, you'll have to turn it off to correct the typo. Just press **Scroll Lock**, erase your error, and turn the recorder on again to finish the sequence. Next, test your program:

1. Call a text file to the screen.
2. Type a word, intentionally putting in a transposition.
3. Put the cursor on the second letter.
4. Press **F5** (Clear Command Line).
5. Type **RUN** PROGRAMNAME.PGM.
6. Press **F9** (Execute).
7. The letter the cursor is on and the one to its left should switch places.

Finally, an optional step to make the program readily available—load it to a Save/Get key:

1. Press **F5** (Clear Command Line).
2. Type **LDPM** PROGRAMNAME.PGM,# (The # stands for the letter or number key you want to hold the program).
3. Press **F9** (Execute).
4. "Done" displays on the prompt line.
5. **Call** a text file to the screen.
6. Type a word, intentionally putting in a transposition.
7. Put the cursor on the second letter.
8. Press **Alt** and the key to which you loaded the program.
9. The letter the cursor is on and the one to its left should switch places.

For instructions on making the Save/Get permanent, review the Save/Get chapter.

The XyWrite Program Language   This one of the major features that sets XyWrite apart from all other word processors. It's a unique feature in a word processor. Programmers find many standard tools here; curious non-programming tinkerers can have a field day. XyWrite provides seven types of programming tools:

- Commands that insert values into a program
- Save/Gets
- Flow Control Commands
- Relational Operators
- Logical Operators
- Arithmetic Operators
- String Operators

These can be combined and intertwined with XyWrite's keystroke recording facility to build a wide variety of customized applications that are run from the mother program.

In XyWrite, there are commands that insert values into a program.These commands get information from XyWrite, from a user, or from another program. They're used to pass the information into the program that's running and act on it. A listing of "values" commands includes:

Argument Insert (AS) Stores the command string that causes a program to run. Typically, a XyWrite program is started when a line like RUN PROGRAM,STRING is executed from the command line. **AS** stores the STRING part of the command for reuse by the program. You could insert the STRING into the text file the program is massaging or use it in a testing situation.

The other common way to run a program is to load it on to a Save/Get key. When the Save/Get combination is executed, **AS** checks the command line to see if a STRING is there and stores whatever it finds.

Column Location The **Column Location** of the cursor (**CL**) holds the number of the column the cursor is in when the program is executed.

Character Position The **Character Position** of the cursor (**CP**) holds the number of characters between the beginning of the file and the cursor when the program is executed. **CP** is used in the XyWrite-written program called MARK.PGM, a program that ought to be in everyone's bag of XyWrite tools. Directions for writing MARK.PGM and GOTOMARK.PGM are given in the Procedure section.

Error (ER) This is used in a True/False test that checks on the last command issued. If there was an error in the previous command, **ER** is set to TRUE. If there wasn't an error, **ER** is set to FALSE. You might use it to monitor the progress of a **Search** or a **Change** command. When all the searches or changes have been made and the command is executed one more time, XyWrite returns a "Not Found" message on the prompt line, which is an error. The **ER** condition switches from **FALSE** to **TRUE**.

Read Character (RC) The **RC** pauses the program until the operator presses a key. **RC** takes on the value of whatever key was pressed. This might be used to store the answer to a Yes/No question, when someone presses **Y** or **N**. The contents of **RC** can be referenced by other parts of the program.

Value of Variable (VA) XyWrite uses a number of variables to store file names, directory paths, and other information. **VA** accesses a variable and stores the information. You can use the contents of the variable in a program, or it can be inserted directly into text. A complete list of values is in the Value section.

Save/Gets This family of commands manipulates two of the three types of Save/Gets. They work with regular Save/Gets that are assigned to the letter and number keys and to a thousand temporary Save/Gets numbered 000 to 999. They don't work with the special &A-&Z and &0-&9 Save/Gets that are linked to function calls.

Get Save/Get (GT S/G) Inserts all the text or runs the program stored on the Save/Get key that's normally accessed by pressing **Alt** and a letter or number key.

Insert Save/Get (IS S/G) In programming, **IS** is used in an IF statement to compare the contents of two Save/Gets. If **IS** is used outside an IF statement, it functions as the regular **Insert Save/Get in Text** (**IS**) command does.

Put Value (PV S/G) When **PV** is used by itself, it functions much like the **Get Save/Get** command. **PV** inserts the text contents of a Save/Get one character at a time. (**GT** inserts the text as a block.) If a program is assigned to the Save/Get, **PV** executes the program. If **PV** is used inside an expression, such as an IF statement, it reads the expression, typically a temporary Save/Get, and generates a numeric result.

Save Subroutine (SU S/G, String) **SU** saves a fragment of a program string, such as an executable **Save** or **Call** command, to the named Save/Get. The subroutine can then be executed as another step in the program with the **GT** command.

Save String (SV S/G, String) SV operates like **SU**, except the string characters that are saved are stored as text, not as a part of the program.

Save Numeric (SX S/G, Numeric) SX is a cousin of **SV** and **SU**, but it only stores numeric expressions.

The following group of flow control commands regulate the progress of a program:

Exit and Continue (EX) EX is used to end a subroutine and return to the main program. If it's used in the main program, it stops the program.

Exit and Stop (EX1) EX1 halts the program.

Go to Label (GL Label) GL works with the **LB** command. It causes the program to jump to the specified label.

If Condition and End If (IF EXPRESSION TRUEBRANCH EI FALSEBRANCH) This command contains two parts, **IF** and **EI**. **IF** is self-explanatory—it sets the stage to evaluate a statement and determine if it's TRUE or FALSE. If the statement is TRUE, the program continues. If it's FALSE, the program jumps to the **EI** command and goes on from there.

Label (LB Label) LB is the front part of the **GL** command. **LB** identifies the place in the program that the **GL** jumps to. The label can be any length. **LB** can also be used to comment on the program, identifying what is going on.

Relational Operators These are used with **PV** to compare two numeric expressions, or with **IS** to compare to string expressions:

- Equal ==
- Not equal <>
- Greater than >
- Less than <

- Greater than or equal >=
- Less than or equal <=

Logical Operators These are boolean operators that evaluate numeric or string expressions. They're used within IF statements:

- Or !
- And **&**
- Exclusive Or **@XOR**
- Not **@NOT**
- Convert letters to uppercase **@UPR**
- Takes a key read by RC and converts it to a function call **@CNV**
- Returns a value equal to the number of characters in a string **@SIZ**

Arithmetic Operators These are the four operators that are used on numeric values:

- Add +
- Subtract -
- Multiply *
- Divide /

String Operators These are the two operators that are used on two string expressions:

- Concatenate (join) +
- String exists within a string ∈

Procedure Providing a full tutorial on programming is beyond the scope of this book. Actually creating a program, however, relies on a small set of operations. This example shows how to write two simple programs that insert a marker in text and return the cursor to the marker. Other good examples of programming, more involved, are provided in the Program chapter.

First, create the marker. Use the **Save Numeric** command and let the **Character Position** command generate the numeric expression:

1. Press **F5** (Clear Command Line).
2. Type **NEP** PROGRAMNAME.PGM. "MARKER.PGM" identifies the program nicely.
3. Shift to Expanded Display by pressing **Ctrl** and **F9** and press **F5** (Clear Command Line).
4. Type **SX 999** (Save Numeric in temporary Save/Get 999).
5. Press **F9** (Execute). «SX999» appears on the screen.
6. Move the cursor onto the second European quote and press **,** (the comma).
7. Press **F5** (Clear Command Line) and type **CP** (**Character Position**).
8. Press **F9** (Execute). «SX999,«CP»» appears on the screen.
9. Store the program.

Next, create the program that returns you to the marker:

1. Press **F5** (Clear Command Line).
2. Type **NEP** PROGRAMNAME.PGM. "GOTOMARK.PGM" works well.
3. Shift to Expanded Display by pressing **Ctrl** and **F9** and press **F5** (Clear Command Line).
4. Toggle the keystroke recorder on by pressing **Scroll Lock** then press **F5**, type **jmp**, and press **F9**.
5. **BC** jmp **PC** should appear on screen.
6. Toggle the keystroke recorder off by pressing **Scroll Lock**.
7. Move the cursor onto the **XC** and press **Spacebar**.
8. Press **F5** (Clear Command Line) and type **PV 999** (Put Variable, contents of Save Get 999).
9. Press **F9** (Execute). «PV999» appears on the screen. Then store the program.

A La Carte Program features aren't available through the A La Carte menus. Use the standard XyWrite procedure.

P

Examples   XyWrite's programming facility can be used to automate many every day tasks, and to greatly enhance the power of the program. Look in the separate Programming chapter for a sampler of how XYQUEST programmers and XyWrite users have put the XyWrite Program Language to work.

Tips   If you've never even thought about writing a program, don't automatically assume you can't do this.

XyWrite's keystroke recorder might be the easiest way in the world to write a program. Start with that! You'll be able to build a host of useful tools that are customized for your particular application.

Also, since every XyWrite program is an ASCII file you can call to the screen and edit, don't be afraid to peek inside other people's programs. All the programs reproduced in this book are in the public domain or are used with XYQUEST's permission, so they can all be modified as you wish.

See Call Program, New Program, Pausing during execution, Program Function Call, Programs chapter, Run, Save/Gets, and Values

---

PROMPT (PR)

Overview   **PR** is embedded in a regular text file to display a message when the file is printed. Use it to tell the user what to do next, or to pass along some other message.

Procedure   1. Move the cursor to the place in the document where the message should appear.
2. Press **F5** (Clear Command Line).
3. Type **PR** MESSAGE.
4. A bright command triangle is inserted in the text.
5. When the file prints, the message displays on the prompt line.

A La Carte The **PR** command isn't available through the A La Carte menus. Use the standard XyWrite procedure.

Examples   If your printer is a distance from your computer, such as you find in an office with a large networked group of PCs, insert a **PA** at the end of your documents that says "Printing is Complete." It'll save you time waiting around the printer for your document.

See Pause

PUT EDIT AND PUT EDIT VERIFY (PE AND PEV)

Overview   The **PE** and **PEV** commands are the final step in redlining, the electronic editing process built into XyWrite. They insert edits into the document by changing the special redlining modes in which the edits were written, to whatever text mode is in effect.

Procedure   The **PE** command inserts all edits, from the cursor position to the end of the file. The **PEV** moves from one edit to the next, giving you the choice to insert or not insert each edit. To insert all edits:

1. Move the cursor to the point where you want to being inserting edits—typically the beginning of the file.
2. Press **F5** (Clear Command Line).
3. Type **PE**.
4. Press **F9** (Execute).
5. All the edits are automatically inserted in the text.

   To insert individual edits:

1. Move the cursor to the point where you want to begin inserting edits—typically the beginning of the file.
2. Press **F5** (Clear Command Line).
3. Type **PEV**.
4. Press **F9** (Execute).

5. The cursor moves to the first edit and a menu displays on the prompt line. Press:
- **A** to **Abort** the edit-insert process. The cursor returns to the starting point.
- **Q** to **Quit** the edit-insert process. The cursor stays at the current location.
- **S** to **Stop** the edit-insert process *after* the current change is inserted. The cursor returns to the starting point.
- **N** to signal "**No,** do not insert the change." The cursor goes on to the next choice.
- **Y** to signal "**Yes,** insert the edit" and move the cursor to the next choice.
- **U** to **Undo** this change and go on to the next choice.

A La Carte   Redlining functions are not supported by A La Carte menus. Use the standard XyWrite procedure.

Examples   "Redlining" is XyWrite's term— and tool—for revising documents. The redlining function allows other people to insert comments or changes in an electronic document. When a copy of the file is returned to the author, the edits can be reviewed, inserted with these **PE** and **PEV** commands, or erased with the **Clear Edits** (**CE**) and **Clear Edits Verify** (**CEV**) commands.

See Clear Edits and Redlining

PUT FIELD (PF)

Overview   **Put Field** is used in mail merge operations to identify and to place fields in the main file. When the main file is merged with a data file, the fields are filled in with the data file's unique information.

Procedure   1. Move the cursor to the point in the main file where the field should be inserted.
2. Press **F5** (Clear Command Line).

3. Type **PF** FIELDNAME.
4. Press **F9** (Execute).
5. A bright command triangle and a non-printing field label are inserted in the text.

Alternate procedure:

1. Move the cursor to the point in the main file where the field should be inserted.
2. Press **F5** (Clear Command Line).
3. Type **PF**.
4. Press **F9** (Execute).
5. A window opens so you can type in the filed label. Press **F3** when you're done.
6. A bright command triangle and a non-printing field label are inserted in the text.

A La Carte Mail merge operations are not directly supported by the A La Carte menus. Use the regular XyWrite procedure.

Examples   If you use mail merge for any operations, **PF** is an essential. It's the command that links a blank in your main file (the "letter") with information from the data file (the addresses, product information, or whatever personalizes the letter).

Warnings   For mail merge to work, the field names you insert with **PF** and those in the **FI** (**Field Identification**) embedded command must be an exact match. Check for misspellings.

See Field Identification and Mail Merge

PUT (EXECUTE) A FUNCTION CALL (PFUNC)

Overview   **PFUNC** is a shortcut normally used when editing a XyWrite program file. **PFUNC** executes any function call from a program just as **FUNC** does from the command line. It can be inserted in the file without shifting into programming mode.

Procedure   To use **PFUNC**, you should have a program file open on your screen. The beauty of the command is that you needn't have opened the program file with the standard **CAP** command:

1. Move the cursor to the point in the program where you want the function call executed.
2. Press **F5** (Clear Command Line).
3. Type **PFUNC** FUNCTIONCALL.
4. Press **F9** (Execute).
5. Store the program.
6. When the program is run, the function call is executed as if it was a regular program function.

A La Carte Programming functions aren't supported by the A La Carte menus. Use the standard XyWrite procedure.

Examples   **PFUNC** is ideal for those situations when you need to make a minor change in a program and simply forgot to open the file with a **CAP** command. Instead of closing the file and reopening it, **PFUNC** can insert the necessary change.

Tips   **PFUNC** is useful for tune-ups, but it doesn't come close to replacing the full-blown program mode for usefulness. It is ideal for simple routines that depend on established function calls.

See Function Calls and Programming

QUIT

Overview **Quit** ends your XyWrite session by shutting down the program.

Procedure 1. Press **F5** (Clear Command Line).
2. Type Quit.
3. Press **F9** (Execute).
4. If any files are open, XyWrite tells you and asks if you want to quit anyway. If you press **Y**, the program shuts down, aborting the open file. Any changes you made to it since the last save are lost. If you want to check on the open files, press **N**. Pressing **Ctrl** and **F10** displays the Window Menu which lists any open files. You can either go to the window and close the file, or abandon the menu and issue the **Quit** command again.
5. Your operating system prompt displays.

A La Carte
1. Press **F6** (A La Carte menus).
2. Press **X** or **W**, or select **XyWrite**.
3. Press **Q** or select **Quit**.
4. The Quit XyWrite screen displays.
5. Press **Y** or select **Yes** to quit, or press **N** or select **No** to remain in the program.

RAGGED TYPE

See Flush Left, Flush Right, and Flush Center

RECORD SEPARATOR (RS)

Overview   XyWrite uses two carriage returns to mark the end of each record in a mail merge data file. You can change this default with the **RS** command.

Procedure   The **RS** command and its companion, the **Field Separator** (FS), are entered in a printer file. When the file is loaded into memory, the commands take effect.

NOTE: By changing the **RS** setting, you change the parameters of any existing data files that use the default. If you don't want to change your data files to match the new setting, consider building a printer file with nothing in it but your separator settings:

1. Open the printer file just as you would a text file, with the **Call** command.
2. Your printer file may already have a **RS** entry. Check by issuing a **Search** command:
   • Press **F5** (Clear Command Line).
   • Type **SE** /RS/.
   • Press **F9** (Execute).
3. The search will probably fail and return a "Not Found" message. If an entry exists, your cursor moves to it (if you have an entry, skip the next few creation steps and modify your existing settings).
4. Move your cursor to a clear area near the top of the printer file.
5. Type a semi-colon and a brief note describing the new separator setting. If your note is longer than one line, end each line with a carriage return and begin each one with a semi-colon.
6. Type **RS** SEPARATOR.
7. Use the **Store** command to close the file.
8. Load the file with the **Load** command.

A La Carte There aren't any special A La Carte menu commands for the **RS** command. Use the standard XyWrite procedure.

Examples   Unless you import a data file from a very unusual program, you'll probably never have to change this setting, since most database programs use the same default setting as XyWrite—two carriage returns.

If you do, it may be more practical to execute a **Change (CH)** command to replace the unusual character in the imported file with XyWrite's double carriage returns.

Tips   If you need to change the defaults with **RS**, think about putting the setting in a separate printer file from the one you normally use. That way the XyWrite default is preserved for use with mail merge files that don't require the unusual default. And you can load the small special file in an instant when you need to.

Creating the file is simple. Just create a file as you normally do. Convention dictates that the file have a .PRN extension for identification, but even that's not required.

The first line of the file must have an identifying code of a semi-colon, a PR, and another semi-colon, like this: ;PR;

After that unique first line, follow the procedure outlined in the first part of this section for inserting the **RS** command and the new separator characters. Remember that any comment lines must fit on one line, begin with a semi-colon and end with a carriage return; word wrap is not allowed.

See Defaults, Field Separator, and Mail Merge

REDLINING (RED ON AND RED OFF)

Overview   Redlining draws its name from the legal field. When attorneys revise a document, they may draw a red line through lines that should be deleted.

In XyWrite, redlining provides a sophisticated way for a document to be revised. Edits can be suggested in XyWrite, then inserted or deleted at the author's discretion. The suggestions can be additions to the original document or deletions from it.

Procedure

The editing process usually consists of at least three steps: preparing the first draft, editing and revising, and reviewing the edits and preparing the second draft. These steps, of course, are often repeated several times.

Redlining is tailor-made to provide a useful function for both the people who write the drafts and those who edit them. Thoughtfully used, redlining speeds up the editing process while maintaining an edit audit trail of changes, including who suggested what.

Three commands are used in redlining:

- **Red On** and **Red Off** to toggle the feature so edits can be suggested and bundled into the text.
- **Clear Edits** (**CE**) and **Clear Edits Verify** (**CEV**) to delete suggestions.
- **Put Edits** (**PE**) and **Put Edits Verify** (**PEV**) to incorporate suggestions.

There aren't any special steps involved in creating a document that's going to be redlined. Just prepare it as you usually would. It's prudent to make a copy of the finished original and rename it so there is a baseline document preserved without any changes.

There's only one difference between editing with redlining and editing without—executing the **Red On** command. Once redlining is turned on, anything that's done to the original document is done in a special format that keeps it separate until the author decides to keep the change or delete it.

To turn redlining on:

1. Press **F5** (Clear Command Line).
2. Type **RED** ON.
3. Press **F9** (Execute).

4. A capital R displays in the upper right corner of the monitor to indicate that redlining is on.

To turn redlining off:

1. Press **F5** (Clear Command Line).
2. Type **RED** OFF.
3. Press **F9** (Execute).
4. The capital R in the upper right corner of the monitor disappears.

As edits are made, deletions and additions are marked with special display modes. Nothing is actually deleted; it's converted to another hidden mode. All other XyWrite functions work as they normally do. If the document is printed, for instance, the deletions and additions print in special modes that reflect their status. There are two exceptions:

- Redlining doesn't work in the expanded display mode. It only functions in normal display.
- Redlining is active in whatever window the **Red On** command is executed in. It's not activated for an editing session. If redlining is active and you shift to a different window, redlining doesn't go with you.

After a document has been reviewed and edits have been made, you can decide to include or ignore the comments and deletions. You have three choices—accept everything as it stands, accept selected edits, or ignore all the suggestions.

Reviewing edits usually follows a fairly fixed pattern, depending on your work environment. It's a good idea to copy and rename the redlined document just as you did the first draft. This copy adds to the edit audit trail so you can track changes from version to version. (See the **Compare** command section for information.)

Most people review the entire document without touching the edits on their first pass. If any of the edits trigger ideas that the reviewer didn't cover, turn redlining on yourself so your second pass changes are recorded. If you're maintaining an edit audit, make a third copy of the file for your archive.

After the overall thrust of the edits is understood, execute the **Put Edit Verify** (**PEV**) command to go through the document from one edit to the next. You can accept selected comments on an individual basis. For some documents, in situations where there is no discretion, executing the **Put Edit** (**PE**) command to accept all edits unconditionally is quicker.

Once the edits you want to use are in place, you can erase the ones you don't want. A **Clear Edits** (**CE**) command removes all the remaining unused edits at once. To keep some of the remaining edits in place a little longer, perhaps because they raised issues that need to be clarified, use the **Clear Edits Verify** (**CEV**) command to selectively clear the unneeded comments.

A La Carte   Redlining functions aren't available through the A La Carte menus. Use the standard XyWrite procedure.

Examples   Too much paper on your desk? You can begin reducing the quantity with redlining. If documents are constantly being revised, edited, and approved in your work, XyWrite's redlining function can also increase the speed with which changes are incorporated and paperwork is processed.

The type of work done in legal offices, real estate offices, newspapers and magazines, technical document preparation, and a host of other sites lends itself to redlining.

Tips   Edit audit trails are mentioned in the Procedure section. If it's important to keep track of who is making what change when, this is critical:

- Make a copy of the document when it first goes out, so you have a record of the original.
- Make another copy when the first revisions come in.
- Make a third copy after the revisions are in place and the second (and the third, and the fourth) draft is ready for review.

- If there's any question about the document and how it was prepared later on, you can pinpoint the change.

For security, and to keep as much space as possible available on your hard disk, it's a good idea to make the copy on a floppy disk. Keeping the edit audit trail on floppy also increases its security, since it's not automatically available on the computer.

If copies of a document go out to many people for review and you want to keep their comments straight, you have a couple options. The first is to incorporate each reviewer's comments individually into a single master file. This typically involves using the XyWrite **Compare** feature or juggling lots of paper. It's a little clunky but it's manageable if your work group isn't huge.

Another option involves juggling display modes. XyWrite keeps redlining comments separate from the text by using different display modes. This table shows what the standard display modes are and what the linked redlining modes are. The Standard display is the mode used by XyWrite when the text is prepared. The Insert and Delete modes are inserted automatically when a change is made when redlining is on. (See the Display section for a comprehensive description of display modes.) Remember that these modes vary from computer to computer and printer to printer. Your settings may not match these exactly.

TABLE 15   **Insert and Delete Modes**

MODE NAME	STANDARD	REDLINE INSERT	REDLINE DELETE
Normal	MD NM	MD IN	MN DN
Bold	MD BO	MD IB	MN DB
Underline	MD UL	MD IU	MN DU
Reverse (form)	MD RV	MD IR	MN DR
Bold underline	MD BU	MD IL	MN DL
Bold reverse	MD BR	MD IV	MN DV
Superscript	MD SU	MD IS	MN DS
Subscript	MD SD	MD ID	MN DD

It's possible to customize each reviewer's printer file so that each person inserts and deletes in a unique color or prints with a unique font or attribute. Again, this is practical if you have good equipment that can support what might be several hundred different modes.

Third, you can create a customized keyboard or set of Save/Gets that automatically insert each person's initials or name with their comment.

Finally, there's a great little program designed just for work-group editing and revision that integrates very well with XyWrite. It's For Comment, published by Broderbund Software. For Comment is designed for one purpose—to allow many people to make changes to a document.

Each person in a work group receives a copy of the original on floppy disk. They make their changes with For Comment's mini word processor and return the disk to the author. The author runs a simple program that incorporates each reviewer's comments into a separate file while keeping the comments isolated. The author then pages through and uses or ignores the comments, just as he or she would in XyWrite. Finally, the completed document is imported back into XyWrite for final polishing and printing.

The program—and the process—works well and the program is inexpensive. If your material is edited by many people on a regular basis, look at this option.

If you use redlining fairly often, why not remap a keyboard key so you can turn the feature on and off with a single keystroke? See the section on Keyboard Files for instructions. The function call to use is **RO.**

Remember that XyWrite can be set to make backup copies of files automatically, with the **BK=1** default setting. (This is entirely different from making a copy and renaming it. The automatic backup setting keeps the last edited version on disk until it's overwritten the next time the file is edited. Making a copy of the file and renaming it keeps it from being changed unless you do it intentionally.)

See Clear Edits, Clear Edits Verify, Put Edits, and Put Edits Verify

355

REFERENCES IN TEXT

Overview   XyWrite tracks your chapters and pages automatically, so you can refer readers to a different part of your document. You can also track other text elements such as illustrations, tables, or footnotes, so their locations can be inserted in text.

The location-tracking feature uses two linked commands, an "anchor" that is inserted in the text that's referred to (the subject text), and a reference command inserted in the "reference text" that directs readers to the subject text.

Procedure   There are two types of "anchors" in XyWrite: labels and labeled counters (a counter that's identified by its own label). There are three types of reference commands: to a page, to a chapter, and to a counter.

Building a document reference is a two-part operation. First, use the **Label (LB)** command to identify the text element, or use the **C#** command to insert a labeled counter in text. Second, use one of the reference commands—**Reference Page**, **Reference Chapter**, or **Reference Counter** in your text. (All five commands are explained in their own sections.) The **Reference Page (REP)** reports the page number of the anchor. The **Reference Chapter (REC)** reports the chapter number of the anchor. The **Reference Counter (REF)** reports the value a labeled counter. Counters are always used in a numbering operation, so they always contain a value. The **REF** command can't be used with a label because a label is an identification tool; it doesn't have a value. (There is one exception, footnotes, and it is discussed in the **Reference Counter** section Tips area.)

This table shows what type of "anchor" works with which reference command:

TABLE 16

Anchors

LABEL	LABELED	COUNTER
REP (Page)	Yes	Yes
REC (Chapter)	Yes	Yes
REF (Counter)	No	Yes

Examples

The **REP** and **REC** commands track the pages and chapters that hold labels and counters, the **REF** command can keep track of almost anything. You can use a labeled counter to identify any text element, a footnote, figure, illustration, or chart, for instance.

If you wish, you can link all the reference commands in the same sentence to generate a line like:

See Page 77 in Chapter 8, Foofoo Goes for a Walk.

In expanded display mode, the line might look like this:

See Page «REPJOHN»in Chapter «RECWALKING», Foofoo Goes for a Walk.

Tips

The reference commands generate just the number of the page, chapter, or counter. They don't generate any text. You have to supply the words that identify the reference. Remember to include a space in your text to separate the number from the last word you type.

The **Reference Chapter** command is intended to be used with a special counter, **C0**, which is only used to track chapter numbers. Read the **Counters** section for instructions on inserting the command.

Warnings

If you're operating in a single file, the references and labels can be placed anywhere within the file— a reference on page 1 can refer to a label on page 8. If you're working in a large document with multiple files that are chained together, however, there's a problem. A reference can only refer to a label that occurs in a previous file, not in one that comes after it in the document. This means you can't insert an automatic reference in chapter 4 to something that exists in chapter 8. A reference in chapter 8 that refers to an element in chapter 4 works fine.

XyWrite doesn't check to see if there is more than one label with the same name. If your reference doesn't generate the proper number, check to be sure you haven't created two labels with the same name.

See Counters, Label, Numbering, Reference Chapter, Reference Counter, and Reference Page

---

REFERENCE CHAPTER (REC)

Overview   The **REC** command is XyWrite's specialized tool for keeping track of chapters that are referred to in text. **REC** tracks labels and counters assigned to chapters and generates the proper chapter number.

Procedure   Using **REC** is a two-part procedure. First, use the **CO0** command with an attached label to identify the chapter. Second, use **Reference Counter** (**REC**) in your text to call out that chapter's number. Insert a counter:

1. Move the cursor to the beginning of the chapter you want to track.
2. Press **F5** (Clear Command Line).
3. Type **C0** LABELNAME (the **LABELNAME** must be unique).
4. Press **F9** (Execute).
5. The labeled counter is inserted in the text. It does not print out.

When you're ready to refer to the chapter:

1. Type the text that refers to the chapter (**See Chapter** ...).
2. Press **F5** (Clear Command Line).

3. Type **REC** LABELNAME.
4. Press **F9** (Execute).
5. A bright command triangle is inserted in text.
6. When the document is printed, the reference command prints the appropriate chapter number.

A La Carte First, insert the label:

1. Press **F6** (A La Carte menus).
2. Press **E** or select **Edit**.
3. Press **R** or select **Reference**.
4. The Reference Labels screen displays.
5. Press **C** or move the cursor to the "**label tied to a counter**" entry.
6. Press **Return.** You're prompted for a unique LABELNAME.
7. Press the down arrow to move to the Counter number blank. Type **0**. (Counter set 0 is reserved for chapter numbering.)
8. Press **Return** to insert the labeled counter in text.
9. The label is inserted in text.

Second, insert the chapter reference:

1. Move the cursor to the place where the reference should appear.
2. Press **F6** (A La Carte menus).
3. Press **E** or select **Edit**.
4. Press **R** or select **Reference**.
5. The Reference Labels screen displays.
6. Press **H** or move the cursor to the "**cHapter reference**" entry.
7. Press **Return.** You're prompted for the chapter's LABELNAME. Type it in and press **Return** again.
8. The reference is inserted in text.

Examples   **REC** tracks a chapter which is referred to in the text. The label it refers to is inserted at the beginning of the chapter text itself. No matter how many chapters are inserted between the labeled counter and the **REC**, **REC** keeps identifying the proper chapter number for you.

Tips The **REC** command can also report what chapter number labels or other labeled counters (besides the C0 set) occur in. To keep track of any other element, just insert the item's LABELNAME in place of the chapter's. No matter what chapter the label or counter occurs in, the proper chapter number appears where the **REC** command is inserted.

See Counters, Numbering, and References in text

REFERENCE COUNTER (REF)

Overview The **REF** command is one of XyWrite's three tools for keeping track of text elements that are referred to in text. **REF** is used to track labeled counters inserted in text to mark passages, illustrations, or other elements. When the element is mentioned in the text, **REF** is used to identify it by its number.

Procedure Using **REF** is a two-part procedure. First, use the **C#** command to identify the text element. Second, use **Reference Counter** in your text to call in the value of the labeled counter:

The **REF** command doesn't report the exact position of a text element in a document, it reports the value of a counter that keeps track of how many elements are identified.

Suppose you were including charts in a document. You can number them automatically (for example, Chart 1, Chart 2...) with a **C#** command. If you also label the counter, you can refer your readers to the proper chart number ("See Chart 2") even though you don't know how many charts you'll use before you finish the document, or where they'll be placed.

If you label one chart "profits" and a second chart "losses" you can use the **REF** command to refer to them by chart number, even though the number is generated by the program. The "See Chart 2" line is actually generated by a **REF** command that keeps track of the chart labeled "losses." If you insert another chart, or a hundred charts between "profit" and "losses," your reference to

"See Chart #" is still accurate because the program keeps track of the current number of charts and keeps your reference up to date.

First, insert a labeled counter by the element you want to track (the "chart"). You can also label a counter and use that name, instead of having to insert both a counter and a label command to identify the same element. This would be more convenient if you were automatically numbering charts or illustrations in your document.

Labeling a counter is explained in the section on Counters, but the basics are the same as when using the **LB** command:

1. Move the cursor to the counter location.
2. Press **F5** (Clear Command Line).
3. Type **C#** LABELNAME. (**#** stands for the number of the counter used, 1-14. The **LABELNAME** must be unique.)
4. Press **F9** (Execute).
5. The labeled counter is inserted in the text.

Insert **REF** in text when you're ready to refer to the labeled text item:

1. Type the text that refers back to the labeled text item (**See Chart** ...).
2. Press **F5** (Clear Command Line).
3. Type **REF** LABELNAME.
4. Press **F9** (Execute).
5. A bright command triangle is inserted in text.
6. When the document is printed, the reference command prints the appropriate number.

A La Carte First, insert the labeled counter :

1. Press **F6** (A La Carte menus).
2. Press **E** or select **Edit**.
3. Press **R** or select **Reference**.
4. The Reference Labels screen displays.
5. Press **C** or move the cursor to the "**label tied to Counter**" entry.

6. Press **Return.** You're prompted for a unique LABELNAME. Type it in and press **Return** again.
7. The label or counter is inserted in text.

Second, insert the reference:

1. Move the cursor to the place where the **REF** should appear.
2. Press **F6** (A La Carte menus).
3. Press **E** or select **Edit.**
4. Press **R** or select **Reference.**
5. The Reference Labels screen displays.
6. Press **R** or move the cursor to the "**Reference to counter**" entry.
7. Press **Return.** You're prompted for the LABELNAME. Type it in and press **Return** again.
8. The reference is inserted in text.

Examples   **REF** tracks a text element other than a page or chapter that is referred to in the text. Most often, this is a footnote, illustration, or chart. You'd use **REF** to create a line that reads "See Figure 1-2." The **REF** command would be inserted in the actual text. The counter it refers to is embedded by the figure.

No matter how many more figures are inserted into the document between the labeled counter and the **REF**, **REF** keeps identifying the proper figure for you.

Tips   If you're going to make extensive use of this feature be sure to review the chapter on numbering. You'll want to set up a numbering scheme that is easy to use, easy to remember, and probably one that can be built into a set of Save/Gets.

You can also use the **REF** command to refer readers to a particular footnote. For this particular application, you embed a **Label** (**LB**) command in the footnote itself instead of using a **C#** command. The very first character of the footnote must be the **LB** command.

Once that's taken care of, use the **REF** command as outlined in the procedure here, referring to the footnote by it's label, just as the labeled counter is. A line like "See footnote number 6" results.

Warnings   XyWrite doesn't check to make sure that the label name you use is unique. If the reference doesn't print with the right page number, check to be sure that you haven't created two labels with the same name.

See Counters, Numbering, and References in text

REFERENCE PAGE (REP)

Overview   The **REP** command is XyWrite's specialized tool for keeping track of what page holds a particular text passage that is referred to in text. **REP** tracks labels assigned to text elements and reports their location when the document is printed.

Procedure   Using **REP** is a two-part procedure. First, use the **Label** command to identify the text element. Second, use **Reference Page** in your text to call out the text's location. Insert a label:

1. Move the cursor to the text item you want to track.
2. Press **F5** (Clear Command Line).
3. Type **LB** LABELNAME (the **LABELNAME** must be unique).
4. Press **F9** (Execute).
5. The label is inserted in the text. It does not print out.

Insert **REP** in text when you're ready to refer to the text again:

1. Type the text that refers to the passage (**See page** ...).
2. Press **F5** (Clear Command Line).
3. Type **REP** LABELNAME.
4. Press **F9** (Execute).
5. A bright command triangle is inserted in text.

6. When the document is printed, the reference command prints the appropriate page number.

A La Carte   First, insert the label in the text:

1. Move the cursor to the beginning of the passage you want to track.
2. Press **F6** (A La Carte menus).
3. Press **E** or select **Edit**.
4. Press **R** or select **Reference**.
5. The Reference Labels screen displays.
6. Press **T** or move the cursor to the "**label in Text**" entry.
7. Press **Return**. You're prompted for a unique LABELNAME. Type it in and press **Return** again.
8. The label is inserted in text.

Second, insert the page reference:

1. Move the cursor to the place where the reference should appear.
2. Press **F6** (A La Carte menus).
3. Press **E** or select **Edit**.
4. Press **R** or select **Reference**.
5. The Reference Labels screen displays.
6. Press **P** or move the cursor to the "**Page reference**" entry.
7. Press **Return**. You're prompted for the text's LABELNAME. Type it in and press **Return** again.
8. The reference is inserted in text.

Examples   **REP** tracks a text passage that's referred to elsewhere in the text. The label it refers to is embedded in the text itself. Then, no matter how many pages are inserted between the labeled text and the **REP**, **REP** keeps identifying the proper location for you.

See Counters, Numbering, and References in text

RELATIVE TABS (RT)

Overview   **RT** is a default setting that determines whether tab stops are established relative to the edge of the paper or to the left margin.

Procedure   Since **RT** is a default setting, you can enter the command in your printer file or in your STARTUP.INT file. If you do, the tab setting remains the same each time XyWrite starts. For complete instructions, see the Procedure portion of the Default listing.

You can also issue **RT** from the command line to set tab stops for a single editing session:

1. Press **F5** (Clear Command Line).
2. Type **DEFAULT** RT=1 (**0** is the regular default, setting tab stops relative to the page—a **1** toggles the setting "on" to make tab stops relative to the left margin).
3. Press **F9** (Execute).
4. "Done" displays on the prompt line.

A La Carte You must be in an empty window (have a blank screen) to access the default menus.

1. Press **F6** (A La Carte menus).
2. Press **X** or select **XyWrite**.
3. Press **D** or select **Defaults**.
4. The View and Change Defaults screen displays.
5. Press **N** or **S** or select **defaults N-S**.
6. Move the cursor to the **RT** entry and type **0** or **1** to turn **Relative Tabs** off or on.
7. Press **Return**. The Update Default File screen displays. You're asked if you want to make the default settings permanent.
8. Press **Y** or **N**. If you select **Y**, the program writes the new default settings to a special file and returns you to the A La Carte Menu Screen. If you select **N**, the settings are used for the current edit session.

Examples XyWrite's **Relative Tab** can seem confusing at first glance. Most people assume a tab stop is a tab stop. The **RT** setting gives you more flexibility than simply setting a tab position.

In the standard XyWrite setup, if you have a left margin set to a number greater than eight and you look at the ruler line on the XyWrite screen, you'll probably see a triangular tab stop symbol to the left of your margin. That's because the standard XyWrite configuration is **RT=0**, or "off." The tab stops are spaced at eight-character intervals across the top of the screen and the top of the page of paper.

If you turn **RT** on, the tab stops are measured from the left margin, wherever it happens to be. If a tab stop is set eight characters in from the margin, it will continue to be eight characters in even if the margin setting changes.

See Tabs and Defaults

REMOVE

Overview **Remove** erases a single Save/Get from memory. It doesn't affect the permanent file of Save/Gets that's stored on disk.

Procedure 1. Press **F5** (Clear Command Line).
2. Type **REMOVE** KEY (**KEY** is the single letter or number key that holds the Save/Get you want to remove).
3. Press **F9** (Execute).
4. "Done" displays on the prompt line.

The change isn't permanent unless you use the **STSGT** command to store the modification on disk for reuse. See the Save/Get section or the **STSGT** listing for details.

A La Carte The A La Carte menus support the Save/Get commands, except **Remove**. Use the standard XyWrite procedure.

Examples   The **Remove** command is used most often to edit the permanent file of Save/Gets that's usually loaded each time XyWrite starts. Many times your Save/Get needs change and you'll want to clear out some keys that aren't used very often.

You can, of course, just load a new Save/Get to that key and overwrite the old command, but if you don't have an application in mind, you can streamline things with **Remove**.

See Save/Gets

REMOVE DIRECTORY (RMDIR)

Overview   XyWrite's **Remove Directory** command works exactly like the DOS command that erases directories.

Procedure   The operation and syntax of **RMDIR** is the same as the corresponding DOS command and the rules are the same. There can't be any files in the directory and you can't remove a directory that you're in.

1. Press **F5** (Clear Command Line).
2. Type **RMDIR** DRIVE:DIRECTORYNAME.
3. Press **F9** (Execute).
4. "Done" displays on the prompt line.

You can also point-and-shoot at the directory you want to remove with the **Tree** command:

1. Press **F5** (Clear Command Line).
2. Type **TREE**.
3. A graphic representation of the file system displays.
4. Press **F5** (Clear Command Line).
5. Type **RMDIR**.
6. Press **F10** to move the cursor into the directory listings.
7. Move the cursor to the directory you want to remove.

8. Press **F9** (Execute).
9. "Done" displays on the prompt line.

A La Carte
1. Press **F6** (A La Carte menus).
2. Press **D** or select **Dir**.
3. Press **R** or select **Remove**.
4. The Remove Directory screen displays. Type in the complete path name of the directory to erase.
5. Press **Return**.
6. The directory is removed.

Examples   This is another of XyWrite's file manipulation commands that let you change your file structure without leaving the program. It's the opposite of **MKDIR**, the command that creates directories.

See Make Directory, Change Directory, and Tree

REMOVE SCREEN (RS)

Overview   **RS** allows you to close an inactive window without going through the Window Management menu. It's needed to manage windows in manual mode.

Procedure   1. Clear the window with the **Store** or **Abort** command.
2. Press **F5** (Clear Command Line).
3. Type **RS**.
4. Press **F9** (Execute).
5. The empty window closes and you're returned to the window that was last active.

A La Carte A La Carte uses the standard XyWrite Window Management menu to open and close windows (accessed by pressing **F10**), so there aren't any special A La Carte procedures for the **RS** command. Use the standard XyWrite procedure.

Examples   If you don't have the **New Window** (**NW**) setting turned "on" you should make a habit of closing windows when you're through with them.

Tips   If you haven't experimented with the **NW** setting that opens and closes windows automatically, try it. Many people find it less cumbersome than juggling them manually.

See Windows and New Windows Setting

RENAME

Overview   **Rename** is a file management command that lets you change the name of a file that's stored on disk without leaving XyWrite. It operates exactly like the DOS Rename command.

Procedure   The operation and syntax of **Rename** is the same as the corresponding DOS command. The file to be renamed must stay in its directory:

1. Press **F5** (Clear Command Line).
2. Type **RENAME** OLDNAME NEWNAME.
3. Press **F9** (Execute).
4. "Done" displays on the prompt line.

A La Carte   You must be in an open window (have a blank screen) to rename a file:

1. Press **F6** (A La Carte menus).
2. Press **F** or select **File**.
3. Press **R** or select **Rename**.

4. The Rename File screen displays. Type in the current filename, then press the down arrow key to enter the new filename.
5. Press **Return**.
6. The file is renamed.

Examples   This is another of XyWrite's file manipulation commands that let you change your file structure without leaving the program. It does not make a new file; it changes the name of an existing file.

REVIEW (RV)

Overview   The **Review** command is the older form of the **Type to Screen** (**Types**) command. Both commands do the same thing—format a copy of the open, or the specified file, and bring it to the screen for a visual review.

Procedure   Just as you can print a document that's displayed or stored on disk, you can **RV** a document in either place.

To see how the document on screen will print:

1. Make sure there isn't a block defined—press **F3** (Release Define).
2. Press **F5** (Clear Command Line).
3. Type **RV**.
4. Press **F9** (Execute).
5. XyWrite opens another window. Depending on how quickly you computer operates and how long the document is, it may seem that nothing else is happening.
6. The formatted document displays as it will print. Your working document is still displayed in the window you issued the **RV** command from.

To see how a document stored on disk will print:

1. Press **F5** (Clear Command Line).
2. Type **RV** FILENAME.
3. Press **F9** (Execute).
4. XyWrite opens another window. Depending on how quickly you computer operates and how long the document is, it may seem that nothing is happening.
5. The formatted document displays, just as it will print.

To clear the screen after you've reviewed the formatted document:

1. Press **F5** (Clear Command Line).
2. Type **AB** (**Abort**).
3. Press **F9** (Execute).
4. The screen clears.

A La Carte
1. Press **F6** (A La Carte menus).
2. Press **T** or select **Type**.
3. Press **S** or select **typetoScreen**.
4. The file is displayed in another window.

Examples   The **RV** command is very useful for any application where you need to see exactly where lines and pages are going to break; for mail merge operations where you want to check before committing to the printer; for previewing header and footer effects, to make sure references are being picked up properly; or for any number of other jobs.

Of course, you save lots of paper using **RV**—you can catch your mistakes on screen, before they roll through the printer.

Tips   **RV** doesn't let you review just a few pages, one of its drawbacks. If you don't want to process a large document, mark out the portion you need to see with a defined block. Use the **Save Define** command to send the block to a file and follow up with an **RV** on the mini-file.

RULER MARKERS (RL)

Overview   The third line of the XyWrite screen is a ruler that indicates where margins, tab stops, paragraph indent settings and the cursor are. Each of the symbols can be changed to another ASCII character with the **RL** default setting.

Procedure   Since **RL** is a default setting, you can enter the command in your printer file or in your STARTUP.INT file. If you do, your ruler settings are used each time XyWrite starts. For complete instructions, see the Procedure portion of the Default listing,

You can also issue **RL** from the command line to set a unique display mode for a single editing session, to try out different characters.

The **RL** setting controls a number of characters so the syntax is a bit involved. The command you issue must include nine settings after the **RL** command:

> Marker for Flush Left Tabs
> Marker for Flush Right Tabs
> Marker for Flush Center Tabs
> Marker for Decimal Tabs
> Marker for the first IP (Indent Paragraph) setting
> Marker for the second IP (Indent Paragraph) setting
> Marker for the cursor position
> Marker for the LM (Left Margin)
> Marker for the RM (Right Margin)

Any ASCII character can be used for any setting. They're accessed in the normal manner, either by typing the character number in directly or inserting if from the ASCII help screen. (See the ASCII character section for instructions.)

1. Press **F5** (Clear Command Line).

2. Type **DEFAULT** RL,m,m,m,m,m,m,m,m,m. (**m** stands for the marker character).
3. Press **F9** (Execute).
4. "Done" displays on the prompt line.

A La Carte The **Ruler Markers** command isn't supported through the A La Carte menus. Use the standard XyWrite procedure.

Examples Changing your ruler markers isn't something that occurs to a lot of people, but XyWrite's markers can be improved. In fact, in the regular manual, XYQUEST provides an example of using the letter **L** for the left margin entry and an **R** for the right, as well as some alternative entries for the tab stops indicators. Using a **D** to indicate a decimal tab seems more understandable.

If your copy of XyWrite is used by people without much experience, you may want to change the markers to increase understanding of what's happening on the screen.

See Defaults

RUN A XYWRITE PROGRAM (RUN)

Overview The **Run** command executes a XyWrite program or a macro. This is the method used to execute programs that aren't loaded onto Save/Get keys for quick execution.

Procedure 1. Press **F5** (Clear Command Line).
2. Type **RUN** PROGRAMNAME.
3. The program is executed.

If you're not sure of the name of the program, or if you have group of programs you only use occasionally, you can use the "point-and-shoot" method to run the program:

1. Press **F5** (Clear Command Line).
2. Type **DIR DIRECTORYNAME** (the name of the directory where your programs are stored).
3. Press **F5** (Clear Command Line).
4. Type **RUN**.
5. Press **F10** to move the cursor into the directory listing.
6. Move the cursor to the program to run.
7. Press **F9** (Execute).

A La Carte   There isn't an A La Carte menu function to run a program. Use the standard XyWrite procedure.

See Programs

RUNNING FOOTER (RF, RFE, RFO)

Overview   XyWrite's **RF** commands generates a consistent message at the bottom of every page in a document. **RF** generates the same message on all pages, or you can use the **Running Footer Even** and **Running Footer Odd** to paginate facing pages in a complementary fashion.

Procedure
1. Move the cursor to the top of the document by pressing **Ctrl** and **Home**.
2. Press **F5** (Clear Command Line).
3. Type **RF** (or **RFE** or **RFO** if you're going to set a different message on facing pages).
4. Press **F9** (Execute).
5. A window opens on the screen. Type in whatever you want printed at the bottom of the page. You can use any XyWrite formatting command. To center the page number on each page:
   - Press **Return**. This creates a line of white space between the footer and any text.
   - Press **F5** (Clear Command Line).

- Type **FC** (**Flush Center**).
- Press **F9** (Execute).
- A bright command triangle is inserted.
- Press **F5** (Clear Command Line).
- Type **PN** (**Page Number**).
- Press **F9** (Execute).
- A bright command triangle is inserted.
6. Press **F3** to close the window.
7. A bright command triangle is inserted in text.

If you were printing a document that was going to be duplicated with printing on each side of the paper, you could easily make a minor change in the procedure to place the page number on the outside edge of each page:

1. Move the cursor to the top of the document by pressing **Ctrl** and **Home**.
2. Press **F5** (Clear Command Line).
3. Type **RFE** (**Running Footer Even** pages).
4. Press **F9** (Execute).
5. A window opens on the screen.
    - Press **Return**. This creates a line of white space between the footer and any text.
    - Press **F5** (Clear Command Line).
    - Type **FLR** (**Flush Left**).
    - Press **F9** (Execute).
    - A bright command triangle is inserted.
    - Press **F5** (Clear Command Line).
    - Type **PN** (**Page Number**).
    - Press **F9** (Execute).
    - A bright command triangle is inserted.
6. Press **F3** to close the window.
7. A bright command triangle is inserted in text.

1. Press **F5** (Clear Command Line).
2. Type **RFO** (**Running Footer Odd** pages).
3. Press **F9** (Execute).
4. A window opens on the screen.

- Press **Return**. This creates a line of white space between the footer and any text.
- Press **F5** (Clear Command Line).
- Type **FR** (**Flush Right**).
- Press **F9** (Execute).
- A bright command triangle is inserted.
- Press **F5** (Clear Command Line).
- Type **PN** (**Page Number**).
- Press **F9** (Execute).
- A bright command triangle is inserted.

5. Press **F3** to close the window.
6. A bright command triangle is inserted in text.

A La Carte

1. Move the cursor to the top of the document by pressing **Ctrl** and **Home**.
2. Press **F6** (A La Carte menus).
3. Press **P** or select **Page**.
4. Press **H** or select **Header/footer**.
5. The Define Running Header and Footers screen displays. In the first fill-in blank, type a **F** to specify a footer. Press the down arrow key. In the second fill-in blank, press **A** to print the same entry on every page, **E** to print on even numbered pages, or **O** to print it on odd numbered pages.
6. Press **Return** and a text entry window will open on the screen.
7. Enter the text of the footer, as described in the standard procedure section.
8. Press **F3** to close the window.
9. A bright command triangle is inserted in text.

Tips   Don't try to cram a lot of information on the bottom of the page. Most style guides favor a simple single line for a running footer, if one is used at all.

Warnings   Look at a **RF** command in expanded display mode and you'll see that the command is written as **RFA**, for **Running Footer All** (instead of **Running Footer Even** or **Running Footer Odd**). Don't erase the A in the expanded command—XyWrite looks for it; if it's not there, you won't get a footer.

See Running Header

RUNNING HEADER (RH, RHE, RHO)

Overview   The **Running Header** commands generate a consistent page header throughout a document. Use the **RH** command to put the same message on every page, or the **Running Header Even** (RHE) and **Running Header Odd** (RHO) to paginate facing pages in a complementary fashion.

Procedure   1. Move the cursor to the top of the document by pressing **Ctrl** and **Home**.
2. Press **F5** (Clear Command Line).
3. Type **RH** (or **RHE** or **RHO** if you're going to set a different message on facing pages).
4. Press **F9** (Execute).
5. A window opens on the screen. Type in whatever you want printed at the bottom of the page. You can use any XyWrite formatting command. To center the title of the document on each page:
   • Press **F5** (Clear Command Line).
   • Type **FC** (**Flush Center**).
   • Press **F9** (Execute).
   • A bright command triangle is inserted.
   • Type the title of the document.
   • Press **Return** twice to create a line of white space between the header and any text.
6. Press **F3** to close the window.
7. A bright command triangle is inserted in text.

If you were printing a document that was going to be duplicated with printing on each side of the paper, you could easily make a minor change in the procedure to alternate the document title with the chapter title, and place the page number on the outside of each page:

1. Move the cursor to the top of the document by pressing **Ctrl** and **Home**.
2. Press **F5** (Clear Command Line).
3. Type **RHE** (**Running Header Even** pages).
4. Press **F9** (Execute).
5. A window opens on the screen.
   - Press **F5** (Clear Command Line).
   - Type **PN** (**Page Number**).
   - Press **F9** (Execute).
   - Press **F5** (Clear Command Line).
   - Type **LD** (**Leadering**).
   - Press **F9** (Execute).
   - A bright command triangle is inserted.
   - Type the name of the document.
6. Press **F3** to close the window.
7. A bright command triangle is inserted in text.

1. Move the cursor to the top of the document by pressing **Ctrl** and **Home**.
2. Press **F5** (Clear Command Line).
3. Type **RHO** (**Running Header Odd** pages).
4. Press **F9** (Execute).
5. A window opens on the screen.
   - Type the chapter title.
   - Press **F5** (Clear Command Line).
   - Type **LD** (**Leadering**).
   - Press **F9** (Execute).
   - A bright command triangle is inserted.
   - Type **PN** (**Page Number**).
   - Press **F9** (Execute).
   - Press **F5** (Clear Command Line).
6. Press **F3** to close the window.
7. A bright command triangle is inserted in text.

A La Carte

1. Move the cursor to the top of the document by pressing **Ctrl** and **Home**.
2. Press **F6** (A La Carte menus).
3. Press **P** or select **Page**.
4. Press **H** or select **Header/footer**.
5. The Define Running Header and Footers screen displays. In the first fill-in blank, type an **H** to specify a footer. Press the down arrow key. In the second fill-in blank, press **A** to print the same entry on every page, **E** to print on even numbered pages, or **O** to print it on odd numbered pages.
6. Press **Return**. A text entry window opens on the screen.
7. Enter the text of the header, as described in the standard procedure section.
8. Press **F3** to close the window.
9. A bright command triangle is inserted in text.

Tips

Running headers are able to carry slightly more information than footers, but they shouldn't be crammed with information. Just as with footers, most style guides favor a single line for a running header, but there are many more variations of headers than there are of footers.

For lists, like a phone list or glossary, it's standard practice to use the first and last entry in the header.

Other types of common headers include:

Even Page	Odd Page
Author's name	Book or article title
Book title	Chapter title
Chapter title	Main topic of page
Last main header	Chapter title

XYQUEST ships a short file of different style headers with XyWrite. Look for a file named HEADERS on your program disks. It is not automatically copied to a working directory, so you may have to move it to your working area. Then use the **TY** command to print a copy of it.

379

The file includes a number of headers suitable for business and legal documents as well as more standard article or book-style headers. Any of them can be copied into one of your real documents easily:

1. Open your document and issue a **Running Header** command.
2. Open another window if necessary, then press **F5** (Clear Command Line).
3. Type **CA** HEADERS.
4. Move your cursor to the header that strikes your fancy and press **F4** (Define Line) until the entire header is a defined block.
5. Either switch windows directly to your document and press **F7** (Copy Define) to move the header into place, or press **F2** and a letter or number key to create a temporary Save/Get. Then move to your document and press **Alt** and the letter or number key to insert the Save/Get into the header environment.
6. Don't forget to issue an **Abort** command to close the HEADERS file.

Warnings Look at a **RH** command in expanded display mode and you'll see that the command is written as **RHA**, for **Running Header All** (instead of **Running Header Even** or **Running Header Odd**. Don't erase the A in the expanded command—XyWrite looks for it; if it's not there, you won't get a header.

See Running Footer

SAVE (SA)

Overview **Save** writes a copy of the currently active document to disk without closing the file. Use **SA** while you're writing, to protect your work.

Procedure   To save an open document to the same name and disk location:

1. Press **F5** (Clear Command Line).
2. Type **SA**.
3. Press **F9** (Execute).
4. "Done" displays on the prompt line.

You can save your active document to a disk that isn't the current default by specifying the drive letter after the command. If your documents are normally stored on your hard drive, drive C:, but you want to make a backup copy of the document on floppy drive A:

1. Press **F5** (Clear Command Line).
2. Type **SA** A:.
3. Press **F9** (Execute).
4. "Done" displays on the prompt line.

If you wish, you can save the open file to a differently named file. This keeps the original document open on the screen under its original name and creates a copy of the file (as it appears on screen) on disk.

1. Press **F5** (Clear Command Line).
2. Type **SA** NEWNAME.
3. Press **F9** (Execute).
4. "Done" displays on the prompt line.

A La Carte
1. Press **F6** (A La Carte menus).
2. Press **F** or select **File**.
3. Press **S** or select **Save**.
4. The Save File screen displays. If you want to save the file under a new name, type in the name.
5. Press **Return**.
6. "Done" displays on the prompt line after the file has been written to disk.

Examples

Of all XyWrite commands, **SA** is the one you'll use most often. Most people who use computers believe wholeheartedly in the last line of Murphy's law: "If anything can go wrong, it will." Experienced computer users save their work at every opportunity because they've all lost hours of work to carelessness, a power failure, or a computer malfunction.

When something bad happens to your computer or your document file, if you've written your work to disk, you're protected from absolute disaster. If you lose a file from your screen, for whatever reason, all you have to do to recover is call the file and recreate a portion of it—not the whole thing.

How often should you use **Save**? The answer to that is another question: How much of your work are you willing to lose? Protect yourself and your work—save early and often!

Tips

To make saving your files easier and faster, put the **Save** command on a Save/Get key. It's an easy program to write—just three keystroke combinations to record! See the Programming section for details. Your file should end up looking like this:

BC sa**XC**

If you want to make an automatic backup copy of the file, save to the original location and to a floppy disk at the same time:

BC sa**XC BC** sa B:**XC**

If you want to make saving even more automatic, XyWrite's technical support department can provide a program called AUTOSAVE.PGM that saves a file every 1,000 keystrokes. It slows your typing speed down a bit, but if you're a slow typist or have a fast computer, you'll never notice it. The program is reproduced in the Programs chapter and is available through XyWrite's technical support department or its bulletin board service.

See Store and Abort

SAVE CODE (SAVEC)

Overview   The **Savec** command unloads a section of the XyWrite program from operating memory and writes it to a special file on disk. If the section of code is needed for an operation, the file is accessed by the parent code in the computer memory instead of being reloaded.

Procedure   **Savec** was intended for people using personal computers with floppy disks, or with small amounts of RAM (Random Access Memory). It's also useful for people with newer machines that have memory over and above the old 640K DOS limitation, which XyWrite can't address.

NOTE: The **Savec** procedure only frees about 50K of memory. It might not be worth the trouble, unless you're really pressed for disk space and memory.

The original idea behind **Savec** is intriguing: create a memory management tool that can use disk storage space as memory. If you want to use all XyWrite III's features on a computer with dual floppy drives, you have a problem—the features (especially the spelling dictionary and thesaurus word list) take up more room than there is on most floppy diskettes. Even on computers with hard disk drives, if you're editing a large file, it's possible to use all your computer's available memory during some operations (it's occurring if you see a "Can't Scroll, Define, or Display" message on your prompt line).

Once features are loaded into computer memory from a master diskette (usually the one that lives in the A: drive on a floppy-drive system), the original program code isn't accessed again.

This means that the original XyWrite diskette, the one that was in drive A: when the program was started (call it MASTER#1), can be removed and replaced with another floppy (call it MASTER#2) that holds whatever features couldn't fit on the original diskette. It also means that the seldom-used portions of code in memory can be removed and written to the MASTER#2 diskette (with **Savec**), freeing computer memory for XyWrite's regular operations.

When you use **Savec**, you're making the computer think you have a super-size floppy disk with as much storage space as two regular floppies.

XyWrite divides its features into several chunks of computer code. These are the modules that are stored on disk by **Savec**:

TABLE 17   **Feature Codes**

FEATURE NAME	NUMBER
All features	0
Load	1
Math and Programming	2
Spelling checker/dictionaries	3
Standard dictionary	-
Help	4
Hyphenation	5
Sorting	6
Printing	7

Savec doesn't permit you to unload memory to a designated drive; it uses whatever drive is the default. If your default drive is not A:, make the appropriate adjustments. If necessary, switch the default drive from B: to A:

1. Press **F5** (Clear Command Line).
2. Type **A:** .
3. Press **F9** (Execute).
4. "Done" displays on the prompt line.

Next, execute the **Savec** command:

1. Remove the MASTER#1 diskette from A: and insert the MASTER#2.
2. Press **F5** (Clear Command Line).

3. Type **SAVEC** # (# is the number of the memory module to save). An entry of **0** unloads all features and frees the most room. To review what's in memory during the procedure, press **Ctrl** and **M** to display the Memory Management Menu.
4. Press **F9** (Execute).
5. "Done" displays on the prompt line. The feature's code is stored in a file named A:EDITOR.OV# (# is the number of the memory module).

Unload the features from your computer's memory:

1. Press **Ctrl** and **M**.
2. The Memory Management Menu displays. Select Unload Program.
3. Press the number of the memory module you specified when you executed the **Savec** command.

A La Carte The **Savec** command isn't available through the A La Carte menus. Use the standard XyWrite procedure.

Tips

Savec was designed for floppy drive systems, but it seems to offer an advantage to users who don't mind tinkering with their machine's memory a bit, and to people who work with large files.

XyWrite can't address memory over 640K directly, although many computers come with more memory. If your computer has more memory, try configuring the chips above 640 as a RAM disk (directions should be in your user's manual or your DOS manual). Then, configure your AUTOEXEC.BAT file so the RAM disk is included in your DOS PATH command statement. Make your RAM disk the default drive, copy the program files (spelling dictionaries, etc.) to it, and use **Savec** to unload features to it. Then use the Memory Management Menu to unload those features and free the lower memory for your regular writing operations.

The entire sequence of executing **Savec** and unloading memory requires more keystrokes than it should. It's a prime candidate for automation with a keystroke-recording macro or a program that does the juggling with function calls.

See Memory

SAVE A DEFINED BLOCK (SAD OR SAVEDEF).

Overview   The **SAD** command saves a portion of a document as a separate file.

Procedure
1. Define a block of text.
2. Press **F5** (Clear Command Line).
3. Type **SAD** FILENAME.
4. Press **F9** (Execute).
5. "Done" displays on the prompt line.
6. The block stays defined; release it by pressing **F3**.

A La Carte
1. Define a block of text.
2. Press **F6** (A La Carte menus).
3. Press **F** or select **File**.
4. Press **D** or select **saveDefine**.
5. The Save Defined Block to File screen displays. Type in a filename.
6. Press **Return**.
7. "Done" displays on the prompt line after the file has been written to disk.

Examples   The **SAD** command provides a quick and easy way to disassemble a document. It's useful for saving a few paragraphs of a letter for use in another document, for preserving a text passage if it has to be cut for some reason, or for editing a lengthy passage to manageable size.

    If you access large databases and download information, **SAD** is perfect for cutting the short part from the middle of a large file without destroying the parent file.

See Blocks

SAVE/GETS

Overview　　A Save/Get is a storage area that keeps text or a XyWrite program (also called a macro) ready for use.

Save/Gets are probably the most powerful tool within XyWrite. They're one of the special features that set the program apart from the herd of run-of-the-mill word processors. Between saving and inserting text and running programs, almost any writing, editing, or computer management task can be greatly speeded up or automated.

A Save/Get can be linked to a letter or number key, ready for recall or use. They are accessed by pressing **Alt** and the key to which the Save/Get is assigned. When the key combination is pressed, the text that's stored on the key is inserted in the active document file or the program that's stored on the key is executed.

Save/Gets can be either temporary or permanent. Temporary Save/Gets are usually created on the fly and used during a single editing session. Permanent Save/Gets are stored as a special file on disk.

Up to 36 permanent Save/Gets (one for each letter and number key) can be active at a time. A collection of Save/Gets can be stored together as a disk file and loaded or unloaded as needed. There's no limit on the number of Save/Get collections you can store, although only one set can be active at a time. You might have a set specifically for file and directory maintenance, one for letter writing, one for mail merge operations, one for academic writing, and so on. There are three types of Save/Gets.

Text Storage Save/Gets　These are storage areas for words and sentences. They're usually created by writing the text in a regular file, defining it as a block, and saving it to a specific key. They're great for storing boilerplate passages and inserting them into a document with a single key stroke combination.

Program/Macro Storage Save/Gets　These are also storage areas, but are for programs or macros that perform an operation

387

when the key combination is pressed. They're usually created in two steps. First the program or macro is created and tested, then it's stored on a letter or number key so it can be executed quickly. Both these types are identified in keyboard files as &A-&Z.

A subcategory of the regular text and program storage Save/Get is the "function key Save/Get". This is another set of storage areas identified by the 36 letter and number keys. These Save/Gets are not mapped directly to an existing keyboard, however. They're identified in function calls and keyboard files as @A-@Z and @0-@9 (and can be tied to a remapped keyboard).

These can be used as storage areas for text, programs, or values, just as the regular pre-mapped Save/Gets are, but they can only be loaded through a program operation or with the **LDPM** command.

Temporary Programming Save/Gets Another distinct category of Save/Gets are used for special programming functions. There are a thousand (numbered 000 to 999) of these temporary storage areas that are only accessed during a program. They're buffers that contain counter values or text that's being manipulated. Most XyWrite users don't use these because their needs are met by the text storage and program storage Save/Gets.

NOTE: The temporary programming Save/Gets and the second set of Save/Gets (the ones identified by a @ sign) are discussed in the Programming and Keyboard Files sections, since they're limited to performing functions related to programming. The rest of this section deals with text and program storage Save/Gets, the ones that are accessed by pressing **Alt** and a key.

Text Storage Save/Gets give the Save/Get function its name because you can *save* text to a key and *get* it back later. While writing, use text storage Save/Gets to:

- Move text around a document, between documents, or between windows.
- Store and insert boilerplate paragraphs, pages, or entire documents into files.
- Store and insert formatting commands.

• Remove a text passage from a document on a trial basis, to see how it reads without it—and be able to reinsert the text or move it to a different location.

To "save" text to a Save/Get key:

1. Define the block of text you want to save.
2. Press **F2** (Make Save/Get).
3. Press the letter or number key you want to store the text on.
4. "Done" displays on the prompt line.

To "get" the stored text back:

1. Move your cursor to the place the text should be inserted.
2. Press **Alt** and the letter or number key you stored the text on.
3. The text is inserted.

When you use this procedure, keep in mind that the stored text remains attached to the key. It's not erased or removed after you perform the "get" operation. You can insert the text as many times as you want.

A program written by recording a series of keystrokes or using the XyWrite Programming Language can be stored on a Save/Get key. When **Alt** and the key are pressed, the program is executed.

There's a special command for storing a program to a Save/Get, **Load Program** (**LDPGM**). Don't bother creating a program Save/Get until you're sure the program you've written works. Test the program with the **Run** command:

1. Press **F5** (Clear Command Line).
2. Type **LDPGM** PROGRAMNAME,# (# is the letter or number key used as the Save/Get key).
3. Press **F9** (Execute).
4. "Done" displays on the prompt line.

Both the text "save" procedure and the **LDPGM** command create a *temporary* Save/Get that stays in place during your current editing session. The Save/Get exists in the computer's memory; as soon as the XyWrite session ends, it's gone. To preserve the

Save/Get for use in other editing sessions, you must save it by writing it to disk. Since Save/Gets tend to travel in herds, you save all your currently loaded Save/Gets as a set with the **Store Save/Gets** (**STSGT**) command. To store a set of Save/Gets on disk:

1. Press **F5** (Clear Command Line).
2. Type **STSGT** FILENAME. (The XyWrite default filename is "GETS," but anything can be used. If you use several sets of Save/Gets for different purposes, be careful—don't specify the wrong filename!)
3. Press **F9** (Execute).
4. "Done" displays on the prompt line.

The **Store Save/Gets** (**STSGT**) procedure stores the file. To use the set of stored Save/Gets in another editing session, they must be loaded with the **Load Save/Gets** (**LDSGT**) command. To load a set of Save/Gets from a disk file:

1. Press **F5** (Clear Command Line).
2. Type **LDSGT** FILENAME.
3. Press **F9** (Execute).
4. "Done" displays on the prompt line.

If you use more than one set of Save/Gets during an editing session, be aware that loading a new set does not automatically remove the old set. The only keys that change are those that are used by both sets. If a key that's used in the first set is not over-written by the new set, it stays in effect.

To completely remove a set of Save/Gets, use **CLRSGT**:

1. Press **F5** (Clear Command Line).
2. Type **CLRSGT**.
3. Press **F9** (Execute).
4. "Done" displays on the prompt line.

To remove a single Save/Get, use **Remove**:

1. Press **F5** (Clear Command Line).

2. Type **REMOVE**,# (# is the key on which the Save/Get is stored).
3. Press **F9** (Execute).
4. "Done" displays on the prompt line.

The **F2** function key is dedicated to managing Save/Gets. It does four jobs:

- **Pressing F2 by itself** is used when a text Save/Get is created. Its use was illustrated in the **Save** procedure.
- **Pressing Shift and F2**, followed by a letter or number key, appends a defined block of text to an existing Save/Get.
- **Pressing Ctrl and F2**, followed by a letter or number key, displays the Save/Get that's stored on that key.
- **Pressing Alt and F2** displays a directory of all the current Save/Gets.

You can print the contents of a single Save/Get key with **Type %** or save a single Save/Get key's contents to a file on disk with **Save %**. These are useful if a program listing or text passage is too long to be viewed on the Save/Get directory, or if the program that's loaded to a key has been erased:

1. Press **F5** (Clear Command Line).
2. Type **TYPE** %# (# is the key on which the Save/Get is stored).
3. Press **F9** (Execute).
4. The contents of the key are printed.

To write the contents to a file:
1. Press **F5** (Clear Command Line).
2. Type **SAVE** %# (# is the key on which the Save/Get is stored).
3. Press **F9** (Execute).
4. The contents of the key are written to a file named #.SAV (# is the key on which the Save/Get is stored).

A La Carte   A La Carte provides access to most of the Save/Get commands mentioned here. They're grouped together on one menu:

1. Press **F6** (A La Carte menus).
2. Press **E** or select **Edit**.
3. Press **G** or select **save/Get**.
4. The Save/Get screen displays. The choices on it are:
   - saVe   Copy Defined text into Save/Get
   - **Append** s/g   Append defined block to end of Save/Get
   - **Get**   Insert Save/Get contents in a file
   - **Store** s/g   Store all Save/Gets onto disk as file
   - **Load** s/g   Load all Save/Gets from file on disk
   - **Clear** s/g   Clear current Save/Get set
   - **Display**   Display contents of Save/Gets
5. Press the capitalized letter or select the entry with your cursor, then press **Return**.

Tips

Many people use a single set of Save/Gets for most editing tasks. It can be loaded automatically by including a line in the STARTUP.INT file. (See the STARTUP.INT section.)

If you regularly switch between several sets of Save/Gets, you can write a short program or help file (that can be loaded onto another Save/Get) that lets you switch quickly between sets. If you write a help file, you can display the names of the sets and generate the **LDSGT** command from that screen, menu-style. See the Help file section for instructions.

If you write a program to do the loading, you could have it generate a directory listing of the stored sets (assuming you give them a common filename attribute such as a .GET extension), clear the command line, put the **LDSGT** command in place, and drop the cursor back down into the directory of Save/Get files.

At that point, you can move the cursor to the set you want to load and press **F9** to execute the **LDSGT** command.

Warnings

The file that stores permanent Save/Gets is a special format that cannot be edited. Although it can be opened with a **Call** command, don't add or delete anything. If you do open it, don't use **Store** (**ST**) to close it, since that can write corrupted data to disk and destroy the file. Always abandon it with **Abort** (**AB**).

See Clear Save/Gets, Function Keys (F2), Insert Save/Get, Load Save/Gets, Load Program, Programming, Programs, Remove, Save %, Store Save/Gets, and Type %

SAVE %

Overview
The **Save** % command writes the contents of a single Save/Get key to disk.

Procedure
1. Press **F5** (Clear Command Line).
2. Type **SA** %# (# is the letter or number key on which the Save/Get is stored).
3. Press **F9** (Execute).
4. "Done" displays on the prompt line.
5. The file is stored under a filename made from the letter or number of the key and a .SAV extension (for example, Q.SAV or 4.SAV).

A La Carte
1. Press **F6** (A La Carte menus).
2. Press **E** or select **Edit**.
3. Press **G** or select **save/Get**.
4. The Save/Get screen displays. Press **G** or select **Get**.
5. Press **Return**.
6. The Insert Save/Get Contents in File screen displays. Press the letter or number key that controls the Save/Get you want to write to disk.
7. Press **Return**.

Examples
If you use Save/Gets to store text, **Save** % could become one of your favorite commands. It makes it easy to edit the contents of a Save/Get. Just use **Save** %, open the file with a regular **Call** command, edit the procedure, and reload it to a key.

See Save/Gets

SAVE STYLE (SS)

Overview   The **Save Style** command creates a collection of formatting commands. Either the default format settings in effect or those specified when the command is issued are included.

Procedure   To record the default formatting settings in effect:

1. Press **F5** (Clear Command Line).
2. Type **SS** STYLENAME.
3. Press **F9** (Execute).
4. A bright command triangle is inserted in the text.

To create a new style collection by specifying styles, first decide just what the text element you're going to format requires so you know what to include in the style bundle. Any document format settings that can be used as a default setting can be included. A complete listing is included in the Defaults section, but some you might consider including are:

- Left and right margin settings (**LM** and **RM**)
- Paragraph indent (**IP**)
- Line leading or line spacing commands—**Automatic Leading** (**AL**), **Line Leading** (**LL**) or **LS**
- Justification (**JU**) or no justification (**NJ**)
- Text position—Flush Right, Center, or Left (**FR**, **FC**, or **FL**)

Different print type (**PT**) and print mode (**MD**) settings, tab stops, printer control codes, pausing between pages, and different form depths can also be included. Then, in an open document file:

1. Press **F5** (Clear Command Line).
2. Type **SS** STYLENAME,setting=value,setting=value. There's no limit to the number of settings you can include.
3. Press **F9** (Execute).
4. A bright command triangle is inserted in the file.

A La Carte The **Style** commands aren't available through the A La Carte menus. Use the standard XyWrite procedure.

Examples A style bundle created with **SS** can format an entire document or just a small portion of one.

Some people use a style bundle for a letter, report, press release, or magazine article. Others may use half a dozen style bundles in the same document—one for a heading, another for a subheading, two or three different bundles for different styles of body copy, perhaps one for epigraphs.

Tips The **SS** command gathers a collection of formatting commands together into a style bundle; it doesn't invoke them. You need to do that with a **Use Style (US)**, **Previous Style (PS)**, or **Next Style (NS)** command.

When you create a style bundle with **SS**, think about how it's going to be called. If you want to use the **Next Style** and **Previous Style** commands, the order in which the styles are created (or arranged in the file) is important. If you're going to use the **Use Style** command, which invokes a style by name, the order of the **SS** commands isn't important, but naming them with easy-to-remember names is. Don't tag a style bundle with an ambiguous word that forces you to peek into the bundle to see what's there.

The position of the **SS** command in the file isn't critical, but it must occur before the command that invokes it. For convenience, it's a good idea to place the **SS** commands you'll use at the top of your text file, where you don't have to hunt for them.

XYQUEST seems to have set up their style management tools to juggle styles within a single document, but it's easy to gather several styles and reuse them as a template for many similar documents. Look over the section on Style Sheets for some ideas.

See Defaults, Next Style, Previous Style, Style Sheets, and Use Style

SCREEN LENGTH (SL)

Overview   XyWrite can be configured to work well with many different combinations of computer equipment. The **SL** default setting is used to match XyWrite to the number of lines your monitor can display.

Procedure   The **SL** setting is a default, so you can enter the command in your printer file or in your STARTUP.INT file to set the display mode correctly each time XyWrite starts. For complete instructions, see the Procedure portion of the Default listing.

If you have an unusual display setup, you can also issue **SL** from the command line to test different settings during a single editing session:

1. Press **F5** (Clear Command Line).
2. Type **DEFAULT** SL=# (# is the number of lines your monitor can display).
3. Press **F9** (Execute).
4. "Done" displays on the prompt line.

A La Carte You must be in an empty window (have a blank screen) to access the default menus.

1. Press **F6** (A La Carte menus).
2. Press **X** or select **XyWrite**.
3. Press **D** or select **Defaults**.
4. The View and Change Defaults screen displays.
5. Press **N** or select **defaults N-S**.
6. Move the cursor to the **SL** entry and type in the number of lines your screen can display.
7. Press **Return**.
8. The Update Default File screen displays. You're asked if you want to make the default settings permanent.

9. Press **Y** or **N**. If you select **Y**, the program writes the new default settings to a special file and returns you to the A La Carte Menu Screen. If you select **N**, the settings are used for the current edit session.

Examples   Most IBM PC compatible computer monitors display 25 lines, the standard XyWrite setting. A few exceptions include EGA and VGA monitors, which are controlled by the special **EG** command; special monitors designed for desktop publishing, which display a full page of 66 lines; and some monochrome display setups that can display 43 lines.

   If you're in doubt about the number of lines your screen can display, check the monitor manual.

Warnings   Unless you're sure that your equipment requires a setting that's different than the standard 25 line display, don't change this setting.

   See Defaults

SEARCH FOR A FILE (FIND)

   See Find

SEARCH FOR TEXT (SE, SEA, SEB, SEBA)

Overview   XyWrite's four search commands locate text passages in active, open documents or in documents that are stored on disk. You can search either forward or backward for an exact match or a non-case sensitive match.

   The search commands can also use wildcards if you're not sure of the exact wording of the text passage.

Procedure   XyWrite searches in one direction at a time: either from the cursor location to the end of the file or from the cursor location to the top of the file. To search from the cursor location to the end of the file:

1. Press **F5** (Clear Command Line).
2. Type **SE** /PASSAGE/ (you can also use **Search** instead of **SE**).
3. Press **F9** (Execute).
4. If the passage is found, the cursor moves to its location. If it's not located, "Not Found" displays on the prompt line.
5. To repeat the search for the next occurrence of the same passage, press **F9** again.

To search backwards from the cursor location to the top of the file:

1. Press **F5** (Clear Command Line).
2. Type **SEB** /PASSAGE/ (you can use **Searchb** instead of **SEB**).
3. Press **F9** (Execute).
4. If the passage is found, the cursor moves to its location. If it's not located, "Not Found" displays on the prompt line.
5. To repeat the search for the next occurrence of the same passage, press **F9** again.

The **Search (SE)** and **Search Backwards (SEB)** commands are not case sensitive. They ignore the case of the letters in the **PASSAGE** entry. There are similar commands to search for a specific mix of capital and lower case letters: **Search Absolute (SEA)** and **Search Backwards Absolute (SEBA)**.

To do a case sensitive search from the cursor location to the end of the file:

1. Press **F5** (Clear Command Line).
2. Type **SEA** /Passage/.
3. Press **F9** (Execute).
4. If the passage is found, the cursor moves to its location. If it's not located, "Not Found" displays on the prompt line.
5. To repeat the search for the next occurrence of the same passage, press **F9** again.

To do a case sensitive search backwards from the cursor location to the top of the file:

1. Press **F5** (Clear Command Line).
2. Type **SEBA** /Passage/.
3. Press **F9** (Execute).
4. If the passage is found, the cursor moves to its location. If it's not located, "Not Found" displays on the prompt line.
5. To repeat the search for the next occurrence of the same passage, press **F9** again.

You can't run a search for a passage in a file on disk if there's anything on your screen. Use the Window Management Menu (**Ctrl** and **F10**) to open a second window if you don't want to close an active document.

XyWrite uses the **SE** or **SEA** command to search for a text passage in stored files on disk:

1. Press **F5** (Clear Command Line).
2. Type **SE** DRIVE\DIRECTORY\FILENAME/PASSAGE/ . To conduct a case sensitive search, use the **SEA** command instead of the **SE**. If you don't specify a **DRIVE** or **DIRECTORY** listing, XyWrite uses whatever drive and directory are active. You must specify some type of **FILENAME**, but the command works with the standard DOS filename wildcards (* and ?).
3. Press **F9** (Execute).
4. If the passage is found, the file containing it displays on the screen and a menu displays on the prompt line. The menu offers four choices:
   - Press **C** to continue the search to the next occurrence of the passage. (This could be in the same file that's open.)
   - Press **O** to open the file that's displayed.
   - Press **S** to stop the search.
   - Press **N** to skip the file that's displayed and continue the search in other files.
5. If the passage isn't located, "Not Found" displays on the prompt line.

If you select **O** to open the file, the search stops. If you want to repeat the search for another occurrence of the same passage, issue the command again.

When you use **O** to open a file that contains a "hit," you're dropped at the top of the file, rather than at the location of the text for which you searched. You have to repeat the **SE** or **SEA** command without the file qualifier to find the string again.

If you're not sure of the exact wording of the passage you're searching for, you can substitute a wildcard character to represent the characters of which you're not sure. XyWrite provides both multi-character and single-character wildcards.

All XyWrite wildcards are typed by holding **Alt** and **Shift** down while typing the wildcard indicator.

Pressing **Alt** and **Shift** and typing **W** generates the multi-character wildcard. It represents up to 80 characters. To use this in a search command, you must specify at least one "hard" character.

In the **SEBA /WP/** search string, the W represents the wildcard and the capital P is the "hard" character. This particular string finds any passage that ends with a capital P.

In the **SEBA /AWP/** search string, the W still represents the wildcard. The capital A and the capital P are "hard" characters. This particular string finds any passage that begins with a capital A, ends with a capital P, and has 80 or fewer characters between the two. It wouldn't find a passage that contains "AP" because there aren't any characters in the middle.

Pressing **Alt** and **Shift** and typing **L** generates the single-character wildcard that represents a letter. You can use this to represent any letter, upper or lower case.

The **SEB /ALP/** search string finds passages such as "asp," "ASP," "gasp," "GRASP," "alps," "ALPS," "MaCalpin," and so on.

Pressing **Alt** and **Shift** and typing **N** generates the single-character wildcard that represents a number.

Pressing **Alt** and **Shift** and typing **A** generates the single-character wildcard that represents either a letter or a number.

Pressing **Alt** and **Shift** and typing **X** generates the single-character wildcard that represents any character, including a space or other separator. It can be any of the 256 ASCII characters.

Pressing **Alt** and **Shift** and typing **S** generates the single-character wildcard that represents a separator—a space, parenthesis, bracket, punctuation mark, or math symbol.

If you need to, you can combine several wildcards in a search command.

The **SE** /NSSA/ search string finds passages such as "1. A" and "104. a."

A La Carte
1. Press **F6** (A La Carte menus).
2. Press **S** or select **Search**.
3. Press **T** or select **searchText**.
4. The Search screen displays. Type the text you want to locate between the vertical lines. Use the down arrow to move down the fill-in form, selecting whatever options are needed.
5. Press **Return** to begin the search.

Tips

To stop a search that's in progress, press **Ctrl** and **Break** (**Break** is sometimes attached to the **Pause** key).

XyWrite's search commands can locate any of the 256 ASCII characters, including carriage returns, a XyWrite command, or graphic characters:

- To generate a carriage return press **Ctrl** and **Return.**
- To generate the European quote marks that fence XyWrite's commands, press **Ctrl** and < or >.
- Full instructions on generating the other special ASCII characters are in the ASCII section.

In the Procedure section, the / is used as a separator to define the beginning and end of the **PASSAGE.** You don't have to use the slash though—any character that isn't in the **PASSAGE** works, even letters. The ability to use any character lets you search for a passage that contains the string, using different separators: **SEA p\FOO\p** would look for a passage containing \FOO\.

You can also use a space as a separator, which lets you skip several keystrokes if you're searching for a single word:

1. Press **F5** (Clear Command Line).
2. Type **SAE**, press **Return** twice (once to separate the command from the passage, the second time to use the space as a passage separator), then type the **Passage** to search for.
3. Press **F9** (Execute).
4. If the passage is found, the cursor moves to its location. If it's not located, "Not Found" displays on the prompt line.
5. To repeat the search for the next occurrence of the same passage, press **F9** again.

If you're searching for a passage that contains spaces, like a sentence or phrase, you can't use the space as a separator, use a hard character.

See Find

SET FOOTNOTE NUMBER (SF)

Overview   The **Set Footnote Number** is an optional command that determines the type of symbol used to identify footnotes and the number with which to begin the sequence. If the command isn't issued, standard Arabic numbers beginning with 1 are used.

Procedure   XyWrite provides eight numbering styles for each of its three sets of footnotes, so you have a choice or two to make before issuing the command. Remember that the system default is to number footnotes with standard Arabic numbers. If you don't issue a **SF**, those are used.

The syntax of the **SF** command is simple, though. If you're using more than one set of footnotes, identify the set you're talking about by adding a **1**, **2**, or **3** to the **SF** command when you issue it—**SF1**

S

for set number one, **SF2** for set number two, and **SF3** for set number three.

XyWrite provides eight numbering styles for footnotes:

TABLE 18   **Footnote Numbering Styles**

STYLE	SYMBOL
Unnumbered	none
Arabic numbers	1
Upper case roman numerals	I
Lower case roman numerals	i
Upper case letters	A
Lower case letters	a
Asterisks	*
Customized symbol set	* or # and the number of the counter string that defines the symbols to use.

To make footnote set number one use upper case roman numerals:

1. Press **F5** (Clear Command Line).
2. Type **SF**1 I.
3. Press **F9** (Execute).
4. A bright command triangle is inserted in text.

To make set number two unnumbered:

1. Press **F5** (Clear Command Line).
2. Type **SF**2.
3. Press **F9** (Execute).
4. A bright command triangle is inserted in text.

To make footnote set number three use lower case letters:

1. Press **F5** (Clear Command Line).
2. Type **SF**3 a.
3. Press **F9** (Execute).
4. A bright command triangle is inserted in text.

To begin numbering with a number other than 1, just issue the command using the symbol from the set of numbers you want to begin with. To make footnote set number one use upper case roman numerals and begin with L:

1. Press **F5** (Clear Command Line).
2. Type **SF**1 L.
3. Press **F9** (Execute).
4. A bright command triangle is inserted in text.

To make footnote set number three use upper case letters and begin with E:

1. Press **F5** (Clear Command Line).
2. Type **SF**3 E.
3. Press **F9** (Execute).
4. A bright command triangle is inserted in text.

If you want to use upper or lower case letters on a set and begin counting with a letter that's also a roman numeral, you've got a problem. XyWrite interprets a letter that's also roman numeral (C, c, L, l) as a roman numeral. When you issue the **SF** command, put a double quotemark in front of the letter. This tells XyWrite it's not just a roman numeral (for example, "C).

When creating page-numbered footnotes, XyWrite normally numbers all footnotes sequentially in either the current file or in a series of chained-together files. You can, however, simply number the footnotes on each page and restart the numbering on the next page. Issue the normal **SF** command, but precede the starting number with a hyphen:

1. Press **F5** (Clear Command Line).
2. Type **SF**3 -1.
3. Press **F9** (Execute).
4. A bright command triangle is inserted in text.

If you have a multi-file document (a book that contains each chapter in a separate file) and want to number footnotes sequentially throughout the series, you have to issue two **SF** commands. First, place the "master" **SF** command in the first file of the series. Second, put a modified **SF** command in the succeeding files in the series, using a question mark in front of the style designator:

1. Press **F5** (Clear Command Line).
2. Type **SF**1 ?1.
3. Press **F9** (Execute).
4. A bright command triangle is inserted in text.

This particular command continues the standard Arabic numbering scheme. The question mark is a flag that tells the program to get the starting number from the previous chapter.

A La Carte
1. Press **F6** (A La Carte menus).
2. Press **P** or select **Page**.
3. Press **F** or select **Footnotes**.
4. The Enter Footnotes and Set Format screen displays.
5. With your cursor, select the Set Footnote # entry.
6. The Set Footnote Number screen displays. Enter the starting number in the appropriate format.
7. Press **Return**.

Warnings   XyWrite only supports a single customized counter string. If you use it for numbering footnotes, for instance, you probably don't want to also use it for page numbers.

See Footnotes, Counters, and Superscript

SET PAGE NUMBER (SP)

Overview   Use **SP** to manually change page numbers. The **SP** command instructs XyWrite to use the number you specify as the page number on the current page and increments all following pages' numbers. **SP** is not used with page numbering that begins with 1.

Procedure
1. Move the cursor to the first line of the page you want to change the number on.
2. Press **F5** (Clear Command Line).
3. Type **SP** # (# is the number to put on the page).
4. Press **F9** (Execute).
5. A bright command triangle is inserted in text.

As with all XyWrite numbering and counting commands, you have a choice of formats. If you want to number your pages with upper or lower case letters, roman numerals, or symbols, substitute the appropriate indicator for the Arabic number.

TABLE 19

Numbering Formats

NUMBERING SYSTEM	SYMBOL
Arabic numbers	1
Upper case roman numerals	I
Lower case roman numerals	i
Upper case letters	A
Lower case letters	a
Customized symbol set	* or # and the number of the symbol set.

A La Carte
1. Move the cursor to the first line of the page where you need to set the number.
2. Press **F6** (A La Carte menus).
3. Press **P** or select **Page**.
4. Press **S** or select **Setpage#**.
5. The Set Starting Page Number screen displays. Enter the beginning page number using the numbering system of your choice.
6. Press **Return**.

Examples　　If you're working on a document that has multiple chapters, each in a separate file, use a special **SP** command at the beginning of each chapter—**SP ?1**. The question mark tells the program that the current page number is unknown and to begin the sequence with the last page of the previous chapter. When the chapters are printed as one document with a "chained files" **Type** command, the chapters will be numbered properly.

　　There's a special procedure for starting a sequence of "lettered" page numbers with a letter that is also a Roman numeral—an I, C, M, or any of the others. Precede the letter with a double quote mark command—**SP "C**.

　　The **SP** command is especially useful if you're writing text that's going to be inserted into a complete document. You can match the page number exactly, and even create loose-leaf document style insert/revision pages, if required.

　　It's also very useful if you're writing a document that has formal "front matter," like an introduction, that is usually numbered with lower case roman numerals. When you swing into the regular text chapters, issue the **SP** command to reset the page numbering scheme to Arabic numbers beginning with 1.

Warnings　　XyWrite only supports a single customized counter string. If you use it for numbering footnotes, for instance, you probably don't want to also use it for page numbers.

　　See Page Number

SET RECORD TEXT (SR IX)

Overview　　The **Set Record** commands are used while formatting an index or table of contents. They position marked text as an entry in the listing with either a page number or a chapter and page number.

Procedure The **SR** commands are used during the second part of building an index, setting the format. The **SR IX** command positions a passage from the text that is also an entry in the index or table of contents. This text is flagged with an **I#** command. The **Set Record Page Number (SR PN)** and **Set Record Chapter Number (SR CH-)** commands generate the page number or the chapter number and page number associated with the marked text.

This procedure also appears in the Index and Table of Contents sections. During the format procedure:

1. Move the cursor to the place in the document where the indexing should end. (Press **Ctrl** and **End** to move the cursor to the end of the main document).
2. Press **F5** (Clear Command Line).
3. Type **X#** (**#** is the number of the index set, **1** through **9**).
4. Press **F9** (Execute). A window opens.
5. Enter the page format of the index. You can use any formatting commands, such as **Left Margin (LM)**, **Right Margin (RM)**, or **Line Spacing (LS)**.
6. Enter the line format of the index with the **Set Record (SR)** command. A typical entry might be:
   - Press **F5** (Clear Command Line).
   - Type **SR** IX (Place Marked Text).
   - Press **F9** (Execute).

   - Press **F5** (Clear Command Line).
   - Type **LD** . (Use Periods As Leadering).
   - Press **F9** (Execute).

   - Press **F5** (Clear Command Line).
   - Type **SR** CH- (place Marked Text's Chapter and Page Number, with a hyphen as separator—other characters can be used).
   - Press **F9** (Execute).

Instead of generating a chapter number and a page number, you might want just the page number:

1. Press **F5** (Clear Command Line).
2. Type **SR** PN (Place Marked Text's Page Number).
3. Press **F9** (Execute).

When the format looks good, press **F3**. The window will close and you can store the document.

A La Carte Index functions aren't available through the A La Carte menus. Use the standard XyWrite procedure.

See Indexing and Table of Contents

SEQUENTIAL PAGES (SQ)

Overview The **SQ** default setting lets you refer to pages in a document by either their physical locations or their logical locations. This command is only important during a **Type** command operation that prints a few specified pages.

Procedure In normal operation, XyWrite identifies each page in a document by the page number that would be printed on it. If you have a five-page document and use a **Set Page Number** command to number those five pages as 64-68, XyWrite sees them as (logical) pages 64 through 68, rather than as (physical) pages 1 through 5.

If you change the **SQ** setting from the default value of 0 to 1, XyWrite homes in on the physical number of the page in the document, ignoring the printed page numbers. In the example above, although the pages would print with the correct numbers (64-68), XyWrite would refer to them as pages 1 through 5.

Since **SQ** is a default setting, you can enter the command in your printer file or in your STARTUP.INT file. If you do, the page numbering scheme you prefer is used each time XyWrite starts. For complete instructions, see the Procedure portion of the Default listing.

You can also issue **SQ** from the command line to test its effect, or to use it during a single editing session:

1. Press **F5** (Clear Command Line).
2. Type **DEFAULT** SQ=# (**0** is the standard XyWrite setting; **1** changes the setting to reference physical pages rather than logical pages).
3. Press **F9** (Execute).
4. "Done" displays on the prompt line.

A La Carte You must be in an empty window (have a blank screen) to access the default menus.

1. Press **F6** (A La Carte menus).
2. Press **X** or select **XyWrite**.
3. Press **D** or select **Defaults**.
4. The View and Change Defaults screen displays.
5. Press **N** or select **defaults N-S**.
6. Move the cursor to the **SQ** entry and type **0** or **1**.
7. Press **Return**.
8. The Update Default File screen displays. You're asked if you want to make the default settings permanent.
9. Press **Y** or **N**. If you select **Y**, the program writes the new default settings to a special file and returns you to the A La Carte Menu Screen. If you select **N**, the settings are used for the current edit session.

Examples   This command only has an impact when you want to print a few selected pages from a document that also uses page numbering that's been altered with a **Set Page Number** command.

If you toggle **SQ** to **1**, you can issue a command like **TYPE FILENAME,5-8** to print the fifth through eighth pages, regardless of their page numbers. If **SQ** remains at the XyWrite default (**0**), you'd have to issue a command that referenced whatever page numbers they carried,**TYPE FILENAME,65-68** .

Tips　　　If you prepare technical documentation or loose-leaf documents that include revision pages, you might want to experiment with the **SQ** setting.

See Defaults and Set Page Number

SHOW HYPHENS (SHOHYP)

Overview　　The **SHOHYP** command lets you see exactly where the possible hyphenation points are in a list of words, but the procedure is sort of clunky.

Procedure　　**SHOHYP** works by reading all the words in a file and generating a second file that shows where the hyphenation points are in the first list. The original file can't have any XyWrite formatting commands in it, so it must be especially prepared.

　　If you have a long file to check, the easiest way to strip all the commands in one step is with the STRIP.PRN process.

　　XYQUEST supplies a handy file called STRIP.PRN with XyWrite. It's a special printer file that removes all formatting codes from a document. To use STRIP.PRN, use the **Load** command to place STRIP.PRN in memory, just as any printer file is loaded. Then use the **Typef** command to create a second file on disk that only contains the words from the original file.

　　If you just have a short list of words you're curious about, type them into a file by themselves:

1. Press **F5** (Clear Command Line).
2. Type **SHOHYP** FILENAME.
3. XyWrite prepares a new file named HY.TMP containing the list and the word's possible hyphenation points. It's an ASCII file that you can open and view as you would any other file.

A La Carte　The **SHOHYP** command isn't available through the A La Carte menus. Use the standard XyWrite procedure.

Tips   **SHOHYP** is useful if you're concerned about where unusual words break if they fall at the end of a line, but the procedure isn't straightforward.

It's usually easier to specify where the word should break by inserting a conditional hyphen (by pressing the tilde key) as you're typing the word in the first place.

See Hyphenation

SHOW TABS (ST)

Overview   **Show Tabs** is a default setting that determines whether tab stops display as a visible character in expanded display mode.

Procedure Since **ST** is a default setting, you can enter the command in your printer file or in your STARTUP.INT file. If you do, your tab setting is used each time XyWrite starts. For complete instructions, see the Procedure portion of the Default listing.

You can also issue **ST** from the command line to set a unique display mode for a single editing session:

1. Press **F5** (Clear Command Line).
2. Type **DEFAULT** ST=# .(**0** or **1**. A **0** hides tabs; they are displayed as spaces. A **1** makes them appear as an ASCII character.)
3. Press **F9** (Execute).
4. "Done" displays on the prompt line.

A La Carte You must be in an empty window (have a blank screen) to access the default menus.

1. Press **F6** (A La Carte menus).
2. Press **X** or select **XyWrite**.
3. Press **D** or select **Defaults**.
4. The View and Change Defaults screen displays.

5. Press **N** or select **defaults N-S**.
6. Move the cursor to the **ST** entry and type **0** to hide tabs or a **1** to show them.
7. Press **Return**.
8. The Update Default File screen displays. You're asked if you want to make the default settings permanent.
9. Press **Y** or **N**. If you select **Y**, the program writes the new default settings to a special file and returns you to the A La Carte Menu Screen. If you select **N**, the settings are used for the current edit session.

Examples   Visible tab stops make some editing tasks easier, but even if you turn your **ST** setting on, the tab stops are only visible in expanded display mode.

Warnings   Although the XyWrite manual says the program default hides tabs, most XyWrite installations display them. Check your setup by typing several tab stops and shifting into expanded display (by pressing **Ctrl** and **F9**) before modifying the setting.

See Defaults, Tab Stops, and Relative Tabs

SNAKING COLUMNS (SN)

Overview   The newspaper, or snaking, column feature (the **SN** command) sets up several columns on a single page and flows text into each subsequent column. Text fills the first column, jumps to the top of the second column, fills that and moves on to the third.

The newspaper column feature is very different from XyWrite's parallel column feature. Newspaper columns unify a single story or stream of text on one or more pages. The column table command establishes several separate unrelated columns on a page.

See Columns (Snaking)

SORT

Overview   The **Sort** command alphabetizes a file or a defined block. Any group of words or letters that ends with a carriage return is sorted.

Procedure   **Sort** operates a bit differently when it sorts an entire file than when it sorts a defined block. The **Sort** command doesn't modify your original file when it sorts it. Instead, **Sort** creates a second file containing the rearranged data:

1. Press **F5** (Clear Command Line).
2. Type **SORT** ORIGINALFILENAME,SORTEDFILENAME.
3. Press **F9** (Execute).
4. "Done" displays on the prompt line when the sort is finished.
5. The sorted file is a normal XyWrite ASCII file that's ready to open and work on.

After you've defined which block to sort:

1. Press **F5** (Clear Command Line).
2. Type **SORT**.
3. Press **F9** (Execute).
4. The defined block disappears from the screen, then reappears, sorted.

A La Carte   There are two sorting procedures in A La Carte: one for sorting the entries in a defined block, the second for sorting a file of entries.

To sort a defined block:

1. Define the block.
2. Press **F6** (A La Carte menus).
3. Press **O** or select **Option**.
4. Press **R** or select **soRt**.

You can't have an open document on the screen when sorting a file of entries. Move to an open window or close your active document:

1. Press **F6** (A La Carte menus).
2. Press **O** or select **Option**.
3. Press **R** or select **soRt**.
4. The Sort a File screen displays. Type the name of the file to sort, then press the down arrow key. Type in the name of the target file, the file that will hold the sorted data.
5. Press **Return**.

Examples   The **Sort** feature is an outgrowth of XyWrite's automatic indexing feature. It wasn't originally intended to be used for heavy-duty text manipulation, so **Sort** isn't quite as sophisticated as some other XyWrite features. Combined with the **SK** setting and the **Sort Table**, however, you can accomplish most text ordering tasks.

Sort uses a built-in set of parameters to arrange data. There are two ways to customize the **Sort** command to your particular needs. You can change the way **Sort** operates by modifying the **Sort Key** (**SK**) default setting. If your sorting needs are *very* different from the standard defaults, you can totally reorganize things by creating a unique **Sort Table**. See the **Sort Table** section for information. In its standard configuration, XyWrite's built-in **Sort** parameters can:

- Arrange "entries," which XyWrite defines as any group of words or letters that ends with a carriage return. If you sort a simple list of items, one to a line, each line is an entry. If you're sorting a regular text file the program uses the first 80 characters of a text passage as its entry.
- Entries that begin with numbers are placed at the top of the sorted file. Next come lines that begin with spaces, those that begin with punctuation, then those that begin with letters. Any hidden type codes or formatting codes are ignored.

- **Sort** is not case sensitive. It doesn't matter whether a letter is upper or lower case; it's arranged as it comes in the alphabet.
- Duplicate entries are preserved.

Tips   The **Sort** command itself doesn't allow much flexibility in the way entries are arranged. If the command doesn't meet your needs, read the **Sort Key** (**SK**) default setting section and the **Sort Table** section.

The **SK** setting is especially useful since it provides quick access to most of the sorting tools people require. It takes more time to build a Sort Table, although it is more useful for repetitive sorting tasks that are a regular part of your routine.

See Sort Key

SORT KEY (SK)

Overview   The **Sort Key** default setting provides some additional control over how XyWrite's **Sort** command operates.

Procedure The **SK** setting controls how entries are sorted, the number of characters to use in each entry during the sorting process, and the number of the column to sort on. The syntax of the command is:

SK=HOW,No.CHARACTERS,No.COLUMNS

The first argument in the **SK** setting is a number that's built from the following chart:

S

TABLE 20   **Sorting Values**

VALUE	APPLICATION
0	Sorts numerical entries in ASCII order.
1	Sorts numerical entries in decimal order (the built-in default).
2	Sorts entries in reverse order (Z-A, 9-0).
4	Delete duplicate entries.
8	Determines whether the third argument (number of the column to sort on) defines the number of tab stops to skip over, or the number of columns to skip.

If you want to specify just one application, the number you enter after the **SK** setting is the number that corresponds to that application. If you want to specify more than one application, add the values of each application together and use that number. For example, if you wanted your list sorted in reverse order, you'd type your command entry as:

SK=2,No.CHARACTERS,No.COLUMNS

If you wanted your list sorted in reverse order and duplicate entries removed, add the value of reverse (2) and the value of remove duplicates (4) to get an entry of 6:

SK=6,No.CHARACTERS,No.COLUMNS

If your list included any entries that started with numbers, you'd probably want to add a 1 to each entry, to insure that they were sorted in decimal order, rather than ASCII order.

Specify Character Number To Use In A Sort The XyWrite default entry for this is 80 characters. If you're sorting a very large file you may want to reduce the number of characters to conserve memory and speed up the operation.

Specify The Column To Sort On The third argument in the setting can be very useful. Suppose you've got a list to sort that's preceded by useless information—say a parts list that begins with parts numbers, when you want to sort on descriptions that begin in the tenth column.

Your entry for this argument would be 11, to skip over the ten-digit part number and sort on the first word of the part description.

If your items are separated by tab stops rather than spaces and you want to skip over tab stops, you need to increase the amount of the value in the first **SK** argument by eight (to tell the program you're going to skip tab stops) and then decide on your entry for this third argument based on how many tab stops to skip over.

Enter The SK Setting   The **SK** setting is a default setting, so you can enter the command in your printer file or in your STARTUP.INT file. If you do, the setting is used whenever you issue a **Sort** command. For complete instructions, see the Procedure portion of the Default listing.

You might not want to include this particular setting as a full-time default setting. **SK** may be more useful to you if you issue it from the command line to set a unique sort order for a single editing session. Also, issuing the **SK** from the command line lets you test different arguments more quickly and easily than modifying and reloading a file does. Issue **SK** from the command line until you know exactly what your arguments should be:

1. Press **F5** (Clear Command Line).
2. Type **DEFAULT** SK=HOW,No.CHARACTERS,No.COLUMNS.
3. Press **F9** (Execute).
4. "Done" displays on the prompt line.

A La Carte   You must be in an empty window (have a blank screen) to access the default menus.

1. Press **F6** (A La Carte menus).
2. Press **X** or select **XyWrite**.
3. Press **D** or select **Defaults**.
4. The View and Change Defaults screen displays.
5. Press **S**.

6. A special Sort Options screen displays. Enter the parameters for the **SK** setting as they're described in the standard XyWrite procedure.
7. Press **Return**.
8. The Update Default File screen displays. You're asked if you want to make the default settings permanent.
9. Press **Y** or **N**. If you select **Y**, the program writes the new default settings to a special file and returns you to the A La Carte Menu Screen. If you select **N**, the settings are used for the current edit session.

Examples   The **SK** setting gives you a quick way to modify XyWrite's **Sort** command. Together with the Sort Table you can create a powerful set of data management tools within your word processor. These could be of great assistance in ordering information from other programs—mailing lists, bibliographic material, stock quotations.

See Defaults, Sort, and Sort Table

SORT TABLE

Overview   The Sort Table is the third part of XyWrite's sorting toolkit. Use it to modify and customize the way XyWrite performs its sorting operations.

Procedure   The **Sort Table** is a special file that's created and loaded into the program to perform a special sorting operation. It's only needed if the built-in sort table doesn't sort your unique material properly.

    The Sort Table is a standard ASCII file, created just as any other text file is. Create the file with the regular **New** command. It's a good idea to identify the file with a special extension, so you can recognize it as a sort table (for example FILENAME.SRT).

XyWrite can sort any of the 256 ASCII characters, not just letters and numbers. Any characters that you omit from your sort table are ignored by the **Sort** command.

1. Press **F5** (Clear Command Line).
2. Type **NEW** FILENAME.SRT.
3. The very first characters in the file must be XyWrite's unique identifier code. Type **;SO;** .
4. Press **Return**.
5. Type a semi-colon and a note explaining what the sort table does. If you need more than one line, end each line with a carriage return and begin each new line with a semi-colon.
6. On the next line, type the character or characters you want sorted first. In XyWrite's internal table, the entry is a space. If you want to make lower and upper case letters equal, you would type **aA**. If you wanted to give precedence to upper case letters, you might type **A** by itself. Press **Return** to leave the first sorted characters on a line.
7. Repeat the process, typing in the character or characters to sort next.
8. When you've finished building the list, use **Store** to close the file.

Next, load the sort table into memory:

1. Press **F5** (Clear Command Line).
2. Type **LOAD** FILENAME.SRT.
3. "Done" displays on the prompt line.
4. When you execute the **Sort** command, the new sort table is used to order the output.

A La Carte There isn't a special facility within A La Carte to create a sort table. Use the standard XyWrite procedure.

Examples A fairly common reason for building a unique sort table is to work around the built-in tables' setting that treats lower case and upper case letters equally. You may want to sort a list so that entries that begin with capital letters are indexed separately from those that begin with lower case letters. Or you may want to stagger the sort, so that upper case As are indexed, then lower case As, upper case Bs, lower case bs, and so on. Or you could choose to index only upper case entries, or only lower case entries. It's even possible to totally ignore all letters entirely and just sort on numbers, something that could be handy for sorting parts numbers, invoices, dates, or dollar amounts.

Warnings   The **Sort** feature is an outgrowth of XyWrite's automatic indexing feature. Even if you use it for other tasks, it's still used by the indexing function to build indexes and table of contents. If you set up an alternate sort table, it can mess up the built-in indexing and table of contents generation features.

If you're performing out of the ordinary sorts using a custom sort table and performing index and table of contents generation, be careful. Don't forget that you have a custom sort table installed! Use your custom sort table during a **Sort** operation, then unload it from memory before you get around to indexing or building the table of contents.

To unload your custom sort table from memory:

1. Press **Ctrl and M** (Memory Management Menu).
2. Move the cursor to the UNLOAD FILE entry.
3. Press **F6**.
4. Press **Esc** to remove the menu.

See Sort and Sort Key

SPELL CHECK (SPELL)

Overview   The **Spell** command invokes XyWrite's electronic proof reader.

Procedure   You can spell check your files three ways:

- Interactively check the file you have open, or a portion of it.

- Check a file that's stored on disk and put the possible misspellings into a separate file for review. Corrections are inserted with the **Correct** command.
- Check a series of files that are chained together (a series of chapters that are printed—and checked as one document). They must be stored on disk and the possible misspellings are written into a separate file for review. Corrections are inserted with the **Correct** command.

It's also possible to spell check one word while you're writing. Put your cursor on the word and press **Ctrl** and **S**. XyWrite displays an "OK" on the prompt line if the word is in a dictionary or displays the correction menu if it isn't. The correction menu is described next.

If you want to check a portion of the active file, define the portion as a block (press **F1** at the beginning of the block, cursor to the end, and press **F1** again).

If you want to check the whole file, press **Ctrl** and **Home** to move the cursor to the top of the file. If you want to check the file from your cursor position to the end of the file, just begin the numbered steps below.

NOTE: If you run the spell check in normal display mode, only the words in the main text are checked. If you switch to expanded mode by pressing **Ctrl** and **F9**, you include the text that's in headers and footers, footnotes, labels, index entries, and all text that's normally hidden:

1. Press **F5** (Clear Command Line).
2. Type **SPELL**.
3. The spell checker begins running. If it finds a word that isn't in the active dictionaries, the spell correction menu displays. The unrecognized word is highlighted and any near matches are offered as substitutes. If you like one of the replacements, move the cursor to highlight your choice and press **Return** to insert it.

If no near matches are found, or they're all incorrect, move the cursor to highlight the suspect word and type in your correction.

If you press **Return**, the correction is inserted in the text. You can also insert it into the text and into a dictionary for reuse by pressing **F4** or **F6** . There are several other options on the menu. Press:

- **Esc**—to abort the spell check process.
- **F1**—to ignore the unrecognized word and continue the spell check.
- **F2**—to abort the spell check process, but leave the **Spell** command in the header, so the command is ready to execute again.
- **F3**—to add the unrecognized word to a temporary dictionary that's only used during the current editing session.
- **F4**—to insert the corrected word in the text and add it to a temporary dictionary that's only used during the current editing session.
- **F5**—to add the unrecognized word to your personal spelling dictionary on disk.
- **F6**—to insert the corrected word in the text and add it to your personal spelling dictionary on disk.

After you've made a decision, the program goes on to the next unmatched word. When it can't find any other questionable words, a short report displays on the prompt line, specifying how many were checked and how many were questionable.

To check a closed file, XyWrite uses the same dictionaries and program to spell check a closed file which is stored on disk that it uses to proofread an open file:

1. Press **F5** (Clear Command Line).
2. Type **SPELL** FILENAME,TARGETFILENAME. (The TARGETFILENAME is optional; XyWrite uses SPELL.TMP if you don't supply a name.)
3. Press **F9** (Execute).
4. "Done" displays on the prompt line when the spell check is completed.

When you check a file this way, XyWrite reads the file, checks its contents against the dictionaries, and builds a list of unmatched words in a second file. You open the "list" file to make corrections and, when you're done, execute the **Correct** command to insert the changes in the original file.

The "list" has the name of the file it's linked to on the first line in reverse type. Each line under that contains an unmatched word.

While you're editing the "list," you can add a correct word to one of your personal dictionaries so it won't be flagged the next time. Press **Ctrl** and **S** as you would to spell check a single word, then **F5** or **F6** to add the word to your personal dictionary.

The procedure for checking a series of linked files is the same as it is for checking a single file in background, with one difference. Instead of typing the filename to check, type the "parent" filename. The parent file is a short text file that lists the names of each linked file. It's required in order to print the linked files as a single document, so it may already exist. It's fully discussed in the section on **Typing** linked files. To create the parent file:

1. Press **F5** (Clear Command Line).
2. Type **NEW** PARENTFILENAME.
3. Press **F9** (Execute).
4. Type the names of the files you want to link together, in the order they should be printed (or spell checked). Put just one filename on a line. Your file should look something like this:
   FILENAME.1
   FILENAME.2
   FILENAME.3
   FILENAME.4
5. Press **F5** (Clear Command Line).
6. Type **ST** (**Store**).
7. Press **F9** (Execute).

To check the series of files:

1. Press **F5** (Clear Command Line).
2. Type **SPELL** @PARENTFILENAME,TARGETFILENAME. (The TARGETFILENAME is optional; XyWrite uses SPELL.TMP if you don't supply a name.)

3. Press **F9** (Execute).
4. "Done" displays on the prompt line when the spell check is completed.

To correct any spelling errors, edit the TARGETFILENAME just as you would the file that comes from a single file. When you open this multi-file word list, you'll see a reverse video entry for each linked file.

A La Carte   There are separate procedures for checking an open document and checking one that's stored on disk. To spell check the active document, or a defined block from it:

1. Define the block of text or move the cursor to the point in the document where you want to begin the spell check.
2. Press **F6** (A La Carte menus).
3. Press **O** or select **Options**.
4. Press **S** or select **Spell**.
5. The Spelling Check screen displays. Press **S** or select **Spell check**.
6. Press **Return**.
7. If any unmatched words are found, the standard XyWrite correction menu displays.

To spell check a document on disk, or a series of linked files:
1. You must be in an open window to perform this procedure.
2. Press **F6** (A La Carte menus).
3. Press **O** or select **Options**.
4. Press **S** or select **Spell**.
5. The Check Spelling screen displays. Type in the filename to check.
6. Press **Return**.
7. If any unmatched words are found, they're written to the SPELL.TMP file for editing.

To customize the spell checker to meet your needs, it's important to understand how it works. XyWrite doesn't arbitrarily decide that a word in a document is spelled incorrectly; it compares the words in your files against a list of correctly spelled words in one or more special "dictionary" files. If one of your words isn't in a dictionary, your word is flagged as questionable when you run the spell checker.

XyWrite provides one main spelling dictionary. It's built from entries in seven published dictionaries: *American Heritage; Merriam Webster's Collegiate; Merriam Webster's Unabridged, Third Edition; Oxford English; Random House College; Random House Unabridged;* and *Webster's Ninth Edition.*

XyWrite also supplies supplementary dictionaries containing "other" words. Two are called LEGAL.SPL and BUSINESS.SPL. They contain jargon and words used in particular fields. A third is named PERS.SPL and contains a list of useful words that many people use in their writing. It's a good idea to rename PERS.SPL with your name, both so you can keep an accurate record of your additions and to keep one copy of the dictionary in original, uncorrupted form.

The original PERS.SPL can be copied again to provide foundation for other personal dictionaries you want to construct.

The main dictionary is loaded automatically as part of the program. The supplementary dictionaries are loaded by a specific command, so they're only used in addition to the main dictionary if you want them to be. (See the **Load** command section for instructions.)

If several supplementary dictionaries are loaded at the same time, any words you add during a spell check session are added to the dictionary that was loaded first.

Tips The temporary spelling dictionary that's an "add" choice on the correction menu exists only in computer memory during your editing session. It can be preserved, though. The **Stspell** writes it to disk, where it can be edited, or words moved from it into your personal spelling dictionary. You can even reload it into memory again. In addition to the words you add during the spell check session, it always contains the contents of the personal dictionaries you already have in memory. See the **Stspell** section.

Spell checking files in background is a quick way to build the automatic replacement portion of your personal dictionary. After you've checked several files, you'll probably notice several words you habitually misspell or mistype. When you've identified a word, try this procedure to include it in your dictionary:

1. Move the cursor to the misspelled word in the "list" file.
2. Immediately after the word, press the **Spacebar** and type the word correctly. Your entry should look like this:
   hte the
3. Press **F4** (Define Line).
4. Press **F5** (Clear Command Line).
5. Type **APPEND** FILENAME (the filename is your personal spelling dictionary).
6. Press **F9** (Execute).
7. "Done" displays on the prompt line.
8. Press **F3** (Release Define).
9. Erase the incorrect word.

Typing Shortcuts The structure of XyWrite's spelling function lends itself to typing shortcuts. The automatic replacement part of a personal spelling dictionary is designed to substitute a correctly spelled word for a common misspelling. You can use this feature to make the dictionary substitute a series of words when you type a short code word.

As an example, suppose you write a lot of letters and always type the same return address. You can set up an automatic substitution string to insert those four lines when you type **RA** .

To do that, open your personal spelling dictionary. Move the cursor to the portion at the bottom of the file where the replacement words are listed. On a line by itself, type **RA**, a space, and the address. Instead of pressing **Return** to end each line in the address, though, hold down **Ctrl** and **Alt** and type **13**. The **Ctrl/Alt/13** sequence inserts the ASCII number 13 character, the carriage return. Store the file. When you run the spelling checker or turn on the automatic correction feature, each "RA" is changed to the return address.

Abbreviations Abbreviations can't be added automatically to a personal spelling dictionary; it won't accept periods. You can add them manually by opening the dictionary as you would a text file and typing abbreviations. Store the text file. When you run the spell checker the next time, it makes sure you typed the period.

Warnings The spell checker is a nice feature, but it doesn't have brains of its own. It won't check to make sure that the proper word is in the proper place. If you care about your work, don't forget to check it over after you've run the spell checker!

See Auto Correct and Correct

SPELLING DICTIONARY, TEMPORARY (STSPELL)

Overview The temporary spelling dictionary created during an interactive spell check session is saved for reuse by **Stspell**.

Procedure 1. Press **F5** (Clear Command Line).
2. Type **STSPELL** FILENAME.SPL .
3. Press **F9** (Execute).
4. "Done" displays on the prompt line.

A La Carte   The **Stspell** command isn't available through the A La Carte menus. Use the standard XyWrite procedure.

Examples When you use **Stspell**, the contents of all the dictionaries in memory (except the main one) are written to disk. That means any personal dictionaries you loaded are written to the same file as the temporary dictionary.

   The file can be reloaded, if you wish, using the normal **Load** command, or it can be edited and words can be moved to your regular personal dictionary.

Warnings   Since the file created by the **Stspell** command includes the contents of any personal dictionaries you loaded, it duplicates the contents of those dictionaries. Don't keep loading a series of stored temporary dictionaries and personal dictionaries; they'll only waste computer memory.

See Spell

SPLIT SCREEN DISPLAY

See Windows

STARTUP.INT FILE

Overview   The STARTUP.INT file configures XyWrite each time the program is started. STARTUP.INT can be modified easily to customize XyWrite to suit personal preferences, or for a particular application.

It runs automatically, just as an AUTOEXEC.BAT file runs under DOS. It's also a short program.

A STARTUP.INT file normally loads the XyWrite support files (a printer file, a keyboard file, spelling dictionaries, hyphenation dictionary, and so on), sets system default settings, and may perform some programmed tasks (generating a directory listing).

Any task that you can perform from the XyWrite keyboard that you'd like the program to do automatically when it starts, can be programmed into STARTUP.INT. This annotated STARTUP.INT file is a good example:

BC LDDDICT DICTION	Loads hyphenation dictionary.
BC LDHELP NEW.HLP	Loads a customized help file.
BC DEFAULT BK=0	Turns the backup file feature off.
BC DEFAULT PL=54,60,50	Sets default Page Length values.

BC DEFAULT TP= 6,LM=10,RM=75	Sets default top, left, and right margins.
BC LP HERCULES.PRN	Loads Hercules Graphics Card Plus printer file.
BC LP 3IBMPRO.PRN	Loads regular printer file.
BC LDSGT GETS	Loads permanent Save/Get file.
BC LOAD ART.SPL	Loads personal spelling dictionary.
BC LOAD ART2.KBD	Loads customized keyboard file.
BC CM W	Executes CM command to modify CM/PRMPT display.
BC DEFAULT DD=192	Sets a default color value for defined blocks.
BC CD \x\	Clears the command line and puts a blank Change Directory command in place, ready to switch to a text storage subdirectory.

The bright **BC** entry that begins each line is the function call that results when you press **F5** to clear the command line. Although they're not visible in this printout, when you open your STARTUP.INT, you'll see that each line ends with a carriage return—which executes the command. The sample file above contains one exception to that general rule. The last line, which begins a **Change Directory** command, isn't executed automatically with a carriage return. That STARTUP.INT ends when the **CD** and the first part of the directory path is typed on the command line so the user can supply the final directory information by hand, depending on where he or she wants to move.

Procedure   Before modifying STARTUP.INT, remember that it is possible to make fatal mistakes while editing any file. STARTUP.INT is critical to XyWrite's operation, so make a copy of the file before you begin:

430

1. Press **F5** (Clear Command Line).
2. Type **COPY** STARTUP.INT STARTUP.OLD.
3. Press **F9** (Execute).
4. "Done" displays on the prompt line. You have a copy of your original STARTUP.INT saved under the STARTUP.OLD name, just in case anything goes wrong.

There are several ways to make changes in your STARTUP.INT. The easiest, perhaps, is to open the file as you would a text file, with the **Call** command. You can delete or modify anything in the file in normal text operation.

If you'd like to enhance the file by adding a command or two, pick a line in the file that's similar to the command you want to add. Put your cursor on the line, press **F4** to define it and **F7** to copy it. Then modify the copied line with your new command. Until you press **F3** (Release Define), you can make more copies of your original line by pressing **F7** again.

When you're done, use the usual **Store** to write the new STARTUP.INT to disk. Then test your modifications without rebooting XyWrite:

1. Press **F5** (Clear Command Line).
2. Type **RUN** STARTUP.INT.
3. Press **F9** (Execute).
4. All the commands in your new STARTUP.INT are executed as they would be if the program was starting for the first time. Stay alert and watch the prompt line while the file runs—any error messages will flash by very quickly.

If you've looked over the section on Programming, you might notice that the **Run** command used in the previous procedure is the command used to execute a XyWrite program. STARTUP.INT is a XyWrite program file, so you can use any of the techniques normally associated with programming to modify it. One of the most flexible is the keystroke recorder, which keeps a record of your keystrokes as you perform a function, saving them for later playback. If you open STARTUP.INT with a **Call Program** (**CAP**) command instead of the regular **CA**, you can use this tool to modify the file. Complete instructions are given in the Programming section.

If you want the STARTUP.INT to run a XyWrite program you've already written, you have two choices. Use the **Merge** command to insert your program in STARTUP.INT or modify a line in STARTUP.INT to read **BC** RUN PROGRAMNAME.PM. Either strategy works, although if you use the second, make sure your program returns control to STARTUP.INT so that the program can complete its run.

A La Carte The STARTUP.INT file used by A La Carte is a standard ASCII file, so it can be opened and modified using standard A La Carte procedures. It contains several A La Carte specific commands, but nothing out of the ordinary. Use the standard XyWrite procedures to modify the file.

Examples   There are few things you can't do in STARTUP.INT. After you've used XyWrite for awhile, you'll think of ways to modify the program to your liking, and recall that STARTUP.INT is one of the easiest ways to do that. Simply put, anything you can accomplish by issuing commands can be built into STARTUP.INT.

Tips   The STARTUP.INT file is also an ideal place to start if you use XyWrite for several radically different tasks and need to totally revamp the program during a working session.

Suppose you use XyWrite every day for routine writing tasks, but also operate a mailing business. Also suppose that the mailing business uses a different printer, you've created custom Save/Gets to automate your mail merge operation, and you have an entirely different set of default settings in place.

The quickest way to redo XyWrite isn't to load each "mailing" file separately. Why not make a copy of STARTUP.INT and rename it MAILER.INT? Then modify that file to install all your new settings in one pass. When you need to switch hats, execute a RUN MAILER.INT command.

Warnings　　Remember that STARTUP.INT is a critical XyWrite file, and it only takes a second to copy your "known-good" copy of STARTUP.INT to a safe place. Make it a habit to copy STARTUP.INT before you try out new modifications.

See Programming

STORE A FILE (ST)

Overview　　**Store** is one of most basic commands. It writes an open file to disk for storage.

Procedure　　1. Press **F5** (Clear Command Line).
2. Type **ST**.
3. Press **F9** (Execute).
4. The file is written to disk and the screen is cleared for another editing operation.

A La Carte
1. Press **F6** (A La Carte menus).
2. Press **F** or select **File**.
3. Press **T** or select **sTore**.
4. Press **Return** to store the active file under its own name, or type a new filename in the blank, then press **Return**.

Examples　　Both **Store** (ST) and **Save** (SA) write files to disk for safekeeping, but there's an important difference.

　　SA doesn't close the file you have on screen; it writes a copy of it to disk. **SA** should be used often during an editing session.

　　ST writes the file to disk and clears the screen. It's only used when you want to quit editing your current document.

Tips
The **ST** command can change a filename or its location as it writes the file to disk. To change the current file's name:

1. Press **F5** (Clear Command Line).
2. Type **ST** NEWFILENAME.
3. Press **F9** (Execute).
4. The file is written to disk under the new filename. If the file that was open had already been stored on disk under its original name, that copy is still available, undisturbed, as it was when it was last saved.

To change the current file's location:

1. Press **F5** (Clear Command Line).
2. Type **ST** NEWDIRECTORYNAME:\NEWPATHNAME.
3. Press **F9** (Execute).
4. The file is written to disk in the new location. If the file that was open had already been stored on disk under its original name, that copy is still available, undisturbed, as it was when it was last saved.

These options can be combined to change the file's location and name in one pass.

See Abort and Save

STORE SAVE/GETS (STSGT)

Overview
The **STSGT** command writes whatever Save/Gets are in memory to a file for disk storage.

Procedure
1. Press **F5** (Clear Command Line).
2. Type **STSGT** FILENAME (usually GETS, but can be anything).
3. Press **F9** (Execute).
4. "Done" displays on the prompt line.

A La Carte
1. Press **F6** (A La Carte menus).
2. Press **E** or select **Edit**.
3. Press **G** or select **save/Get**.
4. The Save/Get screen displays.
5. Press **S** or select **Store s/g**.

Examples   Unless you use the **STSGT** command to preserve them, Save/Gets are lost when you end your XyWrite session. You can store as many different sets to files as you wish, but there are a few caveats involved in reloading and using them. See the Save/Get section for details.

See Save/Gets and Load Save/Gets

STYLE SHEETS

Overview   A style sheet in word processing is a template, a set of formatting commands, that control how a document formats. Style sheets aren't included in XyWrite, although it's a function that's easy to create from XyWrite's "style" tools.

Style sheets make producing similar documents very easy. When you want to create a letter, you just specify the "letter" format and a template containing predefined formatting commands for a letter is inserted in your file. If the next document you write is a press release, call the "press release" style sheet.

Procedure   There are two steps involved in using a style sheet: creating the template and calling it into a document.

Most style sheets contain a separate style for each text element you'll use. A business letter is an ideal document to control with a style sheet. It usually follows the same general format but contains a number of distinct parts. To create the style sheet, first create a new file to hold the style sheet:

1. Press **F5** (Clear Command Line).
2. Type **NEW** BUSINESS.STY.
3. Press **F9** (Execute).
4. The new file opens on your screen.

Next, imagine the letter. Starting at the top of the page, the first thing to define is the date and return address area. For this letter template, let's put it at the top of the page, on the right hand side, and use a medium-size type font that matches the letterhead:

1. Press **F5** (Clear Command Line).
2. Type **SS** RETURN,LM=50,PT=3.
3. Press **F9** (Execute).
4. A bright command triangle is inserted in the file.

These commands set a left margin of 50 to move the return address over to the right side of the page and call Print Table 3, which contains the font that matches our letterhead.

The next part of the letter is the recipient's address. For this, we change the left margin back to the usual position and change the type font:

1. Press **F5** (Clear Command Line).
2. Type **SS** ADDRESS,LM=10,PT=13.
3. Press **F9** (Execute).
4. A bright command triangle is inserted in the file.

The salutation is the next part of the letter, but it can be controlled by the ADDRESS style. The next element that requires a different format is the actual body of the letter. For this, we'll switch from our default of a single-spaced line setting to space-and-a-half for easier reading and begin indenting the first line of paragraphs. The type isn't justified and prints in normal mode. The margins are normal settings of 10 and 75:

1. Press **F5** (Clear Command Line).
2. Type **SS** BODY,PT=2,MD=NM,LS=1.5,LM=10,RM=75,IP=5,NJ.
3. Press **F9** (Execute).
4. A bright command triangle is inserted in the file.

Within the body of the letter, a demand for payment is sometimes inserted. We want this to stand out, so we use a different font, print the demand in bold type, single-space it, indent it from each margin an additional half inch, but don't indent the first line, and justify the type:

1. Press **F5** (Clear Command Line).
2. Type **SS** DEMAND,PT=5,MD=BO,LS=1,LM=15,RM=70,IP=0,JU.
3. Press **F9** (Execute).
4. A bright command triangle is inserted in the file.

This particular letter never ends with a DEMAND; it returns to the BODY style. The only other text element is the close and signature, which can be controlled by a single style. The only change from the BODY style that's in effect is the left margin, since the signature should print to the left, under the return address:

1. Press **F5** (Clear Command Line).
2. Type **SS** CLOSE,LM=50.
3. Press **F9** (Execute).
4. A bright command triangle is inserted in the file.

At this point, the BUSINESS.STY file contains five style bundles represented by bright command triangles. As soon as it has been closed with **Store**, it's ready to use. To use the style sheet, create your business letter file as you normally would. Once the letter file is open:

1. Press **F5** (Clear Command Line).
2. Type **ME** BUSINESS.STY.
3. Press **F9** (Execute).
4. The five bright command triangles are inserted.

Invoke the first style:

1. Press **F5** (Clear Command Line).
2. Type **US** RETURN.
3. Press **F9** (Execute).
4. A bright command triangle is inserted.
5. Type the return address information.

Switch to the ADDRESS style:

1. Press **F5** (Clear Command Line).
2. Type **US** ADDRESS.
3. Press **F9** (Execute).
4. A bright command triangle is inserted.
5. Type the address information.

Next comes the BODY:

1. Press **F5** (Clear Command Line).
2. Type **US** BODY.
3. Press **F9** (Execute).
4. A bright command triangle is inserted.
5. Type the text of the letter.

The DEMAND:

1. Press **F5** (Clear Command Line).
2. Type **US** DEMAND.
3. Press **F9** (Execute).
4. A bright command triangle is inserted.
5. Type the request for payment.

Then more BODY:

1. Press **F5** (Clear Command Line).
2. Type **US** BODY.
3. Press **F9** (Execute).
4. A bright command triangle is inserted.
5. Type the rest of the letter.

The CLOSE:

1. Press **F5** (Clear Command Line).
2. Type **US** CLOSE.
3. Press **F9** (Execute).
4. A bright command triangle is inserted.
5. Type the close and the signature line.

The letter's complete, written with far fewer commands being issued than if each section was formatted with a series of individual commands.

A La Carte Since XyWrite doesn't have a style sheet function, neither does A La Carte. Use the standard XyWrite procedures.

Examples   The procedure outlined here is a small example of what you might do with style sheets.

A person who writes academic papers could go wild with style sheets, since most formal papers are prepared to strict formatting guidelines. An academic paper may require several styles of headlines, subheads, epigrams, and quotations.

Tips   You can select a style in two ways: by issuing a **Use Style** (**US**) command, or cycling through a series with **Previous Style** (**PS**) and **Next Style** (**NS**) commands. For most people, the **US** command is easier to use, since the styles are referenced by name rather than the order in which they were created.

See Next Style, Previous Style, Save Style, and Use Style

SUBSTITUTION TABLES

Overview   Many printers can generate characters that aren't members of the standard ASCII character set XyWrite uses. A substitution table lets you generate these characters from XyWrite if you want to include them in a document.

Procedure   For this procedure, assume that you have a special printer that can generate an unusual character, a circle about a quarter of an inch across. The exact list of special characters a printer can generate is usually included in the printer manual.

The special character your printer puts on paper can't be displayed on the screen because the character only lives inside the printer. Your computer can, through XyWrite, send special instructions to the printer that cause the circle to be printed.

Tell XyWrite where you want to print the circle by typing an ASCII character that isn't usually used in a document. XyWrite recognizes the ASCII character as a representative of the circle. When the circle's stand-in appears in a file that's being printed, the program looks up the stand-in character in the printer file or stand-alone character substitution table and reads the special printer instructions that are listed with the character. The special printer instructions are sent to the printer, which reads them and generates the circle. To make this happen, you have to build a character substitution table. The table can exist as a stand-alone file, but it's usually included in a printer file:

1. Do some research. Select an ASCII character you don't use from the XyWrite help file list or an ASCII character chart. Also, review the printer manual to find a string of characters that causes your printer to generate the special symbol—in this case, the circle.
2. Press **F5** (Clear Command Line).
3. Type **CA** PRINTERFILENAME.
4. Move the cursor to the section of the file, usually near the bottom, where standard substitution tables are. You may find a listing like this (this is just the first part of a longer table):

   ;
   ; SUBSTITUTION TABLE TO ACCESS FOREIGN CHARACTERS
   ;
   SU:FOREIGN
   ¥=R\R
   £=R#R
   ì=RR
   º=R[R
   ¡=R[R
   ¿=R]R
   ñ=R|R

5. If a character substitution table is already in use, the easiest way to proceed is to modify the existing table. If you have a table in place, skip steps 4-7, move the cursor to the table and begin with step 8.

6. Note that the table is identified by a comment line that begins with a semi-colon and with a line that names the table—"SU:FOREIGN."

7. Press **Return** several times to give yourself some working room. On the first line, type a semi-colon and a short note to identify your new table.

8. On the next line, type **SU=NAME** and press **Return**.

9. Next, on a line by itself, type the ASCII character you want to use to represent the circle, an equal sign, and the instruction string your printer should receive to generate the circle.

(The characters that make up the special instruction string should be listed in the printer manual along with the list of special characters the printer can make. Quite often, they include special ASCII characters that aren't letters or numbers. A printed listing may call for the **Esc** key. It's represented in the XyWrite file by the right-pointing triangle.)

If you're building a new table and are through inserting character substitution lines, go to a new line, type **ET**, and press **Return**. Use **Store** to close the file, then **Load** to place it in memory. When you type the representative ASCII character, the printer should generate the special circle.

If you don't want to include a character substitution table in your regular printer file, you can create a separate file that doesn't contain anything but the table. This special file is essentially a modified printer file without any printer information; it usually contains just the substitution table.

The procedure for creating the file follows the procedure for creating a table closely:

1. Press **F5** (Clear Command Line).

2. Type **NEW** FILENAME.PRN.

3. The very first characters in the file must be a file identifier. Type **;SU;** .

4. Press **Return**.

5. Follow the directions above to create a standard substitution table in the new file.

A La Carte   The A La Carte menus don't have any special facilities for editing printer or character substitution files. Use the standard XyWrite procedure.

Examples   Many printers can generate similar "foreign" characters and symbols; quite a few can put graphics and other symbols on paper. The exact application you have for a character substitution table or file is determined almost entirely by the capabilities of your printer.

Tips   Quite a few printers provide some sort of graphics capability. You might be able to use this to draw line boxes around different parts of your documents, using character substitution tables.

Warnings   XYQUEST recommends using a substitution table in a printer file rather than in a separate file. If you choose to use a file, remember that it is a type of printer file that needs to be loaded into memory with the **Load** command.

See Printer Files

SUPERSCRIPT (SC)

Overview   The **SC** command causes the footnote reference numbers that print with the footnote text to print in superscript mode instead of normal mode, as they usually do.

Procedure   The **SC** command can only be entered within a **Footnote Format** (**FM**) command. Within the command, issue **SC** in this format: **FM**

SC=1 (to make reference numbers print in superscript) or **FM SC=0** (to restore normal mode printing).

A La Carte
1. Move to the beginning of the file by pressing **Ctrl** and **Home.**
2. Press **F6** (A La Carte menus).
3. Press **P** or select **Page.**
4. Press **F** or select **Footnotes.**
5. Select **Formats.**
6. A screen with possible options for footnote formats displays.
7. Move the cursor to the **SC** entry and type **1** to make reference numbers print in superscript.
8. Press **Return.**
9. A bright command triangle is inserted in the text.

See Footnote Format

TAB CHARACTER (TB)

Overview   **TB** is a default setting that controls whether a tab stop is printed as a tab stop or as a series of spaces.

Procedure   Since **TB** is a default setting, you can enter the command in your printer file or in your STARTUP.INT file. If you do, tab stops will print as you want them to every time XyWrite starts. For complete instructions, see the Procedure portion of the Default listing.

You can issue **TB** from the command line to print tab stops in a unique way for a single editing session:

1. Press **F5** (Clear Command Line).
2. Type **DEFAULT** TB=# . (**0** causes tab stops to print as groups of spaces. It's the initial XyWrite setting. A **1** causes tab stops to print as true tab stop characters.
3. Press **F9** (Execute).
4. "Done" displays on the prompt line.

A La Carte You must be in an empty window (have a blank screen) to access the default menus.

1. Press **F6** (A La Carte menus).
2. Press **X** or select **XyWrite**.
3. Press **D** or select **Defaults**.
4. The View and Change Defaults screen displays.
5. Press **T** or **Z** or select **defaults T-Z**.
6. Move the cursor to the Tab Character entry and type **0** to cause tab stops to print as groups of spaces. Type a **1** to cause tab stops to print as true tab stop characters.
7. Press **Return**.
8. The Update Default File screen displays. You're asked if you want to make the default settings permanent.
9. Press **Y** or **N**. If you select **Y**, the program writes the new default settings to a special file and returns you to the A La Carte Menu Screen. If you select **N**, the settings are used for the current edit session.

Examples   The **TB** setting is used if you're preparing a file for special applications, particularly using **Typef** to print the file to disk, but retaining the tab stops. You might want to do this is you are exporting a file to a database program, a spreadsheet, or sending the file to some typesetters.

See Defaults and Tab Stops

TAB RESET (TR)

Overview   The **Tab Reset** command restores the original XyWrite tab stop types and locations after they've been modified with a **TS** command.

444

Procedure   1. Move the cursor to the place in your document where the tab
          stops should return to the original settings.
          2. Press **F5** (Clear Command Line).
          3. Type **TR**.
          4. A bright command triangle is inserted in the text.

          A La Carte
          1. Press **F6** (A La Carte menus).
          2. Press **R** or select **foRmat**.
          3. Press **T** or select **Tabs**.
          4. The Set Tabs by Number screen displays.
          5. Press the down arrow key. Type an **R** in the small blank.
          6. Press **Return**.
          7. A bright command triangle is inserted in the text.

Examples   **TR** provides a quick reset to the original XyWrite tab stops after
          you've modified them with a **TS** command. It eliminates the need
          to issue a second, long **TS** command to re-establish the system
          defaults. **TR** does not override a change in the system default **TS**
          setting.

Tips   If you change tab stop settings frequently, you might want to
          create a macro that inserts your standard **TS** setting, followed a
          few blank lines down by a **TR**.

          See Tab Set

TAB STOP SETTINGS (TS)

Overview   XyWrite provides four types of tab stops that create decimal tabs
          and tabs that make text under them set up flush right, left, or
          centered.

Procedure   Tab stops can be set through a special menu, from the command line, or as a default setting. The command line method only works with an open document on screen. The default method changes XyWrite's original settings for all editing sessions. The menu method implements changes in an open file if it's accessed from the file; if there isn't a file open, the new settings become temporary default settings for the editing session.

No matter which method you use, you have the same four types of tab stops to work with:

- Normal tab (sets text flush left against the stop)
- Flush Right tab (sets text flush right against the stop)
- Flush Center tab (centers text under the stop)
- Decimal tab (lines up a column of numbers on a decimal place under the stop)

Using Tab and Margin Selection Menu   This menu provides a good visual tool to show you just where the tab stops you're creating or deleting are.

If you're going to modify your default settings, begin the numbered steps now. If you want to modify the tab settings in a specific document, move your cursor to the point where you want to set new tab stops before you perform the numbered steps:

1. Press **Alt** and **Tab**.
2. The Tab and Margin Selection Menu displays. The cursor displays on the ruler line across the top of the screen.
   - Remove all existing tab stops by pressing **Z**.
   - Remove a single tab stop by moving the cursor to its position and pressing **X**.
   - Create a regular (flush left) tab stop by moving the cursor to the right position and pressing **T**.
   - Create a flush right tab stop by moving the cursor to the right position and pressing **G**.
   - Create a flush center tab stop by moving the cursor to the right position and pressing **C**.
   - Create a decimal tab stop by moving the cursor to the right position and pressing **D**.

3. When you've set up the tab stops, press **F9** (Execute) or **Return**.

4. If you accessed the menu from an open document, a bright command triangle is inserted in text. If you accessed the menu from an open window to change default settings, they're written to memory and used for that editing session. They're not permanently stored in a file.

Set Tab Stops From Command Line This command overrides the default tab stop settings that are established every eight characters. The command is stored as part of a document:

1. Move the cursor to the point in the document where the new tab stops should take effect.
2. Press **F5** (Clear Command Line).
3. Type **TS** #,#,#,# (# is the number of the column where the tab stop should be placed).
   - Typing a number by itself establishes a normal tab stop.
   - Typing a number and **R** establishes a flush right tab stop (for example, **TS 10R,15R**).
   - Typing a number and **C** establishes a flush center tab stop (for example, **TS 10C,15C**).
   - Typing a number and **D** establishes a decimal tab stop (for example, **TS 10D,15D**).
4. Press **F9** (Execute).
5. The new tab stops are displayed on the ruler line.

Establish New Default Tab Stops The **TS** command can be used as a system default setting in your printer file or in your STARTUP.INT file. Your favorite tab stops are established each time you start XyWrite and are used for all your documents. For complete instructions, see the Procedure portion of the Default listing. The command format is exactly the same as is used when issuing the command from the command line:

1. With the file open, type **DEFAULT** TS=#,#,#,# (# is the number of the column where the tab stop should be placed).
   - Typing a number by itself establishes a normal tab stop.

- Typing a number and **R** establishes a flush right tab stop (for example, **DEFAULT TS=10R,15R**).
- Typing a number and **C** establishes a flush center tab stop (for example, **DEFAULT TS=10C,15C**).
- Typing a number and **D** establishes a decimal tab stop (for example, **DEFAULT TS=10D,15D**).

You can also issue **TS** from the command line to set unique tab stops for a single editing session. Using the Tab and Margin Selection Menu is easier.

1. Press **F5** (Clear Command Line).
2. Type **DEFAULT** TS=# (# is the number of the column where the tab stop should be placed). The **R**, **C**, and **D** settings may all be used.
3. Press **F9** (Execute).
4. "Done" displays on the prompt line.

A La Carte
1. Press **F6** (A La Carte menus).
2. Press **R** or select **foRmat**.
3. Press **T** or select **Tabs**.
4. The Set Tabs by Number screen displays.
5. Type the column numbers where you want tab stops in the blank, separated by commas. If you want to make a stop a flush center, flush right, or decimal tab stop, add a **C**, **R**, or **D** after the position number. If you want to clear existing tab stops, press the down arrow key and type a **C** on the small blank.
6. Press **Return**.
7. A bright command triangle is inserted in the text.

You can also set default tab stops in A La Carte. You must be in an empty window (have a blank screen) to access the default menus:

1. Press **F6** (A La Carte menus).
2. Press **X** or select **XyWrite**.

448

3. Press **D** or select **Defaults**.

4. The View and Change Defaults screen displays.

5. Press **T** or **Z** or select **defaults T-Z**.

6. Move the cursor to the Tab entry and type in the tab locations and type indicators, if necessary, separated by commas.

7. Press **Return**.

8. The Update Default File screen displays. You're asked if you want to make the default settings permanent.

9. Press **Y** or **N**. If you select **Y**, the program writes the new default settings to a special file and returns you to the A La Carte Menu Screen. If you select **N**, the settings are used for the current edit session.

Tips   Once you've embedded a **TS** command in a document, you can modify those settings by editing the **TS** command triangle contents in expanded display mode. Press **Ctrl** and **F9** to shift from normal to expanded mode to make your changes. You can shift tab locations and tab stop types without reissuing the **TS** command.

If you changed tab stop locations or types in a document, you can easily restore the original XyWrite tab stop locations with the **Tab Reset** (**TR**) command.

If you use tab stops very often, review the sections on **Relative Tabs** (which allow tab stops to shift as the left margin changes) and the three default settings that control tab display and positions (**Tab Character**, **Tab Set**, and **Show Tab Stops**).

See Defaults, Relative Tabs, and Tab Reset

TABLE OF CONTENTS, EXTRACT (TX#)

Overview   Generating a table of contents in XyWrite is as easy as building an index; in fact, the two procedures are almost identical.

It's a three-step procedure that involves marking text with the **X#** command, setting the table of contents format with the **T#**

command, and building the table of contents itself with the **Table of Contents Extraction (TX)** command.

A XyWrite "table of contents" is a list that's sorted by page numbers. XyWrite uses the term "index" to mean an alphabetically sorted list of words or phrases. You can generate up to nine indexes and nine tables per document.

Procedure   **Part 1—Mark Text** There are three ways to create table of contents entries. You can index a word or phrase in the text, or build a paraphrased entry that doesn't appear in the text. To list a single word in the text:

1. Move the cursor to the space just after the target word. There can be no spaces or hidden mode commands between the cursor and the word.
2. Press **F5** (Clear Command Line).
3. Type **X#** (# is the number of the table of contents set, **1** through **9**).
4. Press **F9** (Execute). A window opens, but don't type anything into it.
5. Press **F3**.
6. A bright command triangle is inserted in the text.

To list a phrase in text, the phrase must end with a carriage return. This is how a title, headline, or subtitle is often written—on a line by itself:

1. Move the cursor to the space just before the target phrase. The cursor must have a space, a tab stop, or a carriage return in front of it. The phrase must end with a carriage return.
2. Press **F5** (Clear Command Line).
3. Type **X#** (# is the number of the table of contents set, **1** through **9**).
4. Press **F9** (Execute). A window opens, but don't type anything into it.
5. Press **F3**.
6. A bright command triangle is inserted in the text.

To build a paraphrased entry (Option 1):

1. Move the cursor to the spot that the entry should reference.
2. Press **F5** (Clear Command Line).
3. Type **X#** (**#** is the number of the table of contents set, **1** through **9**).
4. Press **F9** (Execute). A window opens.
5. Type the phrase or word you want to use as the entry.
6. Press **F3**.
7. A bright command triangle is inserted in the text.

To build a paraphrased entry (Option 2):

1. Move the cursor to the spot that the entry should reference.
2. Press **F5** (Clear Command Line).
3. Type **X#** (**#** is the number of the table of contents set, **1** through **9**) and the phrase or word you want to use as the entry (for example, **X1 FooFoo Goes For a Walk**).
4. Press **F9** (Execute).
5. A bright command triangle is inserted in the text.

Part 2—Set Table of Contents Format   When a table of contents is generated, all marked text that appears before the embedded **TX** command is included. To list an entire document, move the cursor to the end of the main document by pressing **Ctrl** and **End**:

1. Move the cursor to the place in the document where the table of contents should stop listing topics and pages. (Press **Ctrl** and **End** to move the cursor to the end of the main document).
2. Press **F5** (Clear Command Line).
3. Type **T#** (**#** is the number of the table of contents set, **1** through **9**).
4. Press **F9** (Execute). A window opens.
5. Enter the page format of the table of contents. You can use any formatting commands, such as **Left Margin (LM)**, **Right Margin (RM)**, or **Line Spacing (LS)**.
6. Enter the line format of the table of contents with the **Set Record (SR)** command. A typical entry might be:

- Press **F5** (Clear Command Line).
- Type **SR** IX (Place Marked Text).
- Press **F9** (Execute).

- Press **F5** (Clear Command Line).
- Type **LD.** (Use Periods As Leadering).
- Press **F9** (Execute).

- Press **F5** (Clear Command Line).
- Type **SR** CH- (Place Marked Text's Chapter and Page Number).
- Press **F9** (Execute).

7. Instead of generating both a chapter and a page number, you might want just the page number:
- Press **F5** (Clear Command Line).
- Type **SR** PN (Place Marked Text's Page Number).
- Press **F9** (Execute).

8. When the format looks good, press **F3**. The window closes.

9. Store the document.

Part 3—Build The Table of Contents You can either build the table of contents as part of the main document or as a separate file.

To build the table of contents as part of the document:

1. Press **F5** (Clear Command Line).
2. Type **TY** MAINFILENAME.
3. Press **F9** (Execute). As the file prints, the table of contents is generated and printed as part of the document.

Build The Table Of Contents In Separate File To build the table of contents in a separate file you need to include a **No Index** (**NI**) command in the main document or in each file of a document made from a series of chained-together files.

Once that's been done, issue the **TX#** command. If you have a file open when the command is executed, the program uses the open file as the source of the table, unless you specify a different source:

1. Press **F5** (Clear Command Line).
2. Type **TX#** SOURCEFILENAME,TARGETFILENAME (# is the number of the table of contents set, **1** through **9**).
3. Press **F9** (Execute).
4. The table is extracted and placed in the target file you specified.
5. After the table has been generated, it can be opened and edited as any other text file can.

Extract Table Of Contents From Series Of Linked Files The procedure for extracting a table of contents from a series of linked files is the same as it is for a single file, with one difference. Instead of typing a single filename, type the "parent" filename. The parent file is a short text file that lists the names of each linked file. It's required in order to print the linked files as a single document, so it may already exist.

To create the parent file:

1. Press **F5** (Clear Command Line).
2. Type **NEW** PARENTFILENAME.
3. Press **F9** (Execute).
4. Type the names of the files you want to link together, in the order they should be printed. Put just one filename on a line. Your file should look something like this:
   FILENAME.1
   FILENAME.2
   FILENAME.3
   FILENAME.4
5. Press **F5** (Clear Command Line).
6. Type **ST** (**Store**).
7. Press **F9** (Execute).

To process the series of files:

1. Press **F5** (Clear Command Line).
2. Type **TX#** @PARENTFILENAME,TARGETFILENAME (# is the number of the table of contents set, **1** through **9**).
3. Press **F9** (Execute).

4. The table is extracted and placed in the target file you specified.

5. After the table has been generated, it can be opened and edited as any other text file can.

A La Carte   Generating a table of contents is not supported in the A La Carte menus. Use the standard XyWrite procedure.

Uses

Many types of documents, especially academic papers and books, require a table of contents. XyWrite's ability to generate nine separate sorted lists lets you create a chapter title table, a table of illustrations, or almost anything else. As XyWrite builds the table, it automatically removes duplicate entries and combines multiple page numbers on one line.

Tips

Marking text is usually the most time-consuming part of building a table of contents. If you plan ahead and embed markers as you go, it makes the process go faster. In the SUPER.KBD file, XyWrite provides dedicated keys for beginning table of contents entries. You can pirate these entries to your own keyboard, or adopt the SUPER. See the Keyboard section for more information.

At the very least, consider writing a short macro so your table of contents entries can be marked with fewer keystrokes. Read the Save/Get section for instructions.

To generate a multi-level table that groups subordinate listings under a general heading, see the **Index Label** (**IL**) command.

To automatically include break points between entries that begin with different letters of the alphabet, see the **Index Break** (**IB**) command.

If you want to cross-reference entries, or refer to another entry (or an index entry), read the listing on the **End X-Marker** (**EX**) command.

See Indexing, Index Break, Index Label, Index Extraction, Set Record, and Text Marker

TABLES

See Column Tables

THESAURUS (CTRL AND T)

Overview   Along with its built-in spelling dictionary, XyWrite provides a thesaurus that's just a keystroke away. Use it to shop for a word that may be better than the one you used!

Procedure   1. Put the cursor on the word you want to improve.
2. Press **Ctrl** and **T**.
3. A special window opens on the screen. A list of synonyms displays, organized by the parts of speech your word may be.
   - To erase your word and substitute one of those in the list, move the cursor to your choice and press **Return**.
   - To look up the definition of one of the synonyms, cursor to your choice and press **Ctrl** and **PgDn**.
   - To abandon the menu and return to your document, press **Esc**.

A La Carte   The A La Carte menus don't provide a separate procedure to access the thesaurus. Use the standard XyWrite procedure.

TIME (TM)

Overview   The **TM** command is embedded in a file to print the current time whenever the document is opened or printed.

455

Procedure
1. Move the cursor to the point where the time should print.
2. Press **F5** (Clear Command Line).
3. Type **TM**.
4. A bright command triangle and the current time are inserted in text.

A La Carte
1. Press **F6** (A La Carte menus).
2. Press **E** or select **Edit**.
3. Press **D** or select **time/Date**.
4. The Time/Date screen displays.
5. Press **T** or select the **soft Time (tm)** entry.
6. Press **Return**.
7. A bright command triangle is inserted in text.

Examples
The **TM** command generates a "soft" time that changes each time the file it's in is opened or printed. It works like a time stamp, showing when the document was processed.

The **Now** command inserts a "hard" time in text that doesn't change from the time it is originally inserted.

Tips
To work properly, all XyWrite's time-and date-related commands depend on the system clock in the computer. Some computers and versions of DOS let you skip entering the correct date and time when they start up. If you use **TM** or any of the other time and date commands, don't skip entering the correct date and time.

See Date, Now, and Today

TODAY

Overview
The **Today** command inserts the current date when the command is executed.

Procedure

1. Move the cursor to the point where the date should print.
2. Press **F5** (Clear Command Line).
3. Type **TODAY**.
4. The current date is inserted in text.

A La Carte
1. Press **F6** (A La Carte menus).
2. Press **E** or select **Edit**.
3. Press **D** or select **time/Date**.
4. The Time/Date screen displays.
5. Press **A** or select the **fixed dAte** entry.
6. Press **Return**.
7. The current date is inserted in text.

Examples

The **Today** command inserts a "hard" date that doesn't change after it is inserted. It works like a time stamp, showing when the document was processed.

The **Date** (**DA**) command inserts a "soft" date that changes each time the file it's in is opened or printed.

Tips

To work properly, all XyWrite's time-and date-related commands depend on the system clock in the computer. Some computers and versions of DOS let you skip over entering the correct date and time when they start up. If you use **Today** or any of the other time and date commands, don't skip entering the correct date and time.

See Date, Now, and Time

TOP MARGIN (TP)

Overview

The **TP** command determines how much white space to leave at the top of each sheet of paper.

Procedure   The **TP** command can be used either as a system default or as an embedded command that is inserted in a document.

The syntax of the **TP** command is given in lines per inch. XyWrite generally prints six lines of type to an inch, so to leave a one inch margin at the top of each page, you'd type a command that specified leaving a six line margin.

Since **TP** can be used as a default setting, you can enter the command in your printer file or in your STARTUP.INT file. If you do, the top margin stays the same on all your documents. The syntax changes slightly if you use **TP** as a default, to **DEFAULT TP=6**. For complete instructions, see the Procedure portion of the Default listing. To embed **TP** in a document:

1. Move the cursor to the point in the document where you want to set the top margin. (Press **Ctrl** and **Home** to move to the top of the document.)
2. Press **F5** (Clear Command Line).
3. Type **TP** #. (# is the number of lines to leave at the top of the page. For most printers, leave a one inch margin by typing **TP 6**.)
4. Press **F9** (Execute).
5. A bright command triangle is inserted in text.

A La Carte   A La Carte provides tools to set a top margin in a particular document and to alter the system default settings.

To set a top margin in a document:

1. Press **F6** (A La Carte menus).
2. Press **P** or select **Page**.
3. Press **L** or select **Layout**.
4. Move the cursor to the **TP** entry and type the number of lines of white space to leave at the top of the page.
5. Press **Return**.
6. A bright command triangle is inserted in text.

You must be in an empty window (have a blank screen) to access the default menus. To set a new default value for the top margin:

1. Press **F6** (A La Carte menus).
2. Press **X** or select **XyWrite**.
3. Press **D** or select **Defaults**.
4. The View and Change Defaults screen displays.
5. Press **T** or **Z** or select **defaults T-Z**.
6. Move the cursor to the **TP** entry and type in the number of lines you want to leave as white space at the top of the page.
7. Press **Return**.
8. The Update Default File screen displays. You're asked if you want to make the default settings permanent.
9. Press **Y** or **N**. If you select **Y**, the program writes the new default settings to a special file and returns you to the A La Carte Menu Screen. If you select **N**, the settings are used for the current edit session.

Tips Like the left and right margins, this is one command that's usually entered as a default setting, so you don't have to embed a command in each document you print.

See Page Length, Top Margin (Ignore), and Margins

TOP MARGIN, IGNORE (TF)

Overview **TF** is a default setting that instructs XyWrite to ignore any **Top Margin** (TP) settings embedded in a document.

Procedure Since **TF** is a default setting, you can enter the command in your printer file or in your STARTUP.INT file. If you do, any **TP** commands embedded in any document are ignored when the files are printed. For complete instructions, see the Procedure portion of the Default listing.

More often, you will issue **TF** from the command line to set a unique printing mode for a single editing session:

1. Press **F5** (Clear Command Line).
2. Type **DEFAULT** TF=#. (**0** is the original XyWrite default. It honors any **TP** commands. **1** causes the program to ignore any **TP** commands in documents.)
3. Press **F9** (Execute).
4. "Done" displays on the prompt line.

A La Carte You must be in an empty window (have a blank screen) to access the default menus.

1. Press **F6** (A La Carte menus).
2. Press **X** or select **XyWrite**.
3. Press **D** or select **Defaults**.
4. The View and Change Defaults screen displays.
5. Press **T** or **Z** or select **defaults T-Z**.
6. Move the cursor to the **TF** entry. Type **0** to honor any **TP** commands. Type **1** to ignore any **TP** commands in documents.
7. Press **Return**.
8. The Update Default File screen displays. You're asked if you want to make the default settings permanent.
9. Press **Y** or **N**. If you select **Y**, the program writes the new default settings to a special file and returns you to the A La Carte Menu Screen. If you select **N**, the settings are used for the current edit session.

Examples   The **TF** setting is used most often to print documents prepared on one system for a particular type of printer to be printed nicely on a second system.

See Defaults and Page Length

TREE

Overview   The **Tree** command generates a graphic display of all the directories and subdirectories on the default drive. It also allows you to change directories quickly, by pointing to the one you'd like to move to.

Procedure
1. Press **F5** (Clear Command Line).
2. Type **TREE**.
3. A graphic representing all the directories and subdirectories on the default disk drive displays. It looks something like this:

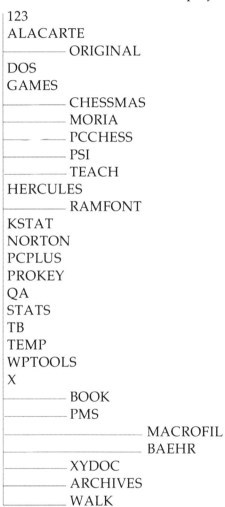

```
123
ALACARTE
─────────── ORIGINAL
DOS
GAMES
─────────── CHESSMAS
─────────── MORIA
─── ─── PCCHESS
─────────── PSI
─────────── TEACH
HERCULES
─────────── RAMFONT
KSTAT
NORTON
PCPLUS
PROKEY
QA
STATS
TB
TEMP
WPTOOLS
X
─────────── BOOK
─────────── PMS
─────────────────── MACROFIL
─────────────────── BAEHR
─────────── XYDOC
─────────── ARCHIVES
─────────── WALK
```

4. The command also places a **Change Directory** (**CD**) command on the command line. If you want to move to another directory:

5. Move the cursor up or down until it rests on the directory you want to move to.
6. Press **F9** (Execute).
7. "Done" displays on the command line.

Remove the **Tree** display with an **Abort** (**AB**) command.

A La Carte   You must be in an empty window (have a blank screen) to access the **Tree** command:

1. Press **F6** (A La Carte menus).
2. Press **D** or select **Dir**.
3. Press **T** or select **Tree**.
4. Press **Return** to see a listing of directories on the current drive. To change drives, press the down arrow key and type the letter name of the new drive in the blank. Press **Return**.

Examples   The **Tree** command is a wonderful navigation aid if you're working on a hard disk drive. It's not uncommon to have 30, 40, or more directories on a large drive, and sometimes it's hard to know just where you are. **Tree**'s graphic lets you point-and-shoot to the directory you want.

See Change Directory, Make Directory, and Remove Directory

TYPE (TY)

Overview   TY is the command that prints your documents.

Procedure   **Type** prints whatever document is active, or can be used to print a document that's stored on disk. If the active document contains a defined block, the contents of the block are printed.
        To print an open, active document:

1. Press **F5** (Clear Command Line).
2. Type **TY**.
3. Press **F9** (Execute).

To print a document on disk:

1. Press **F5** (Clear Command Line).
2. Type **TY** DISK:\DIRECTORYNAME\FILENAME. (The disk and directory name are optional. If they're not specified, XyWrite assumes the current drive and directory.)
3. Press **F9** (Execute).

Type has a number of modifiers that let you print only selected pages or let you pause the printing process after each page.

To print a range of selected pages, use the standard **Type** command, followed by a space, a comma, and the range of pages. Up to five ranges can be specified, separated by slash marks:

1. Press **F5** (Clear Command Line).
2. Type **TY** ,4-17.
3. Press **F9** (Execute).

or:

1. Press **F5** (Clear Command Line).
2. Type **TY** DISK:\DIRECTORYNAME\FILENAME ,3-5/8-10/20-24.
3. Press **F9** (Execute).

To start printing a document on a page other than the first page, issue the command as you would for a range, but leave off the second number:

1. Press **F5** (Clear Command Line).
2. Type **TY** ,4-.
3. Press **F9** (Execute).

To print a single page, specify only the selected page number:
1. Press **F5** (Clear Command Line).

2. Type **TY** ,5.
3. Press **F9** (Execute).

To print just even or odd pages, or to pause after each page, add an **E**, **O**, or **P** to the command. (The **P** switch can be used with **E** or **O**). If a range of pages isn't specified, separate the modifier from the command with two commas:

1. Press **F5** (Clear Command Line).
2. Type **TY** FILENAME,,E.
3. Press **F9** (Execute).

or:

1. Press **F5** (Clear Command Line).
2. Type **TY** FILENAME,3-,E.
3. Press **F9** (Execute).

or:

1. Press **F5** (Clear Command Line).
2. Type **TY** FILENAME,2-40,EP.
3. Press **F9** (Execute).

A La Carte
1. Press **F6** (A La Carte menus).
2. Press **T** or select **Type**.
3. Press **P** or select **typetoPrinter**.
4. The Type to Printer screen displays.
5. Select the file to print:
6. Press **Return** to print the current document (without options).
7. Press the down arrow key and fill in the filename to print a file on disk (without options). Press **Return**.
8. Set options: Press the down arrow key and move into the options fields to select page ranges to print, select even or odd pages, or to pause between pages.
9. Press **Return**.

Examples   The **TY** command is one of the most often-used commands, since printing a document is the goal of word processing. XyWrite provides enough options with its print commands to let you select exactly what and how you're going to put words on paper.

Since few printers are as fast as we want them to be, you can save a lot of time by becoming familiar with the options of the **TY** command. To review interim drafts of documents, investigate the **Types** command, a cousin of **Type** that generates an electronic version of your document that you can review on screen.

Tips   If you're printing documents stored on disk, a number of files can be stacked up by issuing a series of **Type** commands. They'll be printed in the order in which they were sent out. If the files are part of a set of documents, you can print them all with one command—see the **Type @** section.

To stop the printing process, issue a **Kill Type** (**KT**) command:

1. Press **F5** (Clear Command Line).
2. Type **ST**.
3. Press **F9** (Execute).

The printing won't stop immediately because parts of the document have already left the computer and are stored in the printer's memory. No additional material is sent, however. To completely stop printing in its tracks, you'll need to shut off or reset the printer.

See Type to File, Type to Screen, and Type @

TYPE A FILE TO DISK (TYF)

Overview   TYF "prints" a document to a disk file. It provides an accurate electronic preview of your paper documents. It is not usually edited or used as a working file.

Procedure   In almost every aspect, the **Typef** command behaves like the **Type** command, except the output goes to a disk file rather than a printer. All the modifiers that work with **Type** also work with **Typef**. The file on disk can be called to the screen and inspected. It can also be printed by using the DOS COPY command, with the output directed to the printer port.

If **Typef** is executed while there's an active document open in the window, or a defined block exists in whatever document is active, that's the document that's written to disk.

You can specify the name of the file you create with **Typef**, or XyWrite will use FO.TMP.

To print an open, active document:

1. Press **F5** (Clear Command Line).
2. Type **TYF ,TARGETFILENAME**.
3. Press **F9** (Execute).
4. "Done" displays on the prompt line when the document has been processed.

To print a document that's stored on disk:

1. Press **F5** (Clear Command Line).
2. Type **TYF DISK:\DIRECTORYNAME\FILENAME**.   (The disk and directory name are optional. If they're not specified, XyWrite assumes the current drive and directory.) This target file name is the system default, FO.TMP.
3. Press **F9** (Execute).
4. "Done" displays on the prompt line when the document has been processed.

Typef works with all the modifiers **Type** supports. You can "print" only selected pages.

To "print" a range of selected pages, issue the standard **Typef** command, followed by a space, a comma, and the range of pages. Up to five ranges can be specified, separated by slash marks:

1. Press **F5** (Clear Command Line).
2. Type **TYF ,TARGETFILENAME,4-17**.

3. Press **F9** (Execute).
4. "Done" displays on the prompt line when the document has been processed.

To **Typef** a single page, specify only the selected page number:

1. Press **F5** (Clear Command Line).
2. Type **TYF** ,5.
3. Press **F9** (Execute).
4. "Done" displays on the prompt line when the document has been processed.

To **Typef** just even or odd pages, add an **E** or **O** to the command. If a range of pages isn't specified, separate the modifier from the command with two commas:

1. Press **F5** (Clear Command Line).
2. Type **TYF** FILENAME,TARGETFILENAME,,E.
3. Press **F9** (Execute).
4. "Done" displays on the prompt line when the document has been processed.

A La Carte

1. Press **F6** (A La Carte menus).
2. Press **T** or select **Type**.
3. Press **F** or select **typetoFile**.
4. The Type to File screen displays.
5. Select the file to print:
6. Press **Return** to print the current document (without options) to the default FO.TMP file.
7. Press the down arrow key and fill in the file name to print a file on disk (without options).
8. If you wish, press the down arrow key again and type in a file name for the output.
9. Set options, press the down arrow key and move into the options fields to select page ranges to print or to select even or odd pages and press **Return**.

Examples   The **Typef** command generates a file exactly like the one that is sent to the printer when you execute the **Type** command. It includes all the embedded printer codes you normally don't see.

It is useful for checking out the printer and the printer file, especially for verifying that a character substitution table is inserting the proper characters or that a modified line end string is working.

See Type, Type to Screen, and Type @

TYPE A FILE TO SCREEN (TYS)

Overview   **Types** is similar to **Type** and **Typef**, but in this case, a formatted file is sent to the monitor screen. It's an accurate preview of what the paper printout will look like.

In almost every aspect, the **Types** command behaves like the **Type** command, except the output goes to the monitor screen rather than a printer. All the modifiers that work with **Type** also work with **Types**.

Procedure   **Types** prints whatever document is active and can be used to print a document that's stored on disk. If the active document contains a defined block, the contents of the block are printed to the screen.

To preview an open, active document:

1. Press **F5** (Clear Command Line).
2. Type **TYS**.
3. Press **F9** (Execute).
4. Another window is opened automatically. When the file has been formatted, it displays.

To preview a document on disk:

1. Press **F5** (Clear Command Line).

2. Type **TYS** DISK:\DIRECTORYNAME\FILENAME. (The disk and directory name are optional. If they're not specified, XyWrite assumes the current drive and directory.)
3. Press **F9** (Execute).
4. Another window is opened automatically. When the file has been formatted, it displays. It may take a minute or two to appear.

Types has a number of modifiers that let you preview only selected pages. To preview a range of selected pages, type the standard **Types** command, followed by a space, a comma, and the range of pages. Up to five ranges can be specified, separated by slash marks:

1. Press **F5** (Clear Command Line).
2. Type **TYS** ,4-17.
3. Press **F9** (Execute).
4. Another window is opened automatically. When the file has been formatted, it displays.

To preview a single page, specify only the selected page number:

1. Press **F5** (Clear Command Line).
2. Type **TYS** ,5.
3. Press **F9** (Execute).
4. Another window is opened automatically. When the file has been formatted, it displays.

To preview just even or odd pages, add an **E** or **O** to the command. If a range of pages isn't specified, separate the modifier from the command with two commas:

1. Press **F5** (Clear Command Line).
2. Type **TYS** FILENAME,,E
3. Press **F9** (Execute).
4. Another window is opened automatically. When the file has been formatted, it displays.

A La Carte

1. Press **F6** (A La Carte menus).
2. Press **T** or select **Type**.
3. Press **S** or select **typetoScreen**.
4. The Type to Screen screen displays.
5. Select the file to print: Press **Return** to print the current document (without options). Press the down arrow key and fill in the file name to print a file on disk (without options). Press **Return**.
6. Or to set options, press the down arrow key and move into the options fields to select page ranges to print or to select even or odd pages.
7. Press **Return**.

Examples **Types** shows you everything you can see on the final printed page—except the paper. All formatting commands are displayed just as they are on paper; all headers and footers are in place; any labels, index entries, or references are shown as they print; page breaks and line breaks are reflected accurately. And **Types** is faster than printing, and it certainly doesn't use as much paper.

Tips Get in the habit of using **Types** to preview pages, especially if you're experimenting. The command saves time and paper.

See Type and Type to File

TYPE @

Overview The **Type @** command is used to process and to print a series of files that are linked together as one document. Two variations of **Type @**, **Type to File** (**Typef @**)and **Type to Screen**(**Type @**) work just as their single file cousins do.

T

Procedure   The **Type** @ commands require a preparatory step. The group of
individual files that form the document are linked by having their
names listed in a "parent" file. The parent file can be used by the
Type @ commands and several other operations—linked file spell
check, index building, and table of contents generation.

To create the parent file:

1. Press **F5** (Clear Command Line).
2. Type **NEW** PARENTFILENAME.
3. Press **F9** (Execute).
4. Type the names of the files you want to link together, in the
   order they should be printed. Put just one filename on a line.
   Your file should look something like this:
   FILENAME.1
   FILENAME.2
   FILENAME.3
   FILENAME.4
5. Press **F5** (Clear Command Line).
6. Type **ST** (**Store**).
7. Press **F9** (Execute).

All three **Type** @ commands operate as the single file varieties
do. All the printing options remain the same.

To print a document:

1. Press **F5** (Clear Command Line).
2. Type **TY** @DISK:\DIRECTORYNAME\PARENTFILENAME.
   (The disk and directory name are optional. If they're not
   specified, XyWrite assumes the current drive and directory.)
3. Press **F9** (Execute).

To start printing a document on a page other than the first page,
issue the command as you would for a range, but leave off the
second number:

1. Press **F5** (Clear Command Line).
2. Type **TY** @PARENTFILENAME,40-.
3. Press **F9** (Execute).

471

To "print" just even or odd pages to a disk file, add an **E** or **O** to the **TYF @** command. If a range of pages isn't specified, separate the modifier from the command with two commas:

1. Press **F5** (Clear Command Line).
2. Type **TYF @PARENTFILENAME,TARGETFILENAME,,E**.
3. Press **F9** (Execute).
4. "Done" displays on the prompt line after the files have been processed.

To preview a document:

1. Press **F5** (Clear Command Line).
2. Type **TYS @PARENTFILENAME**.
3. Press **F9** (Execute).
4. Another window is opened automatically. When the files have been formatted, they display.

A La Carte
1. Press **F6** (A La Carte menus).
2. Press **T** or select **Type**.
3. Press **P** or select **typetoPrinter**.
4. The Type to Printer screen displays.
5. Select the file to print: Press the down arrow key and fill in the name of the parent file. Be sure to type the @ sign just before the filename.
6. To set options, press the down arrow key and move into the options fields to select page ranges to print, select even or odd pages, or to pause between pages.
7. Press **Return**.

Examples   For people who write or edit large documents, **Type @** makes life easier. When a series of files are linked together, each component stays a reasonable size. It can be processed faster, since the computer doesn't have to juggle hundreds of pages. Each chapter can be worked on independently, a benefit to work groups or anyone who writes on deadline.

Other XyWrite commands support the **Type** @ command. With automatic page numbering, each page in the linked document is numbered sequentially. The indexing and table of contents generation features pull information from each file listed in the parent file. The entire multi-file document can be spell checked and corrected as easily as a single file.

Tips

Type @ does a few special tricks. Page breaks are automatically inserted so each individual file begins printing on a fresh page.

Unless you need to change page formats part of the way through a document, you can use a single set of formatting commands in the first file of the series to control all subsequent files. When dealing with page numbers, chapter numbers, and footnote numbers, you have several options. Generally, each sequence can continue through the entire document, or restart in each chapter.

If you need to stop a **Type** @ printing job, a single **Kill Type** (**KT**) command does the job. You don't have to kill each file.

Warnings

NOTE: The **Type** @ parent file in the Procedure section lists each file separately so the same parent file can be used in other XyWrite processes. **Type** @ supports one option that has the potential to disrupt other XyWrite operations such as the table of contents generation, index extraction, or a spell check.

In a **Type** @ parent file, files can be grouped into sets within the larger document. If this option is used when an index is generated, a separate index is generated for each set instead of a single index for the entire document. The same thing happens with a table of contents.

To generate a **Type** @ parent file that groups files into sections within a larger document, the **Type** @ commands require a preparatory step. The group of individual files that form the document are linked by having their names listed in a "parent" file. The parent file is used by the **Type** @ commands and several other operations—linked file spell check, index building, and table of contents generation. To create the parent file that groups files into sections within a larger document:

1. Press **F5** (Clear Command Line).
2. Type **NEW** PARENTFILENAME.
3. Press **F9** (Execute).
4. Type the names of the files you want to link together, in the order they should be printed. Each section should be on a separate line, separated by a space. Put just one section on a line. (A file can be a section by itself; it doesn't have to be linked to other files.)

If you want to put several files into a separate section, separated form the text of the document, your file might look something like this:

INTRODUCTION.TXT DEDICATE.TXT ACKNOWLEDGE.TXT
CHAPTER.1
CHAPTER.2
CHAPTER.3
CHAPTER.4

5. Press **F5** (Clear Command Line).
6. Type **ST** (**Store**).
7. Press **F9** (Execute).

The **Reference** command can only be used to reference text that occurs before the reference—Chapter 3 can contain a reference to Chapter 1, but not vice versa.

The **Final Page** command doesn't work when printing a chained file—it doesn't have a way to count the total number of pages in the chained document.

See TYPE, TYPEF, and TYPES

TYPE THE CONTENTS OF A SAVE/GET (TYPE %)

Overview   The **Type %** command prints the contents of a single Save/Get key.

T

Procedure   1. Press **F5** (Clear Command Line).
2. Type **TYPE** %# (# is the letter or number key on which the Save/Get is stored).
3. Press **F9** (Execute).
4. The contents of the Save/Get are sent to the printer.

A La Carte   The **Type** % isn't available through the A La Carte menus. Use the standard XyWrite procedure.

Examples   If you use Save/Gets religiously, especially as text storage areas, **Type** % could become one of your favorite commands. It makes it easy to see what's on every key. Just use **Type** % on each of your text storage keys and you have a complete listing.

Tips   The **Save** % command is the cousin of **Type** % and equally useful. **Save** % writes the contents of a Save/Get to a disk file, where it can be called up and edited, then reloaded to a key.

See Save/Gets and Save %

UNBREAKABLE BLOCKS

See Blocks and Breakable Blocks

UNDERLINE SETTING (UL)

Overview   The **UL** default setting determines how XyWrite underlines text and spaces.

Procedure   There are four possible ways to underline text, depending on how you set **UL**:

- Underline everything
- Underline everything but tabs
- Underline everything but tabs and spaces
- Underline only letters and numbers

XyWrite's original setting is **UL=1**, which is underline everything but tabs.

Since **UL** is a default setting, you can enter the command in your printer file or in your STARTUP.INT file to insure that the underline mode stays the same each time XyWrite starts. For complete instructions, see the Procedure portion of the Default listing.

You can issue **UL** from the command line to test different settings or set a unique display mode for a single editing session:

1. Press **F5** (Clear Command Line).
2. Type **DEFAULT** UL=# (**0** underlines everything, **1** underlines everything but tabs, **2** underlines everything but tabs and spaces, **3** underlines only letters and numbers).
3. Press **F9** (Execute).
4. "Done" displays on the prompt line.

A La Carte   You must be in an empty window (have a blank screen) to access the default menus.

1. Press **F6** (A La Carte menus).
2. Press **X** or select **XyWrite**.
3. Press **D** or select **Defaults**.
4. The View and Change Defaults screen displays.
5. Press **T** or **Z** or select **defaults T-Z**.
6. Move the cursor to the **UL** entry and type **0**, **1**, **2**, or **3**.
7. Press **Return**.
8. The Update Default File screen displays. You're asked if you want to make the default settings permanent.

9. Press **Y** or **N**. If you select **Y**, the program writes the new default settings to a special file and returns you to the A La Carte Menu Screen. If you select **N**, the settings are used for the current edit session.

See Defaults

UNLOAD

Overview   The **Unload** command removes programs and support files from XyWrite's memory, making room for large files or different versions of the same type of support file (two different sort tables, for instance).

Procedure   XyWrite divides its features into several blocks of computer code. These are the modules that can be removed with **Unload**.

TABLE 21   **XyWrite Features**

FEATURE NAME	FEATURE NUMBER
All features	0
Load	1
Math and Programming	2
Spelling checker and user dictionaries	3
Standard dictionary	-
Help	4
Hyphenation	5
Sorting	6
Printing	7

Each feature usually has supporting files attached to it. The spell checker has both main and user dictionaries; the hyphenation program has its own dictionary.

1. Press **F5** (Clear Command Line).
2. Type **UNLOAD** #,#F. (The first # is the feature number. The second # is also the feature number, but of the support file. You can also unload the main spelling dictionary by typing its name, **DICT.SPL** instead of using the F switch.)
3. Press **F9** (Execute).
4. "Done" displays on the prompt line.

A La Carte   The **Unload** command isn't available through the A La Carte menus. Use the standard XyWrite procedure or the memory management menu.

Examples   **Unload** duplicates the features of the Memory Menu (press **Ctrl** and **M** to see the menu). If you know what segments of memory or files you're going to remove, **Unload** can save you several keystrokes. It's can also be used if you're writing a program that unloads some features or programs.

See Memory Menu and Savec

UPPER CASE (UC)

Overview   The **UC** command changes a lower case letter, or all the lower case letters in a defined block of text, to upper case (capitals).

Procedure   To change a single letter:

1. Put the cursor on the lower case letter you want to make a capital.
2. Press **F5** (Clear Command Line).
3. Type **UC**.
4. Press **F9** (Execute).
5. The letter changes to lower case.

To make a defined block of text upper case:

1. Define the block.
2. Press **F5** (Clear Command Line).
3. Type **UC**.
4. Press **F9** (Execute).
5. All letters in the block change to upper case.

A La Carte
1. Press **F6** (A La Carte menus).
2. Press **E** or select **Edit**.
3. Press **C** or select **Case**.
4. Press **U** or select **Upper case**.
5. The cursor returns to the text. Move it to the character you want to change.
6. Press **F9** (Execute).

Examples   **UC** is a quick fix for the typing errors created when you were a split-second off hitting the **Shift** key. Go over them with **UC** instead of retyping them.

Tips   In single-character correction situations, **UC** does the same thing as **Change Case** (**CC**). It's just a question of which command is easier to remember.

See Automatic Upper Case, Change Case, and Lower Case

USE STYLE (US)

Overview   **US** invokes a style sheet containing a set of formatting codes into a document.

Procedure   Before the **US** command can be issued, you must have created a style with **Save Style** (**SS**). Part of the **SS** procedure involves naming the style (H1, SUBH, LETTER). Once the style has been saved under a name, it can be reused in the same document:

1. Move the cursor to the point in the document where the new style should be inserted.
2. Press **F5** (Clear Command Line).
3. Type **US** STYLENAME.
4. A bright command triangle is inserted in text. If text already exists in a document, it conforms to the new style commands.

A La Carte There isn't a special procedure for style commands in the A La Carte menus. Use the standard XyWrite procedure.

Tips

Most people think that **US** is an easier way to invoke styles than the **Next Style** and **Previous Style** commands since it references the styles by name, rather than by the order in which they were created.

If you type a lot of similar documents, review the Style Sheet section. They can save you a lot of time and keystrokes!

See Next Style, Previous Style, Save Style, and Style Sheets

VALUE OF A VARIABLE (VA)

Overview

XyWrite contains a number of variables that store information for the program—the name of the current file, the cursor position, and so on. **VA** reads the value of a variable and displays it in text.

Procedure

The following table lists the different XyWrite variables.

TABLE 22   Variables

VARIABLE NAME	VA CODE	DESCRIPTION
Bad Words	$BD	Contains the number of unrecognized words the spelling checker found when last used.
Display Mode	$DT	Contains a code number that indicates how the active file is being displayed (the display mode in use). The numbers are:
	0	Expanded Display.
	1	Normal display. Command triangles displayed, page/line numbers not displayed.
	2	Normal display. Command triangles displayed, page/line numbers displayed.
	3	Normal display. Page/line numbers displayed.
	4	Normal display.
	5	File is processed with Types (Type to Screen).
	6	File is processed with Type (Type to Printer).
Filename	$FI	Name of the active file.
Drive, Path, Filename	$FP	Drive, directory, and filename of active file.
File Status	$FS	Indicates if a file is open.
	0	Means no files are open.
	1 (or other no.)	Means at least one file is open.
Line Number	$LN	The line number of the cursor position.
Memory available	$ME	Shows the amount of computer memory available after XyWrite is loaded.
Current Drive, Path	$PA	Shows current drive and path.
Current Page	$PG	Shows current page number, if the page/line number display is on.
Word Count	$WC	Shows the number of words counted the last time a word count program or the spell checker ran.
Window Number	$WN	Shows number of the current active window.
Window Status	$WS	Indicates the status of the current active window. The codes are:
	0	Window is empty.
	1	File is open.
	2	Directory is displayed.

The contents of any of the variables can be displayed in text or used by a program. The contents themselves are not inserted. A bright command triangle is inserted; the triangle displays the contents of the variable, just as the **DA** command triangle generates the current date.

1. Press **F5** (Clear Command Line).
2. Type **VA** VARIABLE.
3. Press **F9** (Execute).
3. A bright command triangle is inserted in text and the contents of the variable displays.

A La Carte The A La Carte menus don't have any special capability for generating the **VA** command. Use the standard XyWrite procedure.

Examples There are any number of uses for the **VA** command. You can print the current path and file name at the top of each page, get an accurate count of line, insert a marker in text that shows the number of words or lines to that point—the list goes on and on.

Remember that all the values generated through the **VA** command are "soft." They change if conditions in the file change. For instance, if you insert a **VA $FP** command to show a file's path and move the file to a different drive, the message returned by the command changes.

Tips Some types of writing, such as magazine articles or newspaper stories, use a "slug line" at the top of each page. You can use a **VA** setting to display either file name variation in a running header, and the **VA $WC** puts the total word count for the story at the top of the piece so an editor can judge the length at a glance.

The variables are also very useful in programming. There's a corresponding **VA** programming command that reads all the same variables.

See Programming

482

WAIT

Overview   Many computer operations are performed as background tasks which means the task is done by the computer or the software without the user doing anything. These are usually performed by part of the computer, so that another part can be free to work on a different task.

Other operations are performed as foreground tasks. These are tasks that require all the resources of the computer.

Writing is usually a foreground task. Printing, once the command has been executed, usually takes place in background.

XyWrite normally prints a file in the background, a process which lets you begin typing again while the file is printing. The **Wait** command makes printing a foreground operation that dedicates all the resources of the computer to processing the file.

Procedure   Immediately after you execute a **Type** command:

1. Press **F5** (Clear Command Line).
2. Type **WAIT**.
3. Press **F9** (Execute).

A La Carte   The **Wait** command isn't available through the A La Carte menus. Use the standard XyWrite procedure.

Examples   **Wait** is normally used in a program that prints a file to disk before doing something to the output. There might not be an application for **Wait** in day-to-day operations.

See Type and Type to file

WIDOW CONTROL (WD)

Overview   When a paragraph begins at the bottom of a page and concludes on the next page, the first few lines at the top of the second page are called "widows." The **WD** sets the minimum number of lines you think are acceptable.

Procedure   **Widow Control** (and **Orphan Control**) are dependent on the settings in the **Page Length** (**PL**) setting. **PL** sets the minimum acceptable page length, the nominal page length and the maximum page length in lines.

XyWrite's default values for **PL** are 54, 60, and 50, meaning that XyWrite tries to fit 54 lines on a page, is satisfied if 50 fit, and has a maximum of 60. The default **WD** entry is 2, meaning that the last two lines of a paragraph are permitted on the top of a page, but that a single line never appears by itself.

Calculate the largest number of lines you can enter in your **WD** command by subtracting the nominal entry in your **PL** from the maximum entry and adding a line. Using the preset values, 54 lines from 60 leaves 6, plus 1, means your largest possible widow entry should be 7 lines. If you use 7, XyWrite would place the last seven lines of a paragraph at the top of a page, but never print fewer than six there.

Once you've checked your **PL** entry (Usually found in the STARTUP.INT file, but can be embedded in a document) and figured the maximum allowable orphan entry, execute the command:

1. Move the cursor to the first line of your document by pressing **Ctrl** and **Home**.
2. Press **F5** (Clear Command Line).
3. Type **WD** # (# is the minimum number of lines).
4. A bright command triangle is inserted in the text.

A La Carte

1. Move the cursor to the beginning of the file by pressing **Ctrl** and **Home**.
2. Press **F6** (A La Carte menus).
3. Press **R** or select **foRmat**.
4. Press **S** or select **Status**.
5. The Status screen displays.
6. Move the cursor to the **WD** entry and type in the number of lines you want to specify as widow lines.
7. Press **Return**.
8. The new setting is installed.

Examples

"Orphans" and "widows" are typographic terms. The "orphan" (controlled by the **OP** command) is the first few lines of a paragraph that print at the bottom of a page. The "widow" (controlled by **WD**) is a few lines that print at the top of the next page.

In most documents, you'll want to make sure that a paragraph is never split in such a way that it prints only a line or two at the top of a page. A line or two at the top of a page make it hard for your reader to follow the idea expressed in the sentence or paragraph. Two lines, the XyWrite preset, is the minimum. Three is a good setting for general purpose work, and more is better for complex documents.

Warnings

The **Widow Control** setting is linked to the **Page Length** (PL) setting. If you change the **PL** setting, remember to check the **OP** and **WD** settings. Conversely, if you increase the number of lines used in **WD**, check your **PL** settings. For **WD** to work properly, the difference between the **PL** "nominal" and "maximum" numbers must be greater than the **WD** or the **OP** setting. For instance, the XyWrite default entry for both **WD** and **OP** is 2 lines. The difference between the modified **PL** setting's nominal and maximum values should be at least 3.

See Breakable Blocks, Orphan Control, and Page Length

WINDOWS

Overview   XyWrite lets you work on up to nine documents or directories by creating a special work area (a window) for each task. Move between windows through the Window Menu or with specialized window commands.

Procedure   XyWrite provides two methods for creating windows, the Window Menu and the **Window** command. Call the Window Menu:

1. Press **Ctrl** and **F10**.
2. The Window Management menu displays. It provides several choices and controls all window-related functions.
   - **Vertical Split** To split the current window (screen) in half vertically and open another window in the right side of your active window, press **V**. The cursor switches to the new window and goes to the command line.
   - **Horizontal Split** To split the current window (screen) in half horizontally and open a window under your active window, press **H**. The cursor switches to the new window and goes to the command line.
   - **Additional Full Screen** To open another full-screen window, press **N** or a number from the window selection list that's *"not in use."* The cursor switches to the new window and goes to the command line.

   To execute the **Window** command, you need to decide the size of the window to create, in lines (the vertical measure) and columns (the horizontal measure):

1. Press **F5** (Clear Command Line).
2. Type **WINDOW** #,#,#,#,#. The first # is the window number, the second is the column that the left side of the window should occupy (0 to 80), the third is the line number where the top of the window should be (0-22), the fourth is the

width of the window in columns, and the fifth is the depth of the window, in lines.

- To create a full screen window type **WINDOW #,0,0,80,22**.
- To create a window in the bottom third of the screen type **WINDOW #,0,15,80,7**.
- To create a window on the left side of the page, just wide enough for the file names in a directory listing, type **WINDOW #,0,0,14,22**. You may have to issue a **Left Margin** command of **0** (**LM 0**) to get a good display if the window is displayed on the same screen as another document window.

3. Press **F9** (Execute).
4. The window opens, the cursor switches to it, and moves to the command line.

When deleting windows, XyWrite also provides two methods for deleting windows, the Window Menu and the **Remove Screen (RS)** command.

To call the Window Menu:

1. Clear any documents or directories from the window.
2. Press **Ctrl** and **F10**. The Window Management menu displays.
3. Type **X**.

Execute the **Remove Screen (RS)** command:

1. Clear any documents or directories from the window. The cursor moves to the command line.
2. Type **RS**.
3. Press **F9** (Execute).

When moving between windows, XyWrite uses two Function Key combinations to provide quick access to windows. **Alt** and **F10** moves the cursor back and forth between two windows, the current window and the previous window. **Alt** and **F10** doesn't let you back up through a series of windows you've worked in. **Ctrl** and **F10** moves the cursor through all open windows.

If you know the number of the window that you want to move to, hold down **Ctrl** and **Shift** and press the number of the window. (**Ctrl**, **Shift** and **5** to move to window number 5.)

To set the window size, open a window with the **Window** command to create a window that's a specified size.

You can modify any window's size from the Window Menu, even if it was opened with the **Window** command:

1. Move to the window you want to modify.
2. Press **Ctrl** and **F10**. The Window Menu displays.
   - To modify the top border, press **T**.
   - To modify the bottom border, press **B**.
   - To modify the right border, press **R**.
   - To modify the left border, press **L**.
3. Use the cursor key to position the window border.
5. Press **Return**.

NOTE: If you press **Cancel Borders** (**C**) when the Window Menu displays, it doesn't return a modified window to its previous size—it makes the double line between windows disappear.

A La Carte   A La Carte uses the standard XyWrite Window Menu. Follow the procedures outlined here.

Examples   Multiple windows are a great help for almost any type of writing. They make moving text between two documents and copying text within the same document a breeze. The same document can be open in two windows at once. If you open the same document in two windows, designate one as your "master" and make the changes to it. Changes made in one window aren't made in the second; the computer sees the two windows as separate entities. Also, don't save both copies, or the second one written to disk will overwrite the first. Save the "master" and use the **Abort** command to get rid of other.

If you want to compare two similar files for differences, XyWrite's **Compare Files** feature requires multiple windows.

Multiple windows on the screen also make directory and file management easy. You can keep the **Tree** command's graphic file structure in a long thin window, have a directory listing open in a second, and still have lots of room for a "browse" window to display files.

Tips XyWrite opens and closes windows as needed if you change your **New Window (NW)** default setting. Set **NW** to **1** and XyWrite opens a new window when a file is opened or a **Tree** or **Directory (Dir)** command is issued. The window closes when you issue an **Abort (AB)** or clear the screen and execute the **Restore Screen (RS)** command.

Window Number Indicators When several full screen windows are open, it can be difficult to know just where you are. You have a couple of options. Issue a **CM W** command from the command line to make the active window number display on the prompt line.

Or you can make the window number and its file display on the top line of each window as they do when you split the screen horizontally, if you're willing to give up a line of editing room. As you open each new window, move its top line down one line, so each window is stacked on top of the others like a deck of cards. You can adjust the size with the Window Menu, but it's even easier to do if you create your windows with the **Window** command. As you issue the commands, just drop the starting line down a notch:

For the second window, type **WINDOW 2,0,1,80,22**.
For the third, type **WINDOW 3,0,2,80,22**.

If you like the effect, you can make it semi-permanent—see the next tip.

Automatic Window Creation There isn't a way to set window size defaults in XyWrite, but you can create windows more quickly than the menu or the **Window** command does. Decide on the window structure you want. If you usually open one window at a

489

time, write a set of Save/Gets that opens each window with the **WINDOW** command. Once your keystroke combination is recorded, you can create the window with a single keystroke combination instead of 20.

If you always use multiple windows (like the staggered display) create a Save/Get or keystroke program that executes all the commands needed to create the windows. You can execute the sequence as a Save/Get, run it as a program, or even include it in your STARTUP.INT file so they're set up each time you use XyWrite. See the sections on Programming, Save/Gets, and STARTUP.INT for more information.

Quitting With Documents In Several Windows When you want to stop writing, but have documents open in several windows, XyWrite can be slower to shut down than necessary since you have to move through the sequence of windows, storing documents and closing windows. The job's a prime candidate for a Save/Get or program.

Just record your keystrokes as you press **Shift** and **F10** to cycle through the windows, executing **Store File (ST)** commands as you go. If you want to get fancy, build in a testing sequence that uses **VA** commands to read variables and decide when all the windows were closed and issue the **Quit** command for you (but the program works well without it, it just stops when it runs out of windows.) What if in a window there's a directory listing that you don't want to save? At the end of the program, add one more command, one that erases any file that has a .TMP extension.

Warnings   Be careful when you have a number of windows open and habitually close them with the **Abort (AB)** command. It's easy to dump a file you meant to save.

See New Window, Remove Screen, Box Colors (Window Border Colors), and Window Border Characters

WINDOW BORDER CHARACTERS (WB)

Overview   The **WB** default setting specifies what ASCII characters frame the XyWrite windows.

Procedure   Since **WB** is a default setting, you can enter the command in your printer file or in your STARTUP.INT file. If you do, XyWrite's windows are constructed from your favorite characters each time XyWrite starts. For complete instructions, see the Procedure portion of the Default listing.

You can also issue **WB** from the command line to set a unique display mode for a single editing session, or to test an effect. The **WB** setting has six arguments, four for the corners and one for each set of parallel sides. The syntax of the command looks like this:

WB left, upper right, horizontal sides, lower left, lower right, vertical sides

1. Press **F5** (Clear Command Line).
2. Type **DEFAULT** WB<,#,#,#,#,#.
3. Press **F9** (Execute).
4. "Done" displays on the prompt line.

NOTE: The syntax of this command is different from other default settings. Most use an equal sign between the letter code and the arguments; **WB** requires a less than sign "<" (because the equals sign can be used as a graphic character for a side).

A La Carte   The **WB** setting isn't available through the A La Carte menus. Use the standard XyWrite procedure.

Examples   The **WB** setting is a command that's fun to play with, since there isn't a real compelling reason to change the double rule XyWrite uses to frame its windows.

See Box Colors (Window Border Colors), Defaults, and Windows

WORD COUNT (WC)

Overview　　The **WB** and **WCB** commands count the number of words in a file or defined block.

Procedure　　The **WC** command counts words from the cursor position to the end of a file. The **WCB** command counts words from the cursor position back to the top of the file. The basics are the same, however.

　　　　To count words in a defined block, or from the cursor position to the end of the file:

1. Either define the block of text you want to count the words in or move the cursor to the point the count should begin.
2. Press **F5** (Clear Command Line).
3. Type **WC**.
4. The number of words displays on the prompt line.

　　　　Count words from the cursor position to the top of the file:

1. Move the cursor to the point the count should begin.
2. Press **F5** (Clear Command Line).
3. Type **WCB**.
4. The number of words displays on the prompt line.

A La Carte
1. Press **F6** (A La Carte menus).
2. Press **O** or select **Option**.
3. Press **C** or select **wordCount**.
4. The Word Count screen displays. Press **Return** to count forward from the cursor position to the end of the file or to count the words in a defined block. To count words from the cursor position backwards to the top of the file, press the down arrow key to move to the option blank. Type **B**, then press **Return**.

Examples   Either **Word Count** command is ideal for those situations where you're writing to size—a 2,000 word story or a 10,000 word paper.

Tips   In some situations, such as preparing magazine articles or newspaper stories, displaying the word count at the top of the piece is routine. You can either manually transfer the numbers from the **WC** command or use the **VA $WC** command to display the results automatically.

Warnings   You'll get different results from **WC** and **WCB** depending on whether the command runs while your document is in normal display or expanded display mode. In normal display, only text words are counted. In expanded display, the words in footnotes, headers and footers, index and table of contents marker, and any other "hidden" text is included in the total.

WORD OVERSTRIKE (WO)

Overview   The **Word Overstrike** default setting determines how XyWrite implements the Overstrike typing mode that's toggled on and off by pressing the **Ins** key.

Procedure   You can make XyWrite type over existing text in three different ways. A **WO** of **0** lets you type over all existing text and word separators except carriage returns and tab stops. A **WO** of **1** won't overwrite space characters, carriage returns, or tab stops. A **WO** of **2** lets you overwrite text characters, but not word separators.

　　Since **WO** is a default setting, you can enter the command in your printer file or in your STARTUP.INT file so the program behaves the same way each time you use it. For complete instructions, see the Procedure portion of the Default listing.

　　You can also issue **WO** from the command line to test the different setting or set a unique mode for a single editing session:

1. Press **F5** (Clear Command Line).
2. Type **DEFAULT** WO=# (0, 1, or 2).
3. Press **F9** (Execute).
4. "Done" displays on the prompt line.

A La Carte You must be in an empty window (have a blank screen) to access the default menus.

1. Press **F6** (A La Carte menus).
2. Press **X** or select **XyWrite**.
3. Press **D** or select **Defaults**.
4. The View and Change Defaults screen displays.
5. Press **T** or **Z** or select **defaults T-Z**.
6. Move the cursor to the **WO** entry and type **0**, **1**, or **2**. (The memo beside the blank says to select either **0** or **1**, but you can insert an entry for **2** if you wish.)
7. Press **Return**.
8. The Update Default File screen displays. You're asked if you want to make the default settings permanent.
9. Press **Y** or **N**. If you select **Y**, the program writes the new default settings to a special file and returns you to the A La Carte Menu Screen. If you select **N**, the settings are used for the current edit session.

Examples   The **WO** setting limits the destruction you can cause when you toggle into overstrike typing mode from the normal insert mode. Essentially, the three settings limit the amount of text you can overtype automatically to a paragraph that's ended by a carriage return which can't be crossed; a phrase which is delimited by a word separator like a comma; or a single word that's set off from its neighbors by a space.

See Defaults

494

Programs

PROGRAMS

Overview   Everyone who writes has strong opinions about the perfect word processor. It should change itself as the writing task changes. Lean, mean, and speedy for a news story. Able to spell-check proper nouns. Multi-computer-lingual to read any file. Simple enough for a grade school paper. Powerful enough for a thesis. Flexible enough to keep track of index entries, tables of contents, illustrations, figures, charts, and graphs. Full-featured for outlining. Adaptable for work-group editing.

XyWrite is a special gift. It's the fastest word processor in the field and it comes packed with tools to make dreams come to life on the small screen.

Over the years, a number of people have built their own word processors using XyWrite's keystroke recorder to create macros. Many XyWriters have taken the time to share their work with others, often providing their labors for free. As many as possible have been included in the section that follows—it's a sampler of what's available and what can be built.

Procedure   The listings that follow include macros, full-blown programs, keyboard files, help files, printer files—probably every part of XyWrite that can be customized.

The programs listed here have been kept relatively short. You can recreate them using the procedures in the Programming section simply by copying the text you see on these pages. All programs are available as ready-to-run files. If the program author included a description of his work, that is also included in quotation marks. The original sources, and the places many of the files can be obtained include:

CompuServe   Someone, usually the program author, uploaded the program to CompuServe's IBM Applications forum Word Processor library, where they're available to the public for downloading. If you do download the program, it's available in its ready to run form. Authors who can be reached on CompuServe are identified by an electronic mail box number in square brackets alongside their names (for example, Art Campbell [72227,1375]).

XYQUEST XYQUEST, the publisher of XyWrite, provides a number of programs to registered users. Several of the company's programs are included here, by permission. The programs are available free to registered users through the company's technical support department and may be available on the company's support bulletin board system. Contact the regular customer support number {(508) 671-0888} for information on what's available in what form.

To make the programs more available, especially to people who don't have modems, all these programs and a number that are too large to list, or arrived too late to include, are available on floppy disk. The disk is offered for $10.00 to cover the cost of materials, copying, and mailing. For a copy of the programs, send a check or money order for $10.00 to:

Art Campbell
P.O. Box 1915
Exeter, N.H. 03833

Be sure to specify if you need a 5.25 inch or a 3.5 inch floppy.

Tips

If you type a program listing, follow the general rules outlined in the Programming section of the book. Many programs include special key strokes indicated by [Esc] and [CR]. These mean to press the Escape or Carriage Return key while typing the program in. They are not literal characters.

Function calls are indicated by bold type in the program listings. If you're not sure what key controls what function call, check the listing in the Function Call section. You may also be able to identify the call through the XyWrite help feature.

Anything in a program listing that's in regular text is typed on the command line or is text that's part of the program.

A number of programs include comments or are documented by the author. Those programs usually begin with the **Label (LB)** command, which looks like this: «**LBtext.**

Warnings   All these macros and programs are available for use, as is, without any guarantee from anyone. All of them may be modified to suit your particular system.

Not all programs work on every version of XyWrite. Also, each program is reproduced here as it was written and made available. Every author writes differently and a number didn't annotate their code. In these programs you may be on your own!

ABORT by Art Campbell CIS [72227,1375]

```
«LBABORT.PM is used with DBLDIR.PM. DBLDIR.PM
displays a directory listing of the current
hard drive directory and a floppy disk in
windows, side-by-side. ABORT.PM clears the
windows and returns the display to a single
full screen—Art Campbell.»BC abXC AS BC abXC
SW fBC abXC
```

AUTOSAV by XYQUEST

AUTOSAVE counts keystrokes. Every thousand keystrokes, the active file is saved to disk to protect it. It's a nice feature since many people neglect to use the **Save** command while they're writing. It's ideal for inexperienced computer users who may forget to save entirely.

```
«sx01,0»«sx02,1000»«sv03,@S
»«lbloop»«sx05,«va$ws»»«sx04,«rc»»«if«is04»==«i
s03»»«prAuto-save
disabled.»«ex»«ei»«pv04»«sx01,«pv01»+1»«if«pv01
»==«pv02»»BC saXC
«sx01,0»«glloop»«ei»«if«pv01»(«pv02»-10)»«prRea
```

```
dy to save»«glloop»«ei»«if«pv05»1»«prNo file
to save.»«ex»«ei»«glloop»[CR]
```

BOLDWORD by Art Campbell CIS [72227,1375]

```
«LBBOLD makes a single word bold. It's easily
modified to make a line, sentence, or
paragraph bold by changing the DW (Define
Word) function call to the appropriate
function call. It's also easy to make the
block be underline or italic by changing the
"M2" entry to the appropriate mode function
call.»DW M2 XD
```

COLEC2.PGM by Jay Brent CIS [72267,3157]

One of the handiest programs around. XyWrite doesn't let you define blocks in several sections of a document or in several documents. COLLECT does. It works by appending defined blocks to a separate file, which can be imported into a file with **Merge** or edited by itself.

```
«GLSTART»This program uses the APPEND command
to collect stuff from other files to a file
named COLLECT.TXT. [CR]
Load this program to a key such as Z.  LDPM
COLLECT.PGM,Z[CR]
Now whenever you find info you are collecting
for some piece you're doing, define it and
hit ALT-Z. Each time you run this program it
will check to see if COLLECT.TXT exists. If
it does exist it gets appended to. If it
doesn't exist it will get created. After
using your collected text you can then rename
COLLECT.TXT if you wish to keep it or erase
it.[CR]
[CR]
```

500

«LBSTART»«sx77,«va$ws»»«if«pv77»==0»**BC** dir **XC**
BC es 0 **XCBC**
«ex»«ei»«SX79,«VANW»»«sx78,«va$eh»»«sx76,«va$df
»»«if«pv76»==0»«pr no text is
defined»«ex»«ei»**BC** D NW=1**XC BC** default eh=0**XC**
BC exist COLLECT.TXT**XC**
«if«ER»==TRUE»«glnofile»«ei»«lbappend»**BC** func
de **XC CL BC** APPEND COLLECT.TXT**XC GT BD BD BC**
D NW=«PV79»**XC BC** d eh=«PV78»**XC BC** «pr
Appended to file, COLLECT.TXT»«ex»[CR]
«lbnofile»«sx75,«va$ws»»«if«pv75»==2»«sx74,«va$
wn»»**AS** «sx73,«va$ws»»«if«pv73»==2»**BC** lb**XC** [CR]
- Pal, you have too many DIRECTORIES open!
Get rid of some Directories.[CR]
[CR]
I can't run with directories in alt windows.
[CR]
[CR]
In this situation we have to open a new file
called COLLECT.TXT. When you open a new file
it replaces the directory. The defined text
or lines in the directory will be lost. To
get around this we use the alternate window
command. Since you have a dir in the
alternate window also, we have a problem. The
new file will get created at the expense of
the alternate directory. [CR]
[CR]
So, bottom line, if you have directories in
alternate windows, change that and then run
the program.[CR]
[CR]
Press F3 to continue[CR]

501

```
«rc»BD BD BD BC «ex»«ei»«lbnodir»BC NEW
COLLECT.TXTXC BC STXC BC rsXC BC window
«pv74»XC «glappend»«ei»«glnodir»[CR]
```

COPYFILE by Art Campbell CIS [72227,1375]

```
«LBCOPYFILE lets you point and shoot at a
file on your hard disk; the file is copied to
a floppy. When the program is executed, the
cursor drops into the directory listing. Move
it to the file you want to copy and press F9
to execute the copy to the floppy command.
The file is copied to the floppy drive. Try
it with the DBLDIR.PM program.»BC copy a:CC
XC
```

CTABLE.ARC by CIS [74017,2463]

"Program CTABLE installs HP Downloadable fonts for XyWrite, Nota Bene, PC-Write, and MS Word. CTABLE reads a font file and produces a fragment of a printer definition file that contains the font selection escape sequence and the character width table necessary Version 1.41sw adds improved support for XyWrite and Nota Bene. This shareware version generates character width tables only for the normal alphabet, and only font files up to 40K bytes in size are supported."

CLEANU.ARC by Ernie Wallengren CIS [71360,2206]

"If you use XyWrite and you have a hard disk, you will want CLEANUP.PM, which is a disk maintenance utility written in XPL. It is specifically targeted at the genuinely lazy (myself included) who absolutely loathe cleaning up after themselves. Now if I can only figure out a way to get it to work on my back yard." Ernie Wallengren

```
«glStart»[CR]
CLEANUP.PM[CR]
June 11, 1988[CR]
```

Copyright (c) 1988 E. F. Wallengren[CR]
Use and distribute this program freely.[CR]
«lbStart»**SI XD** «sv350,[CR]
****
*»«sv13,[CR]
»«sv27,[ESC]»«sv30,[ESC][CR]
»«sv65,A»«sv67,C»«sv68,D»«sv70,F»«sv83,S»«sv77,
M»«sv78,N»«sv89,Y»«sx100,0»«sx101,0»«sx102,0»«s
v103,Y»«sv300,[CR]
»«sv301,FILES.VAR»«sv255,sx397,«va$ws»»«if«pv39
7»==1»**BC** Screen must be empty to
proceed.«prAborting»«ex»«ei»«sx398,«vanw»»«if«p
v398»0»**BC** d nw=0**XC** «ei»**BC** es 1**XC BC** ca *.***XC**
«lbTest»«sx302,«va$fp»»«if«is301»«is302»=0»**BC**
ab**XC EN**

«glTest»«ei»«sx397,«va$ws»»«if«pv397»1»«glEnd»«
ei»«lbTestP»**BC** This file: ave elete ove
lag ollect OR: Abort programHM «prView file
using cursor
keys»«lbReadTest»«sx99,«rc»»«sx99,@upr(«is99»)»
«if«is99»==«is83»»**XC** ab**XC EN**
«glTest»«ei»«if«is99»==«is68»»«glDel»«ei»«if«is
99»==«is77»»«glMove»«ei»«if«is99»==«is70»»«sx10
2,1»«sx300,«is300»+«is302»»«sx300,«is300»+«is13
»»**BC** ab**XC EN**
«glTest»«ei»«if«is99»==«is67»»«glCollect»«ei»«i
f«is99»==«is65»»«glAbort»«ei»«if«is255»«is99»=0
»«pv99»«ei»«glReadTest»[CR]
[CR]
«lbCollect»**TF** «gt350»[CR]
[CR]
DF From «pv302» on **BC** today**XC** :**DF M2 XD** [CR]
[CR]

«if«pv101»==1»«glcollect2»«ei»**BC** exist
files.var**XC** «if«ER»»**GT DF   DF BC** sad
files.var**XC XD BD** «ei»«lbcollect2»«sx101,1»**BC**
append files.var**XC BC** ernv «pv302»**XC BC** ab**XC**
EN «glTest»[CR]
[CR]
«lbDel»**BC** ernv «pv302»**XC BC** ab**XC EN**
«glTest»[CR]
[CR]
«lbMove»«sx303,«va$fi»»**BC** MOVE TO: irectory
loppy «prPress Esc to
abort»«lbReadMove»«sx99,«rc»»«sx99,@upr(«is99»)
»«if«is99»==«is68»»«glDirM»«ei»«if«is99»==«is70
»»«glFlopM»«ei»«if«is99»==«is27»»«glTestP»«ei»«
glReadMove»[CR]
[CR]
«lbDirM»**BC** Destination (Press ENTER when
ready): \«prPress Esc to
abort»«lbReadDirM»«sx99,«rc»»«if«is99»«is30»==-
1»«pv99»«glReadDirM»«ei»«if«is99»«is30»==0»«glT
estP»«ei»**EL RC RC RC RC RC RC RC RC RC RC RC
RC RC RC RC RC RC RC RC RC RC RC RC RC RC
RC RC RC RC RC RC RC RC RC RC RC** copy
«pv302»**XC**
«if«ER»==TRUE»«glXErr»«ei»y«glDel»[CR]
[CR]
«lbFlopM»«if«is103»==«is89»»«glGetDr»«ei»**BC**
copy «pv302» «pv103»:**XC**
y«if«ER»==TRUE»«sv103,Y»«glXErr»«ei»«glDel»[CR]
[CR]
«lbGetDr»**BC** PLACE A DISK IN DESIRED DRIVE,
then type target drive letter: «prPress Esc
to

```
abort»«sx103,«rc»»«sx103,@upr(«is103»)»«if«is10
3»==«is27»»«glTestP»«ei»«pv103»«glFlopM»[CR]
[CR]
«lbXErr»BC Error accessing target drive or
directory.«prPress any
key»«sx99,«rc»»«glTestP»[CR]
[CR]
«lbAbort»BC Are you sure you want to quit
(y/n)? «lbRead
Abort»«sx99,«rc»»«sx99,@upr(«is99»)»«if«is99»==
«is89»»BC
abXC«sx100,1»«glEnd»«ei»«if«is99»==«is78»»«glTe
stP»«ei»«prType Y or N»«glAbortDel»[CR]
[CR]
«lbEnd»BC d nw=«pv398»XC BC es 0XC BC
«if«pv102»==1»BC es 1XC BC ernv flag.varXC BC
es 0XC BC ne flag.varXC «gt300»TF BC These
are the files you wanted to
flag:«ex»«ei»«if«pv100»==0»«prNo more
files»«ex»«ei»«prDone»«ex»
```

DEFINE.PGM by XYQUEST

This is the XYQUEST program called DEFINE.PGM. It's used to put a defined block of text on the command line. It's designed to be used during a search or a search-and-replace operation where a long string might need to be defined. The number 9 occurs in two places in the listing, it can be changed to any letter or number key that can serve as a temporary storage buffer for a SAVE/GET. The Save/Get it uses must be one of the letter or number keys; the program doesn't work properly with one of the upper register temporary Save/Gets. The program should be loaded to a SAVE/GET key other than the one listed in the program (for example, if 9 is in the listing, don't load the program to key 9.)

```
SV 9GH «pv9»GT «ex»
```

DEFQU3.PGM by Jay Brent CIS [72267,3157]

"The third iteration of DEFQUOTE PROGRAM. This version will run on older versions of XYWRITE. I forgot that v. 3.54, not older versions, allows use of higher save/gets to store defined characters <sv115>. The program will now allow older versions to use it, but you will have to give up one of your lower save/gets. I have used number 4. You can easily change it to another lower save/get by using the instructions in the program. Jay Brent"

«glstart»DEFQUO2.PGM is the new version of my quotes program that will help you and/or your children while editing the documents. It is only for editing (adding quotation marks) after the text has been created. Since about 80 percent of writing is editing, there should be some value here.
This program will, with some intelligence, put quotations around your defined text. Define a word, sentence, or paragraph. Use ALT-F4, CTRL-F4, or SHIFT-F4. You can also use the Define Line (F4) key. If you use the F1 key, be careful not to include too many spaces (all the ones before and after words, that's one or two spaces, are okay). Load the program to a key and try it. Enjoy it and maybe learn something— Jay Brent, CIS 72267,3157

Punctuation rules from "Punctuate It Right", Harry Shaw, publ. Barnes and Noble, p. 123.

The comma and period always come inside
quotation marks.
The semicolon and colon come outside the
quotation marks.
A question mark, or exclamation point, or
dash comes outside the quotation marks unless
it is part of the quotation. Put the question
mark inside the quotation when both the
nonquoted and the quoted elements are
questions.
The last part of the above paragraph is a
little too complicated for this simple
program. So we put the question mark, the
exclamation point, and the dash outside the
quotation mark ALL THE TIME. A special window
will open and show you some examples of
correct usage of the quotation marks with the
? or ! or. You will then be prompted for a
change or leave as is.
[CR]
«lbstart»«LBcheckerr»«sx105,«va$ws»»«if«pv105»1
»«pr Need file
open»«ex»«ei»«sx104,«va$df»»«if«pv104»1»«pr
Nothing is defined»«ex»[CR]
«ei»«LBsvcomp»«sv108,,»«sv109,.»«sv110,?»«sv111
,!»«sv112,-»«sv113,[CR]
»«sv114, »«sv117,;»«sv118,:»**SI BC** se /**WA** /**XC
CL "XD DF CL DF** «sv115»**XD**
«lbtryagain»«if(«is115»==«is108»!«is115»==«is10
9»)»**CR**
"«glend»«ei»«if(«is115»==«is117»!«is115»==«is11
8»)»"«glend2»«ei»«if«is115»==«is114»»«glspace»«
ei»«if«is115»==«is110»!«is115»==«is111»!«is115»
==«is112»»«gl?!-»«ei»«if«is115»==«is113»»«glret

507

urn»«ei»«if«is115»«is113»==0»«pr
????»«glreturn»[CR]
[CR]
[CR]
«lbend»**BC CC** «pr it's a . or ,»«ex»[CR]
«lbend2»**BC CC** «pr it's a : or ;»«ex»[CR]
«lbspace»**DF CL DF** «sv115»**XD**
«if«is115»==«is114»»**CL**
«ei»«if«is115»==«is112»»«gltryagain»[CR]
«ei»**CR "BC CC** «pr No punctuation marks
here!»«ex»[CR]
«lbreturn»**BC** p There is a [CR]
 in this define trying to screw things up...
Wait.**XC XC XC XC XC XC XC XC XC XC BC** seb /**WA**
/**XC CR DF CR DF** «sv115»**CL XD** «gltryagain»[CR]
[CR]
«lb?!-»«gl?mark»[CR]
«lb?mark»**BC** lb **XC** - A question mark, or
exclamation point, or dash comes outside the
quotation marks unless it is part of the
quotation. Put the question mark inside the
quotation when both the nonquoted and the
quoted elements are questions.[CR]
Examples:[CR]
Did Jim say, "I have enough money"?[CR]
Jim asked, "Have I enough money?"[CR]
What is meant by "an eye for an eye"?[CR]
[CR]
Press F3 to continue[CR]
«RC»**BD "BC** Press C to change it or Esc key to
leave as is and end
task.«sv93,c»«sv92,C»«sx91,«rc»»**BC**
«if«is91»==«is92»!«is91»==«is93»»«glyes»[CR]

```
«ei»«pr Done»«ex»«lbyes»BC CC CR DF CL DF CL
MV CR «PRChanged»«ex»[CR]
 Jay Brent, CIS 72267,3157[CR]
```

DIRPM.ARC by Ernie Wallengren CIS [71360,2206]
"DIR.PM is an XPL routine that virtually turns XyWrite into a point-and-shoot file and directory manager. It allows tagging of files for copying, deleting and printing. It will load keyboard and printer files, run other XPL routines and execute external .EXE and .COM files. It has plenty of other options, as well, and is extremely simple to use. All it costs is the price of the download time!" Ernie Wallengren

DBLDIR by Art Campbell CIS [72227,1375]
```
«LBTDBLDIR.PM. is used with ABORT.PM.
DBLDIR.PM displays a directory listing of the
current hard drive directory and a floppy
disk in windows, side-by-side. ABORT.PM
clears the windows and returns the display to
a single full screen—Art Campbell»BC dsort
e,fXC BC dirXC BC FUNC SW [CR]
VBC dir a:XC
```

FCS.ARC by Conrad S. Kageyama CIS [76703,1010]
"FCS.PGM provides a method of searching for XyWrite Function Calls in XPL programs utilizing an external module and the undocumented PFUN command." Conrad S. Kageyama

```
«LB*   Function Call Search
V 1.00,»«GLZ»[CR]
[CR]
«LBZ»«SX200,«VA$FP»»«SV107,z_z_z__z.$$$»«SV108,
FCI_MARK.$$$»«SV109,FCO_MARK.$$$»«SV42,[CR]
»XP DX BC es 1XC BC default nw=1XC BC ernv
z_z_z__z.$$$XC BC ernv fci_mark.$$$XC BC ernv
```

509

```
fco_mark.$$$XC «LB-1»DO BC es 1XC BC Enter
two-letter Function Call and C/R, or Q to
End:
«SX113,«RC»»«SX113,@UPR(«IS113»)»«PV113»«SV115,
Q»«SV42,[CR]
»«IF«IS113»==«IS115»»BC
«EX»«EI»«IF(«IS113»«IS42»==0)»«GL-1»«EX»«EI»«SX
114,«RC»»«SX114,@UPR(«IS114»)»«PV114»«IF(«IS114
»«IS42»==0)»«GL-1»«EX»«EI»«SX116,«RC»»«SX116,@U
PR(«IS116»)»«IF@NOT(«IS116»«IS42»==0)»«GL-1»«EI
»BC «PR Working...»DX DO BC DX BC es 1XC BC
ne «PV107»XC BC pfun «PV113»«PV114»XC BC stXC
BC abXC BC sa «PV108»XC DO BC dos /c fcmarkXC
BC ne fcsmark.tmp,«PV109»XC XP DX BC es 1XC
BC ernv «PV107»XC BC ernv «PV108»XC BC ernv
«PV109»XC BC es 0XC DO BC se \\XC «EX»
```

FUNCAL.ARC by various authors
FUNCCALL.WPF is a XyWrite Programming Language (XPL)
routine that allows easy entry of XyWrite function calls into XPL
routines that you are writing. Doc file included. Written by Tom
Robinson, Modified by Andy Glass, Uploaded by Pete Strisik.

GEN(eric)DIR(ectory)by Art Campbell CIS [72227,1375]
```
«LBGENDIR sorts the active directory by file
extension and name, pulls a directory
listing, puts the CA command on the command
line and drops the cursor into the listing.
Move the cursor to the file you want to open
and execute the CALL command by pressing F9.
Art Campbell»BC DSORT E,FXC BC dir XC BC caCC
```

LOCKUP.PML by Tim Baehr
```
«gl0»This program stores your keyclick spec
(if you have specified one), specifies a new
```

keyclick tone, and then locks up the
keyboard. If you press any key, you will
either get no effect (shift), an unimportant
effect (Caps Lock), or a high-pitched beep to
remind you that the keyboard is locked.[CR]
USES: When you need to reach over the
keyboard to make a note or answer the phone,
when· you don't want others to touch your
work, etc.[CR]
RELEASE: Just press Esc. Your keyclick spec
will be restored. Tim Baehr.[CR]
[CR]
«lb0»«sv01,[ESC]»«sx02,«vakc»»**BC** d
kc=256,10400**XC BC** «lb1»«PRKeyboard locked -
press Esc»«sx03,«rc»»«if«is03»«is01»==0»**BC** d
kc=«pv02»**XC BC CC** «PRKeyboard
released»«ex1»«ei»«gl1»

NOTE: If you want to lock your keyboard for security reasons,
you might want to eliminate the "Keyboard locked" message that's
in the **Prompt** command.

MAGNA.ARC by CIS [71131,2734]
Shareware utilities to make the XyWrite III keyboard emulate the
MagnaType keyboard. The operator is virtually unaware of which
editor he or she is using. In addition, a Magna spell dictionary
containing the Magna codeset and ($) mnemonics is included.
When spell checking in XyWrite III, the Magna codes will not be
flagged as misspellings.

NOTE: The "MagnaType" referred to is a typesetting system.
The files aren't reproduced here, since they're only of interest to
those people who use this specific system. If you're one of those
people, however, this package could be valuable.

MAIL.PGM by XYQUEST

MAIL is a XYQUEST technical support program used to convert DbIII data files into XyWrite data file format for mail merge operations. You can get it by calling Technical Support, or through XYQUEST's bulletin board. The program listing reproduced here performs a number of search-and-replace operations.

```
TF BC CI !/,/!/! XC TF BC CI !/,!/! XC TF BC
ci !/!!XC TF BC SE !/!XC CL
«SX01,«CP»«IF«PV01»==0»RC  «EI»«EX»[CR]
```

NUM3.PRG by CIS [70426,1732]

"Line numbering for XyWrite - a program that really works. It uses the FO.TMP file to avoid having to put returns in the original file. The program assumes that you have the STRIP.PRN file available and that you do not want blank lines numbered."

NOTE: The STRIP.PRN file referred to is a special printer file that removes XyWrite formatting codes. It's included on the master program disk but isn't automatically loaded to your working directory.

```
BC default nw=1XC BC ldprn strip.PrnXC BC
tyfXC BC HIT ANY KEY WHEN done APPEARS«RC»BC
ed fo.TmpXC «SX001,0»«SV002,»TF
«LBTOP»«SX001,«PV001»+1»BC se / /XC
«IF«ER»==TRUE»«GLSTOP»«EI»BC FUNC LBCC XC
«PV001»«PV002»LD «GLTOP»«LBSTOP»TF
```

UNDERL.ARC by Ernie Wallengren CIS [71360,2206]

"This font file displays underlined text in place of high intensity text, allowing underlines to display as underlines in word processors such as XyWrite, where the user is able to define the way various text modes are shown on screen. Requires minimal modification to the XyWrite printer file. EGA only!" Ernie Wallengren

NOTE: Some color monitors don't display XyWrite's underline mode as underline; it's shown as a different color. Wallengren's file is very useful for people running EGA (or VGA) monitor systems.

Since this file was posted, XYQUEST made the official solution, a program called, UNDERLIN.EXE, available. It's available free through the XYQUEST technical support department.

NUMXY1.ARC by Jim Franklin CIS [72136,224]

"This archive contains new versions of my line-numbering programs for XyWrite. One numbers all lines consecutively; the other does it by pages. New versions do not require loading special printer drivers and make better use of XyWrite typeface and page formatting abilities." Jim Franklin

NOTE: A different approach to line-numbering than the NUM3 program. Two programs and documentation are included in the archive package. Both work well, providing two different approaches to line numbering.

First, the NUMBERAL program, which hits each line in a file, incrementing the line numbers as it goes from page to page:

```
«lbNUMBERAL.PGM 6/10/88 by J.L.Franklin, CIS
72136,224»«prWorking . . .»DX TF BC es 1[CR]
«lbTESTINS»«sv379,0»TF GT [CR]
CL xxCL CL aaTF BC se //XC BC seb /xx/[CR]
«IF«ER»»«glOVER»«EI»«glINSERT»[CR]
«lbOVER»TF DP RD SI «sv379,20»«glSTART»[CR]
«lbINSERT»CL CL DP RD «glSTART»[CR]
«lbSTART»«sv000,«TS4D,8»«HY0»«PL54,60,50»«WD3»«
OP3»»«gt000»«SV001,0»«SV002,»SP BC se /WA
/«lbLOOP»XC «IF«ER»==TRUE»«glSTOP»«EI»EL
«pv002»«SX001,«PV001»+1»«PV001»«PV002»NI PW
CL «lbCHECK»«if«cl»0»«PV002»«glCHECK»«ei»ER
«glLOOP»[CR]
«lbSTOP»BC es 0[CR]
```

TF «IF«pv379»==20»**CI** «EI»**BC CC SP DO** «prDone
!!!»

NOTE: And the equally effective PAGENUMB program, which numbers each line on a page, then starts over on the next page:

```
«lbPAGENUMB.PGM numbers lines on each page of
XyWrite documents, 6/9/88 by J.L.Franklin,
CIS 72136,224»«prWorking . . .»DX TF BC es
1[CR]
«lbTESTINS»«sv379,0»TF GT [CR]
CL xxCL CL aaTF BC se //XC BC seb /xx/[CR]
«IF«ER»»«glOVER»«EI»«glINSERT»[CR]
«lbOVER»TF DP RD SI «sv379,20»«glSTART»[CR]
«lbINSERT»CL CL DP RD «glSTART»[CR]
«lbSTART»«sv000,«TS2D,8»«HY0»«PL54,60,50»«WD3»«
OP3»»«gt000»SP BC SE /WA
/«lbTOP»«SX001,1»«SV002,»«SX003,«VA$PG»»«lbLOOP
»XC
«IF«ER»==TRUE»«glSTOP»«EI»«SX004,«VA$PG»»«IF«IS
003»«IS004»»EL «glTOP»«EI»EL
«PV002»«PV001»«PV002»«SX001,«PV001»+1»NI PW
CL «lbCHECK»«if«cl»0»«PV002»«glCHECK»«ei»ER
«glLOOP»[CR]
«lbSTOP»BC es 0[CR]
TF «IF«pv379»==20»CI «EI»BC SP DO «prDone !!!»
```

PRNID2.PGM by Jay Brent CIS [72267,3157]

"Will place the printer filename that is active into a four character label at the top of the file. It is a non-printing label. If you change printer files it will not erase the old label or put a new one in, but it will tell you on the prompt which printer file you now have loaded. Protecting that original label is important if you call for PT#s that are not active in the other printer files." Jay Brent

```
«glstart»This program will tell what printer
file you have loaded.  You must identify each
printer file with a DF KC=n,n so that this
program can tell what file is loaded.  [CR]
In this program:[CR]
The 35HP.PRN file has a DF KC=1,0[CR]
The 35HPFORM.PRN file has a DF KC=2,0[CR]
The 3NEC3550.PRN file has a DF KC=3,0[CR]
The STRIP.PRN file has a DF KC=4,0[CR]
Put the program on a key combination and
activate at any time to see a prompt that
tells which printer file is loaded.[CR]
«lbstart»BC
«sx51,«vakc»»«sv41,1,0»«sv42,2,0»«sv43,3,0»«sv4
4,4,0»«if«is51»==«is41»»«pr 35HP.prn is
loaded»«ex»«ei»«gl2prn»[CR]
«lb2prn»«if«is51»==«is42»»«pr 35HPFORM.prn is
loaded»«ex»«ei»«gl3prn»[CR]
«lb3prn»«if«is51»==«is43»»«pr 3NEC3550.prn is
loaded»«ex»«ei»«gl4prn»[CR]
«lb4prn»«if«is51»==«is44»»«pr STRIP.prn is
loaded»«ex»[CR]
;Because of the Load command being able to
handle "+" for combination loads XyWrite
cannot tell you what any printer file name or
value is. There are other reasons also or the
LDPRN or LP command would do it. However, "be
happy and don't worry" — "There is always a
way." Jay Brent - cis,72267,3157[CR]
```

PROOF.ARC by various authors

This is a XyWrite III routine that uses Wordproof II (not included)
to spell check the document on screen. It helps with directory
changes, saving the document, etc. ARC file contains routine and
documentation. It is a routine that someone gave me and that I

have significantly modified. Download with a protocol, unpack with ARC-E. Public Domain.

NOTE: This should be interesting to anyone running an older version of XyWrite (prior to III+) who wants a good spell checker. The original version was written by XYQUEST's technical support department, and modified by the author of this book before Pete improved it. The original version is still available from XYQUEST.

QUITSAVEby Tim Baehr

«LBThis program closes all your active windows so you can QUIT XyWrite quickly. It saves all active files along the way. Tim Baehr. [CR]

[CR]»

«LB0»**BC** P Storing all windows to disk**XC XC #1**
#2 #3 #4 #5 #6 #7 #8 #9 BC es 1**XC BC** st

«AS»**XC** y**BC** rs**XC BC** st «AS»**XC** y**BC** rs**XC BC** st

«AS»**XC** y**BC** rs**XC BC** st «AS»**XC** y**BC** rs**XC BC** st

«AS»**XC** y**BC** rs**XC BC** st «AS»**XC** y**BC** rs**XC BC** st

«AS»**XC** y**BC** rs**XC BC** st «AS»**XC** y**BC** rs**XC BC** st

«AS»**XC** y**BC** es 0**XC BC** «PRAll windows closed.»

QUOTES.ARC by Edward Mendelson CIS [71600,1200]

"XyWrite/Nota Bene programs to convert ASCII quotation marks (") with paired backquotes and apostrophes (" and ") for laser printing. Also converts single quotes within double quotes. Checks for pairing of quotation marks. Version 1.3 works around XyWrite bugs affecting quotation marks immediately followed by embedded commands and wildcard searches. Faster Nota Bene version turns off screen while working." Edward Mendelson

NOTES: One of several quotation mark checking programs in this section. The program reproduced here is one of three programs in the archived file. The other two are a documentation file and a version optimized for Nota Bene, an academic and scientific word processor built on the basic XyWrite program.

```
«glStart»«lb[CR]
[CR]
QUOTES.XY[CR]
[CR]
XyWrite program to change standard ASCII
quotation marks (") [CR]
into paired single quotation marks (`` and
'') for laser printing.[CR]
[CR]
If quotation marks are not properly paired in
your text, the [CR]
program returns the text to its original
condition and returns[CR]
an error message.  The same message appears
if there are no [CR]
quotation marks at all in your text.[CR]
[CR]
If you have single quotation marks within
double quotation marks,[CR]
the program replaces them with the correct
combination and inserts[CR]
a space between the double and single quotes
(`` `and' '').  It will[CR]
also convert opening single quotes within
double quotes when these[CR]
are not adjacent to the double quotes, so it
will give the correct [CR]
format for this:[CR]
                    ``she said `what she said'
''[CR]
[CR]
The extra space inserted between single and
double quotes may look[CR]
```

excessive, so you should experiment with the results.[CR]
[CR]
By Edward Mendelson[CR]
[CR]
Ver 1.2 - tests for initial overwrite mode and converts all inner[CR]
single quotation marks.[CR]
[CR]
ver 1.3 - works around XyWrite bugs involving searches for characters[CR]
followed immediately by embedded commands and searches for wild[CR]
alphanumeric characters.[CR]
[CR]
»«lbStart»«PRWorking . . .»**BC** es 1**XC** «lb[CR]
»«lbTestins»«sv379,0»**XP TF GT** [CR]
CL xx**CL CL** aa**TF BC** se //**XC BC** seb /xx/**XC**
«if«er»»«glOver»«ei»«glInsert»«lbOver»**TF DP RD SI** «sv379,20»«glChange»«lbInsert»**CL CL DP RD** «glChange»«lb[CR]
»«LBChange»«lb[CR]
»**TF BC** se /"/**XC** «if«er»«glCheck»«ei»**CL RC** ''**XC** «if«er»»«glCheck»«ei»**CL RC** '' «glChange»«lb[CR]
»«LBCheck»«lb[CR]
»**BF BC** seb /''/**XC BC** se /''/**XC** «if«er»»«glFiasco»«ei»«lb[CR]
»«lbSingles»«lb[CR]
»**TF BC** ci /'''/'' '/**XC BC** ci /'''/' '/**XC** «lb[CR]
»«lbInnies»**TF BC** se /WS 'WL /**XC** «if«er»»«glRestore»«ei»**CL CL RC** '«glInnies»«lb[CR]

518

```
»«lbRestore»BC es 0XC GT «if«pv379»==20»CI
«ei»BC «prConversion completed »«ex«lb[CR]
»«lbFiasco»«if«pv379»==20»CI «ei»«lb[CR]
»TF BC ci /``/"/XC BC ci /''/"/XC BC es 0XC
BC BC «pr Quotation marks not paired! »
```

SAVER by Art Campbell CIS [72227,1375]

```
«LBSAVER is a quick program that saves an
open file to its home directory and a floppy
drive, for fast backup security.
[CR]
»BC sa[CR]
BC sa a:XC
```

QUOPAR.ARC by Jim Franklin CIS [72136,224]

"Contains QUOSPARA.PGM, a XyWrite program that changes quotation marks from " to pairs of '' and ''. It also changes spacing between sentences and ensures consistent paragraph indent by real spaces, changes required by typesetters such as Atex. Also has QSPSMALL.PGM, which does away with comments and long labels. New version fixes minor bug. See also QUOT1A.ARC for other versions." Jim Franklin

```
«prWorking . . .»DX BC es 1[CR]
«lbA»«sv379,0»TF GT [CR]
CL xxCL CL aaTF BC se //XC BC seb /xx/[CR]
«IF«ER»»«glB»«EI»«glC»[CR]
«lbB»TF DP RD SI «sv379,20»«glD»[CR]
«lbC»CL CL DP RD «glD»[CR]
«lbD»BC se /"'WA /«lbE»XC
«IF«ER»==TRUE»«glF»«EI»CL CL BD ''R3 R2
«glE»[CR]
«lbF»BC XP TF BC ci / `"/ 'R3 R2 ``/[CR]
BC ci /`"/'R3 R2 ``/[CR]
BC ci /"'/''R3 R2 '/[CR]
```

```
BC ci / "/ ''/[CR]
BC ci /"/''/[CR]
BC ci /»"/»''/[CR]
«lbG»BC se /"WA /«lbH»XC
«IF«ER»==«TRUE»«glI»«EI»CL BD ''«glH»[CR]
«lbI»TF BC ci /"/''/[CR]
BC ci /'''/''R3 R2 '/[CR]
BC ci /'' '/''R3 R2 '/[CR]
BC ci /'' '/''R3 R2 '/[CR]
BC ci /'''/''R3 R2 '/[CR]
BC ci /'''/'R3 R2 ''/[CR]
BC ci /.  /. /[CR]
BC ci /?  /? /[CR]
BC ci /!  /! /[CR]
BC ci /''  /'' /[CR]
BC ci /:  /: /[CR]
BC ci /)  /) /[CR]
BC ci /»  '/» '/[CR]
BC SE /»  WA /«lbJ»XC
«IF«ER»==TRUE»«glK»«EI»CL BD «glJ»[CR]
«lbK»«sv32, »«sv13,[CR]
»TF [CR]
NM BC se /WA /«lbL»XC
«IF«ER»==TRUE»«glM»«EI»LL «lbN»DF CL DF SV
1XD
«if«is13»==«is1»«glO»«ei»«if«is1»«is32»»«glN»«e
i»XP CR «glP»[CR]
«lbO»DF CR DF SV 1XD «if«is13»==«is1»»CR
«ei»LL «lbP»UP    NM NP «glL»«lbM»BC es 0[CR]
«IF«pv379»==20»CI «EI»TF RC BC GT DO
«prConversion complete . . .»
```

QUOT1A.ARC by Jim Franklin CIS [72136,224]

"Contains QUOTE1.PGM, a XyWrite program that replaces inch
mark quotes with pairs of single quotes, preferred for use with

laser printers and systems like Atex. Version A better handles
quotes within quotes and properly inserts unbreakable spaces
between single and double quotes. Also includes
QUOTSPAC.PGM, which does all the above plus changes spacing
between sentences from two spaces to one, as required by some
typesetters." Jim Franklin

SAVE.PGM and SAVEPLS.PGM by XYQUEST

These programs let you customize XyWrite to save active files to
different (several, if necessary) directories or drives. In the listings,
the "PATH" statements should be modified to match your system's
requirements. Both programs use more steps than the SAVER
listing to see if files are open and if they already exist on the
designated drives. SAVE works on early versions of XyWrite;
SAVEPLS is intended for version III+.

```
SAVE.PGM
«sx96,«va$ws»»«sv95,0»«if«is96»==«is95»»«glexit
»«ei»XD BC es 1[CR]
«sx00,«va$fi»»BC exist PATH1«pv00»[CR]
«if«er»»BC es 0[CR]
BC sa PATH1«pv00»[CR]
BC es 1[CR]
«gla»«ei»BC erase PATH1«pv00»[CR]
BC es 0[CR]
BC sa PATH1«pv00»[CR]
BC es 1[CR]
«lba»BC exist PATH2«pv00»[CR]
«if«er»»BC es 0[CR]
BC sa PATH2«pv00»[CR]
BC es 1[CR]
«glb»«ei»BC erase PATH2«pv00»[CR]
BC es 0[CR]
BC sa PATH2«pv00»[CR]
BC es 1[CR]
«lbb»BC es 0[CR]
```

521

```
«lbexit»BC

SAVEPLS.PGM:
«sx96,«va$ws»»«sv95,0»«if«is96»==«is95»»«glexit
»«ei»XD BC es 1[CR]
«sx00,«va$fi»»BC exist PATH1«pv00»[CR]
«if«er»»BC es 0[CR]
BC sa PATH1«pv00»[CR]
BC es 1[CR]
«gla»«ei»BC es 0[CR]
BC sa PATH1«pv00»[CR]
YBC es 1[CR]
«lba»BC exist PATH2«pv00»[CR]
«if«er»»BC es 0[CR]
BC sa PATH2«pv00»[CR]
BC es 1[CR]
«glb»«ei»BC es 0[CR]
BC sa PATH2«pv00»[CR]
YBC es 1[CR]
«lbb»BC es 0[CR]
«lbexit»BC
```

STABLE.ARC by Paul O'Nolan CIS [72007,242]
"XyWrite character width table squisher (for people using the HP Laserjet printers). Reads widths generated by John Thomson's CTABLE program, sorts and compresses them to shorten the printer driver. TURBO Pascal 4 source included." Paul O'Nolan

TABNEW.PGM by Jay Brent CIS [72267,3157]
This goody uses tab stops to set up three even columns on a page.

```
«GLstart»«LM10»«RM70»«TS30C,59R,0»This
program allows you to have 3 equally spaced
tab columns in any file[CR]
Example:[CR]
```

```
tab 1tab 2tab 3[CR]
[CR]
```
The first tab is obviously not a tab, it is
your left margin. The second tab is a
computed centered tab. The third tab is a
computed flush right tab.[CR]
The program saved your default relative tab
value (either 0 which is off or 1 which is
on). It then saves the name of the file you
are in and then STores it. Now it can change
the default relative tab to 1 which it needs
to do this task correctly. It calls the file
back up, searches for a Right Margin embedded
command and then goes to the right side of
that line to be sure it is beyond the Left
and Right margin commands. It has to do this
so it can do the math correctly. Now it saves
the value of LM, the value of RM and
subtracts the LM from the RM and divides by
2. This sum is used to find the center tab
position. Now it subtracts the value of the
left margin from the right margin, subtracts
1 more column. This value, as long as rt=1,
will give the proper position for the flush
right tab (we want it one column to the left
of the right margin marker). The TS embedded
command is now placed and the original value
of RT is put back as the default. This
original RT value will not take effect in the
on screen file but it will be in effect on
any other file called up. This is a
considerable amount of work to accomplish so
little, but there are good reasons for it.
The biggest problem is that you can't change

the RT default on the on screen file. So we
had to STore it, change the RT default, and
then CAll it up. [CR]
[CR]
This version has some new checking functions,
i.e. Checks to be sure there is a file open,
if your default RT=1 already it will skip
SToring file and resetting and resetting RT.
It also searches forward for RM and if not
found it searches backward. The TS command is
now placed directly after the RM command and
the cursor will now be put back to where it
was when you started the program. [CR]
[CR]
«LBstart»«sx20,14»«sx19,«cp»»«sx
21,«pv20»+«pv19»»«sx17,«vart»»«sx18,«va$fi»»«if
«pv17»==1«glskip1»«ei»**BC** st**XC** «if«er»**BC**
«glend»«ei»**BC** d rt=1**XC BC** ca «pv18»**XC**
«lbskip1»**XP BC** es 1**XC BC** se /«rm/**XC**
«if«er»»**BC** seb /«rm/**XC** «ei»«if«er»**BC**
«glend»«ei»**SP BC** es 0**XC BC** se /**WA** /**XC CL BC**
«sx10,«valm»»«sx11,«varm»»«sx13,«varm»-«valm»»«
sx14,«pv13»/2»«sx15,«pv11»-«pv10»-1»**BC** ts
«pv14»c,«pv15»r**XC BC** default rt=«pv17»**XC BC**
jmp «pv21» **XC BC CC** «pr Task
completed»«ex»«lbend»**BC** Program terminated
«pr ERROR - Need file open»«ex»

WALK.ARC by Ernie Wallengren CIS [71360,2206]
"WALKing" is an interactive, menu-driven help system for film
and television writers who use XyWrite. This is a beta version that
is nevertheless fairly complete and bug-free. It aids in everything
from creation of specialized save/gets to script pagination and
scene numbering. You *must* have XyWrite version 3.54 in order to
use this package. A hard disk is required." Ernie Wallengren.

WS-KBD.XYW by CIS [72345,147]

Does anyone still use Wordstar? Yes, apparently a lot of people. Including many who learned on WS and moved to XyWrite. This file is a set of "XyWrite macros that emulate WordStar's CTRL-key and ctrl-Q-key functions so you (almost) never have to lift your fingers from the "home" keys. REVISED VERSION includes loadable binary file, new features (delete sentence and paragraph). Cursor moves, screen scrolling and paging, begin/end defines, deletes are all done with alpha keys."

XY.ARC by CIS [72617,1541]

"Mouse menu (w/documentation and "source") for use with XyWrite Version 3.1x & up. Menu is context-sensitive (hence requires recent version of XyWrite); useful for manipulating blocks, changing/setting text attributes. Requires Logitech mouse driver and Logitech's MENU.COM."

NOTE: XYQUEST supplies mouse-related files for Microsoft and Logitech mice, free of charge, through its technical support department.

XY.HLP by CIS [70105,440]

"A collection of tips/techniques and help for XyWrite users who are upgrading to EGA or VGA. This is a binary file. Download with a protocol."

NOTE: Includes a special printer file used to set EGA/VGA colors and modes. Similar to the .DFL printer files discussed in the Printer File section.

XYCLUB.ARC by CIS [71600,1200]

"A collection of small programs and utilities for XyWrite written by members of the Chicago XyWrite Users group. These programs aren't spectacular, but there's a useful CLUB.HLP file that can replace XyWrite's HELP and gives an explanation of the HELP system. Includes two samples from a disk of programs written by someone described as the author of the XyWrite docs."

XYCONV.ARC by Ernie Wallengren CIS [71360,2206]

"XYCONV.ARC contains a routine called CONVERT.PM, which reads XPL routines and converts them into printable listings." Ernie Wallengren

XYDFLT.ARC by Robert Woods [71350,1200]

"Among the drawbacks of XyWrite is the inability of the program to tell which printer file is loaded. Particularly important for those of us who use a laser printer and have several different printer files corresponding with the loaded font, this small XPL program will display the loaded printer driver as well as other major editing defaults. It sure saved paper and toner for me. Download via protocol." Robert Woods

NOTE: This archived package includes the actual working file, a documentation file, and the display file. When the program is installed and executed, it displays a handy display screen like this one:

```
                  DEFAULTS NOW IN EFFECT


          Offset
          Right Margin
          Left Margin
          Top Margin
          Bottom Margin
          Form Depth
          Page Length


          Point Style


          TIME
          DATE


          PRINTER FILE PRESENTLY LOADED:
```

XY-ENV.PGM by Jay Brent and Ernie Wallengren

"Latest envelope program for XyWrite and HP Laserjet II. Allows you to change PT and position of address easily. All in one file. Read explanation in program file. "

```
«glstart»[CR]
;ENVELOPE PRINTING PROGRAM FOR HP LASER II[CR]
;This program defines the 4 address lines on
your letter.  You can change it ;by the
number of DLs shown at the beginning of the
program.[CR]
;Put the cursor anywhere on the first line of
the address and RUN ENV.PGM.  No ;embedded
commands allowed on the 4 address lines.  If
you only have 3 be sure ;the fourth line is a
clean blank one.  The program shows PT 1
which is ;default courier (landscape will be
automatic here).  You can use soft fonts. ;My
PT 4 is 12 times-roman landscape.  Make it
whatever you wish just remember ;to load and
use a landscape soft font.  The top to bottom
print position is ;always be centered and
okay for any envelopes.  If you want to
change the ;position, use the ascii 013.  The
more you add to the existing bunch the
;further down the envelope the address will
go.  To change the print left to ;right
position on the envelope, experiment with the
LM command.[CR]
;I used the LS 1.25 to give an easier to read
address on the envelope.[CR]
;REMEMBER - YOU MUST DOWNLOAD THE LANDSCAPE
SOFT FONT THAT YOUR PT NUMBER ;CORRESPONDS
TO.[CR]
```

```
;Possible Problems.. only if all 9 windows
are in use when you run this ;program you'll
get an error message and the program will
terminate.[CR]
;-- ENJOY!  Jay Brent & Ernie Wallengren
--[CR]
;[CR]
«lbstart»«sx55,«vanw»»«sx56,«vaeh»»«sx57,«vaes»
»«sx58,«vaeb»»BC default nw=1XC BC default
eh=0XC BC es 1XC BC p  Wait... I'm
working....XC XC XC XC DX DL DL DL DL BC new
env.tmpXC «if«er»»DO XD BC      ERROR -
ENVELOPE PROGRAM TERMINATED«pr ALL 9 WINDOWS
ARE IN USE»«EX1»«EI»BC lm 54XC BC rm 95XC BC
pt 1XC BC CC CR [ESC]&llo3HBC al 0XC BC ls
1.25XC CP AS XD AS BC TYXC DO BC p  Place an
envelope in the printer XC XC XC XC XC XC DX
BC default eb=3000,65000XC BC  dirXC XC XC
DO BC p  Place an envelope in the printer XC
XC XC XC XC DX BC ABXC BC default nw=«pv55»XC
BC default eh=«pv56»XC BC es «pv57»XC BC
default eb=«pv58»XC BC DO BC «ex1»
```

XYHEAD.ARC by Edward Mendelson CIS [71600,1200]

"HEADER is a XyWrite program that will insert a default running header into any new file opened in XyWrite. Mostly a demo of XPL tricks and techniques (including undocumented material), but perhaps also useful for its ostensible purpose." Edward Mendelson

```
«lb[CR]
FIRST SAVE ENTER KEY, F9, AND F5 TO
SAVEGETS[CR]
»«sv01,[CR]
»«sv02,XC »«sv03,BC »«lb[CR]
[CR]
```

```
TEST IF FILE OPEN ON SCREEN (VA$WS);[CR]
»«sx95,«va$ws»»«lb[CR]
[CR]
GET CURRENT WINDOW HANDLING (i.e. new window
for new file?)[CR]
AND CREATE SUBROUTINE 21 FOR RESTORING
CURRENT WINDOW HANDLING LATER[CR]
»«sx75,«va$nw»»«su21,BC Default NW=«pv75»XC
BC »«lb[CR]
[CR]
CREATE SUBROUTINE 22 FOR RESTORING WINDOW
HANDLING AND GETTING OUT[CR]
»«su22,(«gt21»«ex1»)»«lb[CR]
[CR]
SUBROUTINE 28 FOR READING KEY AND TESTING FOR
F5 IN ORDER TO GET OUT[CR]
»«su28,«sx10,«rc»»«if«is10»==«is03»»«gt22»«ei»»
«lb[CR]
y[CR]
MAKE WINDOW HANDLING = XYWRITE DEFAULT (i.e.
NO NEW WINDOW FOR NEW FILE)[CR]
»BC default nw=0XC «lb[CR]
[CR]
TEST FOR OPEN FILE; IF NONE IN WINDOW SKIP TO
LABEL N (NEWFILE MENU) BELOW[CR]
»«if@not(«pv95»==1)»«glN»«ei»«lb[CR]
[CR]
LABEL F -- IF FILE ON SCREEN, PUT s, a ,r
(Save, Abort, Return) KEYS ON SGTS [CR]
»«lbF»«sv45,s»«sv46,a»«sv47,r»«lb[CR]
[CR]
DISPLAY MENU FOR USE WHEN FILE ON SCREEN[CR]
»BC p  S store, A abort, R/F5 return to file
XC «lb[CR]
```

[CR]
USE SUBROUTINE 28 FOR READING KEY; IF NOT ONE
OF THE LEGITIMATE KEYS [CR]
GO BACK AND READ KEY AGAIN[CR]
»«lbFF»«gt28»«if@not((«is10»==«is45»)!(«is10»==
«is46»)!(«is10»==«is47»))»«glFF»«ei»«lb[CR]
[CR]
IF KEY PRESSED IS R THEN GO TO SUBROUTINE 21
FOR RESTORING WINDOW HANDLING[CR]
AND GET OUT OF THIS PROGRAM[CR]
»«if«is10»==«is47»»**BC** «gt21»**CC** «ex»«ei»«lb[CR]
[CR]
BUT IF KEY IS S THEN STORE THE FILE AND GO TO
THE Newfile MENU BELOW[CR]
»«if«is10»==«is45»»**BC** st**XC** «glN»«ei»«lb[CR]
[CR]
IF IT ISN'T R OR S THEN IT MUST BE A, SO
ABORT FILE AND GO TO [CR]
LABEL N -- WHICH IS THE Newfile MENU[CR]
»**BC** ab**XC BC** «lbN»«lb[CR]
[CR]
PUT N FOR New AND C FOR Call ON SGTS, AND
DISPLAY NEWFILE MENU[CR]
»«sv41,n»«sv42,c»**BC** p N new, C call, F5
other commands **XC** «lb[CR]
[CR]
USE KEY-READING SUBROUTINE 28 AGAIN, COMPLETE
WITH LOOP IF WRONG KEY[CR]
»«lbNN»«gt28»«if@not((«is10»==«is41»)!(«is10»==
«is42»))»«glNN»«ei»«lb[CR]
[CR]
IF USER WANTS TO OPEN NEW FILE GO TO LABEL
P[CR]
»«if«is10»==«is41»»«glP»«ei»«lb[CR]

```
[CR]
LABEL C --IF USER WANTS TO CALL EXISTING
FILE, [CR]
THEN PUT ca ON CMD LINE AND GET INPUT[CR]
»«lbC»«sv06,ca »BC «pv06»«lb[CR]
[CR]
LABEL X -- NOW WE GET FILENAME FROM USER,
LETTER BY LETTER; [CR]
IF F5 PRESSED GO TO SUBROUTINE 22 AND GET OUT
[CR]
»«lbX»«sx10,«rc»»«if«is10»==«is03»»BC
«gt22»«ei»«lb[CR]
[CR]
NEXT TESTS FOR ENTER KEY (see manual) OR F9,
AND IF FOUND GOES TO LABEL T[CR]
»«if(«is10»«is01»==0)!(«is10»==«is02»)»«glT»«ei
»«lb[CR]
[CR]
NEXT PUTS USER'S CHOICE OF FILENAME ON CMD
LINE AND RETURNS TO LABEL X[CR]
»«pv10»«glX»«lb[CR]
[CR]
LABEL T -- SEND FILENAME TO XYWRITE, AND
CHECK FOR ERROR MESSAGES[CR]
»«lbT»XC «sx76,«va$er»»«lb[CR]
[CR]
IF FILE EXISTS GO BACK TO LABEL C[CR]
»«if(«pv76»==055)!(«pv76»==003)»«glC»«ei»«lb[CR
]
[CR]
IF ALL IS WELL RESTORE WINDOW HANDLING, PUT
CURSOR IN TEXT, AND END PROGRAM[CR]
»«gt21»CC «ex»«lb[CR]
[CR]
```

```
LABEL P -- WHERE WE OPEN A NEW FILE BY
PUTTING ne ON CMD LINE [CR]
AND GETTING KEYBOARD INPUT FOR FILENAME[CR]
»«lbP»«sv05,ne »BC «pv05»«lbY»«lb[CR]
[CR]
READ KEYS AND IF IT'S F5 GO TO SUBROUTINE 22
TO GET OUT[CR]
 »«sx10,«rc»»«if«is10»==«is03»»BC
«gt22»«ei»«lb[CR]
[CR]
IF IT'S ENTER OR F9 THEN GOTO LABEL M WHICH
EXECUTES COMMAND[CR]
»«if(«is10»«is01»==0)!(«is10»==«is02»)»«glM»«ei
»«lb[CR]
[CR]
PUT FILENAME ON CMD LINE AND WHEN THROUGH
GOTO LABEL Y TO END THINGS[CR]
»«pv10»«glY»«lb[CR]
[CR]
LABEL M WHERE WE EXECUTE COMMAND AND CHECK
FOR ERRORS[CR]
»«lbM»XC «lb[CR]
[CR]
IF THE NEW FILE HAS THE NAME OF EXISTING ONE
WE GO BACK TO LABEL P, ABOVE[CR]
»«sx77,«va$er»»«if«pv77»==001»«glP»«ei»«lb[CR]
[CR]
IF ALL'S WELL WE INSERT THE RUNNING HEADER
AND THAT'S THE END[CR]
»«gt21»BC RHXC BC FCXC BC PNXC [CR]
BC FLXC [CR]
XD
```

XYNEW.ARC by David Auerbach CIS [72261,402]

"A bunch of useful XyWrite programs featuring a replacement for XC, that stacks the command line and does other useful command line filtering. It is arced and there is a documentation file." David Auerbach

NOTE: This package includes a number of files that support the single program called STACK. STACK functions like the UNIX history command; it records commands and lets you replay them for re-execution with UNSTACK, a companion program.

XPLPRM.ARC by David Auerbach CIS [72261,402]

"Update to xplprmpt; now includes documentation. A sample of xpl programs that illustrate various techniques, especially user input." David Auerbach

XYPROG.ARC by Ernie Wallengren CIS [71360,2206]

"New upload of XyWrite routines CAPTURE.PM and MAKEWIN.PM. MAKEWIN allows windows to be "drawn" on the XyWrite screen using simple cursor movement. Previous version crashes and burns under III+. This one runs fine. CAPTURE allows any number of keystrokes to be captured and replayed. An additional feature in this upload is a Pause switch, suspending captured keystrokes during execution so that text can be entered before resuming playback." Ernie Wallengren

XYWRIT.MAC by Pete Strisik [76556,2651]

"This is a collection of several macros written for XyWrite III. Download the file as binary with a protocol, load into XyWrite to read. Instructions and comments are contained within. This is a first attempt at a XyWrite macro upload" Pete Strisik

Index